BENEVENTO

Ariano Irpino

P A N

Mercogliano
(Montevergine)

Bagnoli Irpino

MONTI ALBURNI

AVELLINO

Volturara

N

I

Acerno

S. Gregorio

Sarno

A

Sicignano
degli Alburni

S. Marzano

Nocera

Eboli

Pagani

SALERNO

Vietri

Battipaglia

Sele River

Maiori
Amalfi

BAY OF SALERNO

Roccadaspide

Capaccio

Paestum

C I L E N T O

Ogliastro

Agropoli

Castellabate

S E A

Acciaroli

Naples
at Table

5.10.01

For Irena,
Great meeting you.
Enjoy!

Arthur Schwartz

HarperCollins*Publishers*

NAPLES AT TABLE

COOKING IN CAMPANIA

More than
250 recipes from

AVELLINO

BENEVENTO

CASERTA

SALERNO

THE AMALFI COAST

CAPRI

& ISCHIA

ARTHUR SCHWARTZ

The photographs and other illustrations reproduced in this book were
provided with the permission and courtesy of the following:
Pier Luigi Bassignana and Nigella Lawson, *Il Museo Immaginario della
Pasta*. Rome: Umberto Allemandi & Co., 1995: title page; pages 42, 129,
131, 165, 177. Museo Nazionale delle Paste Alimentari, Rome: title
page; pages xxi, xliv, 133. Alessandro Veca, Umberto I Gallery, Naples:
title page. Chiara Turturiello Kaleidos, Naples: page xi. Claudio
Vitale/Grazia Neri, Milan: title page; page 65. Copyright Tom Eckerle,
pages 226 and 227, Paul Pugliese: endpaper maps; page xlvi. All remaining photographs were taken by or are in the collection of the author.

HarperCollins books may be purchased for educational, business, or
sales promotional use. For information please write: Special Markets
Department, HarperCollins Publishers, Inc., 10 East 53rd Street,
New York, NY 10022.

FIRST EDITION

Designed by Joel Avirom and Jason Snyder

Schwartz, Arthur (Arthur R.)
    Naples at table : Cooking in Campania / Arthur Schwartz.
      p. cm.
    Includes bibliographical references and index.
    ISBN 0-06-018261-X
     1. Cookery, Italian—Southern style. 2. Cookery—Italy—Naples.
I. Title.
TX723.2.S65S34   1998
641.5945'7—dc21   98-17628
                                      CIP

00 01 02 RRD/❖ 10 9 8 7 6 5

For my muse, Iris Carulli,
without whom this book
could not have been written

CONTENTS

ACKNOWLEDGMENTS

ONE OF THE REASONS I gravitate to the region of Campania is the openness and warmth of its people, the way they readily—even eagerly—draw you into their lives, families, and homes. This quality has made the research and writing of this book a great life experience, as well as much easier than I dared expect. One friend has led to another, one kitchen to another, and I now have many home cooks, restaurant chefs, discerning eaters, and food chroniclers to thank.

I must start where I began, at Tenuta Seliano in Paestum, the farm and Agri-Tourism inn of Baronessa Cecilia Bellelli Baratta, where I went several years ago to convince myself that this was a project I should undertake. It didn't take more than a day with Cecilia, her adult sons Massimino and Ettore, and her right-hand kitchen assistant Anna D'Amato. I have spent many glorious, educational, hard-working, hard-playing, tear- and laughter-filled days with Cecilia. I have seen Massimino grow into a good cook himself and Ettore become an accomplished organizer of the many parties nowadays catered at Seliano. I've learned much about the inner life of Campania through the hospitality, observations, and connections of Cecilia and her extended family, which includes her mother, Elvira, in the Art Deco family villa in Battipaglia, her sister Laura and  brother-in-law Savj Marano in Salerno, and her sisters Rosaria and Enrica and their families, also of Salerno.

Back in New York, I have long admired the Neapolitan-style cooking of Ida Cerbone, a native and still part-time resident of Pignataro Interamna, who owns the restaurant Manducatis in the borough of Queens with her husband Vincent, a native of Naples. At their home in Italy, now occupied full-time by their American-born sons, Piero and Joseph, Joseph's wife Leila Evangelista, and Joe and Leila's young children Beatrice and Vincenzo, I was accepted as one of the family—and as one of the in-laws by Modestina, Arcangelo, and Lucilla Evangelista, Leila's parents and sister. Through the Cerbone sons and the Evangelistas, I was also privileged to meet and spend kitchen time with Antonio and Gina Evangelista of the restaurant Sordella 1919, Elisa and Carmine Evangelista of the restaurant L'Espero, and Marisa Marano, the woman who cooked for Modestina Evangelista's family when she was a working mother.

From the beginning, I was encouraged by Marchese Franco Santasillia di Torpino, Neapolitan gastronome and author of *La cucina aristocratica napoletana*; my very old friend Antonio Mastroberardino, whose Campanian wines have long been considered among the best wines of southern Italy; Antonio's son and American daughter-in-law, Carlo and Kelle Mastroberardino, who are carrying the family's winemaking tradition into its third generation; New York pal Anna Teresa Callen, the Italian cooking teacher and cookbook author; and my soul-brother Francesco de Rogati, who is Genovese but has summered in Ischia for so long that I sometimes forget he is from the north. ("My father was Neapolitan," he always reminds me.)

Among my greatest inspirations and most encouraging cheerleaders were the brothers Maurizio and Bruno De Rosa and their mother Rita, who divide their time between a New York restaurant, Pierino, an apartment in the Vomero section of Naples, and a wonderful house in Scauri, a beach-side enclave of Neapolitans in southern Lazio. I have spent many hours and days in New York and Italy cooking with them, at table with them, and going through many trials and tribulations of life with them.

In the heart of Naples, in the old quarter of Spaccanapoli, I am indebted to Rosario Mazzella, the noted Neapolitan painter, his wife, Rosa, and their son Marcello, an artist in New York who introduced me to them. No one knows Naples better than Rosario, and his guided walks and drives around the city have made me at times feel like a native, too. I think of Rosa as my Neapolitan sister. We bonded immediately. Enough said.

Michi Ambrosi, who, with her daughter Bianca, runs the Neapolitan cooking school and catering company Il Peperoncino, took the time to write me a list of the essential dishes of *la cucina napoletana*, explain it all for me one afternoon in her sprawling apartment, and give me a precious copy of Nello Olivero's *Storie e curiosità della cucina napoletana*. Camilla Giannuzzi Savelli, another generous new friend, loaned me her copies of the cookbooks published by *Il Mattino*, the Neapolitan newspaper, and got me VIP seats to witness the Miracle of San Gennaro.

In Capua, Francesca Pasca di Magliano, proprietor of the elegant Agri-Tourism farm Masseria Giòsole, was generous with her knowledge of her native Naples and adopted home in the province of Caserta. And in the city of Caserta itself, water buffalo breeder Onofrio Piccirillo not only taught me what I needed to know about the cheeses of Campania, but drove and guided me to places and experiences in his province that I would have otherwise never seen or had. In Frasso Telesino, Gianna and Pasquale Amore and their extended family helped me understand the differences between the food of Benevento and the rest of Campania.

On the Internet, I discovered Chiara Lima of Ravello, who I am sure will be a lifelong friend. Through her, I had the privilege of meeting her mother, Agata, one of Ravello's finest cooks, who now teaches cooking in her home kitchen. Netta Bottone of Ravello's best restaurant, Cumpà Cosimo, let me badger her in the kitchen, as did Maria Desiderio at her restaurant, Da Giorgio, in Capri. In Sant' Agata sui Due Golfi, Alfonso and Livia Iaccarino of restaurant Don Alfonso 1890 were also most generous with their time and knowledge.

Without teacher and cookbook author Nick Malgieri's recipes and advice, the dessert chapter would be sorely lacking. I am also indebted to Carole Walter and Michele Scicolone for baking advice, Susan Loden, director of the four Kings supermarket cooking studios in New Jersey, and Sandy Daniels, director of the Silo cooking school in New Milford, Connecticut. Both let me teach my work in progress and get some of the kinks out. Thanks also to Allaire Brumfield for providing archeological research and to Bob Harned for being my personal ancient history professor.

On the most personal level, I could not have gotten through this project without the encouragement, support, and understanding of my nearest and dearest—my soulmate, Bob Harned; my sister Andrea and her husband Milton Alexander; my impressive nephew and niece, Brian and Rachel; my soul-sister, the chef and cookbook author Rozanne Gold and her wise husband, the international food consultant Michael Whiteman; friend and advisor Robin Zucker; and dear Alison Alifano, who not only gives me unqualified love but enthusiastically did kitchen prep, washed pots and pans, and re-tested recipes. For all their moral and other kinds of irreplaceable support, I am also eternally indebted to my friend Daniel Young, the restaurant critic of the *New York Daily News*; my radio mentor and "on-air wife," Joan Hamburg; my "Food Talk" producer, Christopher Thompson, on whose calming influence I depend so much; my brilliant and always accessible agent, Alice Martell; and my trustworthy friend, travel companion, and accomplished editor, Susan Friedland, who gives the best publishing experience in the cookbook business.

Above all, and as the dedication to this book says, *Naples at Table* would not have been possible, as most of my life for the last seven years would not, without Iris Carulli, conscientious assistant, deft translator, inspirational muse, and friend. This is as much her book as mine.

INTRODUCTION

Naples is a paradise. In it everyone lives in a sort of intoxicated self-forgetfulness.
. . . If in Rome one can readily set oneself to study, here one can do nothing but
live and go about with people who think of nothing but enjoying themselves.

JOHANN WOLFGANG VON GOETHE, *TRAVELS IN ITALY*, 1787

IT IS VERY TELLING that Neapolitan cooking is "what the whole world knows as Italian," as the late American food writer Waverly Root put it, and that two of the most popular foods in the world—spaghetti with tomato sauce and pizza—are Neapolitan. It speaks of the poverty that drove hundreds of thousands of people from Naples and its countryside to seek opportunity elsewhere, creating what amounts to a Neapolitan diaspora. It speaks of the strong ties these people had with their food, passing their traditions on for generations, their cultural identity defined by their zest for the table and their knowing ways with dried pasta, vegetables, tomatoes, sausage, seafood, and sweets. And it proves that *la cucina napoletana*, the vivid, sometimes lusty, sometimes refined cuisine that is a melding of rustic Campanian country cooking with the foods and foodways introduced during centuries of successive foreign occupations, has nearly universal, even primal appeal. Nowadays, they're even gobbling up pizza in India and China.

What the world knows now as Neapolitan cuisine emerged in the late sixteenth century, when Naples—the urban center of Campania, the most important capital of southern Italy, and, after Paris, the second city of Europe—was rife with poverty, possibility, and new ingredients from the New World. But its story starts eons earlier, with Vesuvius.

It's worth taking a ferry trip from Naples to one of its offshore islands, Capri, Ischia, or Procida, if only to see the city from the sea.

On the middle right and slightly behind Naples is Vesuvius, the volcano that looms over Naples's skyline and its convoluted history. No matter how blue, how clear, how utterly benign the Mediterranean sky over the vast crescent Bay of Naples may be, a whiff of mist or cloud is always at Mount Vesuvius's jagged, magnificent peak—nurturing and reassuring, taunting, threatening. Visible in every city view and from an amazing distance in the northern hinterlands, Vesuvius is the only active volcano on the European mainland (Etna is on the island of Sicily) and an ever-present symbol of nurture and destruction. Over millennia its lava has decomposed into the rich soil that gives Campania its fertility, while its unpredictable furies of fire and ash have burned and buried cities.

Living on the edge of the volcano. Even today, it makes every minute count, and Campanians have always been known for their ability to enjoy life, to find joy—even when times are catastrophic—in the simple pleasures of daily living—eating, drinking, singing, dancing, joking, loving.

Stretching behind the vast volcano is a ridge of the Apennines that curves around it and forms the mountainous Sorrento peninsula, which juts into the sea, encloses the Bay of Naples on the south, separates it from the Bay of Salerno on its other side, then pops out of the azure waters as Capri, an island sentinel standing guard over the harbor. On the left, protecting the bay on the northern end, is the slim, low spit of land called Capo Miseno, with Ischia and tiny Procida off its point, more island guardians of the bay. With Capri, they are called "pearls of the Mediterranean."

Entering the bay, Naples is in the center, fanned out on hills that slope down to one of the world's greatest and most anciently used natural harbors; a city built like an amphitheater whose stage is the blue beyond. An early twentieth-century English guidebook writer, Cecil Headlam, said the earth, sky, and sea here "mingle in a rapture of physical delight." And with this vista, he went on, "the Great Landscape Painter has thrown down a challenge to all those lesser artists whom He created in His own image, drawing the outlines of His design in elemental sea and rock, and washing them over with colors that are forever changing and forever lovely, even as the sunshine, sea and air of which they are composed." It is a sight beyond art, though. The forms—the crescent bay, the massive cone of Vesuvius—the vivid colors, the special light. They never fail to strike deep chords of recognition in anyone who sees them. Perhaps the ancients were right to invest this place with spiritual intrigue.

Beyond the city and the string of suburban towns with which it shares the bay—names with historical resonance like Pozzuoli, Posillipo, Portici, Ercolano, Pompeii, Torre del Greco, Torre Annunziata, Castellamare di Stabia—is the rest of Campania, one of Italy's twenty regions, itself divided into five provinces. There is Avellino (east of Naples and bordering on the region of Puglia), the once desperately poor interior province where hazelnut trees and grapevines cover the many hills. In equally mountainous Benevento (the northeastern province that neighbors Molise on the north), and Puglia (on the east), there is even more vineyard land. It is a veritable garden of grapes. The province of Caserta, also north of Naples, starts at the feet of Molise's and Benevento's mountains, but it is mostly a huge, sea-level plain supporting fruit trees, vegetables, tobacco, and the water buffalo whose milk is made into mozzarella, Campania's most distinctive agricultural product.

Finally, south of Naples and on the other side of the Sorrento peninsula, is the province of Salerno, the largest province of modern Italy. It has its own protected crescent bay, the Bay of Salerno, site of the city of the same name, which is nestled against the peninsula's highlands. South of the city, the province opens to another low plain, like that of Caserta but smaller and triangular. It also supports orchards and vegetable farms, as well as those all-important water buffalo.

The Salerno plain opens to the bay, its shore the sandy beaches where the Allies landed in 1943. Behind the plain are three mountain ranges. The highest peaks are those of the Cilento, a stubby peninsula that forms the southern enclosure of Salerno Bay. The verdant hills to the north of the plain are the same as those in neighboring Avellino. Between them are the arid peaks of the Monti Alburni.

Living on the edge of the volcano. Or near the entrance to hell, as Virgil and Dante thought. The land still lifts and falls in and around Naples, as they both observed in their days. To the north of the city, neighboring Pozzuoli was under water as recently as 1980, and an earthquake left more than 100,000 Neapolitans homeless. Next to Pozzuoli, only a few minutes' drive from the center of Naples, Italy's two major seismic fault lines intersect at the Phlegraean fields. There, in a barren sandy crater called the Solfatara, the earth continually seethes and bubbles with sulfuric gases. To the east of Naples, the forested hills of the province of Avellino were ravaged by earthquakes in 1981, the devastating shocks reaching south into Salerno's Monti Alburni. Only recently have these areas fully recovered.

The land is still and the volcano is quiet these days. Vesuvius's slopes are lushly green and achingly beautiful. Grape vines brought by the Greeks spin up, down, and around it. Attesting to the richness of the earth made by millions of years of activity and decay, there are walnuts, hazelnuts, chestnuts, citrus fruits, figs, peaches, apples, pears, grapes, tomatoes, peppers, cabbage, broccoli, escarole, turnips, peas, beans, artichokes, herbs, sheep, goats, cows, and water buffalo thriving on it, or in the valleys around it. Nearby, the Sorrento peninsula is terraced with oranges and lemon groves. Lush flower gardens spread before grand, antique villas surrounded by vine-covered pergolas and topiary evergreens, bay trees, and rosemary shrubs. Tile-roofed houses hang over deep ravines. Luxury resorts mingle with stone hovels on steep, shrubby hills stepping down to the sea. In Salerno there are vegetable fields as far as the eye can see, which is to the mountains, themselves covered in olive trees. In the high woods above the Caserta plain, roads climb through dense chestnut forests.

But the volcano can erupt again. It has done so at least seventy times since it buried the Roman pleasure cities of Pompeii and Herculaneum in A.D. 79. To name just two of its most tragic later eruptions, it wiped out a vast population in 1631, and, as recently as 1944, its most recent eruption, it destroyed villages and spewed inches of ash and stone onto the streets of Naples and Salerno only months after the Allies had "liberated" them; or, as the locals like to say, after they threw the Germans out.

The seismologists and vulcanologists expect the land under Campania will someday again act with violence. It always has, and that fact has helped shape its people.

The ancient Greeks thought Campania was a land of mystery and deadly seduction. They placed the myth of the Sirens on its shores. They said the Sibyl and the Cyclops lived in caves just north of Naples.

The Romans called it the "happy countryside" or "fortunate countryside," *Campania felix* in Latin. They built pleasure palaces on the teeming, life-giving sea, and were awed by how large vegetables grew in its easily tillable, volcanic soil, heated by an average 230 days of sun a year.

In the eighteenth century, cosmopolitan, Baroque Naples was, as Goethe said, "a paradise," perhaps not a physical one, but certainly an intellectual one, at least for the artists and aristocrats who flocked there to indulge in the city's free-thinking atmosphere and many sensual pleasures.

In the last half of the nineteenth century, the Victorian English made pilgrimages for these pleasures. Escaping, as the ancient Romans did, the repressive prudishness of their country, they joked that adulterers went to Naples, divorcées to Sorrento, homosexuals to Capri—perhaps not coincidentally, all places for great pastry.

Naples has seen it all, remembers it all, and somehow always manages to overcome it all.

It was anything but Goethe's paradise in 1969 when I made my first trip, on a night train from I-don't-remember-where up north. The city had not yet recovered from the deep trauma of the Second World War, or the misguided attempt after the war to make it an industrial port in an age when planes, trucks, and trains carried cargo, not to mention a century of Italian unification and natural calamities. I recall that the makeup of the passengers changed dramatically after we pulled out of the station in Rome. It felt, as a prejudiced friend in Florence said it would, like I had entered another country, and a dangerous one. I didn't dare sleep that night.

At the Naples train station, I was accosted by cab drivers, baggage carriers, and boys and women selling cigarettes, "Omega" watches, and various personal services.

Somehow I managed, without being conned into buying something I'd regret, to get safely to the Santa Lucia hotel, a luxury palace I could ill-afford but felt I needed for its security. I merely had to pay the cab driver double the meter to get my luggage.

As a New Yorker accustomed to fending off a street hustle, and having grown up surrounded by southern Italians, I acclimated quickly. The palm trees in the park along the sea seduced me. The decrepit Baroque splendor of the city stunned me. I couldn't keep my eyes off the laundry famously hanging over the narrow streets of the old quarters. It seemed to me that each clothesline told a story, and a tale very different from the look of the facade from which it was strung. And, of course, there was the food. The catering shops carried all kinds of macaroni-filled pastries, individual size and huge ones to cut a wedge from; cakes of fried pasta, fried balls of rice, stacks of vegetable frittatas, baked lasagne, and ziti. There were fry shops with fritters and croquettes, trendy pizzerias with long pies sold by the meter, and traditional pizzerias, every surface white marble, where I first learned to eat pizza with a knife and fork. I indulged in pastries and babà every morning and afternoon, drank short, powerful coffees all day, and finished each evening with a stroll and a gelato. I ate linguine with clams in Posillipo (then took a nap on a jetty on the sea); drank Greco di Tufo (white wine) and stuffed myself with buffalo mozzarella at every opportunity. I could see right away it was a tough place to eat through, so I kept going back for more.

There were still warm almond-studded taralli, rings of crisp lard dough, from a street vendor by the sea, pasta and beans in a nineteenth-century trattoria, lamb ragù and cavatelli in the hills of Benevento, goat ragù and fusilli in the Monti Alburni, squid and potatoes on Capri, rabbit braised in tomatoes on Ischia, fish stew at the beach near Gaeta, and lemon chicken in Ravello.

So many things have changed in Naples and on its countryside since 1969. And so many things have fortunately remained the same. The region has become more affluent in recent years. It's still very hard to find work, but there is no apparent poverty. While young people wait for jobs they get higher educations. Naples itself (and Salerno, too) is now better organized under a new mayor. There are fewer hustlers. The garbage is picked up every night. Street crime is under control, at least as much as can be expected in Italy's third largest and most densely populated city. New subway lines are being built. Museums, churches, and municipal offices keep to schedules (well, within reason for Italy). The city is recognizing itself again as a culture capital and refurbishing its astounding architectural heritage. A new contemporary art museum has been opened in the Capodimonte Palace of the Bourbon royalty, the

PULCINELLA

Pulcinella is the mascot of Naples, but more than a clownish sidekick and sometimes protector against the evil eye, he is the tragicomic embodiment of the Neapolitan character. Through double entendre, parody, ridicule, and graphic gestures, he expresses the Neapolitans' fears, imaginations, and obsessions.

The Commedia dell'Arte playwright Silvio Fiorillo, a Neapolitan, invented the character called Pulcinella in 1609 for a play called *La Lucilla Costante* (*Constant Lucille*), published in 1632. But clown characters like Pulcinella (Pulicinella, in Neapolitan dialect)—comic heroes, ritualistic buffoons, theatrical comedians, tricksters—are universally present in primitive mythologies. (The English puppet Punch is a derivative of Pulcinella.) Indeed, these are the characters, rather than the seriously heroic figures (today's "superheros"), who are more thoroughly fleshed out. Incarnating the ideals of the populace as they do, the Pulcinellas of world literature have complex, ambivalent, ambiguous personalities. They mirror our dark sides as well as our godly sides, our honorable devotions along with our impulses to give in to temptation.

A legend has it that Pulcinella was hatched from an egg made by two witches and placed by Pluto in the mouth of Vesuvius. Hence the name, little chicken. The costume dates from the seventeenth century. He sometimes appears as a tiny shepherd among the toys offered to the baby Christ figure in the Christmas *presepe*, but otherwise he wears a pointy, cone-shaped white hat and is dressed in baggy white pants, a blousy, sashed white shirt with buttons down the front, and a crenelated Elizabethan-style collar. With his beak-like nose, he is the prototypical clown.

The exaggerated nose comes from the hooked bill of the chicken. Chickens in Western cultures often stand for buffoons, transgressors, the insane, and, above all, the sexually ambiguous.

Pulcinella may act dumb or docile, but he is eloquent and courageous. He is always hungry. He is always in love. He is in touch with the sacred and the mysterious, yet he is carnal and prone to make obscene, even scatological jokes. He can be stupid or cunning, the obliging or deceitful servant, the messenger who cannot speak, the underdog who wins, or the noble guardian of work or home. Pulcinella also protects the community from outside threats. For centuries, his figure was put on top of church steeples, echoing the Germanic custom of putting the rooster's image on bell towers and steeples (and the American custom of using rooster figures for weathervanes). Tavern keepers and melon vendors, just to cite two businesses, would always have Pulcinella on their signs as a guarantee of authenticity.

"The Boss," a story by Giuseppe Marotta that was made into one of the segments of the 1954 film *The Gold of Naples* (*L'Oro di Napoli*) by Vittorio de Sica, is a typical Pulcinella story. The little man triumphs over the big. Metaphorically, the individual triumphs over the system and Naples over its many foreign occupations, including that of the north since Italian unification.

Meek, kind, gentle, loving Don Savj, played by Totò, the Neapolitan actor most famous in the twentieth century for embodying the Pulcinella character, has been tyrannized by a childhood friend, Don Carmine (Pasquale Gennaro), the once schoolyard bully, now neighborhood boss. Thirteen years earlier, on the occasion of the early death of Don Carmine's wife, and merely out of polite kindness and not any particular closeness or blood relation, Don Savj's wife had said to Don Carmine, "Please call on us if there is anything we can do." Since then, Don Carmine has lived in Don Savj's apartment, ruled his young children, scolding his wife over her laundry and cooking, and, most significantly, deciding what is for dinner.

The story opens on the morning of Christmas Eve, and Don Savj has brought home the traditional baccalà (dried salt cod). "Have you gone mad, you know as well as I do that it upsets him," says Savj's wife when she smells what's in the paper package he's placed on her ironing table. "That's why I bought it," says Don Savj, for the first time announcing his intention to rebel against Don Carmine. When Don Carmine comes home that afternoon, crying that he has just been diagnosed with a bad heart and that any loud noises, surprises, or stresses will certainly kill him ("Perhaps you should send the children to their aunt," he suggests), Don Savj collects all the plates from the dinner table and, with certainty, dignity, and power, drops them behind Don Carmine's back. The boss lives. But Don Savj now has the courage to excise Don Carmine from his life. In a rage, he pushes Don Carmine out the door and throws his possessions off the balcony. Then he happily brings home some lively eels, another Christmas Eve tradition we are to presume was not a favorite of the boss.

In the end, Don Carmine finds out he is not dying after all. He returns to Don Savj's apartment. The family is celebrating their freedom and Christmas Eve dinner with champagne. There is no turning back. The family stands together and stares the bully down. The last shot is the doorknob as Don Carmine leaves forever.

WHO IS CAMPANIAN?

No one in Campania would ever call himself Campanian. Hardly anyone in Italy identifies himself with a region. The furthest border they consider theirs is the provincial border. To explain the system, think of an Italian region (there are twenty) as equivalent to a state in the United States, and think of a province as equivalent to a county. Campania is divided into five provinces. They are Naples, which includes the city itself and a semicircle of *borghi,* or suburbs; Caserta, north of Naples; Benevento, northwest of Naples; Avellino, west of Naples; and Salerno, which is south of Naples and not only Campania's largest province, but Italy's largest, too. The islands of Ischia and Procida are in the province of Naples. Capri is in Salerno.

For the purposes of this book, I have used the word Campanian when I mean to generalize about a region-wide dish or foodway. Even though the people of one province will argue that they are very different from the people of a neighboring province, to the outsider there are more similarities than differences. Cuisine, language, and customs don't pay attention to political borders, either. There are provincial differences, and dishes and foodways can change slightly from one town to the next, but there are no dramatic differences over small distances, even from one region to the next. For instance, in the northern reaches of Campania, the food may be more similar to Molise or Lazio than it is to Salerno or Agropoli, which, although they are in the same region, are much farther away. Another example: In the northwestern province of Benevento, the food has some similarities to neighboring Puglia. Still, since Naples has been the pace-setter of southern Italy for so many centuries, one can prudently say that all of Campania cooks *la cucina napoletana.*

same building in which the Farnese collection of antiquities and Renaissance paintings has been magnificently remounted. The gardens of the Caserta palace, which vie with those of Versailles, are used for outdoor concerts. Except during the worst weather, a flea market is held every weekend in the Villa Comunale, the palm-lined park along the bay in Naples. Traditional Neapolitan songs are gaining popularity among the young, even if in reggae or country western arrangements, and Naples is said to be the main spawning ground of talent for Milan's recording industry. Art is on the streets. Musicians are in the restaurants. Posters everywhere advertise film series, painting exhibitions, and theatrical entertainment, often classic Neapolitan farce and satirical comedy. And, of course, there is San Carlo, Italy's oldest and largest opera house.

Yet, as residents of a city and region that has survived by defying and living around the rules and taxes of oppressive foreign occupiers, Neapolitans remain wary of the government's law. They subscribe only to the laws of humanity that develop from living so close to one another—with, literally, one's laundry hanging out to dry.

Organized crime still reigns—there was recently a scandal about the Camorra taking over the main street of Caserta and raising all the prices. Black-market vendors, mainly old women, are still on the corners selling counterfeit or stolen goods—cigarettes, watches, designer perfume. And everyone in Naples seems to agree that the traffic signals are "only a suggestion" (*"solo un consiglio"*) and that one-way street signs are to be ignored after dark.

Only a couple of years ago, I asked a hotel clerk where I might get a book photocopied, even though, as I told her, I knew it was illegal to photocopy copyrighted material. "Excuse me, sir," she said, taking that backward step people do when they are amazed or insulted, "nothing is illegal in Naples." More recently, at a famous luxury hotel on the Amalfi Coast, the hotel's owner was showing me and a friend around. My companion commented on the luminous blue of the new ceramic floor tiles, and how well they matched the old ones. "Oh yes," said our hostess, "they contain lead, which is illegal now. But if you pay the ceramic people enough they'll put it in anyway."

If you think Italy in general is sort of an unreliable, disorganized place, let me point out that Campania is considered quintessential Italy. But even with its dark side, sunny Italy indeed.

ANCIENT TIMES

When the ancient Romans called it *Campania felix*, they meant the "happy countryside" or "fortunate countryside," although Campani was already the name of the area in the language of the native population. These were the Oscans, centered in Capua, on the plain near the sea, and the Samnites, who spoke the Oscan language but lived further inland, in the hills around Benevento.

Through a mountain pass south of their city, the Latin-speaking Romans found a land with easily tillable, unbelievably productive volcanic soil, a climate that afforded several crop cycles a year, and a sea coast not only teaming with edible life but with beautiful low-lying beaches and protected bays. And let's not underestimate this: The locals were a notoriously carefree, welcoming, and warmhearted people.

Although the Romans did not bother much with what is the northeastern province of modern Campania, Benevento (which is to this day the least like the rest of the region), most of the rest of this countryside became Rome's vegetable garden and grain field, its coast their playground. It was mainly along the fine beachy stretches of the Campanian shore that the aristocracy built their country retreats. It was, for the richest and highest class, a place to withdraw from the political intrigues and hectic life of Rome, and a more politic and receptive place to let off steam than their surprisingly staid and prudish capital. Emperors and patricians alike, including Lucullus, the great Roman gastronome, built grand villas here. It was at these Campanian estates that many of those infamous Roman orgies were held. Most of the houses and palaces were long ago swallowed up by the Tyrrhenian Sea, but ruins of two of the grandest are open to tourists. In Sperlonga, which continues to be a fashionable Roman getaway near the port city of Gaeta—the spiritual if no longer actual northernmost point of modern Campania—tourists can visit Caesar Tiberius's fish farm, an adjunct to his villa, in a cave by the sea. The cave was once adorned with monumental statuary that is now displayed in a museum by the road, and it gives some idea of the opulence one might have met at the villa itself. On Capri, the small island at the southernmost end of the Bay of Naples, off the tip of the Sorrento peninsula (the Amalfi Coast), there are ruins of the villa from which Tiberius actually ruled the empire for twenty-three years. It was here, in the luminous sea waters of the Grotta Azzurra, the Blue Grotto, that he is supposed to have "frolicked" with young men.

His behavior was apparently not so unusual in his day; at least not for Romans in Campania. Let's not forget how priapic Pompeii was! Campania was, and still is in some ways, a place with different moral standards from the regions north of it. The prejudices of the north are not entirely unfounded. For instance, little is known about Oscan and Samnite culture, but we do know that they had a tradition of theater from which grew the populist Commedia dell'Arte. Oscan theatricals were so vulgar to the Romans that the word Oscan eventually became the word "obscene." More importantly, all of southern Italy was, from about the eighth century B.C., part of "Greater" Greece, a culture that had much more liberal ideas about pleasure than Rome.

Campania continues in many respects to be more a Greek place than a Roman place. Only recently, a young Neapolitan told me—by way of explaining the sensual aliveness and atmosphere of his city, the welcoming warmth, openness, and independence of its people—"Of course, Napoli is Magna Grecia." To him, anything north of Rome is "Germany," just as anything south of Rome is "Africa" to those who live north of the capital.

The seductiveness of Naples and Campania, is, after all, the subject of Greek myth. The story of the Sirens was first written by Homer in the *Odyssey*, but it could be a continuation of a local Oscan belief that the rivers and streams that once trailed down the hills of Naples into the sea were inhabited by a river god and his daughters. According to the Greek version, the Sirens were human-size, birdlike creatures with claws and the heads of women.

GREEK NAPLES TODAY

The stamp of the Greeks is forever physically on Naples, as well as culturally. The Greeks' distinctive grid street plan, laid down in about 600 B.C. and later adopted by the Romans for their other cities, dominates what is still the heart and historic center of the city—Spaccanapoli, literally "split Naples." The grid consists of long rectangular blocks of roughly north-south running streets crossed perpendicularly by wider east-west streets. In Naples, the wide streets are still very important. Via Tribunali, the main and central one, takes pedestrians across Spaccanapoli. Via San Biagio dei Librai, which changes to Via Benedetto Croce along its course and is informally called Spaccanapoli by those in the neighborhood, is a busy shopping street full of booksellers. And Via Anticaglia is another street full of shops.

Other outstanding remnants of the Greeks are columns and decorations from Greek temples built into churches, and a tour of underground Greek ruins can be privately arranged. But the main public vestige of Greek architecture is the bit of city wall that has been excavated at Piazza Bellini, next door to the Pizzeria Bellini.

They lived on the islands and rocks offshore. Among these are the Galli islands in the Bay of Salerno; the Faraglioni, the two prominent rocks next to Capri that are depicted on postcards and the covers of tourist guides, and sometimes stenciled in sugar on a local cake (torta caprese); and the so-called Mushroom Rock at Ischia, whose fungal shape is also the subject of contemporary souvenirs and antique art.

The Sirens' "call," which is described in literature as either a high-pitched tone or an indescribably beautiful song, was irresistible. Sailors passing the Campania shore would be compelled to jump into the water to meet the calls, and they would perish. Knowing this, says Homer in the *Odyssey*, Ulysses (or Odysseus) had his crew stuff their ears with wax and had himself tied to a mast so he could hear the tempting call but couldn't respond. There is a famous Greek vase depicting the story. On it, the Sirens are shown flopping all over the boat while Ulysses, bound to the mast, has a mighty erection. Eventually, the Sirens began to be depicted in art and literature as women with fish tails instead of as birds; in other words, mermaids. Today, *sirena* means mermaid in Italian (and Disney's *Little Mermaid* is, by the way, *La Sirenetta*).

The Siren named Parthenope (meaning Maiden Face) is particularly identified with Naples. She was supposedly so depressed when she couldn't seduce Ulysses that she committed suicide, throwing herself against the rocks. Her body washed up onto the shore of the Bay of Naples, giving her name to the area at the foot of the hill (now Pizzofalcone) where the Greeks eventually settled in about 600 B.C. They called it Parthenope in her honor. Still today in Naples, the street along that stretch of the sea—where the grandest hotels are—is Via Partenope. And when republicans controlled the Kingdom of Naples for a few months in 1799, they called it the Parthenopean Republic.

The Greeks settled in Campania about 160 years before they founded Parthenope, however. Sometime about 760 B.C., they formed a colony on Ischia, on a cliff above the current town of Lacco Ameno. It was their first settlement in the western Mediterranean. From Ischia, they could trade more conveniently with the Etruscans, whose territory reached south to the Oscan lands and to whom they were already selling their iron wares. Archaeologists propose several reasons for the Greeks choosing Ischia, which they called Pithecusae, such as the presence of iron deposits on the island, or perhaps easily accessible fuel for them to forge iron. The possible reasons for their leaving only about ten years later include volcanic eruptions or earthquake activity—a problem all over the region to this day. We do know, however, that the Greeks next settled on the mainland, across a narrow strait from Ischia, founding what they called Cumae and is now Cuma.

Growing in number and reinforced with colonists from Rhodes, they flourished in Cumae. They got rich from their trade with the Etruscans and from selling Hellenic and Eastern wares to the Oscans and Samnites. From Cumae, which is now a rather dumpy suburb of Naples, they expanded southeast. They founded the seaport of Dikaearchia, which was called Puteoli by the Romans when they harbored their navy there, and is now Pozzuoli. It is still such a strategically important, beautifully protected port that a large NATO naval force is stationed there.

From Pozzuoli, which is today, in essence, a suburban extension of Naples (and most famous in popular culture as the birthplace of Sophia Loren), it was natural to move on and settle in the next and bigger bay, to the shore on which the mythological Parthenope had been washed up.

One of the first stories we have about the Greeks who lived on the big bay foreshadows the character that is still associated with Neapolitans—an independent people who win with their wits, not war, people who compromise for survival, bending with the times, the government, the conquerors, but never breaking, never giving up their distinctiveness or truly submitting.

There were, in fact, two tiny settlements on the grand bay—Parthenope and neighboring Neapolis, which means New (*nea*) City (*polis*). In time, the name Parthenope gave way to the name Paleopolis, Old City. When, in 328 B.C., the Romans, who had already made themselves masters of the northern coast of Campania and the chief power on the peninsula, laid siege to the two southern Greek cities, the Neapolitans did not do battle. They negotiated. Some historians say the Paleopolitans did fight, and thus perished. In any case, the name Paleopolis was never mentioned again, while Neapolis survived.

The Neapolitans accepted Roman domination, but were granted full equality of rights, exemption from military service, and peace. They retained their Greek constitution, the Greek language, and humanistic Hellenic culture, and when, in 89 B.C., the Romans granted citizenship to all their Italian allies, the Neapolitans were still allowed to continue with their own government, laws, magistrates, customs, and language.

By the time the Romans were invading Naples, the Oscan and Samnite cultures had faded. Through trade, the Neapolitans had Hellenized and assimilated the native tribes. Archaeologists know little about Samnite culture, although some artifacts of theirs can be seen in a museum in Benevento, the center of their civilization. They know much more about the Oscans, whose museum is in Capua, their ancient capital. Given that, it's ironic that many people in the modern province of Benevento

THE MIRACLE OF SAN GENNARO

There are no street fairs in Naples on the Feast Day of San Gennaro, September 19. There are no sausage and pepper sandwiches, no zeppole, and no midway games and gambling as there are at the Feasts of San Gennaro in Little Italys across North America. Sure, since every Neapolitan moment needs a food to go with it, vendors set up tables outside the Duomo, the cathedral, and sell torrone, almond nougat from candy bar sizes to chocolate-swirled and covered pieces in the shape of San Gennaro's bishop's hat. It's not the food on the street but what goes on inside the church that Neapolitans focus on. Will the saint's blood liquefy and guarantee good times for the city, or will it remain solid in its monstrance and portend catastrophe? The Feast of San Gennaro has been called the world's "greatest display of collective paranoia."

Gennaro, or St. Januarius, the bishop of Benevento, was martyred by the Romans in Pozzuoli, right outside Naples, in A.D. 305. The story is that he came from Benevento to save some of his clergymen who had previously traveled there. Naturally, he, too, was captured by the Romans and sentenced to be burned alive in a furnace. When the Romans looked into the furnace, however, they found the bishop sitting, very much alive, the flames burning around him, praying with a heavenly chorus.

Next, Gennaro and his followers were thrown into the arena with the lions. Hungry as they were, the wild beasts would not touch the Christians, who were on their knees in prayer. Finally, Gennaro was beheaded.

Followers collected the blood of the martyr, which is supposed to have liquefied in the hands of St. Severus as he carried Gennaro's relics from Pozzuoli to Naples. It is this blood that is said to be held in the two glass vials housed together in a crystal and silver monstrance in a chapel inside the Duomo. Twice a year (it used to be three times), at the Duomo on September 19, which is the saint's birthday; and at the church of Santa Chiara on the first Saturday in May, commemorating the transfer of his relics to Naples, Neapolitans await Il Miracolo di San Gennaro, the miracle of the saint's blood. Solid and dark, as anyone in the church can see, it turns brighter red and liquefies—or not. Neapolitans can correlate almost every eruption of Vesuvius, every earthquake, every cholera epidemic, war, and lost soccer championship, to San Gennaro's blood remaining solid.

The ceremony is always called for nine A.M. Even though the proceedings are broadcast on television these days, thousands of believers attend, spilling onto the street to eagerly await notice. While most observers are seated in the pews of the huge church, a group considered to be *i parenti di San Gennaro*, the relatives of the saint (it's not clear how one proves this), are allowed to stand behind a guarded VIP section in front of the altar. They exhort the saint, if necessary—and curse him if he doesn't produce the miracle.

To begin, accompanied by choir and organ, the silver monstrance with the vials of blood and a golden reliquary containing the saint's head and torso are carried to the altar by a procession of priests, altar boys, and a committee of nobles and representatives of the people. This group is charged with the maintenance of San Gennaro's chapel. The committee members, dressed in white tie and tails and with red sashes across their chests, are seated on the altar with the archbishop while he delivers a sermon, then prays with the congregation for the liquefaction of the blood.

The praying is very loud and earnest, especially among the relatives of San Gennaro. Up on the altar, the archbishop turns the monstrance upside down a few times. If the blood doesn't liquefy, he asks the congregation to pray again. The blood usually doesn't liquefy, and the praying gets louder and more earnest. Eventually, usually, the blood liquefies. It happens almost always a little after ten, as it did the day I witnessed it, "after the soloist of the day performs during the second round of prayers," a nonbelieving Neapolitan friend assures me.

When the miracle occurs, the chairman of the chapel committee waves a white handkerchief, and everyone in the cathedral applauds politely—strangely politely, given the ardor of their prayers and the usual exuberance of Neapolitans. (They are also oddly restrained in theaters.) The archbishop shows the liquefied blood to the TV cameras first, then to the VIPs seated in front of the altar. It is customary to kiss the monstrance when he offers it.

As superstitious as Neapolitans are, many swear that the monstrance is rigged. "I don't think the current clergy has anything to do with it," a friend assured me in all seriousness, "but I'll bet back in the fifteenth century, they put something in there to make it happen."

consider themselves descended from the Samnites, *I Sanniti,* and to this day call their cooking *cucina sannita,* while not a soul in Capua ever considers saying he is descended from the Oscans.

A HISTORY OF OCCUPATION

The history of Naples and Campania is a series of foreign occupations and dominations. As Carlo Levi said about Campania in his 1945 autobiographical novel, *Christ Stopped at Eboli* (Eboli is a town in the hills of Salerno), "Nobody ever came here except as a conqueror, an enemy, or an unappreciative visitor." Through sheer strength of character, however, the people have always managed to resist fully capitulating to their conquerors. Instead, they've used them and their culture, or won them over, to enhance their own. It's the Neapolitan way of shrugging off adversity.

After the Romans, the Neapolitans got no respite. In A.D. 330, the Emperor Constantine established a new eastern capital of the Roman Empire in Byzantium, renaming it Constantinople, and in 395, the empire was divided into a stronger eastern and much weaker western branch. It took no time at all for Germanic tribes from the north to fill the void in the west and pounce on the Italian peninsula. Alaric sacked Rome in 410, and on his march to Sicily, he pillaged Naples. The city suffered similarly in 455, when Genseric's Vandals stopped by. The last emperor of the Western Empire, Romulus Augustulus, was forced to flee. He took cover in the Villa of Lucullus (the long-gone famous Roman gastronome), situated on a rock that juts into the Bay of Naples exactly where the body of the Siren Parthenope is supposed to have washed ashore. He died there. It is now the site of the medieval fortress called the Castel dell'Ovo. These days, prosaically filled with offices and surrounded by a cluster of cafés and restaurants, it is still one of Naples's most prominent and monumental landmarks; a spot where Virgil supposedly had a vision, the place where the Roman Emperor Tiberius may have died, and home to many other legends.

Soon after the Vandals came the Goths, who were routed temporarily by Emperor Justinian, ruler of the Byzantine Eastern Empire, under his General Belisarius. Justinian was determined to drive the Ostrogoths out of the Italian peninsula, but it wasn't easy. In 543, the Goths recaptured Naples, and it wasn't until ten years later that the Eastern Empire gained control again, under Justinian's General Narses.

Even under Byzantine rule, the Neapolitans managed to keep control of their city. The emperor declared them a duchy, but the Neapolitans made sure they got to elect the duke.

Now the "savage" Lombards came in 568, marching into the peninsula from Eastern Germany and Hungary under their chief, Alboin. Within a few years, the Lombards were the masters of most of Italy, but notably not of Naples, Salerno, or Paestum, this last the ancient Greek settlement on the plain south of Salerno. These cities on the sea were able to hold out, while the rest of the peninsula remained under tenuous and disastrous Lombard control. After Alboin's death, the Lombard chiefs fought with each other over their territories, creating the havoc that is often blamed for the disappearance of the large Roman plantations of grain and vegetables that thrived so remarkably on Campania's volcanic soil. By the time the Lombards had sorted their differences out and finally divided their conquered lands into thirty-six Lombard duchies, all that was left were smaller, less productive plots of land, farms that could support only a family or a small local economy and that were more susceptible to the vagaries of nature.

ANECDOTE: NONAGREEMENT PACT

One of the first things you learn sitting at table in Campania is that no one agrees on anything, and with more drama than no one agrees on anything in the rest of Italy. Even within the same household, where everyone has learned to cook from the same grandmother or mother, there can be debate on the right or wrong, better or worse way of preparing any and every dish. I've witnessed these squabbles many times, but one day in Frasso Telesino, the debate got particularly heated among the daughters and granddaughters of the extended family. In the end, one of the younger women turned to me, lifted her espresso cup, and said, defeated and exasperated, "Listen, in our family, we can't even agree on how to make coffee."

Eventually, another Lombard chief, Zotto, named himself the Duke of Benevento. Though Zotto laid siege to Naples in 581, the Neapolitans, still loyal to the emperor and led by their bishop, repulsed him. Zotto's successor, Arichis, claimed most of the rest of southern Italy, but Naples, Salerno, and Paestum still held firm. It wasn't until 640 that the Lombards conquered Salerno and Paestum, and in 717 they grabbed Cuma.

Surrounded by the Lombard duchies of Rome, Benevento, Capua, and now Salerno, the Imperialist Duchy of Naples was small, but remarkably rich and blessedly independent. Although technically under the emperor, it was physically so far from the rest of the empire that it could behave like a sovereign and practically republican state. Both the offices of duke and bishop became more or less hereditary, but their positions were at least ratified by the citizens before being confirmed by the emperor.

During the seventh and eighth centuries, Naples was virtually alone among the nominally Byzantine areas of Italy in its independence from the Lombards, although the going was never easy. It maintained its population, which was about 40,000, its Greek language, character, and culture, but it was literally surrounded and always under the threat of Lombard siege. Perhaps that is why the Neapolitans developed a commercial relationship with the Moslem Saracens (coming from northwest Arabia), who pirated Naples's neighbors up and down the coast but never plundered Naples.

In the 840s, Arabs coming from North Africa first conquered Sicily, and by 880 they controlled most of southern Italy, except Naples. The Arabs did change Campania, though. Through them, via Sicily, came the orange and lemon trees that are now so prominent on the landscape of Campania. The Neapolitans' love of sweets made with the candied peels of those fruits, almonds, and flower waters is an Arab legacy, and the Neapolitan habit of adding raisins and pine nuts to otherwise savory dishes is said to be Arab also.

The ninth century also saw Naples lose its nominal control over Salerno and Amalfi, which had grown as seaports and had become Naples's new rivals, along with Gaeta up the coast. Along the Amalfi Coast, one also sees the Arab influence in the colorfully tiled domes of churches. And anyone who has ever listened to Neapolitan songs can readily hear the Arab influence in the alternating minor and major key changes.

Neapolitan independence and prosperity lasted for nearly 400 years, until the beginning of the 12th century. Then along came the Normans, descendants of the Vikings who conquered England, Ireland, and the Normandy region of France that is named for them. Starved for lands at home, the Normans, on their return from the Holy Land in 1030, set up their first principality in Aversa, only a few miles north of Naples. There they laid plans to conquer the rest of southern Italy. By 1053, they controlled so much of the south that Pope Leo IX led an army against them, only to be defeated. The cost of the defeat was declaring one of the ruling Normans, Guiscard, Duke of Apulia and Calabria. And when, in 1084, the Normans freed Pope Gregory VII from German Emperor Henry IV's siege of the Vatican, they essentially became the rulers of Italy from the toe of the boot to the Tiber. By 1091, another Norman, Roger of Calabria, had taken Sicily from the Arabs, and in 1128, Roger's son, Roger II, wheedled the title "king" of Sicily out of Pope Anacletus II. Finally, in 1139, the city of Naples itself fell to the Normans after a long siege that left many citizens starving.

By this time, the port of Naples had been eclipsed by the neighboring ports of Salerno and Amalfi. Naples had become a small town, about the size of Florence, but smaller than Venice, Rome, or Milan, the other important Italian cities. And so it was a turn of good fortune for Naples that the Normans decided to quash the independence of Salerno and Amalfi and concentrate on strengthening Naples, which they must have realized had a grander, deeper, better harbor and a more felicitous position on the sea.

With southern Italy united under the Normans, the wars between the Lombard city-states over, and trade now flowing from the interior to the coast under the protection of a unified Norman rule, Naples enjoyed a renaissance. It became the trading hub between France, Spain, North Africa, and Sicily. Traders from Salerno and Amalfi opened offices there. In the thirteenth century, the Genovese came. The Normans made it a cultural hub, too, tolerating all religious practices, including Moslem and Jewish, and, as great assimilators themselves, they blended Latin, Greek, and Arab cultures. In the late tenth century, they founded the first medical school in the Western world, in Salerno, which to this day continues to attract students from all over the world.

It was an accident of inheritance that put Naples in the temporary but beneficent hands of the Germans. The Norman William II, William the Good, was about to go on his Third Crusade when he died childless in 1189. Through the usual tangle of marriages used in those days to create political alliances, his heir ended up being Frederick I Barbarossa, a Hohenstaufen prince raised in the Sicilian court of Palermo. Frederick, who ruled from 1215 to 1250 as Holy Roman Emperor, turned Palermo into the cultural center of Europe. Among many other things, he broke the tradition that poetry could be written only in classical Latin and he encouraged works in the "vulgar" Italian language.

Frederick preferred Naples, though, and appreciated the unique protective qualities of the nearby port of Pozzuoli. The weather was better, and he could be nearer his problematic northern border with the papal state, as well as closer to his lands in Germany. He built up the city, and to seize the religious and philosophical high ground from the pope, he established the University of Naples in 1224. Not only was it open to all, but Frederick forbade his subjects from going elsewhere, lest they take lessons from the pope. (Thomas Aquinas, one of the most influential thinkers of the Middle Ages, was one of the university's students.)

After Frederick's death in 1250, the pope, Urban IV, a Frenchman, offered the kingdom, still called the Kingdom of Sicily but including all of the southern half of the peninsula from the toe of the boot to the papal state in Rome, to Count Charles of Anjou. Said the pope: It would be only a matter of killing Frederick's heir, Manfred. And that's what Charles of Anjou did in 1266, with the help of his wife, Beatrice of Provence, who hocked her jewels to send her husband to war against Manfred. As her three sisters were already queens, she was determined to be one, too.

Charles, now Charles I of the Kingdom of Sicily, chose Naples, not Palermo, as his capital and immediately started calling his new realm the Kingdom of Naples. It was just as well. After the twenty-year so-called War of the Vespers in Sicily, he lost the island to the Aragonese.

Charles I of Anjou and his heirs, the Angevins, brought Naples into a period of international importance and influence, prosperity, and cultural brilliance. The years of war during Charles I's reign, the family's possessions in Anjou, Provence, and the Piedmont, immediately gave a boost to Naples's economy. Merchants from around the Mediterranean, from Marseilles, Catalonia, and even Florence, set up offices in Naples. A new manufacturing district rose near the waterfront. Bankers and investors clustered in another new section of the city. Charles dredged a new harbor, built the castle of Belforte, now the Castel Sant'Elmo, the fortress that is gorgeously illuminated each night on one of Naples's highest hills, and the Castel Nuovo, a new fortress on the bay. Locally, Castel Nuovo is called the Maschio Angioino, in honor of Charles, and it now houses the city council.

It was in this progress-minded milieu that the first Neapolitan cookbook was written by a courtier of Charles II. Called *Liber de coquina* (Book of Cooking), it was written in Latin and was meant to establish a new tradition around this new French family in Naples. The book mixes recipes from both the French and Neapolitan courtly traditions, but also from the other groups that lived and traveled in southern Italy: the Arabs, Spanish, Genovese, and Tuscans. Naples was becoming an international city.

As much as Charles I and II improved the lot of Naples, Charles II's son, Robert I (the Wise), and his second queen, Sancia of Majorca, were the Angevins who really brought Naples to the forefront of European culture. Their court became a meeting place for poets, scholars, theologians, reformers, writers, artists, and musicians. The king was known for his learning. Dante immortalized his sermonizing. Petrarch tells of his interest in antiquities and his deep knowledge of the city's legends. Boccaccio wrote about Naples's sophisticated mores and vivid personalities. Another Neapolitan cookbook appeared, written anonymously, and alternately written in Latin and the relatively new Italian language. The *Due libri di cucina* (The Two Books of Cooking) describes the costly, complicated dishes of the court. At least one recipe remains a favorite of Neapolitans: blancmange, or milk pudding.

Naples grew. In about 1340, the population was 100,000. With Venice, Milan, and Florence, it was among the largest cities in Europe. To put it in perspective, Paris's population was then about 80,000; Constantinople, the largest city in the West, was at about 200,000.

But the Neapolitans were living on the edge of a volcano, and on a periodically trembling land. In the early 1340s, earthquakes destroyed a portion of the city and sank ships in the bay. In 1347, bubonic plague arrived from the Crimea via the shipping trade routes and killed 63,000 people in and around Naples. The plague hit again in 1362, 1382, 1399, and 1411.

It wasn't just natural calamities that ripped apart what the early Angevins built. The kingdom was not served well after Robert the Wise died in 1343. His heir died before him, and his throne went to his nymphomaniac granddaughter, Giovanna I. She had four husbands and numerous lovers, and she is said to have been under the spell of a Franciscan named Robert of Mileto. After taking the wrong side in the "Great Schism" between the French pope, Clement VII, and the Roman pope, Urban VI, she was excommunicated, then murdered by her successor, a cousin, Charles (III) of Durazzo. He seized the throne in 1381. For the next few years, the court was in so much confusion that the noble families of Naples were able to usurp power and, in 1386, they elected six nobles and two merchants as a city government.

The last of the line of Angevins was another Giovanna, and Giovanna II got worse treatment from the historians than her ancestor. To stave off the growing power of the Neapolitan barons, she had love affairs with and made marriages to many influential men. In 1423, she even adopted a lover, Alfonso V, King of Aragon and Sicily. But she soon disowned him.

The adoption, however, gave the Aragonese a claim on the Kingdom of Naples, and when Giovanna died in 1435, it was Alfonso who finally won the city from the legitimate Angevin heir. It was 1442 and the beginning of the Renaissance.

Alfonso's reign was so beneficial to the Neapolitans that he became known as Alfonso the Magnanimous, and the kingdom became a major cultural center of the period. Alfonso repaired the roads, palaces, and churches. He established a humanist center at his court, refurbished and enlarged the royal library, sponsored philosophical and literary discussions, and revived the university, which had been closed during the Angevin reign. He established a permanent class of well-educated professionals and a bureaucracy of middle-class citizens to counteract the power of the local barons.

Another devastating earthquake shook Naples in 1450, but the Aragonese continued to beautify and enrich the city. In the next fifty years, under Alfonso II and his successors, the city became known for its elegant villas and gardens, and the city limits were expanded. In 1487, Alfonso began to build the Renaissance-style royal palace, the Palazzo Reale, which remains a centerpiece of the city.

By the beginning of the 1500s, Naples's population had rebounded and exceeded its former 1340s high point. With an estimated 150,000 citizens, it was now larger than Venice and Milan, and twice the size of London. By 1550, the numbers were up to 210,000, while Constantinople, still the largest city in the West, topped 400,000.

In 1503, however, through yet another battle over claims to the throne, Gonsalvo de Cordoba, who had taken Granada from the Moors, won the entire Kingdom of Naples for "Ferdinand the Catholic," as in Ferdinand and Isabella of Spain. Now began a 230-year rule under Spanish viceroys—the first one was Cordoba himself—then another 230-year rule by the Bourbons, a dynasty descended from the French Philip, Duke of Anjou, who became King of Spain in 1700.

Though the managing viceroys of Naples were Spanish, they were actually under the control of the Hapsburg Emperor Charles V of the Holy Roman Empire. In 1516, as Charles I, he became Ferdinand's successor as king of a newly unified Spain and also ruler of all Europe except for the Papal States, Venice, England, and France. This was to prove to be a very important distinction and an advantage to the Neapolitans.

Again the Neapolitans managed to maintain some rule over themselves. The viceroys allied themselves with the local aristocracy against the urban poor and allowed the Neapolitans some home rule—their own courts, a parliament to air grievances, and the privilege of appealing to the king of Spain directly. Despite repeated but locally thwarted Spanish attempts to introduce the Inquisition and suppress the university, the city had a free atmosphere and became a haven for religious dissidents and intellectuals of all types.

A TURNING POINT

The period of the Spanish viceroys is often depicted as the lowest point of Neapolitan history, yet it was anything but. It was, rather, a major turning point, and no less in gastronomy than in anything else. Besides easing intellectual and artistic restraints, the viceroys improved the city's infrastructure, building roads, expanding the city, building some of the wide avenues that still intersect the city, building a new port, and encouraging trade. As part of Charles V's empire, Naples could trade freely with almost the whole continent, and by the middle of the sixteenth century it was a prime producer of luxury textiles, including linens and silks, lace, braids—trimmings of all kinds. Florence and Venice were the big markets for Naples's raw materials, and trade with Spain also brought wealth.

The Spanish viceroys are blamed, however, for, among other things, a system of taxation that further impoverished the already poor rural population and drew them into the city looking for food, housing, and work—and generally in that order. Even though there was another black plague in 1562, by 1595 the population had doubled to 300,000. Naples was now twice as populous as Venice and second only to Paris in Europe. Meanwhile, the Kingdom of Naples (all of the south of Italy, including Sicily) grew, too, tripling its population from 1 million to 3 million in less than a century.

The nobles continued to build lavish homes in the city, and cultural life flourished, but with its booming population the city became increasingly more impoverished, squalid, and crime-ridden. The overtaxed rural population streamed in but found less and less work, becoming homeless, beggars, and bandits. This all had a major impact on the food people ate, as did, very importantly, the stream of new foods coming from the New World—tomatoes, peppers, squash, potatoes, chocolate, and beans unlike any they had seen before. Because of its Spanish connections, Naples was among the first places to receive the new foods. Because of their poverty, Neapolitans were among the first to eat them. Says Maria Giovanna Fasulo Rak, in *La cucina napoletana in cento ricette tradizionali* (Neapolitan Cooking in 100 Traditional Recipes): "The spice route to the eastern Mediterranean was closed, but the tomato route to America opened." Maybe for that reason, chili peppers came to dominate over black pepper (see page 4).

In many respects, the new flavors profoundly changed Neapolitan cooking between the sixteenth and seventeenth centuries.

THE PASTA EATERS

Until the last half of the sixteenth century, both the urban and rural populations were largely vegetable eaters. Naples was celebrated for its great variety and quality of fruits and vegetables. They were sumptuously displayed in the markets, decorated with roses and jasmine, with great attention paid to the colors and forms of the displays. Until the middle of the sixteenth century, the people were called *mangiafoglie* (leaf eaters) by foreigners, and the main flavors were those of the Middle Ages—sweet and sour. The most common vegetable was broccoli, as it still is today, and Neapolitans relished it cooked with anchovies, fried garlic, and lemon juice, as they still might. Fish was abundant, and the fish were displayed with the

"SEE NAPLES AND DIE"

"See Naples and die!" was the cry of eighteenth-century English travelers, the well-heeled, cultural adventurers who took the "Grand Tour" of the Continent as part of their education. The exclamation was meant to suggest that after one had seen the glories and experienced the pleasures of Naples, there was nothing left to do but die. It's akin to the American expressions "It's the living end" or "It's to die for!" ("Da morire!" in contemporary Italian.)

Naples was then second only to Paris, the European center of music and opera, painting, architecture, fashion, and archaeology. The excavations at Pompeii, which began in 1731 and coincided with the beginning of the rule of the lavish Spanish Bourbons, made Naples the focus of European attention. The expression took on unfortunate meaning as the stylishness, cleanliness, and safety of Naples seriously declined in the late nineteenth and first half of the twentieth century, after the unification of Italy.

same flair as the produce. Meat was cooked with plums, garlic, pine nuts, raisins, sugar, almonds, and cinnamon, notions picked up from the Arabs.

Among the dishes that come down to us from that time (all in this book) are broccoli rabe cooked with garlic; various leafy greens cooked with anchovies, raisins, and pine nuts; and minestra maritata, a pot of greens and broth created from preserved and fresh pork products.

Ricotta, mozzarella, provola, and various other cheeses were being made, and the convents specialized in making perfumed waters—rose, mixed flowers, myrtle. The nuns also made pastas—lasagne, ravioli, gnocchi (strangolaprieti) and macaroni, sometimes stuffed with fresh cheeses. Sweets also came from the convents; mostaccioli, the popular Christmas spice cookies, among them.

Supplying perishable vegetables to a city so populous and still expanding became a problem near the end of the sixteenth century. And so Neapolitans were encouraged to depend more on storable, dried pasta—maccheroni—as the Sicilians already did. Wheat for flour was brought in from the Ukraine. The war-, earthquake-, and plague-devastated Campanian countryside was no longer able to produce as it did in Roman times. This flour wasn't taxed in order to placate the impoverished masses. The viceroys also set out great feasts of pasta. "There were more than 10,000 people that his Excellency delighted in seeing gorge themselves with macaroni Neapolitan style [eaten] with their hands," wrote a diarist in 1617.

Soon the Neapolitans started creating new pasta shapes: ziti, vermicelli (what we and the rest of Italy call spaghetti), fusilli, bucatini, linguine, and paccheri among them. They are still the major macaroni forms.

The basic way to eat pasta remained the same for at least 100 years. Still dripping with cooking water, it was dressed with grated cheese and ground black pepper, then eaten with the hand. Except for the tomato, the seasonings we use now were sometimes used then, too: garlic, oregano, onion, meat, fish, and shellfish. Some historians say the tomato started to be put on flat bread about this time—the late 1600s—creating Neapolitan pizza, although some others set the date at the mid–1700s.

The arrival of chocolate transformed all of Europe, but first Spain and then Naples. One of the Spanish chocolate desserts that went around Naples was "softened by the aroma of jasmine and citrus," observed Francesco Redi in 1685 in *Bacco in Toscana, annotazioni* (Bacchus in Tuscany, Annotated).

THE FRENCH INFLUENCE

By the beginning of the eighteenth century, with Naples still under the Spanish viceroys, French cuisine started to eclipse the local cooking on the tables of the nobility. All over Europe, a new lightness and refinement in cooking coincided with the desire for moderation brought about by the Enlightenment. French style started to prevail.

In 1731, the government changed again. Through the political machinations of his mother, Elizabeth Farnese, Grand Duchess of Parma and Piacenza, Carlos I, whose father was Philip V of Spain, became the first reigning monarch who actually lived in Naples. Carlos was sent to Tuscany and Parma to reclaim his mother's family's lands from the Austrians. To make a long, politically complicated story very short, in the end Carlos got Naples and all of the south of Italy, including Sicily, while the Austrians remained in Parma.

Carlos I reigned for almost thirty years. He ascended the throne of Spain in 1759 as Charles III, leaving the Kingdom of Naples to his third son, Ferdinand IV, now called Ferdinand I of Naples. They presided over the most glorious days of the city, when all of intellectual and artistic Europe crossed paths in Naples. But both father and son were noto-

IL CARRO DELLA CUCCAGNA
The Cart of Abundance

During early Bourbon times, in the middle of the eighteenth century, it was the custom for the four Sundays before Carnevale (the end of January, the beginning of February) for the king to put out decorated wooden carriages full of foodstuffs in the Piazza del Plebiscito, which is still the central square of the city. One week there would be breads, one week meats, one week vegetables, and one week fish. Armed guards protected the carriages until the signal sounded from the king. Then the people would attack them. This became so disorderly and dangerous that it finally had to be abolished.

FESTE, FARINA, E FORCA

It is said that the Bourbons ruled the Kingdom of Naples (later called the Kingdom of the Two Sicilies) by *feste, farina, e forca.*

Feste: They threw feasts, such as Il Carro della Cuccagna.

Farina: They made flour (from the Ukraine) available and tax-free.

Forca: They sent just about anybody to the gallows.

Feste, Farina e Forca (Feasts, Flour and Gallows) is a book on the subject by Vittorio Gleijeses (3rd edition published 1977).

rious layabouts, favoring hunting and fishing over any other activity, except for sex and eating. They made a few attempts at social reform and support, did a few good deeds—such as establishing the first public housing for the poor (sadly inadequate) and continuing to forbid the Inquisition in the kingdom—but neither of their reigns improved the situation of the average Neapolitan. Their legacy is mainly buildings.

Carlos, competing with his Bourbon relatives in France, built a country palace twelve miles outside Naples, in Caserta, that vies with Versailles in size and grandeur. Besides 1,200 rooms, it has a park that is still awesome for its beauty, including a 250-foot-high manmade waterfall that tumbles into a basin filled with monumental sculptures of Diana and Actaeon. Outdoor concerts are held here today, and the garden and palace are open to the public.

In 1737, he commissioned San Carlo, the opera house named for his patron saint, building it in eight months and attaching it to the Palazzo Reale. It is the oldest and still largest opera house in Italy, seating 3,000.

To compete with his Saxon father-in-law, who owned the world's most famous porcelain factory in Vienna, Carlos founded his own porcelain works in 1740. At first the porcelain laboratories were placed in the gardens of the Royal Palace in Naples, so he could micro-manage them. However, soon finding this arrangement unsuitable, or the laboratories too small, he built a new factory in the Royal Park of his suburban palace, Capodimonte, on a hill high above the city. (The Capodimonte palace now houses both the astonishing Farnese family collections that Carlos removed from Parma before turning the city over to the Austrians, and, on its upper floors, a recently opened contemporary art museum that is part of the city's current cultural rejuvenation.)

It was during the reigns of Carlos and Ferdinand that *la cucina napoletana* came into its own. Carlos's son, Ferdinand, for his part, loved to carouse with the lowest rungs of Neapolitan society, and from them he learned about macaroni. He brought the people's food to court, and may have even had the four-tined fork invented (at his wife's insistence) so he could eat it more politely than with his hands, as the boys on the street did. His queen, Maria Carolina of Austria, a Hapsburg princess and the sister of Marie Antoinette of France, was a stickler about proper court decorum and sent her chefs to Paris so they could prepare and present the local foods and flavors with more refinement. These chefs were called *Monzù*, a Neapolitan corruption of monsieur, and they created a true fusion cuisine, maintaining the vivid flavors of Neapolitan cooking, even some of the dishes themselves, while combining them with or superimposing on them the refinements and elaborate, decorative presentations of Louis XVI's court. Pastry cases for pasta and complex savory compositions came into fashion. And fine forcemeats. Broth and butter were used more freely. Architectural desserts were invented for the Bourbon table.

In a weak moment of high-mindedness, Ferdinand took time out from his nearly daily hunting trips, on which he slaughtered animals until he was waist-high in blood and guts, and built a Utopian city, San Leucio, next to his palace in Caserta. Here, he guaranteed work in his silk factory, housing, and health care for all workers. The endeavor failed, but the buildings stand and San Leucio remains a center of fine silk manufacture.

THE MELDING OF RICH AND POOR COOKING

The rich got richer and the poor got poorer during the Bourbon era, which lasted until the unification of Italy in 1861, and it was exactly that circumstance that created the full blooming of *la cucina napoletana*. The first book that gave a nod to the cuisine was published in 1773. *Il cuoco galante* (The Gallant Cook) by Vincenzo Corrado reflects its era's French taste for food decoration—at least among those who would buy a cookbook—but it also describes simple dishes, food seasoned only with herbs and without sauces made apart from it, which were more in the Campanian country tradition. It has a recipe for tomato sauce as we know it. In 1778, Corrado also published *Il credenziere del buon gusto* (The Steward of Good Taste), which describes the coffee beverages, sorbets, and ice creams that Naples's royal chefs perfected and Neapolitans still adore.

A clue to what the poorer Campanian ate, or at least to what he hoped he could eat in the mid-eighteenth century, is the nativity scene, the *presepe,* that became popular during Carlos I's reign. Father Rocco, a great friend of the king, promoted the *presepe* as a way of spiritualizing the illiterate masses that crowded Naples's slums. (He also, in a typical Neapolitan way, outmaneuvered the criminal element by lighting the streets with shrines to the saints, many of which continue to

THE *MONZÙ* TRADITION

*F*rench taste came to the court of Naples when Maria Carolina of Austria, a Hapsburg princess and the sister of the French queen Marie Antoinette, married Naples's Bourbon king, Ferdinand IV, in 1768.

Neapolitans like to say that Maria Carolina was actually enamored of the local cooking, but all we really know is that her husband preferred it, as he preferred carousing with the common people rather than his courtiers.

Whatever her position was, she sent her court's chefs to her sister's court in Paris for a few French cookery lessons. To "upgrade and ennoble" the cuisine, as one Neapolitan food historian put it, "with a touch of the refined cooks from north of the Alps."

When the cooks returned, they were called monsieur as a title of honor, which became corrupted in Neapolitan dialect to *Monzù*. Naturally, the aristocracy and untitled upper classes followed suit. Everyone had to have a *Monzù*.

According to Franco Santasilia di Torpino, whose book *La cucina aristocratica napoletana* (The Cooking of the Neapolitan Nobility) records some of the *Monzù* recipes, the *Monzù* tradition was mainly verbal. The cooks handed down their recipes, which often took on the names of their employers, who in fact may have helped devise some of them, or at least suggested the ideas for some of them. Only during the Second World War did many families have to give up their family cooks. After the war the *Monzù* became a rarity. Today, many of their dishes live because families have kept them alive or because they've become part of the cuisine in general. Modern-day *Monzù*-style chefs also have catering businesses and cook at private clubs.

be decorated with fresh and plastic flowers each day. Apparently, Neapolitan hoodlums respect church property.) In the *presepe*, from its earliest days, the figures of Mary, Joseph, and the baby Jesus nearly get lost in the crowds of hanging hams and straw-wrapped melons, salamis, sausage, and cheeses; the butchering vignettes; pasta-making and bread-baking scenes; the baskets of fish and fruit. All in miniature. The *presepe* museum at Montevergine, in Avellino, has halls full of them from all over the world. Almost nowhere else is food such a focus. In the monastery of San Martino in Naples, there's an extraordinary display of antique *presepi*.

THE MATURING OF THE CUISINE

At the beginning of the nineteenth century, macaroni was the most popular food, and Neapolitan cooking was continuing to take shape as a combination of various country traditions melded with French, Spanish, and the other foreign influences of its past. By now you could go to a middle-class home and be served food previously considered aristocratic, and go to an aristocratic home and be served food previously considered of the poor. Ippolito Cavalcanti's recipe for spaghetti with tomato sauce in his 1839 book, *Cucina teorico-pratica* (The Theory and Practice of Cooking), is often used to set the date for the beginning of the quintessential Neapolitan dish. I'd like to suggest that the record shows only that by 1839 spaghetti with tomato sauce was being eaten by the rich. It was surely eaten by the poor long before that. As many courtly influences as Neapolitan cooking has, it is truly a cuisine of poor people making pleasure out of necessity.

In 1833, Ferdinand II opened the first pasta factory. Naples, and other towns on the bay, Portici and Gragnano in particular, were, before technology took over the job of the sun and the wind, perfectly suited for drying pasta. The breezes blowing off the sea seem to whirl along the Bay of Naples just so, and a famous sight, described by many travelers well into the twentieth century, is the racks of pasta flapping in the sun, on the roofs of houses, and even in the alleys of Naples.

It was during the nineteenth century that Neapolitan cooking began to become internationally known. Naples was the artistic and intellectual center of the peninsula, and its food was described in detail by the travelers, painters, intellectuals, and diarists who flocked there. Besides the idiosyncratic scenes of hills terraced with pasta racks, the picturesque street vendors drew special attention—the sellers of macaroni, and the street urchins who ate spaghetti with their hands, their heads tilted backward to catch it, a bottle of wine at their feet. The fish man and the woman doling out octopus from a terra-cotta cauldron at a makeshift table. The couples in colorful dress flirting over the fry stand, or dancing around it. There were sellers of shellfish and watermelon, cold mineral waters, ice creams and ices. Etchings, engravings, and watercolors of Neapolitan food vendors, antique, original, and reproductions, sell as souvenirs today, and as always it's hard to tell which is which.

Then, in 1903, Enrico Caruso went to America, and until his death in 1921 made spaghetti for and sang Neapolitan songs to anyone who would eat and listen.

CAMPANIA AND FAT

It is now widely recognized in the region that olive oil is healthier than lard, but until the 1970s, it was pork fat that provided most of the fat calories in the Campanian diet. Lard is still used in many dishes where its distinctive flavor would be missed, such as in family heirloom recipes made for feasts and festivals, or where it is necessary to give baked goods a texture that another fat won't. Under the false assumption that margarine "has less fat," "contains fewer calories," or "is lighter"—I can't tell you how many times I've heard these phrases— it sometimes substitutes for lard, and certainly for butter in baking. In the past, with the exception of the worldly aristocracy, Campanians did not eat much butter. Both the cow and buffalo milk of the region are used to make full fat cheeses, which continue to be a major source of protein (as well as saturated fat) in the diet.

And who wouldn't? Poor country Campanians and Neapolitans had started to flow into the United States in the late nineteenth century as the region came under the grip of another foreign invasion—at least that is how Naples viewed the new ruling Savoy monarchy that had unified the Italian peninsula by the force of General Giuseppe Garibaldi. Caruso had a welcome, homesick audience in America. Against the stereotype of the lazy Neapolitan who lives by his cunning, the Italian immigrants were hardworking and ambitious. They were masons and builders, cooks and grocers, laborers and craftsmen—tailors, leather workers, upholsterers, and house painters. They established communities with their own churches, markets, and political units. They opened restaurants.

Caruso is often credited with popularizing Neapolitan cooking in America. Like every Neapolitan, he had to have his pasta every day, and if Omaha didn't have any, he did, and he would show Omaha how to make it. There was more to the growing popularity of "red sauce" food, though. The restaurants one went to for antipasto and spaghetti, sausage and peppers, and zuppa inglese, had romance—candlelight, checked tablecloths, straw-covered Chianti bottles, and, above all, the knowing, charming, entertaining, and ultimately discreet Neapolitan waiter, a man who knows from his history that a few cents' worth of food tastes so much better when it comes with a flourish, a story, a song, even an argument.

NAPLES AT TABLE

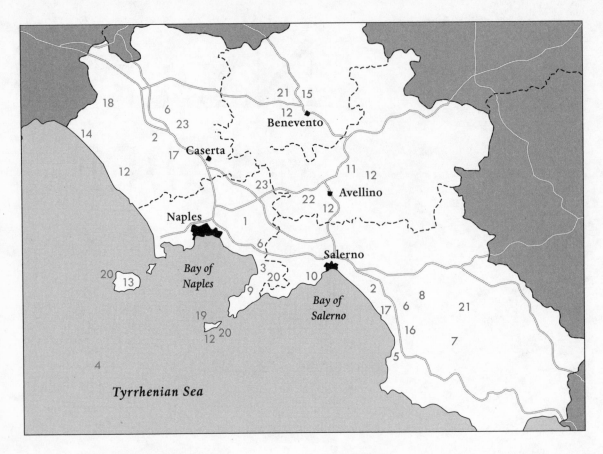

1. TOMATOES (SAN MARZANO)

2. MOZZARELLA DI BUFALA AND OTHER CHEESES

3. PASTA (GRAGNANO)

4. SEAFOOD, INCLUDING CLAMS, SQUID, OCTOPUS, SEA BREAM, OYSTERS, SHRIMP AND OTHER CRUSTACEANS

5. SALTED ANCHOVIES (AGROPOLI)

6. BROCCOLI RABE AND OTHER GREENS AND VEGETABLES

7. CHICKPEAS (CILENTO)

8. WHITE BEANS (MONTI ALBURNI)

9. LEMONS (SORRENTO)

10. WALNUTS (AMALFI)

11. HAZELNUTS (AVELLINO)

12. WINE

13. RABBIT (ISCHIA)

14. QUAIL (MONDRAGONE)

15. TORRONE (NOUGAT) AND OTHER CANDY (BENEVENTO)

16. ARTICHOKES (PAESTUM)

17. CITRUS FRUITS, PEACHES, FIGS

18. CHESTNUTS (ROCCAMONFINA)

19. FAVA BEANS AND PEAS (CAPRI)

20. OREGANO AND MARJORAM

21. LAMB (AVELLINO)

22. BLACK TRUFFLES (BAGNOLI IRPINO)

23. OLIVE OIL

THE NEAPOLITAN PANTRY

BEYOND BREAD, DRIED PASTA, fresh vegetables, fish, cheese, and meat, it doesn't take much to make a dish taste Neapolitan. Following are the ingredients, the seasonings—*condimenti* in Italian—that you need to keep on hand for *la cucina napoletana*. All except the fresh herbs and garlic can be stored for months, if not years.

ANCHOVIES

In the south of Italy, anchovies are eaten fresh, marinated, and salted. All three kinds are eaten for their own sake, but only salted anchovies are used as a flavoring. (The only place I've ever seen a canned anchovy in Campania is in a delicacy store where they also sell things like English preserves and American peanut butter.) All the recipes in this book call for salted, not oil-packed canned, anchovies, and I urge you to find some. They are less salty and aggressive than canned, and in the last few years, very good ones from Sicily have become more widely distributed in the United States. In our specialty food markets, they are usually sold in small amounts—say, by the quarter-pound—out of a wholesale-size tin. A retail-sized twenty-one-ounce tin is also available and well worth the investment if you like anchovies. Kept packed in the salt in their tin, covered with foil in the refrigerator, the anchovies hold up for years, although the top layer may become somewhat dry. If you must, you can substitute canned anchovy fillets. Good ones are firm and not fishy. The province of Salerno is famous for its salted anchovies. (See page 15 for a description of how they are preserved.)

Salted anchovies are sold whole with bones, not filleted. To clean them, rinse them under running water and pull off any fins that may be still attached. While you are running the water over the anchovies, use your fingers to carefully separate the fish into two fillets. The bone will adhere to one of the fillets, but it is easily pulled away. Do not be concerned if some pinbones are too difficult to remove. They are so fine, they won't be detectable.

BASIL

Fresh basil is used mainly to season tomato sauces and dishes with tomatoes. Indeed, the herb is often grown alongside tomatoes because it keeps pests from attacking the precious red vegetable. Basil leaves may be whole, torn, cut, or chopped, depending on the recipe and the cook. They are often added two times to a dish, once at the beginning or middle of the cooking, then again just before it is removed from the heat or before it is served.

BLACK PEPPER

Some Campanians will tell you that they don't often use black pepper to season a dish that is long cooked because the cured berries of *piper nigrum* become a kidney/liver irritant when heated to cooking temperatures. (There is some scientific explanation of this.) Or they might explain that they don't cook with black pepper but use it at the table because the main pleasure of black pepper is its fragrance, and so it is better to season a dish with black pepper at the very end of cooking, or to grind it on at the table, where the full impact of its bouquet can be appreciated.

BREAD CRUMBS

Bread is an important ingredient in Neapolitan cooking, and it is never wasted. After being enjoyed as fresh bread, on the day it is made or the day after it is made, the firm but still pliant dough may be soaked and squeezed out to extend and lighten ground meat, or as the base for a stuffing for a vegetable, or cut into cubes and fried to garnish a soup (zuppa). This interior bread dough is called mollica di pane, and sometimes it is also grated into bread crumbs. The bread crumbs we are more familiar with, however, are called pangrattato and are made from thoroughly dried-out bread. They are used as a binder or a thickener of stuffings, to coat fried foods, or to add a crunchy surface to a baked casserole, or they are fried to top pasta dishes on which grated cheese doesn't go. Fully dried bread is also used to make toasts called pane biscottato, although these are rarely made at home these days. They are available packaged. A few brands from Puglia are available in the United States. See pages 257 and 359 for a discussion of dried bread: freselle and pane biscottato.

CAPERS

Capers grow in Campania, but they are not grown commercially, and there seems to be total consensus in the region that the best capers are from Pantelleria, the small Italian island between Sicily and Tunisia. No matter where the capers come from, they are always salted capers, the bud of the caper bush cured in sea salt to draw out its moisture, then packed in salt for long storage. Large and small capers from Pantelleria and unidentified other sources are sold everywhere in Italy. In North America, it is harder to find them, and they are often expensive, but I urge you to seek them out to make the food of Campania taste like it was made in Campania. (The difference in taste with capers is more dramatic than that between salted and oil-packed anchovies.) Capers packed in brine without vinegar are good, too, but even harder to find. Capers packed in vinegar are the last choice because they taste more like a pickle than a caper. Salted capers have to be rinsed thoroughly, and if they are large, coarsely chopped. (Despite the French word "nonpareil"—without peer—being applied to tiny capers, larger ones taste better.)

GARLIC

Neapolitan cooks make a big point of how subtly they use garlic. More often than not, garlic is lightly smashed with the heel of the hand, or cut in half, then gently cooked in olive oil until it is soft, but not colored. As soon as it begins to color, the garlic is removed. The garlic gives up its flavor to the oil and hence to the dish, but the garlic itself is rarely eaten.

On the other hand, there are dishes where garlic is meant to be a powerful flavor, such as when it is used finely minced and raw with grilled vegetables. And in the mountainous areas of Campania, where the food is heartier than along the coast, garlic is sometimes browned and included in a dish, notably with pasta and beans or pasta and chickpeas.

Another idiosyncrasy of the Neapolitan kitchen is that garlic and onion are hardly ever combined in the same dish. The thought of putting these two related bulbs together is baffling to a Neapolitan. Garlic and onion "cancel each other out," or "are conflicting flavors," or "would be redundant" are the prevailing Neapolitan attitudes.

There are exceptions, but garlic, not onion, is used with fish and seafood, and it's the cook's choice which goes in meat, poultry, and vegetable dishes.

HOT RED PEPPER

Neapolitan food is known in the rest of the world as "spicy" food, but that would be news to a Neapolitan. There are dishes with a fiery punch, and there are Campanians who dump pepper or pepper oil on everything but dessert. (Chile peppers *are* addictive.) There are anomalous eaters like that in every culture. Mostly, hot red pepper—fresh, dried pods, or in flakes—is used as we use black pepper, to give a background flavor and piquancy, not up-front fire.

MARJORAM

Marjoram is a milder, sweeter-smelling version of oregano, and it grows wild all over the region. Capri is noted for it, and it is an essential ingredient in the island's famous ravioli filled with caciotta, a type of basket cheese, usually fresh, but also salted. Marjoram is also used for the classic Genovese sauce of onions flavored with meat. Sometimes, oregano is so sweet in Campania, it is hard to distinguish it from its tamer cousin, and some Neapolitan cooks use them interchangeably.

MINT

Mint, several varieties of which grow wild all over Italy, is much appreciated with grilled fish, zucchini, and some other vegetables. It is sometimes used instead of basil, which is a close relative.

OLIVES

Gaeta olives are the main table and cooking olive of Campania. They are a medium-size olive, roundish, and with pits that are easily removed. For some reason, those that are exported are usually a blackish purple, indicating they are fully ripe or nearly ripe olives, but in Italy they are often brownish-green or mottled, meaning they've been picked earlier. The less mature olives are firmer, but both are equally excellent.

Named for the port city from which they travel the world, "Gaeta" is a government-controlled name for olives grown from Latina to Esperia, in the hills behind the southern coast of Lazio, which is adjacent to modern Campania, but part of the ancient region called *Campania felix*. Actually, the political border was not moved

NAPLES AT TABLE

4

until after the Second World War, which is why even well-educated Campanians insist that Gaeta olives are a product of Campania. In 1861, the Bourbons lost their final battle with Garibaldi's forces in Gaeta, completing the unification of Italy under the Savoy monarchy.

Even with the government's controlled area of origin (DOC), it is often hard to find first-quality Gaeta olives in the United States, although they have started to appear in select supermarkets. The best are cured with salt, never with lye. However, a major grower confided that these days there are many lye-cured olives on the market because it is a faster, cheaper process.

If you can't find Gaeta olives, substitute the round, purple Greek variety—usually called simply Greek olives.

OLIVE OIL

Table olives are not grown in Campania, but the region does produce large quantities of olive oil. It is not as heavy as the green, peppery, eucalyptusy oil of Tuscany, or as light as Ligurian oil. It is a golden oil with a pleasant, fruity flavor. Extra-virgin olive oil is always preferred by those who can afford it, and it is used for all cooking purposes, including some deep-fat frying. Those who do not want to spend what's necessary to buy olive oil for frying often use what Italians generically call "seed" oil—what we call vegetable oil—or mix the two together, but I prefer peanut oil, as many professional Neapolitan cooks do, or canola or corn oil.

Excellent olive oils from Campania are available in the United States. However, because the regional name means nothing in the U.S. olive oil market, you have to look carefully at the label for its origin. A Ligurian oil, a Spanish oil, or a commercial-grade extra-virgin oil, such as Carapelli, which is available nationally in supermarkets, is an excellent substitute.

Oregano

Oregano has different flavors, depending on where it is from. Bags of the wild herb are sold along the roadsides of Sorrento, on Capri, and on Ischia, and it is amazing how different they taste. Sometimes, oregano is very assertive. Sometimes, it is as mild as marjoram. It is almost always used dried.

Pancetta

I've been told that pancetta (cured bacon) is more widely used now than it used to be. Lard, either cut into dice or rendered with bay leaves for a little extra flavor (and then called sugna), used to be the pork fat of choice. With the health concerns of today, however, Campanians seem to think that pancetta, which has lean and fatty portions, is the better choice. In Campania it comes cured with black pepper or rubbed with hot red pepper.

Parmigiano-Reggiano

To Italian Americans accustomed to using the sharp, salty pecorino cheese that has been readily available in the United States for generations, it is surprising how much grating cheese from Parma is used in Campania. It is not only because there is more affluence in Campania the last two decades and it has become more affordable. There is a long tradition of using Parmigiano-Reggiano, dating back at least to the thirteenth century. Still, some Campanians like to cut the sweetness of Parmigiano with the sharpness of pecorino, and the two are often mixed.

Parsley

Parsley is a flavor, not merely a garnish, in Campania, and one of the first things I observed in my explorations into the kitchens of the region is that it is rarely chopped finely. That's because parsley's flavor is extremely volatile, and the more it is cut, the more of that flavor is lost. Campanians are most likely to just cut parsley very finely, drawing the knife through the herb only once. Because parsley in Italy is usually much more aromatic than the commercial product in North America (our garden parsley can be very aromatic), I often include fine parsley stems in my cuttings because stems have so much more flavor than the leaves.

Whole leaves of parsley or other tender, mild herbs, such as mint, are sometimes scattered over dishes, but always individually, never in bunches or branches. For yet another herbal flavor and textural effect, herbs are sometimes torn and bruised before being added to or scattered on a dish.

PECORINO

Very little pecorino is commercially made in the region. The local sheep milk cheese is mainly a farmstead product and is consumed by those who produce it or live in an area where neighbors produce it. Pecorino from Calabria, Puglia, or Tuscany is what most people buy. It is a younger and less sharp cheese than is available in the United States, so, depending on the dish and your personal taste, you may want to mix the pecorino Romano (actually from Sardinia) available here with a small amount to as much as two-thirds Parmigiano.

PINE NUTS

The creamy texture of pine nuts (pignoli) is highly regarded as a textural punctuation in meatballs, the stuffing of braciole, stuffed vegetables, in sauces with raisins, and of course in desserts. If fresh when bought, pine nuts will keep well for up to a year in a tightly closed container in the refrigerator, and for even longer in the freezer.

PROSCIUTTO

Prosciutto "imported" from Parma or San Daniele—to a Campanian, those nearly foreign points north—is today more available and fashionable in Naples and the provinces than the rarer local production, which is strictly artisanal. But at the tables of both affluent urbanites and knowing country people, and among those with a mission to save the old ways and/or the environment, ham cured by a local farmer is preferred. These are denser, darker, more intense in every way, including saltier, than the Parma or San Daniele hams. They actually taste more like the best North American–made prosciuttos, such as those from the Italian-based Citterio made in the hills of Pennsylvania (including the one sliced and packaged in plastic, hanging from a hook in the supermarket meat case). Volpi in St. Louis is another excellent producer.

Coppa or capicollo is pork shoulder cured like prosciutto—both "sweet"-cured with black pepper or "hot" with a coating of ground hot red pepper.

Raisins

Neapolitans mainly use Sultanas, large golden raisins, but any raisin will do in these recipes.

Salami and Soppressata

All types of preserved pork sausage—salumi, which are also called insaccati—are among the most cherished products of the region. There are too many to list, each area having its own slightly different ones, but, in general, they range from four- to six-inch links of dried "sweet" or red-peppered sausages to the giant, four- to five-inch-diameter soppressata, hand-packed with coarsely ground meat, diced fat, and cracked black peppercorns. Good American-made products may be a little hard to find. Some manufacturers use too much preservative, and these products have an unpleasant sting and aftertaste. The nationally distributed Citterio brand, originally from Italy, has a Neapolitan-style soppressata that is excellent, however. It is sold cut to order in specialty stores and presliced in packages in supermarkets. There are small domestic companies that do a respectable job with other salamis and dried sausage.

Tomatoes (Canned)

When fresh tomatoes are not in season, Campanians use canned and jarred tomatoes, often preserved at home. For a full discussion of canned tomatoes, see the recipe for tomato sauce from canned tomatoes, page 50. Canned tomatoes should be used within six months of purchase. Their flavor and texture start deteriorating quickly after that.

Vinegar

White wine vinegar is used much more than red in Campania, and it is a must for making pickled vegetables. Red wine vinegar would change the color of pickles. It can be difficult to find unflavored white wine vinegar in North America, so substitute red wine vinegar if necessary when it seems appropriate.

Antipasti e Fritti

Dearest Mario,

Forty years have gone by and your antipasti have already been swept aside by the asphyxiating pressure of obsessive modern life, which is constantly on the lookout for new sensations, especially those connected with the table.

Those sweet curls of butter, those romantic pink slices of prosciutto and capicollo, the nostalgic anchovies which clung so passionately to tender olives, and the rather assertive, familiar pickles—all arranged on the serving plate with such imagination—these are no longer the object of admiration.

These items which were an indispensable prologue to every outing into the countryside, and to every convivial gathering . . . have been definitively consigned to the archives of Neapolitan gastronomic history . . . and so it is that the simplicity of the slice of prosciutto has been supplanted by the altogether more aristocratic . . . "sliver" of Canadian salmon or smoked swordfish.

—Nello Oliviero, Neapolitan gastronome and writer,
in *Partenope in cucina* (Parthenope in the Kitchen)

THE ANTIPASTI OF Nello Oliviero's lament was also, until twenty years ago, what was meant when you said "antipasto" in English, the assortment you expected when you uttered the word in any Italian-American restaurant or pizzeria. Indeed, the Neapolitan model is so much a part of our culture that the word "antipasto" itself has come to mean an array of cold cuts, cheese, pickled vegetables, and olives. The take-out department of your supermarket may even sell "antipasto salad" made with those ingredients, cubed and tossed instead of arranged on a plate. It's no longer fashionable to serve it here, as there, in urbane restaurants or at tables where a "sliver" of smoked salmon is considered "altogether more aristocratic." But the antipasto the world knows best and loves the most is still the antipasto napoletano, as some Italian cookbooks actually label it, and, despite Oliviero's cry for times gone by, one that many Neapolitans still relish.

In Naples and the other provinces of Campania, no one would think to refer to it as antipasto napoletano, just as no one in New York calls a loin strip steak by the city's name. Yet, platters of all the classic Neapolitan elements are still freely, happily, and proudly offered, although in these days of faster living and lighter eating, not necessarily at one meal. A nibble of pickled eggplant or peppers and a piece of bread will do to start. Or a few slices of salami, or "the simplicity" of a slice of prosciutto for a treat.

Antipasti have definitely evolved from the antique plate of cold cuts and preserved vegetables, and Oliviero's lament did, indeed, strike a chord at a Christmas Eve dinner in Salerno a couple of years ago. At this gastronomic and family ritual, La Vigilia di Natale (the Christmas Vigil), which is traditionally a menu of fish dishes, the first plate passed among this affluent family held Norwegian smoked salmon. Then down the long table came a beautifully molded and garnished salmon roe mousse. Then a plate of pickled herring, at which point I felt compelled by this Scandinavian turn of events to ask, "Why herring?" It was a favorite of their deceased father, one of the middle-aged daughters told me, and, anyway, "Herring is not much different from anchovies." That is how traditions are made.

LA FELLATA

*I*n the seventeenth century, any slice of ham or salumi, also called insaccati—dried sausage, soppressata, salami, capicollo—was referred to as la fellata. Even in today's modern parlance all you have to say to a waiter is *"Gli affettati, per favore"* ("The slices, please"), and you'll get a plate of cold cuts.

La Vigilia is a feast, not an everyday meal, and Campanians don't necessarily or usually start with an antipasto at home, unless they have guests. Then the antipasto might be a small portion of something that isn't per se an antipasto—a wedge of escarole-stuffed pastry or bread dough (pizza di scarola), a slice of lard bread enriched with diced salami (tortano), a few clams steamed open with garlic and parsley (sauté di vongole), mussels steamed with black pepper (cozze impepate), stewed squid (calamari in cassuola), a mixed vegetable dish like ciambotta, a vegetable frittata, a pasta frittata, a stuffed pepper, or eggplant parmigiana. All the recipes in the pizza and savory bread chapter, almost all the recipes in the vegetable chapter, and many in the fish chapter, are served as antipasti, a course to serve before a minestra, zuppa, or pasta.

Fried battered vegetables, croquettes, and fried yeast batter, bread dough, and pastry dough—plain, flavored, filled, or topped—are what Neapolitans truly dote on, what their antipasto dreams are made of. Every neighborhood in Naples has a *friggitoria,* a fries shop, or, as is more prevalent in the hinterlands, a pizzeria where deep-fat frying is done. On the way home from work in the evening, many Neapolitans stop to buy a bag of pasta cresciuta, amorphous blobs of fried yeast dough, usually seasoned only with salt, but most coveted when flecked with seaweed (alghe) or just-born fish so small they are barely visible (cicinielli or neonati). The shops also sell thumb-size potato croquettes rolled in bread crumbs (crocchè di patate), golden rice balls that truly look like little oranges (arancini), and, in their season, battered zucchini, eggplant, artichokes, and asparagus. People take them home to keep the family from being famished until supper is ready, and walking home, almost everyone dips his hand to eat one or two while they're still hot.

Frijenno magnanno (fry and eat) is the dialect expression for the way fried foods are best, and in pizzerias, fritti are rushed from fry pot to table as a first course before the pie. In restaurants with a good fry chef, you can get a series of fried items as antipasti, not to mention an entire fried dinner, a fritto misto, served on one hot plate after another.

Campanians fry plenty at home, too. That's clear once you've seen the large selection of traditional wide and deep-fry pans with baskets and electric deep-fat fryers available in the appliance stores. Besides making all the items sold at the *friggitorie,* home cooks (and professional fry cooks) also make panzerotti, ricotta- or cheese-filled crescents of either bread or pastry dough; pasta cresciuta, fritters with salt cod, or olives, or anchovies, or other little goodies. Pizzette, fried flat rounds of pizza dough, are topped with tomato sauce and grated cheese, or with sauce and mozzarella. Small, whole, floured and fried fish of all kinds—frittura di pesce or simply frittura—are considered the imperial plate of fries; fresh fish is as expensive in Italy as it is here. Squid is much less costly, so quantities of it are fried, too, although it's not now as popular as it is in the United States, perhaps because there are so many other fries to choose from.

For the most part temperamentally incapable of cooking anything exactly the way anyone else does, every Neapolitan also has some idiosyncratic fried item that she prepares to show off her creativity. It could be as simple a difference as adding capers to a classic salt cod fritter, or dicing Gruyère instead of mozzarella into a ricotta-filled savory pastry, but that's enough to cause talk among the neighbors.

All kinds of bruschette, toasts with toppings, are particularly fashionable now. I am told that fresh anchovies marinated in olive oil, vinegar, and garlic (alici marinate) have never been so popular. Certainly, they are ubiquitous in the restaurants, as are substantial balls of true buffalo mozzarella, dripping with freshness and served solitary on a plate, to be eaten with knife and fork. Campania is the home of mozzarella. It's natural that the locals are connoisseurs and take every opportunity to indulge in what they rightly consider one of their region's prime contributions to world gastronomy. Still, to an outsider, it seems strange to see whole cheese consumed that way.

PROSCIUTTO AND FIGS AND MELON

Even in the seventeenth century, prosciutto was eaten with figs, when in season at the end of the summer and in early fall. Closer to Christmas and during the winter, the cured ham was eaten with melons, which were protected, in the days before refrigeration, with a thick layer of straw and hung in a cool place waiting to be consumed. Nowadays, as a vestige of the old way, the green-skinned melons sold during the Christmas season are tied with straw raffia or come in a straw net bag (or a plastic imitation) and have a loop for carrying or hanging. The melons are also common in *presepi*, the nativity scenes (or crèches) that Neapolitans popularized and continue to adore. So much more than vignettes of the Holy Family, *presepi* are genre scenes with food a major feature, both in markets and on the table.

VINEGAR PEPPERS

Papacelle and puppachielle are the dialect words for small, sweet, red peppers—what we would call cherry peppers—that have been preserved in vinegar. They are a popular part of an antipasto napoletano and are combined with pork in several dishes (pages 296 and 297). Some people may still put them up themselves, but most buy them in jars at the supermarket, or from a specialty store where they may or may not have been made on the premises. All the cherry peppers in vinegar I have ever found in the United States have been very hot ones, but sweet ones exactly like those in Italy are beginning to be marketed fresh, both by specialty farmers at their local markets and by supermarkets. It can't be long before someone markets them in jars with vinegar.

Large bell peppers put up in vinegar are easy to find in American supermarkets and substitute very well. Campanians often use them themselves, although the smaller peppers are more coveted. Look for a brand without sugar added, although even the lightly sweetened ones can be fine.

ANTIPASTO NAPOLETANO

All the elements of a Neapolitan antipasto can be purchased in an American supermarket—prosciutto, salami, or other cold cuts; provolone or other cheese; olives, anchovies, and pickled vegetables such as peppers and mushrooms. See "The Neapolitan Pantry" on pages 1–8 for shopping guidance. There are, however, a number of pickled vegetable recipes in this book that can turn what seems like a mundane assortment into a special one. See La Spiritosa (page 319; pickled carrots, fennel, or green beans), Peperoni sott'Olio (page 351; pickled sweet red peppers in oil), Melanzane sott'Olio (page 339; pickled eggplant in oil), and Melanzane sott'Olio Estive (page 338; another pickled eggplant).

ACCIUGHE E BURRO
Anchovies and Butter

Say anchovies and butter in Salerno, Campania's second city and its largest province, and the response will be the southern Italian hand gesture that means "delicious": It looks like turning a key into the corner of the mouth. It's an old-fashioned antipasto, but even a young Salernitano will cry, *"Ottimo!"* ("The best!"). His eyes might roll in a mock swoon, too. This is just for a slice of toast—a hot or lukewarm bruschetta or crostino, a cracker, or a slice of cold toasted white bread—slathered with sweet butter and draped with a shimmering anchovy fillet, or several.

Salerno is famous for its anchovies, especially those preserved in the old ways, either salted and packed into wooden barrels, which is hardly (maybe never) done anymore, or packed into pottery crocks and kept under sea-salt water. You can't find the crocks in stores anymore, but you can sometimes see them at a wholesale fish market. They are so special that the one lone crock of them I spotted at the huge Posillipo fish market one morning was displayed on a crate placed on end, as if the anchovies were a work of art on a pedestal.

I mentioned my interest in these anchovies while visiting the family of an Italian-American friend in Agropoli, one of the southernmost towns of the Campanian coast. It used to be known as a place with superior anchovies, although these days its role as a beach resort and day-trip destination for shopping and zuppa di pesce has eclipsed its renown for salted fish. "Do you know anyone who would sell me some anchovies in crocks?" I asked the matriarch of the family, Marietta Carola, who in her younger days was famous for her deep-fat frying, but now, well into her eighties, was ensconced that raw December evening in the Carola Hotel lobby with an electric heater directed at her blanket-wrapped lap.

"Well, my son Nicola is in the back playing with his crocks right now. You're lucky, it's the season for them," she said.

Nicola is in his mid-sixties and knows the old ways. He guts all the minuscule fish himself, not always so thoroughly that every trace of red entrail is gone. He layers them in white crocks with open-ear handles, then pours in a brine made with sea salt, filling to cover all the anchovies. The anchovies are held under the salt water by a top he fashions from Styrofoam (a nod to modernity) onto which he has glued a little stack of two-inch-long firing strips. This forms a sort of handle for the Styrofoam cover. Across this crudely fashioned handle he balances another, longer slat of wood that he ties at either end to the crock's handles. In this way, the anchovies are kept submerged, and as they are eaten and their level retreats, the string can be tightened and the Styrofoam cover held in place at a lower level.

He instructed me to make a carefully ratioed solution of sea salt and boiled and cooled tap water, and to keep topping off the liquid as it evaporated. I starting eating mine soon

after New Year's, when they were still submerged in the salt-water solution I had already replenished a few times (some did spill out on the way home); but after a while I realized that it is only water that evaporates, not salt, so I stopped adding anything. Somehow, they kept beautifully for over a year, in the refrigerator, most of the time packed only in sea salt without water. I related my experience to a young Salernitano chef, and he agreed that after their initial submersion and cure, the water is not really necessary, although eventually the anchovies do dry out, becoming less pleasantly sharp in flavor, and they lose their nearly fresh texture, the softness that makes them so appealing against cool butter and crisp bread.

Fortunately, one doesn't need quite such superior anchovies to appreciate the combination. Anchovy fillets packed in cans or jars with oil don't quite make it, but salted anchovies that are exported (usually from Sicily) in large cans and are sold by the ounce or quarter-pound in specialty food stores do. They are not only milder than oil-packed anchovies, they are, ironically, less salty and sweeter-tasting, and they have a firmer texture. Do try, however, to find ones either from a fairly recently opened can or from the very bottom of the can, where they remain moist from the juices that have settled there.

LA COLATURA

The juices from salted anchovies, which are red from the traces of entrail left on the anchovies, are called la colatura and much coveted as a seasoning for spaghetti. People still talk about la colatura, but nostalgically, because it's said that for it to be really fine it must come from one of the wooden barrels that once were used to cure the tiny fish. These were old barrels no longer sound enough to age wine. For anchovies, they were equipped with a hole on the bottom to make it possible to draw off the salty red juices that settled there. (Perhaps the wine-impregnated wood gave some flavor to this colatura.) Only a few weeks after the anchovies were packed, and just in time for Christmas Eve's fish dinner—La Vigilia—la colatura would be collected, blended with some garlic-flavored olive oil, and tossed with pasta to make one of the featured plates. The tradition continues in some families today as spaghetti with anchovies (pages 142 and 144).

ALICI MARINATE

MARINATED FRESH ANCHOVIES

Ask a Campanian, "What is the difference between acciughe and alici?" and he will tell you that there is none. Both words mean the same thing: anchovies. But in common parlance, acciughe is used for salted anchovies, alici for fresh anchovies, although salted anchovies are often also called alici salate.

Fresh anchovies, which taste somewhat like their larger cousins, herrings, are a mainstay of the Campanian antipasto table. Carefully filleted and sometimes butterflied, the two halves held together by their tail, the anchovies are first cured in vinegar, then marinated in olive oil with garlic, hot pepper, parsley, and sometimes oregano. Arranged in silvery layers in flat dishes, they are as attractive as they are delicious.

If you can find a source for fresh anchovies, they will most likely be already filleted and marinated. Such anchovies are now sold in fancy American specialty food stores and Italian markets. They are expensive. Much less costly, because the price of laboriously filleting them is not included, are the fresh whole anchovies that can now sometimes be found in American fish markets. If you find these and care to take the trouble of preparing some yourself, here's how to do it:

1.   Clean the anchovies by first cutting off the heads. Then, with a very small, sharp knife, make a slit down the belly and wash out the insides under cold running water. Now split the anchovy in half entirely or allow the 2 halves to remain attached at the tail. With your fingers and the aid of the knife, pull the central bone off the half to which it is attached.

2.   Wash the anchovies again (there's no need to dry them), then place them in layers in a dish with a high rim. When all the anchovies have been cleaned, pour white wine vinegar over them to cover. Use a fork to slightly lift the fish layers, letting the vinegar run around them all.

3.   Refrigerate for 24 hours.

(continued)

4. Drain the anchovies and rinse them again. This time pat them dry. Rearrange them into a neat layer or layers in a serving dish. Cover them, on each layer, with olive oil, a few flakes of hot pepper or pieces of fresh hot pepper, sliced garlic, and just pinches of fine sea salt, and finely cut parsley and/or dried oregano. Let marinate a few hours before serving at room temperature.

To store: The anchovies may be kept in the refrigerator, covered with oil, for a couple of days. Return to room temperature before serving.

BRUSCHETTA
Toasted Bread

The slice of toasted country bread topped with tomato salad that Americans have come to know as bruschetta (pronounced brew-SKET-ta) is only one of many versions of bruschetta nowadays made in Campania and other places in Italy. Campania's favorite is still the tomato version when tomatoes are in season, but a bruschetta with butter and salted anchovies is also treasured, or you can dress a slice of toast with boiled beans flavored with garlic and condiment-quality olive oil, with smothered greens such as escarole, Swiss chard, spinach, or broccoli rabe. In restaurants, bruschette or crostini (an alternate word usually applied to smaller toasts or used on a formal menu) are sometimes dressed with shavings of bottarga, salted and pressed gray mullet or tuna roe, or truffles. In Paestum, on my friend Cecilia Bellelli Baratta's water buffalo farm, she serves oiled bruschette with slices of moist buffalo ricotta, sprinkled with freshly ground black pepper.

On Ischia, Da Peppino di Renata has even become famous for its bruschette. At the restaurant, housed in the cave and attached ancient, primitive farmhouse that was once the summer home of owner Sebastiano D'Ambra's family—down a road so narrow that even a small Fiat has trouble squeezing through—Sebastiano offers a parade of different bruschette with seasonal toppings. Anything goes.

BRUSCHETTA NAPOLETANA

THINK OF THIS AS the prototype for English muffin pizza. In Naples, it might be called pizza finta (fake pizza), because the idea of *finto* anything delights Neapolitans. It's akin to fooling the gods. It's nothing more than toasted bread topped with mozzarella, diced or sliced tomato, an anchovy fillet, a pinch of oregano, and a "string" of olive oil, as Neapolitans put it. It goes into a hot oven or under the broiler flame just until the cheese begins to melt.

For each bruschetta:

1 slice dense, country-style bread

1 or 2 ¼-inch-thick slices mozzarella, to fit the bread in one layer

Juiced, seeded, and diced fresh tomato, sliced cherry tomatoes, or a "fillet"
of canned plum tomato

Optional: 1 or 2 anchovy fillets

Big pinch dried oregano

1 teaspoon extra-virgin olive oil

Freshly ground black pepper

1. Toast the bread until light brown on both sides. Arrange the bread slices on a baking sheet.

2. Top each bread slice with mozzarella to cover the whole slice, except for ¼ inch around the edge. Arrange a few pieces of tomato on each slice of cheese. Drape 1 or 2 anchovy fillets over the top. Season with oregano.

3. Drizzle a tiny bit of olive oil over each slice.

4. Place the sheet of bruschette under the broiler or in a preheated 425-degree oven and cook until the cheese melts, but does not bubble or brown. Barely runny is the goal.

5. Serve immediately, and pass the pepper mill.

CROSTINI FANTASIA DEL FRIGORIFERO

CROSTINI FANTASY OF THE REFRIGERATOR

———

I'VE PUT MY OWN flowery Italian name to this, but it is serious business: an idea, more than a firm recipe, that can save you when you need to drum up an off-hour or cocktail snack, or want a little something extra to accompany a salad or soup. It is nothing more than bits and pieces of cheese and salumi scavenged from the refrigerator, cut into fine dice, bound together with ricotta, and melted on top of a piece of toast. I'm told that you can buy packages of avanzi di salumi, literally "leftovers of cold cuts," in stores in Naples—as a flavoring for various dishes, such as Genovese or a pizza rustica—but I've yet to find them.

Serves 4 to 6

1 ounce Swiss Gruyère, cut into ⅛-inch or smaller dice (about 2 tablespoons)

1 ounce Italian or Danish Fontina, cut into ⅛-inch or smaller dice
(about 2 tablespoons)

1 ounce sweet or sharp provolone, cut into ⅛-inch or smaller dice
(about 2 tablespoons)

2 ounces salami, soppressata, dried sausage, prosciutto, mortadella,
boiled ham, pepperoni, or a combination of the above, cut into ⅛-inch
or smaller dice (about ¼ cup)

¼ to ⅓ cup ricotta

Freshly ground black pepper to taste

Packaged toasts or crackers

1. Preheat the oven to 375 degrees.

2. In a mixing bowl, blend the diced cheeses and meat together with the ricotta and pepper.

3. Spread a tablespoon of the mixture on each of the crostini. Place on a baking sheet or in a shallow pan.

4. Bake for about 5 minutes, until the cheeses begin to bubble and brown very lightly.

5. Serve immediately.

PÂTÉ DELLE DUE SICILIE

MUSHROOM PÂTÉ OF THE TWO SICILIES

THIS IS FROM Marchese Franco Santasilia di Torpino's *La cucina aristocratica napoletana* (The Cooking of the Neapolitan Noblilty), his book of recipes from Naples's *Monzù* chefs. "It was probably invented at the end of the 1920s," says Santasilia, by *Monzù* Cesare, who was the chef to the Caracciolo di Castagnetto family. The pâté is, as one might imagine, a fine and refined paste. The aristocracy used to love beige and white food, to set them apart from the masses whose food is very colorful.

Makes 1¾ cups

12 ounces white mushrooms, cleaned and sliced

2 tablespoons butter

½ teaspoon mixed dried rosemary, thyme, sage, and marjoram

½ cup dry Marsala

1 tablespoon salted capers (not in vinegar!), thoroughly rinsed

1½ tablespoons Gaeta olives, pitted and chopped

½ cup heavy cream, or a little more

Salt

Packaged toasts or crackers

1. In a skillet, over medium heat, cook the mushrooms with the butter and herbs. After the mushrooms have given up their liquid, stir in the Marsala and let all the liquid evaporate.

2. Add the capers and olives. Cook over low heat, stirring frequently, for 15 minutes. This dries the mixture further, and the mushrooms will become lightly browned.

3. Place the mixture in a blender with the cream and process to a stiff puree. If the mixture is too stiff to puree, add a little more cream, a tablespoon at a time. However, in the end, there should be no trace of liquid.

4. Place the mixture in a bowl and stir in salt to taste. Smooth the surface with a knife, cover with plastic wrap, and refrigerate for at least 2 hours.

5. Serve with melba toast.

FRITTI

FRIED SNACKS

FRYING IS NOT COOKING, a Campanian will tell you. It requires a special talent, a special temperament, or at least a special skill. Now that I have been doing quite a lot of it myself, I understand. Frying requires good organization and absolutely full attention, an intensity of focus and a sense of urgency that all fryers seem to agree is meditative and exhilarating at the same time.

The oil is hot and dangerous. It changes temperature and demands constant adjustments. If it's too hot, the outside of the food burns before the inside cooks. If it's too cool, the food absorbs oil and becomes greasy. The fries need to be checked, turned, sometimes nursed along, then removed at the right moment. At the same time all this is happening and needing attention, the upcoming batch has to be battered, floured, rolled in bread crumbs, or patted dry. You're taking food out of the fat and draining it on paper or a rack, trying to get the next shift in quickly so the fat doesn't get too hot again because you haven't added more food to cool it.

It sounds difficult, and it is nerve-wracking at first, but you develop a rhythm with practice. Then you get addicted to the process, not to mention the results.

Electric deep-fat fryers do make it easier. Their temperatures are thermostatically controlled. They have covers with charcoal filters to prevent vaporizing oil from greasing up the atmosphere. They are a very popular home appliance nowadays. The downside of the electric fryers is that they don't get hotter than 370 degrees. I'm told this is because the plastic casings (and perhaps other fittings) cannot take the 375 degrees or more that some foods need to fry perfectly.

Great fryers still swear by a skillet or deep pot on top of the stove. They offer more control. You can get the temperature higher. It's more fun.

The classic, old-time pot is made of tin-lined copper, is four times wider than it is deep, and has two big, outward or upward-angled handles that can be fitted with a draining basket to hang on them. They are not hard to find. I see them hanging decoratively in Neapolitan home kitchens, but I don't see home cooks using them. Most restaurant kitchens use stainless-steel versions, though, and the huge frying vats in the friggitorie are proportioned the same way. They provide a lot of surface to fry on and just enough depth of oil. A skillet is excellent, too. For small fry jobs, a seven- to eight-inch pan saves oil; sometimes all that's needed is a half-inch of oil, about one and a half cups in a small skillet. Black cast iron is perfect. For some jobs, particularly fried yeast batter, pasta cresciuta, and fried pastries where surface flour can cause foaming, a deep pot is best. Heavy aluminum is ideal for this one.

Deep-fat frying doesn't add nearly as much fat to food as is rumored; not when it is done well. I have measured oil before and after frying sessions over and over again, and it is always astounding how little oil has been used. It's possible to fry a slew of antipasti or a fritto misto for four and consume only a quarter to a third of a cup of oil.

What oil to use? It's arguable, but many would say a light- to medium-flavored extra-virgin olive oil is the best for everything. For one thing, it has all those anti-oxidants. But olive oil has a low smoking point, it imparts its flavor and you don't necessarily want that all the time, and good olive oil is expensive. So some people blend it with "seed" oil, which in Italy is usually sunflower, and some people use only seed oil, which at least has a smoking point of nearly 400; hot enough. Peanut oil was recommended to me by several cooks, and I now prefer it. It has a smoking point of 450 degrees, so it is nearly impossible to burn, and it has a clean, almost imperceptible flavor. I've tried grapeseed oil with great success, too. It's also a clean-tasting oil with a high smoking point, but it is expensive—between the price of peanut oil and the least expensive extra-virgin olive oil. I also use canola oil and corn oil. Both have smoking points of about 400 or a little higher. If I prefer a certain oil for a particular job, it's specified in the recipe. Otherwise, it's your choice.

PASTA CRESCIUTA

Yeast Fritters

FRITTO DI VENTO

Fried Wind

———

THIS IS THE MOST basic item of the Neapolitan frying repertoire, a batter of four ingredients: yeast, water, flour, and salt: deep-fried dough. It has universal, primal appeal, even when sprinkled only with salt. Incidentally, the same dough, sprinkled with sugar, is used to make "zeppole" at Italian-American street fairs, although in Campania zeppole are a very different fried delicacy.

Pasta cresciuta, because it is a living mass of microorganisms, frightens some people, but it is a forgiving dough when you get to know it. If it's not quite ready when you are, you can stir it down. You can beat in flavor ingredients after the rise, and it will still puff up gloriously. When the insides of fritters are gluey or doughy, it's most likely that the frying oil is too hot, rather than that the batter is wrong; lower the heat. On the other hand, if they are fried in oil that isn't hot enough, they become greasy. Most residential deep-fat fryers will not get hot enough to fry perfect pasta cresciuta, which needs about 380 degrees, so use a deep pan with about three inches of oil.

Makes 24 to 30 small fritters, serving 4 to 6

1 envelope dry yeast (2½ teaspoons)

2 cups warm water

¾ teaspoon salt

2½ cups all-purpose flour, or slightly less

Peanut, canola, or corn oil for frying

1. In a large mixing bowl, using a whisk, dissolve the yeast in ½ cup of warm water. Let stand for 10 minutes, until fizzing.

2. Whisk in the salt and 1½ cups more warm water. Still using the whisk, add the flour a few tablespoons at a time, incorporating each addition completely before adding the next. You will end up with a soft, smooth dough, neither too liquid nor too stiff, but better on the looser side. You may want to withhold the last 1 or 2 tablespoons of flour.

3.   Cover the bowl with a clean dishtowel and set aside to rise for 50 minutes to 1 hour, until the batter is bubbling and puffed to nearly double its volume. If the batter is ready before you are ready to fry it, stir it down gently and let it rise again.

4.   When the batter is doubled in bulk, season it by stirring in chopped anchovies, seaweed, or salt cod, following the variations below or the recipe on page 26.

To deep-fry:

5.   Heat about 3 inches of oil in a deep, wide pot to about 380 degrees. (A high-temperature thermometer is indispensable for deep-fat frying. These are sold as both candy and deep-fat thermometers.)

6.   Drop the batter, roughly by the tablespoonful, into the hot oil. It will not be of uniform shape. It shouldn't be. In fact, the more irregular, the more extra-crispy parts it will have. Do not overcrowd the pan. You can cool the oil too much by adding too much batter at once. The fritters need some space, and you need room to maneuver them. The fritters fry on the surface of the oil. When they have colored on one side, turn them. I find tongs are the best tool for handling pasta cresciuta, especially since sometimes some balls, depending on their shape, will need to be held in place on their second side for a few seconds to prevent them from turning back over.

7.   When golden all over, drain the fritters briefly on absorbent paper or on a rack, then serve immediately, sprinkled lightly with salt, on a paper-lined plate. Some people do not mind cooled pasta cresciuta, but to be at their best they should be consumed while still hot. They are not good reheated.

Variations:

For Cresciute di Acciughe, fried dough with anchovies, chop at least a dozen anchovy fillets and stir them into the batter after it has risen.

For Cresciute di Alghe, fried dough with seaweed, use the nubby portion of the stringlike seaweed used by North American fish markets. Shellfish are often packed in it, and fish markets are usually willing to give it to you for free. Snip off the ropy part and discard it, and use as much of the nubby portion as desired. They do not need to be chopped. The fritters should be merely dotted with pieces of them.

For Cresciute di Fior di Zucca, fried dough with zucchini flowers, chop the flowers, squeeze out excess moisture, and stir into the batter.

CRESCIUTE DI BACCALÀ, OLIVE E CAPPERI ALLA ROSA MAZZELLA

ROSA MAZZELLA'S FRITTERS WITH SALT COD, OLIVES, AND CAPERS

ROSA MAZZELLA, WHO HAS lived in the oldest part of Naples since she was a child, is the wife of Neapolitan painter Rosario Mazzella, and the mother of New York–based artist Marcello Mazzella. When it comes to pasta cresciuta, she is an artist in her own right. So light are Rosa's fritters that though she makes too many and you cannot stop eating them, when her glorious linguine alle vongole arrives, or her ravioli with semi-ragù, you dig in with gusto and still have room for, say, fish baked in parchment, then, for dessert, the pastiera she buys from a Spaccanapoli baker.

Makes about 24 irregular-shaped fritters

1 recipe Pasta Cresciuta (see previous recipe)

1 pound skinless and boneless baccalà, soaked (see page 259)
and shredded into small pieces

1 tablespoon coarsely chopped and pitted Gaeta olives

1 tablespoon salted capers, thoroughly rinsed, chopped if large

1 tablespoon pine nuts

1 tablespoon raisins

Peanut, canola, or corn oil for frying

1. Prepare the pasta cresciuta according to the recipe.

2. After the batter has risen, stir in the crumbled baccalà and the rest of the ingredients, except the oil. Make sure the ingredients are well mixed in.

3. Heat the oil and fry tablespoonfuls as described in the preceding recipe.

4. Eat immediately.

CROCCHETTE (CROCCHÈ) DI PATATE

POTATO CROQUETTES

POTATO CROQUETTES ARE ALWAYS an element in a Neapolitan-style fritto misto, but they are also eaten as a snack for their own sake. The fry shops—*friggitorie*—often excel at them. But pizzerias offer them, too, and a plate of croquettes, with perhaps some fried mushrooms, artichokes, zucchini, or other vegetable, is a typical way to quell one's appetite while the pizza is being baked or if you are still hungry afterward. The snack shops and *tavole calde* always offer them, too, although unfortunately these days they reheat them in a microwave oven, which renders them gluey and flabby. Better to eat a potato croquette at room temperature than to microwave it. Also unfortunately, because adding flour to the potatoes makes for easier handling, frying, and keeping, you are as likely to get a starchy and stodgy croquette as you are to get one that is light and digests easily. Parsley, tiny cubes of mozzarella, smoked provola, scamorza, or even Gruyère, and/or a fine dice of prosciutto or salami are often added to the potatoes, which makes the mixture the same as for gattò, the Neapolitan potato cake (page 353), except that for croquettes it is shaped into torpedoes and fried.

Makes 24 to 30

2 pounds all-purpose potatoes

2 eggs, lightly beaten

1½ cups (loosely packed) freshly grated Parmigiano-Reggiano

⅛ teaspoon freshly ground nutmeg

¼ teaspoon freshly ground white pepper

½ teaspoon salt

1 egg

1 tablespoon water

2 cups dried bread crumbs

Oil for frying

(continued)

1. Boil the potatoes in their skins until fully tender. Peel them while they are still hot—use a towel to hold them.

2. Also while they are still hot, push them through a potato ricer into a mixing bowl.

3. Immediately, stir in the beaten eggs, the Parmigiano, the nutmeg, the pepper, and the salt. Mix well.

4. Allow the mixture to cool to room temperature or place it in the refrigerator for about 30 minutes to cool it. When cooled, it should be thick enough to handle and shape.

5. In a shallow bowl, beat the third egg with a tablespoon of water. Pour the bread crumbs into another shallow bowl.

6. Shape the potato mixture into croquettes ¾ to 1 inch in diameter and about 3 inches long. Using a table fork to help turn the croquettes, gently roll each in beaten egg, then in bread crumbs, coating them thoroughly. Place the croquettes on a platter for at least 15 minutes, or until ready to fry.

7. Heat ½ inch oil in a skillet and fry the croquettes without crowding the pan. Turn them once or twice so that they brown evenly all over.

8. Drain on absorbent paper and serve immediately, or at least within a few minutes. They may be reheated in a 350-degree oven, but are always best when eaten soon after they come from the fryer—*frijenno magnanno.*

ARANCINI DI RISO

LITTLE ORANGES OF RICE

PALLE DI RISO

RICE BALLS

THE FEW SPOONS OF tomato sauce in these do not add much flavor. They're there to tint the rice, making the crumb-coated, bumpy rice surface even more golden and truly looking like arancini (tiny oranges). In Italian-American communities, rice balls can be huge, and Sicilian arancini are indeed much larger than Neapolitan, but they are also usually stuffed with a little ground meat and pea mixture. Tiny ones like these don't cry out for a filling, but if you want a surprise center or decide to make larger balls where a filling would break up the monotony of all the rice, poke a cube of mozzarella or other good melting cheese into the center, then close up the hole you've made, or mold the rice around the cheese.

Makes 20 to 24 balls

1 cup Arborio rice

2 eggs, lightly beaten

3 tablespoons tomato puree

½ teaspoon salt

⅛ teaspoon freshly ground black pepper

⅓ cup freshly grated Parmigiano-Reggiano, pecorino, or a combination

Fine, dry bread crumbs

Oil for deep-fat frying

1. In a large pot of boiling, salted water, cook the rice until tender, 12 to 15 minutes. Drain well. Put the rice in a mixing bowl and let it cool until tepid.

2. Stir in the beaten eggs, then the tomato puree, the salt, the pepper, and the grated cheese. Refrigerate until cold.

3. Place the bread crumbs in a shallow bowl or on a plate.

(continued)

4. Keeping your hands moist, and using a tablespoon measure to scoop up the rice, form balls of 1 rounded tablespoon each. Roll the balls of rice in bread crumbs to coat well.

5. In a deep-fat fryer or deep pot, heat to 375 degrees enough oil so the rice balls can be submerged in it. Fry the balls 5 or 6 at a time for about 1½ minutes. When done, they should have a deep golden-orange color.

6. Serve immediately.

CROCCHÈ DI BESCIAMELLA

WHITE SAUCE CROQUETTES

FRIED SAUCE: IT SOUNDS IMPOSSIBLE. That it's a sort of kitchen trick makes it even more delectable. Starchy white sauce becomes seductively soft after being shocked by the heat of the oil. Bite in, and it's on the verge of oozing out of its thin, fried egg and bread crumb shell. These are a traditional item in a grand fritto misto, a whole menu of fried foods, and can be sweetened for a dessert instead of flavored with grated cheese. I can't think of a more elegant fry to serve with drinks before dinner, but they absolutely must be served as soon as they come out of the fryer. They get stodgy quickly.

Makes 20 to 24

8 tablespoons (1 stick) butter

½ cup all-purpose flour

2 cups milk

¼ cup loosely packed freshly grated Parmigiano-Reggiano

Few scrapings of nutmeg

½ teaspoon salt

At least 1 cup fine, dry bread crumbs

2 eggs

Oil for deep-fat frying

1.   In a small saucepan, melt the butter over medium heat. Whisk in the flour and, continuing to whisk constantly, let it bubble for 2 minutes.

2.   Add all the milk and, still whisking constantly, bring the sauce to a simmer and let it simmer 1 minute. Remove from the heat and stir in the cheese a tablespoon at a time, then the nutmeg and salt.

3.   Scrape the sauce into a bowl or a plastic container. Cover and refrigerate for several hours, until the sauce is well chilled. It will be firm.

4.   Place the bread crumbs in a shallow bowl or on a plate. In a shallow bowl, beat the eggs to mix well.

5.   With moistened hands, and using a tablespoon measure to scoop out the white sauce, form the mixture into small balls, then flatten them slightly. Dip in egg, coating thoroughly. Roll the patties in bread crumbs, firmly but gently pressing them in to coat well, especially on the sides. (While doing this, it is easy to neaten up the shape.)

6.   Deep-fry at 375 degrees for about 1 minute, until golden. If the crocchè start to erupt, then you are frying them for too long, or at too high a temperature.

7.   Serve immediately.

VARIATIONS:

To the white sauce, you can add finely minced ham, prosciutto, mortadella, dried sausage, etc., or a diced cheese such as smoked mozzarella or provola, provolone, or caciocavallo. Use these sparingly, however. There should end up being no more than a few specks in each piece.

CROSTATE DI TAGLIOLINI

PASTA CAKES

THEY CALL THESE CROSTATE di tagliolini at L.U.I.S.E. on the chic Piazza dei Martiri, the hub of the most expensive shopping area in Naples. It's the best *tavola calda* in town, the oldest and smallest of several L.U.I.S.E. shops. As you walk into the narrow storefront, there is a cheese and cold-cut display case and service counter and, on the opposite wall, shelves of specialty items, including, enclosed behind locked glass sliding doors, English marmalades and preserves. In the rear, where there are counters and stools for sitting and having lunch or a snack, there is a delectable array of baked pastas, timballi, fritattas, fried snacks, and many other hot foods all freshly made on the premises and displayed in a shallow case. Customers are served at a small counter

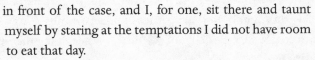

in front of the case, and I, for one, sit there and taunt myself by staring at the temptations I did not have room to eat that day.

The reason the Piazza dei Martiri L.U.I.S.E. is so good is that owner, Antonella Mastrorilli, has such high regard for quality and freshness. There is, for instance, always a small platter of these pasta cakes on the counter. As soon as it's down to the last few, a new batch is fried, the pasta mixture scooped up from a premixed mound ready to shape, crumb, and fry.

Remember that at home, too. The pasta and sauce can be mixed ahead, but cakes should be breaded just before they go in the fryer and served immediately. They don't reheat all that well, but better than some other fried foods. Still, *frijenno magnanno*.

Makes about 15

For the white sauce:

4 tablespoons butter

¼ cup flour

2 cups milk

1 cup freshly grated Parmigiano-Reggiano

Freshly grated nutmeg

½ teaspoon salt

⅛ teaspoon freshly ground black pepper

For the pasta:

1 pound fresh egg tagliolini (fine noodles),
cut into 3- to 4-inch lengths before cooking

3 tablespoons butter

1 cup freshly grated Parmigiano-Reggiano

Plus:

3 eggs

Fine dry bread crumbs

Peanut, canola, or corn oil for frying

To make the white sauce:

1.   In a small saucepan, melt the butter over medium heat. Whisk in the flour and let bubble, whisking constantly, for 2 minutes. Add all the milk and, still whisking constantly, bring to a simmer and let simmer 1 minute.

2.   While the sauce is still hot, stir in the cheese, a couple of tablespoons at a time, then the nutmeg, and the salt and pepper. Set aside.

To assemble:

3.   Cook the pasta in plenty of boiling, salted water. Drain well.

4.   In a large bowl, combine the drained pasta and the butter, tossing until the butter melts and the pasta is coated with butter. A couple of tablespoons at a time, toss the cheese into the hot pasta. (Adding a little cheese at a time prevents the cheese from clumping on the hot pasta.) Add the white sauce and stir to mix thoroughly.

(continued)

5.   Refrigerate for at least 2 hours.

6.   Break the eggs into a shallow bowl—like a soup or pasta bowl—and, with a fork, beat to mix well. Place the bread crumbs in another shallow bowl or on a plate.

7.   With moistened hands and using a ¼-cup measure to scoop up the mixture, form the pasta into patties about ¾ inch thick and 2½ inches in diameter. Dip the patties in egg to cover well. Dredge the patties in bread crumbs to coat well, pressing them into the crumbs lightly. The breaded cakes may be set aside in the refrigerator for several hours before frying.

To fry:

8.   In a skillet, heat about ½ inch of oil to 360 degrees or slightly higher. Ease the pasta cakes into the oil and fry until golden on both sides, which should take about 2 minutes a side.

9.   Drain on absorbent paper. Serve immediately.

VARIATION:

A more elaborate version of these is outlined in Ippolito Cavalcanti's 1839 *Cucina teorico-pratica* (The Theory and Practice of Cooking). Form the cakes with ½ as much mixture, making them ½ as thick but the same diameter. Cut slices of boiled ham into rounds about ½ inch smaller in diameter. Cut thin slices of mozzarella, scamorza, Emmenthaler, or Gruyère cheese the same size as the ham. Make sandwiches of pasta, ham, cheese, and pasta. Press the edges together to enclose the ham and cheese. Fry as above.

ZUCCHINE A FIAMMIFERO

ZUCCHINI MATCHSTICKS

FRIED ZUCCHINI CAN BE as addictive as potato chips, and don't Americans know it. It is one of the most popular appetizers in both old-fashioned Italian-American restaurants and the new "family" chain restaurants. In Campania, you never get thick sticks of the vegetable. The zucchini is either cut into fine strands, as in this recipe, or cut in thin rounds. Buy small zucchini if possible; no bigger than about three to the pound, but preferably smaller.

Zucchini

Fine sea salt

All-purpose flour

Extra-virgin olive oil, peanut, or canola oil for deep-fat frying

Optional: Lemon wedges

1.   Cut the zucchini into matchstick pieces about 3 inches long and ⅛ inch on each side. Sprinkle lightly with fine salt and let drain in a colander. (If making a large amount, make several layers of zucchini with salt sprinkled on each, each time tossing the whole batch with your hands to mix and distribute the salt before adding more zucchini.) Let drain at least 30 minutes, preferably an hour.

2.   Squeeze the zucchini in the colander firmly (but not to mash it) to extract a little extra water.

3.   Place a ½-inch layer of flour on a platter and toss the zucchini—as much as will be fried at once—to cover it lightly with flour. Toss handfuls in your palms, letting excess flour fall back on the platter. (If you want a really light flour coating—you'll learn after a couple of batches how much you like—shake the zucchini in a strainer or your fryer basket to remove more flour.)

4.   Fry in deep fat at 375 degrees until lightly golden—about 8 minutes in an open pan, up to 15 minutes or longer with some electric deep-fat fryers.

5.   Turn out onto a napkin or paper-covered serving plate and serve immediately, with additional fine salt if desired, and/or with lemon wedges.

Carciofi Indorati e Fritti

Batter-Dipped, Fried Artichokes

Indorati means both "gilded" and "dipped in egg." It would be hard to find a more apt word for this type of fry. Almost anything can be *indorato e fritto*—dredged in flour, dipped in egg (usually beaten with grated cheese), then deep-fat fried. The Neapolitan favorites are vegetables, particularly artichokes, asparagus, zucchini, zucchini flowers, eggplant, mushrooms, blanched broccoli and cauliflower, and, if you want to get recherché, borage leaves.

I owe whatever good dip-and-fry technique I have to Rita De Rosa of Naples and New York, and when she used artichokes as my first lesson, her eyes had that sparkle I've learned to know means, "Sonny, are you in for a treat!" In honor of that indelible moment, and because artichoke preparation requires explanation, whereas most vegetables don't, the specifics of this recipe are for artichokes. It should be easy to extrapolate from this recipe how to do other foods. It's just dredge, dip, and fry.

Serve gilded and fried vegetables for their own sake, as an antipasto or aperitivo snack, or as part of a mixed fry, or as a side dish. Don't expect a very crisp coating. Even when the vegetables are eaten directly from the boiling oil, the gilding is tender and soft. Indeed, floured and egg-dipped vegetables are among the few fried items that don't lose any savor or texture by being served at room temperature. And they're better at room temperature than reheated.

Serves 4 to 6

2 lemons

4 large artichokes

Flour

3 eggs

¼ cup freshly grated Parmigiano-Reggiano

Peanut, canola, or corn oil for frying

1. To prepare the artichokes, have at hand a large bowl of cold water. Squeeze in the juice of both lemons. Turn back and break off all the outer, dark green petals of each artichoke, until you get to the petals that are mostly chartreuse. Using a large, sharp knife, cut off the darker green tops of those petals—about the top 2 inches of the artichokes. To prevent the artichokes from discoloring, dip them in lemon water as you work.

2. Trim off the stems. They may be saved for another use or fried separately. With a sharp paring knife, trim off any dark green from the base of the artichokes. Cut the artichokes in half lengthwise, and with the tip of the paring knife, cut out the hairy chokes and purple petals at the center by making a cut that follows the curve of the base. Discard the choke and purple petals. Cut each artichoke bottom (still with some tender outside petals attached) into ¼-inch slices. You should get about 8 slices from each artichoke. Keep the prepared artichokes in the lemon water until ready to cook. (I have kept them in a closed container in the refrigerator for as long as several days.)

3. To fry, heat about an inch of oil in a 7- to 8-inch skillet, until it is very hot, about 375 degrees. You will see the beginning of a boil just before the fat is hot enough. Do not let it smoke.

4. Meanwhile, place some flour on a dinner plate and, in a small bowl, beat the eggs with the grated cheese until well blended. Arrange the plates in front of you, with the bowl of prepared artichokes, next to the heating oil.

5. When the oil is hot, dredge the still-wet artichoke slices, one at a time, in the flour, then dip them in egg, making sure the flour, then the egg, coats thoroughly. Use a fork to manipulate the vegetable in the egg and the other hand to dredge in flour. In that way you don't batter your fingers.

6. Fry the artichokes until golden on both sides, adjusting the heat so that they begin frying as soon as they hit the fat, but not so violently that they brown immediately—before the artichokes themselves are fully cooked. It is, however, better to start with the fat too hot than too cool. If the fat is too hot, besides lowering the heat, lift the pan off the heat for a few seconds. You can fry a few slices at a time, but do not crowd the pan. There must be enough room for each slice to fry on the surface of the oil.

7. As soon as each slice is golden, remove with tongs to a rack or a plate covered with absorbent paper. Serve hot or warm, sprinkled with salt.

INVOLTINI DI ASPARAGI FRITTI

FRIED, HAM-WRAPPED ASPARAGUS TIPS

THESE ARE TIME-CONSUMING to form and fry, but I had to do it at least once, and you might want to try them, too. When I served them, everyone thought they were a miracle of *Monzù* manipulation but wondered who was ever going to bother, in this day and age, to wrap asparagus spears in ham, dip them in flour, egg, and bread crumbs, then fry them and serve them instantly. I would. And the few times I've served them, everyone was very happy I did. Make them for family and good friends gathered in the kitchen for an informal fry night, or as a first, stunning, stand-up nibble for more formal company.

Asparagus spears

⅓ paper-thin slice prosciutto per asparagus spear

Flour

Beaten egg

Fine dry bread crumbs

Peanut, canola, or corn oil for frying

1. Use only the top 4 inches of each asparagus spear. Save the bottoms for another recipe: Peel them, and they can be steamed or boiled and served as a vegetable, or sauté them with butter or pancetta and serve with pasta, as in the pasta with peas recipe on page 104. Wash the asparagus tips and dry them very well.

2. Wrap each asparagus tip with ⅓ slice of prosciutto. It should wrap about 1½ times around the asparagus. It should also stick to itself, like plastic wrap.

3. Arrange a plate of flour, a shallow bowl of beaten egg, and a plate of bread crumbs in front of you. Dredge the wrapped tips in flour, then roll well in beaten egg, then in bread crumbs. They may be prepared ahead and fried later.

4. Heat ¼ inch of oil in a skillet until a pinch of flour sizzles immediately. Fry the breaded tips a few at a time, handling them with tongs.

5. Drain on absorbent paper and serve immediately.

CALZONCINI

FILLED AND FRIED DOUGH CRESCENTS

THERE ARE SO MANY names given to filled and fried turnovers in Campania that the nomenclature is meaningless, except within a family or, one has to suppose, within a small community. It's not so much that there are local names, but that names are used interchangeably for different and the same things in the same and different places. Calzoncini, for instance, are usually made with pizza dough. The name means "small calzoni," even though calzoni themselves are more often called pizze ripiene (filled pizzas). Still, there are recipes for calzoncini that are made with pastry dough, which would made them technically pizzelle or panzarotti to some, although pizzelle and panzarotti are also made with pizza dough. Then there are pizzette, which are generally not stuffed turnovers but fried flat rounds of yeast dough, small fried pizzas, that are eaten topped with tomato sauce and either grated cheese or mozzarella—except when they are not. Take the recipe on the next page. Its creator calls them pizzette, although by qualifying the dish with the word "frolla," she indicates they are made with pastry dough. They are filled turnovers.

Makes 8 to 10

½ recipe pizza dough (see page 71)

Ricotta

Optional: Finely diced salami or boiled ham

Peanut, canola, or corn oil for frying

1. Tear off walnut-size pieces of dough. Roll them into neat balls between the palms of your hands, then flatten the balls and stretch them into 3- to 4-inch disks, using your thumbs and forefingers, as you would for pizza.

2. Put a teaspoon or so of ricotta in the center of each disk. If desired, add a few tiny pieces of salami or ham.

3. Fold the disks in half and pinch the seams together well. To make the seal extra tight, roll the double edge slightly and pinch again.

4. In a skillet, heat about ½ inch of oil to 375 degrees. Fry the filled crescents, turning once, until golden on both sides.

5. Drain on absorbent paper and serve immediately.

PIZZETTE FROLLE DI RITA DE ROSA

Rita De Rosa's Fried Yeast Pastry Turnovers

THIS IS A TOTALLY original dough. Rita has taken a classic short pastry and added yeast, which makes for a particularly tender, flaky, and puffy casing for a filling of mixed cheeses and minced salami. Eliminate the salami if you like. They are delectable as an antipasto, either alone or plated with a small salad.

Makes about 15, serving at least 6

For the dough:

1¼ teaspoons active dry yeast

2 tablespoons warm water

2 cups cake flour

¼ teaspoon salt

6 tablespoons cold butter, in one piece

1 egg, lightly beaten

For the filling:

2 tablespoons salami in ⅛-inch or smaller dice

2 tablespoons freshly grated pecorino

¼ cup mozzarella in ⅛-inch dice

⅔ cup ricotta

Plus:

Peanut, canola, or corn oil for frying

1.   Dissolve the yeast in the warm water and set aside.

2.   In a mixing bowl, combine the flour and the salt. Grate the butter on the coarse side of a box grater into the flour, tossing a few times to coat the butter bits with flour. Add the dissolved yeast and the egg. With a table fork, or your hand, mix the liquids into the dough until it holds together. If it seems dry, add up to a tablespoon of cold water.

3. Remove the dough from the bowl and knead it a few times. Form the dough into 2 disks. Wrap in plastic and let rest in the refrigerator for at least 15 minutes before rolling out. (It can be made hours ahead.)

4. Meanwhile, prepare the filling by blending all the ingredients together.

5. If well-chilled, let the pastry warm up nearly to room temperature before working it. Roll out each disk to ⅛-inch thickness. Use a biscuit cutter or glass to cut the dough into 3-inch circles. Roll out each circle to a 4-inch circle.

6. Place a scant tablespoon of filling in the center of each round, then moisten the edges of the rounds with water, fold each round over its filling, and press the edges together firmly. Use a fork to decorate the edges and press them together even more securely.

7. Set the pastries aside, uncovered on a lightly floured dishtowel to rest for 15 to 30 minutes. (If you want to make them somewhat ahead, keep them refrigerated until 5 minutes before frying them.)

8. In a skillet, heat about ½ inch of oil to about 375 degrees. Slip in a few pastries at a time, and, using a large spoon, immediately baste the tops with hot oil. As soon as the first side is golden, turn the crescents and fry the second side very briefly. It should mostly be cooked from the basting.

9. Drain on a rack and serve immediately.

THE CLASSIC SAUCES: TOMATO SAUCE, IL RAGÙ, AND LA GENOVESE

*F*or centuries, maybe for millennia, pasta has existed. Dressed with cheese and often sweetened with sugar and cinnamon, it was praised, people liked it. But it was dull, inexorably dull. At the beginning of the 16th century, the tomato arrived but few people appreciated it. Two centuries later, its joy exploded, finding in Naples a climate and atmosphere most favorable to its blooming. We don't know who was the first to think of marrying pasta and tomato. He surely deserves a monument. That was the most solemn moment in the history of pasta, for it is only in this union that each finds completion. Just think of the long journey the tomato and the pasta had to take before happy circumstance placed them in each other's path.

—Jeanne Carola Francesconi,
La cucina napoletana (Neapolitan Cooking)

TOMATO SAUCE

THERE IS NO FOOD more Neapolitan than tomato sauce, except perhaps the spaghetti and pizza it goes on. And as Neapolitans are liable to do about anything of their own invention, in her definitive book on Neapolitan cooking, Francesconi goes on and on romanticizing, sentimentalizing, and aggrandizing "this happy coupling of tomato and pasta."

In that vein, Francesconi is not the only Neapolitan to claim that pasta with tomato sauce is perhaps the one food that a human can eat every day. Certainly one can't go more than several days without it, a Neapolitan will say, straight-faced, with complete sincerity. "You can eat American food for two, maybe three days in a row," said my young friend Ettore Bellelli from Paestum when he was visiting New York, explaining why he much preferred to stay home and eat some macaroni and the ragù in my refrigerator rather than the steak awaiting him in a restaurant. And it is possible, as Francesconi says (and any Campanian would agree), to eat pasta and tomato sauce every day because the "inventive and inexhaustible genius of humble housewives has overcome the inevitable monotony of doing so."

All anyone can say to that is, those "humble housewives" definitely knew how to make do. They took the tomato, which grew with ease and in profusion in the rich volcanic soils of Campania, and, to paraphrase Francesconi, by using one herb or another, and either onion or garlic (hardly ever both), and by cooking them with either olive oil or lard, for a short time or for a long time, on a higher fire or a lower flame, and by proportioning the amount of tomato against other possible ingredients, such as olives, capers, fish, and meat, they created an almost endless variety of tomato sauces.

The most elemental is the uncooked *salsa all'insalata*, which is nothing more than diced tomatoes marinated in olive oil with salt and basil. The most elaborate would be ragù, the category of Neapolitan sauces in which the tomatoes cook long and slowly with meat that eventually gives up its color and savor to the tomato, making the red sauce resonate with it and deepening its tone to nearer the color of red mahogany.

It is only with tomato sauce that pasta became famous around the world, which is ironic, given that Neapolitans have, in general, a distrust of sauces made separately from the main food. All their sauces are integral to the dish. To the common Neapolitan mind, sauce cooked separately from the food is the way of French kitchens and is used to cover up less than superior meat or whatever else is being sauced—an opinion in other parts of the world, too. In the old days, only the aristocracy and the rich served sauce on meat or fish, and that was to impress guests with Frenchified food. Nowadays, those pretenses are rare. Everyone knows that sauce is served in international restaurants, and all Neapolitans think a fine tomato sauce or ragù is as noble as food can get.

Indeed, ask Neapolitans to name their favorite pasta, as I have, and they are most likely to say, no matter from which class they come, "spaghetti with a quickly cooked fresh tomato sauce and basil." Nothing could be more basic to their hearts or kitchens. Neapolitans have a reputation for cooking tomato sauce for a very long time (some would say too long) when actually the opposite is true. The fresh tomatoes are peeled or not. If they are cherry tomatoes, certainly not. It would take too much time and effort. Then the tomatoes are chopped, cut into strips, crushed, or pureed, depending on how the sauce will be used. Fresh tomatoes on medium to high heat in a wide pan can be cooked in as little as five minutes, less time than it takes to bring the pasta water to a boil. A slowly simmered puree can be ready to eat in less than half an hour. Put it up a few minutes before the pasta water, and it can be ready at the same time as the spaghetti.

MARINARA

*M*arinara can mean several things in Campania. It's the name of the pizza with the simplest topping—chopped tomatoes with minced garlic, olive oil, and oregano: pizza alla marinara. However, when those same ingredients sauce something other than a pizza, the dish is said to be *alla pizzaiola*, in the style of the pizza maker, and not marinara. (See page 278 for Carne alla Pizzaiola and page 215 for Scamorza alla Pizzaiola.) Marinara is also the name of a sauce for pasta, usually spaghetti or bucatini (also called perciatelli), but it is not the basic tomato sauce that Americans and other Italians might call marinara. Marinara in Campania is most often a tomato-based sauce with Gaeta olives, capers, anchovies, garlic, and sometimes preserved (canned or jarred) tuna. The word "marinara" indicates that fish is included in the sauce. Adding to the confusion, the Campanian marinara sauce can also be called puttanesca (see pages 164 and 166).

Sugo di Pomodoro

Smooth Tomato Sauce—From Fresh Tomatoes

It is said that Naples gave glory to the tomato with this sauce, which, as you can see by glancing at the ingredients, is extremely simple. There is no secret to it except utter simplicity. The sweet taste of the tomato is what is most important. To that end very few seasonings are added to the basic Neapolitan tomato sauce, and it is cooked very briefly. The choice of onion or garlic is up to the dish in which the sauce will be used—garlic with fish and seafood, onion with most other foods—the cook in charge of it, and the whim of the moment. If fresh basil is at hand, that's definitely the herb of choice for pasta, but, in a pinch, there is dried oregano or marjoram. For fish and shellfish, the herb is always fresh parsley.

There is definitely a difference in the flavor and texture of sauce made from peeled and unpeeled plum tomatoes. The puree derived from peeled tomatoes has a slightly lesser density and lighter flavor—one might even say a "fresher" flavor—while a sauce from unpeeled tomatoes has a slightly more concentrated texture and deeper flavor. Both are excellent, and both have their appeal. I make my decision about which to prepare mainly based on the quality of the tomatoes and the amount of sauce I am making. Some tomatoes simply peel cleaner and easier than others, taking less flesh with the skin. So if I have easy peeling tomatoes and a small amount of sauce to make, as in this recipe, I'd probably take the time to peel the tomatoes. However, during the summer, when making a large amount of smooth tomato sauce for keeping (I use the freezer), peeling all those tomatoes, no matter how cleanly they go, seems like an unnecessary and tedious job. I count on a food mill to keep back the skins, as well as the seeds.

Makes about 4 cups, enough for 1½ pounds of pasta, serving 6 to 8

1 medium onion, chopped (about 1 cup)
or 2 large cloves garlic, lightly smashed

2 tablespoons extra-virgin olive oil

3 pounds ripe plum tomatoes, peeled or not, and cut into large chunks

½ cup (packed) whole basil leaves

1 tablespoon salt, or to taste

⅛ to ¼ teaspoon hot red pepper flakes, or to taste

1. If making a sauce with onion, place the onion and the oil in a 6- to 8-quart pot over medium heat, and cook, stirring, until the onion is tender and golden, 8 to 10 minutes. If using garlic, combine the garlic and oil in a 6- to 8-quart pot over low heat and cook the garlic, pressing it into the oil a couple of times to release its flavor, until it *barely* begins to color on both sides. Remove the garlic.

2. Stir in the tomato chunks, increase the heat slightly and, stirring occasionally, cook until the tomatoes have collapsed into a mush, about 20 minutes.

3. Puree the sauce in a food mill, then return it to the pot. Tear the basil leaves into the sauce and add the salt and hot red pepper. Bring to a simmer over medium heat and, stirring occasionally, simmer for another 5 to 15 minutes, or until the sauce has thickened. The timing will depend on the moisture content of the tomatoes.

To store: The sauce can be made ahead and kept in the refrigerator for up to a week, or in the freezer for up to 10 months, at least until the next tomato harvest.

VEGETABLE MILLS

A high-quality, hand-cranked vegetable mill makes pureeing tomatoes a snap and holds back the skins (of fresh tomatoes), as well as the seeds that can make a tomato sauce bitter. Never use a blender or food processor. It is better to make a less pureed sauce or to push the finished sauce through a strainer. I like the kind of vegetable mill with interchangeable graters—using the medium one for this sauce—and with collapsible arms that hold the mill in position over the pot, so the tomato puree falls into it directly.

Chunky Fresh Tomato Sauce

Sometimes you will want or need a chunky fresh tomato sauce or sauce base, instead of a puree. It's good on short tubes of macaroni or to dress slices of meat or fillets of fish.

Makes about 2 cups, enough for 12 ounces of pasta, serving 4

2 pounds ripe plum tomatoes

¼ cup extra-virgin olive oil

1 small or ½ medium onion, cut into ¼-inch dice

½ teaspoon salt

½ cup loosely packed whole basil leaves

1. Place the tomatoes in boiling water for 1 minute. Drain immediately. When cool enough to handle, use a sharp paring knife to pull off the skins. If the tomatoes are very ripe, they come off easily. Cut the tomatoes in half and squeeze out their seeds. Chop the tomatoes coarsely or finely, depending on the consistency of sauce desired.

2. In a 10-inch skillet, sauté pan, or shallow stovetop casserole, combine the oil and onion and cook over medium heat until the onion is tender and golden, 8 to 10 minutes. Add the tomatoes, increase the heat slightly and bring to a simmer, then adjust the heat so the tomatoes simmer gently for about 15 minutes, or until the sauce has reduced to the desired thickness.

3. A minute or so before removing the sauce from the heat, add the salt, then tear the basil leaves into tiny pieces and add them to the sauce. If you make the sauce ahead, add the basil when reheating it.

FILETTO DI POMODORO

FILLET OF TOMATO SAUCE—FROM EITHER CANNED OR FRESH TOMATOES

IN THE UNITED STATES, the expression "filetto di pomodoro" has come to mean, through its use in stylish, supposedly "northern Italian" restaurants, a quickly cooked *fresh* tomato sauce. It should mean exactly what it says, a sauce made with discernible strips of tomato pulp, cooked so quickly they don't turn to sauce. And it is certainly a southern Italian notion, not "northern." One doesn't hear or see the expression "filetto di pomodoro" used much these days in Campania, although most people know what it is, and at the height of summer one is likely to eat it. Instead, it might be called sciuè sciuè, sauce in a hurry (see page 160), or just tomato sauce, sugo di pomodoro. I've also been told that filetto di pomodoro is a bit old-fashioned, that the vine-type cherry tomatoes, which are much easier to handle and even more delicious (certainly sweeter) to many, are being used where tomato fillets used to be.

By the way, good canned tomatoes can taste almost fresh when cooked as these are, in only 5 minutes in a wide pan that promotes evaporation. Keep that in mind some January when you see "fresh" filetto di pomodoro on the menu of a "northern Italian" restaurant.

Makes 1 cup, enough for 6 ounces of pasta, serving 2

1½ to 2 cups well-drained, seeded, canned peeled plum tomatoes,
sliced lengthwise into ¼-inch strips, or an equal quantity of fresh tomatoes,
peeled, seeded, and sliced lengthwise into ¼-inch strips

2 to 3 tablespoons extra-virgin olive oil

1 teaspoon finely minced garlic

1 rounded tablespoon finely cut basil or parsley

⅛ to ½ teaspoon salt (depending on saltiness of tomatoes,
canned needing less than fresh)

Pinch hot red pepper flakes

1. In a 7- to 9-inch skillet, combine all the ingredients and place them over medium-high heat.

2. Simmer briskly for about 5 minutes for canned tomatoes, about 8 minutes for fresh, stirring a few times. The tomatoes should remain in pieces and there should be no liquid in the pan, only reddish oil separating from the tomatoes.

SUGO DI POMODORI PELATI

SMOOTH TOMATO SAUCE—FROM CANNED TOMATOES

CAMPANIANS PUT A PREMIUM on sauce made from fresh summer tomatoes. *Mamma mia!* They practically worship it. But they have absolutely no qualms about using tomatoes preserved in cans or bottles during the rest of the year. Bottled tomatoes are definitely preferred over canned, and many households, even those in the center of bustling, urban Naples, still go to the trouble of putting up what they consider the world's best tomatoes—their own San Marzano, grown at the foot of Vesuvius as well as in gardens and farms all over the region. Bottled tomatoes are also sold in the groceries, as they are beginning to be in North America. In theory, they don't have as strong an acid edge (or metallic edge, if you will) as canned tomatoes, but all processed tomatoes, no matter what brand or in which material they are packed, get more acidic, bitter, and mushier with age. It's best to use canned or jarred tomatoes within six months of their packing.

Brands of canned tomatoes differ dramatically, too. I don't, for instance, use the domestic tomatoes canned with tomato puree. The puree gives the impression that the tomatoes are more flavorful than those that are canned in natural juice, but they are often blander; not a good thing when the recipe requires draining the tomatoes. Both domestic and imported can be good or not so good. Besides Italy, Turkey, Spain, Greece, Chile, and Israel are exporting canned tomatoes. Of course, the brand on special sale is always a temptation. In case you open a weakly flavored, bitter, or acid can of tomatoes, you can compensate by adding a teaspoon to a tablespoon of tomato paste. (I avoid adding sugar.)

Frugal Neapolitans use both the tomatoes and their packing juices when they make tomato sauce from peeled, preserved tomatoes—pelati in Italian. They will even rinse out the jar or can with a bit of water, not wasting a drop of tomato flavor. I will do the same for a long-cooked ragù, and if you have the best flavored tomatoes packed in thick, well-flavored juice, try it. Otherwise, using the tomatoes generally available to us, I've found that draining the liquid from the can, and using only the tomatoes and the juice inside them, reduces the cooking time, produces the same amount of sauce, and results in one that tastes more like fresh and is less apt to have an acidic edge. (The one-half to one cup of juice each twenty-eight-ounce can contains can be saved in the refrigerator for up to a week and used in place of water in a vegetable minestra or for a vegetable broth.)

Makes about 2 cups, enough for 12 ounces of pasta, serving 4

2 tablespoons extra-virgin olive oil

1 small onion or ½ medium onion, finely chopped (about ½ cup)
or 1 large clove garlic, lightly smashed

1 28-ounce can plum tomatoes, drained of the can juices (see note)

½ teaspoon salt

Hot red pepper flakes or freshly ground black pepper to taste

A few leaves of fresh basil or parsley

1.   In a 1½- to 2-quart saucepan, combine the oil and onion and cook over medium heat, stirring frequently, until the onion is fully tender and golden, 8 to 10 minutes. Or, over medium-low heat, combine the oil and the garlic. Cook the garlic, pressing it into the oil a couple of times to release its flavor, until it *barely* begins to color on both sides. Remove the garlic.

2.   With a food mill, puree the tomatoes directly into the pot and stir well. Add salt and either hot red pepper flakes or black pepper to taste. Increase the heat slightly and bring to a brisk simmer. Adjusting the heat as the sauce cooks down, and stirring frequently, simmer briskly for about 12 minutes, until the sauce has thickened and reduced.

3.   Season with herbs according to the recipe you are preparing. For the most basic spaghetti sauce, add a few torn basil leaves or a tablespoon of finely cut parsley to the sauce while it is simmering, then add a little more of either at the very end of cooking.

To multiply the recipe: The recipe can be doubled or tripled, but you don't have to multiply the oil by as many times. Use your judgment and taste. A larger quantity of sauce will take longer to cook.

Note: The easiest way to drain the tomatoes is to open the can but not remove the lid, then use the lid to hold back the tomatoes while the juices run into a cup or bowl.

Variation:

Sometimes you will want a chunky sauce, not a smooth puree. Instead of pushing the tomatoes through a food mill, turn the whole can of tomatoes, drained or not, into the pot with the oil. Using the side of a wooden spoon, a wooden fork, or an old-fashioned American potato masher, break up the tomatoes as desired, then proceed as above.

Il Ragù

Ragù is the grand exception of Neapolitan tomato sauces. Instead of being quick-cooked it is legendary for the length of time it simmers away. To the Campanian mind, however, it is not truly a tomato sauce. They see it more as meat sauce, with tomatoes as the medium into which the meat's flavor is extracted, and a very different thing from tomato sauce.

Ragù does cook a long time, but even in the old days, probably not as long as some old family tales would have it. For one thing, we have to remember that the larger the pot of ragù, the longer it takes to cook, so it would not have been out of line to simmer huge pots of ragù for five, six, seven hours . . . what seemed like all day—*piano, piano*: slowly, slowly—to feed the large families of pre–World War II Italy. People these days have smaller families and make smaller amounts and are proud to tell you that they cook their ragù for only two and a half hours, or two hours, or one and a half hours, at which point some will admit that it is only "semi-ragù." It's the modern, "light" thing to do to cook it short, rather than long. Good Campanian cooks agree, however, that two and a half hours is about the minimum for a small quantity of sauce that you can legitimately call ragù. At some point soon after the two-hour mark, there is a transformation, a big flavor and color change. Suddenly the sauce gets a penetrating flavor.

Rita De Rosa, a modern Neapolitan cook who is nevertheless bound to tradition, speculates, too, that perhaps those ragùs from the old days were not cooked as long as we think and they thought. "They cooked on coal braziers," she explains, "in pottery. And the fuel would always be dimming and going out. They had to take the pot off the fire to add fuel to the fire, or stoke the coals. Meanwhile the ragù cooled a little. Then it had to heat up again. After five hours of cooking the ragù, maybe it really cooked three."

It's no wonder that ragù is also called il sugo della guardaporta (sauce of the door-keeper or concierge). Long cooking also means frequent stirring, not to mention tending the fire in the old days. Who but the woman who lived in the room next to the courtyard entrance and guarded it—whose job it was to be at home all day—had the time for such work? In a typical Neapolitan way, a joke proposes that by the same theory, ragù could as well be the sauce of whores.

Ragù Napoletano

Rraù

Neapolitan Meat Sauce

The queen of all sauces—our beloved, immortal and mouth-watering ragù.

—Nello Oliviero, late twentieth-century Neapolitan gastronome
and writer, *Storie e curiosità del mangiar napoletano*
(Neapolitan Food Stories and Curiosities)

*You can't make ragù distractedly as you can any tomato sauce. It requires
dedication and attention. You must stay with it, guide it, caress it for hours and
hours so that the aromas of its various components can be released and mingle
with each other. For four, five, six hours it must cook slowly and it must never be
abandoned . . . Arm yourself with patience and maybe with a book that is not
excessively interesting, so that it won't absorb you so much that you will let
everything burn. Dedicate yourself to the preparation of the queen of sauces,
give up a part of your day off and do it with love. You won't regret it.
It will give you calm.*

—Jeanne Carola Francesconi,
La cucina napoletana (Neapolitan Cooking)

This is a contemporary recipe for ragù. If you read the old ones you would probably never cook ragù, although I could not help but include one antique version on page 56. Some old recipes have three kinds of fat—batons of pork fat to "lard" the meat, which might be pork, too, plus rendered lard (sugna) and olive oil for browning the meat. There are recipes, though rare, that also throw butter into the mix. Leanness is the word of the day in Italy today, and I've talked to contemporary cooks who don't even add olive oil to the pot, considering the bit of fat rendered from the well-trimmed meat as it sears and then simmers to add plenty of fat texture to their sauce. Then again, Italians use far more olive oil than we consider prudent, and many would brown meat in triple the quantity I've suggested here.

You can make a ragù, according to these directions, with any kind of meat. It can be all beef, all veal, all pork, all lamb, all goat, or any mixture of them. Venison is not a meat of Campania any longer (all the game animals were hunted out long ago), but one of the best ragùs I've ever made was with venison. The kind of meat used depends on locale, as much as on the philosophy of the cook. In the province of Benevento, for example, cooks use at least some lamb, if not all lamb (they also might use garlic instead of onion, or both). In the high Cilento of southern Salerno province, and the Monti Alburni, the lower mountains behind the Cilento, where goats are kept, *capretto* (baby goat) or *castrato* (castrated old goat) ragù is made. On the plains where water buffalo are husbanded for their milk, their meat also makes it into the ragù pot. Braciole, stuffed meat rolls, cooked with tomatoes, also results in ragù (see page 280) and is extremely popular now that the beef for braciole is affordable to more people. It's also considered the height of modernity and sane nutrition. Finally, everywhere in the region, pork sausage may go in a ragù. It not only adds a wonderful flavor to the sauce, but if you add them for only the last half or so of the cooking time, you have some succulent meat for a second course or to slice into a composed pasta dish, such as Lasagne di Carnevale (page 206) or Timballo di Maccheroni (page 186). Ragù made with ground meat, as they do in Emilia-Romagna for ragù bolognese, is called ragù di macinata in Campania (pages 182 and 200).

Makes 4 cups sauce, enough for 1½ pounds pasta, serving 8

½ pound well-trimmed pork cut in large chunks, or sweet Italian sausage

½ pound lean stewing veal, cut in large chunks

½ pound well-trimmed chuck or shoulder, cut in large chunks

1 medium onion, finely chopped

2 tablespoons extra-virgin olive oil

½ cup hearty red wine

2 28-ounce cans peeled plum tomatoes (not drained)

1½ teaspoons salt

Big pinch hot red pepper flakes

1. In a 4- to 5-quart pot or stovetop casserole, combine the meats (except sausage, if using, which gets added later), the onion, and the olive oil. Place over medium-high heat and sear the meat. It will immediately exude juices. Keep cooking, stirring frequently, until the meat juices have evaporated and the meats and the onions are light brown, at least 10 minutes.

2. Add the wine and continue to cook, stirring frequently, until the wine evaporates. The meat will be a much darker brown now.

3. Pass the tomatoes through a food mill—directly into the pot if you like—and stir them into the meat. Add the sausage, if using. Add salt and hot pepper and stir again. Simmer gently for 2½ to 3 hours. Stir every 15 minutes or so, but after about an hour, before stirring, skim any fat off the surface that you consider excess. (If the meats are lean, there is usually no more than a couple of tablespoons of fat, and you'll want to leave it in the sauce.) Also, every time you stir, remember to stir down any sauce that will have condensed on the side of the pot just above its surface. When done, the ragù will have a dark color and a thick consistency.

4. Let the sauce cool slightly, but strain out or pick out the meat while it is still warm. Check for salt and pepper.

5. Serve the sauce very hot on pasta or use it in other recipes as indicated. The meat can be served as a separate course, or on another day. Both the sauce and the meat can be kept in the refrigerator for up to a week, much longer in the freezer. After a week of refrigerator storage, if it is necessary to keep the sauce longer, bring it to a simmer, then refrigerate it again. It will need to be reseasoned when reheated for use.

VARIATION:

For Ragù Beneventano, substitute 1 pound of lamb neck, still on the bone, for the veal, and use 3 large cloves of garlic instead of the onion. Smash the garlic and remove it from the oil when it begins to color, or at least before adding the wine.

RAGÙ DI PUNTINE E CONCENTRATO

Ragù from Pork Ribs and Tomato Paste

THIS IS AN EXTREMELY old-fashioned recipe. It's hard to find Campanians who these days would make a ragù solely from tomato paste, much less with a fatty cut of pork. I think most people would consider it low-class or ignorantly rustic or, at best, quaint. If, however, you are looking for that velvety fatty texture and acid-edged sweetness of an ancestral, immigrant Neapolitan's ragù, this may be the recipe to satisfy you. I find the texture incomparable and a real treat.

Makes 1 quart

2 medium onions, cut into ¼-inch dice (about 2 cups)

2 tablespoons extra-virgin olive oil

2 pounds meaty pork ribs, excessive fat removed

¾ cup red wine

1 cup tomato paste

5 cups water (approximately)

1 teaspoon salt

1.   In a 4- to 6-quart saucepan or stovetop casserole, combine the onions, the oil, and the pork ribs and place over medium heat. Cook, stirring frequently, until the onions and ribs begin to color, 15 to 20 minutes.

2.   Add the wine and let it evaporate over medium-low heat, still turning the ribs frequently, about another 15 minutes.

3.   Dissolve the tomato paste in the 5 cups of water and add just enough to cover the meat. Add salt. Simmer very gently, uncovered, for about 3 hours. Bubbles should just break on the surface. Stir every 15 to 20 minutes, making sure the meat doesn't stick to the bottom of the pot, and adding just enough of the tomato paste and water mixture to keep the meat covered. Also, every time you stir the pot, stir down any sauce that concentrates on the side of the pot just above the surface. If you run out of tomato mixture before the sauce has finished cooking, add water by spoonfuls as necessary. In the end, the sauce should be thick and dark.

4.   Strain the sauce to use on pasta, reserving the ribs for a second course or for another meal.

LA GENOVESE

LA GENOVESE IS A Neapolitan mystery. This puree of onions flavored mainly with meat is considered one of the glories of the Neapolitan kitchen, a dish proudly held up as proof that there was original, even fine cooking in Naples before the tomato. And it is unknown in Genoa. Or anywhere else in Italy, unless a transplanted Neapolitan cook has introduced it to the neighborhood.

One story has it that, in the sixteenth century, Genovese merchants living in Naples, attending to their businesses (the cities always communicated and traded because they were and are still chief ports of the Mediterranean), had private chefs who made such a sauce. The merchants eventually went back to Genoa, but some of the chefs stayed behind, enchanted by their new-found paradise, Naples. They set up shops or stands selling food to the public, many of whom didn't have kitchens in their tiny, one-room apartments (called *bassi*). The sauce that was to become known as la Genovese was their specialty.

The only thing that's believable about this story is that there were Genovese merchants with private chefs. Certainly, frequently famine-stricken Naples of the sixteenth century, governed by the Spanish viceroys, was not entirely an enchanting paradise. And cooking on the street for the people had to be a big comedown from cooking for rich Genovese merchants. Perhaps the chefs were thrown out onto the street. Another version of the story has the chefs in a labor dispute with their employers. Another that the employers lost all their money and didn't take their cooks back home.

In any case, the first printed recipes for la Genovese are nothing like what the sauce is now. As late as 1837, Ippolito Cavalcanti gives a recipe in his *Cucina casarinola co la lengua napolitana* (Home Cooking in the Neapolitan Language) that is essentially a French *glace de viande*, a meat stock reduction. It was not an onion sauce yet. It does contain a French *mirepoix*, though—equal amounts of diced onion, carrot, and celery to flavor the rich stock. Somewhere along the line, later in the nineteenth century, the *mirepoix* got out of whack. The onions took over. The carrots and celery became practically token in relation to the huge quantity of onions. The meat—in Naples an expensive food and not a high-quality one—was reduced to the role of flavoring the onions, not vice versa. Often no beef at all was used, only scraps of salami and ham, a prosciutto rind or bone. Some people even began to make the sauce without any meat. Macaroni with a sauce of only onions, a finta Genovese (fake Genovese), became a fast-day dish. And still is. (See page 63 for a contemporary version.)

As it is often made today, la Genovese is back to being a meat dish. In newly afflu-ent Campania, it is made with enough meat to serve meat as a second course, sliced and dressed with a bit of the onion sauce. A green vegetable would accompany that. Peas are considered the best. The sauce, which tastes quite like the gravy from a Jewish-American pot roast, is really the main event, however. And it always goes on ziti or mezzani, a long tubular macaroni, a slightly larger version of bucatini that's often broken into three- to four-inch lengths or cut into shorter lengths in the factory. Neapolitans would find penne acceptable, too.

La Genovese di Maria Russo

Maria Russo's Genovese Sauce

Maria Russo is a butcher and grocer in Castel Volturno, the town on the sea at the mouth of the Volturno River in the province of Caserta. Even though she has easy access to meat, she sometimes makes her Genovese with only a tiny piece—a half-pound for this recipe with four pounds of onions—bolstering the flavor with bouillon cubes, as so many Italian home cooks do with so many dishes these days. If you want a piece of meat to serve as a second course, however, you'll need about one-third pound of beef per person at the minimum, which is what I have specified.

Maria Russo

Using water to cover the meat and onions, and not relying only on the meat's and onions' own juices to render a sauce, makes this is a very old-fashioned method of making Genovese. Perhaps it is the oldest style, if some historians are correct in speculating that before all the onions were added, the sauce began as a French-type stock reduction, a meat extract or demi-glace. For that matter, the other theory is that it started as a French daube or stew, and this could be a point in its case, too.

There is one striking contemporary touch here, though: the tomato paste as a color enhancer. Tomato is a big no-no to traditionalists who love to point out that la Genovese predates the tomato.

Serves 6, enough sauce for 1 pound pasta, plus meat for a second course

2 pounds (approximately) chuck roast, tied, or a chuck steak

4 pounds onions, halved through the root end and finely sliced,
about 12 cups

1 medium carrot, finely diced (about ½ cup)

½ large, outside rib celery, finely diced (about ¼ cup)

2 teaspoons salt

2 rounded tablespoons finely cut parsley

½ teaspoon dried marjoram

8 cups water

1 cup dry white wine

Optional: 1 tablespoon tomato paste

Optional: ¼ cup or more water

Freshly ground black pepper

For the pasta:

1 pound ziti or penne

Freshly grated Parmigiano-Reggiano

1. Place the meat in a heavy-bottomed, 7- to 8-quart pot. Surround and cover the meat with the onions, carrot, celery, salt, parsley, marjoram, and 8 cups water. Bring to a simmer and cook uncovered over medium-low heat, simmering gently but steadily, and stirring every so often. As the liquid reduces in the pot and the meat becomes exposed, make sure to turn the meat regularly—every 20 minutes or so—so that it cooks evenly.

2. After about 3 hours, most of the liquid should have evaporated, the onions should be almost creamy, and the meat should be tender. Even if the meat is not as tender as you would like, remove it and set it aside. It can be further tenderized when reheated.

3. Raise the heat under the onions and add the wine. Boil, stirring frequently, until the wine has evaporated, about 10 minutes. Then continue to boil, stirring frequently, even constantly, until the sauce has reduced and thickened so much that when it is stirred you can see the bottom of the pot for a second. This can take as long as 20 minutes. If desired for added color, stir in the tomato paste at this point and cook another minute. (If, when reheating, the sauce seems too tight, stir in a little water to loosen it.) Season with plenty of freshly ground pepper. Correct the salt, if necessary.

4.   Save about ½ cup of sauce for the meat. Serve the remaining sauce very hot on ziti and pass the pepper mill and Parmigiano-Reggiano.

5.   The meat can be served as a separate, second course, with a little onion sauce, or refrigerated and eaten at another meal. If the meat did not become entirely tender during its cooking with the onions, slice it and layer it with spoons of the sauce in a baking dish or casserole. Cover (with foil if necessary) and reheat in a 325-degree oven until heated through and almost fall-apart tender.

A NINETEENTH-CENTURY GENOVESE

THIS STYLE OF SAUCE is out of favor in Naples, where more than one cook told me that it was nearly sacrilegious to use any pork cut other than pancetta, if you use pork at all. Yet additions of salami and prosciutto seem so Neapolitan, add so much flavor, and not only is this the way it was done in the late nineteenth and early twentieth centuries, but it is my personal favorite of the three Genovese recipes here. Additions of salami, ham, and pancetta used to be so common, according to Jeanne Carola Francesconi, that butchers would sell minced odds and ends of salumi, all packaged together just for the purpose of seasoning a Genovese. Even though Francesconi's *La cucina napoletana* (Neapolitan Cooking) was revised as recently as 1995, if you ask about this seasoning packet these days, no one knows what you're talking about.

Makes about 1 quart sauce, enough for 1 pound of ziti, serving 6, or 12 ounces of pasta, serving 4, plus a little sauce for the meat course

2 tablespoons extra-virgin olive oil

2 pounds chuck roast, tied

2 ounces Neapolitan or Abruzzese-style salami or soppressata, finely diced

2 ounces fatty prosciutto, finely diced

2 ounces pancetta, finely diced

2 pounds yellow onions, halved and thinly sliced

¼ cup finely chopped celery

½ cup finely chopped carrot

⅓ cup finely cut parsley

½ teaspoon dried marjoram

1 teaspoon salt

1 cup dry white wine

1. In a 6-quart saucepan, warm the oil over medium heat and brown the meat on all sides—about 15 to 20 minutes.

2. Leaving the meat in the pot, add the remaining ingredients, except the wine. Cover and cook over medium heat until the vegetable juices start collecting at the bottom of the pot, about 5 minutes, then adjust the heat so the vegetables simmer gently but steadily with the pot covered. This will take a few minutes of watching and adjusting. Cook over low heat for about 1 hour, then begin turning the meat about every 20 minutes for another 2 hours. In a total of about 3 hours the meat should be fork tender.

3.   Remove the meat and set aside, covered with foil or with a bowl turned upside down over it. Add the wine to the sauce. Cook over medium-high to high heat for about 30 minutes, stirring occasionally for the first 15 to 20 minutes, then stirring frequently, and finally stirring constantly and vigorously, scraping the bottom and sides of the pot, until the sauce is thick, has taken on a darker color, and the onions are very creamy.

4.   Serve the sauce hot on ziti with a generous amount of Parmigiano and freshly ground black pepper. Serve the meat sliced as a separate course, if desired, dressed with a little of the onion sauce.

VARIATION:

For Coniglio alla Genovese (rabbit Genovese style), brown pieces of rabbit (about 3 pounds) instead of beef, then follow the recipe as above.

Cecilia's Genovese

LIKE MOST CAMPANIANS, Baronessa Cecilia Bellelli Baratta cooks what is most available to her kitchen. And on her farm, La Tenuta Seliano, in Paestum, where, among many other things, she raises buffalo for mozzarella and ricotta, she has buffalo meat in spades—sometimes young buffalo meat from slaughtered bull calves, which are hardly as precious as the milk-giving females, and sometimes older meat from females who cannot be milked any longer. A Genovese made with buffalo meat, especially older meat, is a dark and heady sauce, but Cecilia's additions of sage and rosemary, her use of red wine instead of white, and a little red wine vinegar to cut the sweetness of the onions, makes even a beef-based Genovese made by her recipe taste richer and much different from the traditional.

*Baronessa Cecilia
Bellelli Baratta*

**Serves 4, enough sauce for 12 ounces of pasta,
plus meat for a second course (and leftovers)**

1½ pounds onions, sliced thin

8 large leaves of sage

1 rounded tablespoon fresh rosemary leaves

2 large cloves garlic, peeled and lightly smashed

3 tablespoons extra-virgin olive oil

1 tablespoon red wine vinegar

3 pounds chuck roast, rolled and tied

1 teaspoon salt

1 cup red wine

1.   In a casserole just slightly bigger than the roast, combine the onions, sage, rosemary, garlic, and olive oil. Place over low heat and cook, tossing the mixture several times, until the onions wilt, about 10 minutes.

2.   Add the red wine vinegar, raise heat to medium, and cook, again stirring several times, 15 minutes longer or until the onions begin to brown.

(continued)

63

3. Push the onions to the sides of the casserole and add the meat. Turning the meat occasionally, let the meat brown, about another 15 to 20 minutes.

4. Add the salt and red wine. Bring the wine to a gentle simmer and turn the meat in it several times. Simmer gently, partially covered, for 2 to 3 hours, rotating the meat slightly every 15 minutes. Be careful that it doesn't stick to the bottom of the pot and scorch. When the meat is fork tender, remove it from the sauce and set aside on a platter. Skim the sauce of any excess fat, if necessary and desired.

5. Serve the sauce hot on ziti, or, even better, because there will not be that much sauce, toss very al dente pasta in the sauce and let it finish cooking while absorbing some of its flavor. Pass the pepper mill and grated Parmigiano-Reggiano. Serve the meat separately.

PIZZA,
SAVORY
BREADS,
AND TARALLI

PIZZA

A FEW YEARS AGO, when a pizza chef named Saverio Bovino won a national prize with a bizarre pizza topped with lemon cream and amaretti, a reporter for the *Wall Street Journal* asked him how he thought up such a thing. "At night, I either sleep, make love, or think about pizza," he answered. "That night, I was thinking about pizza."

It often seems like Neapolitan life revolves around pizza. Most people still eat their big meal in the middle of the day, then go out for pizza at night. The pizzeria is where you gather with friends or your extended family, or go for the meal you don't want to cook at home, or go for food to take home—not only pizza but deep-fried croquettes and fritters. Cab drivers, hotel clerks, shopkeepers, any person a tourist would meet in Naples, recommends a pizzeria, unprompted, and declares that it is not merely his favorite, but the best. If Neapolitans can create a drama over choosing fruit in the market, which they do, imagine the strong feelings they express about pizza, the food they consider a symbol of their city and their ambassador to the world.

One night at a brand-new pizzeria in Naples, I noticed that the couple at the next table did not look happy. After they had eaten the center, sauced portions of their pizzas, the man called the waiter over and started tapping the uneaten crusty frame of his pie with his knife. "Too tough," said the man, looking the waiter in the eye but still tapping his crust for emphasis. "Too tough," he repeated. And his wife kept shaking her head, affirming her husband's opinion, then pushed her plate away in disgust.

It is generally assumed by all relevant historians, including the typically chauvinistic Neapolitan ones, that no date can be put on the beginnings of the bread part of the pizza. Flat breads like it go back forever. The word "pizza" is obviously related to the word "pita," which is a name for various kinds of yeast-risen flat bread in the Middle East. Edda Servi Machlin, in her *Classic Cuisine of the Italian Jews*, speculates that the Jews brought the flat bread idea with them to Italy when they first arrived in numbers after the Roman conquest of Judea in the first century A.D. It is in any case a good bet that both pizza and pita are descended from the first yeast-risen breads, which were Egyptian. It was the Egyptians, before the exodus of the Jews, who learned to control yeast fermentation and with this knowledge turned the desert nomad's hard, unleavened flat bread into soft risen bread. So can we say that pizza is Egyptian?

At the Autostrada exit to Mercogliano, in Avellino, along with the expected gas station, there's a pizzeria called Il Piramide (The Pyramid) in what we would call a strip mall. The young clerk at my nearby hotel told me it was the main gathering place in town. It was. And that the pizza was good. It wasn't. When I returned and met the hotel manager, a self-styled *buongustaio*, and gave him my report, he exclaimed, "What kind of pizza did you expect from an Egyptian?" Campanians do not give credit where it might be due.

If we are interested in knowing when Neapolitan pizza was first made, the question should be when were tomatoes first put on the flat bread, turning it into the most popular food in the world, especially now that it is taking hold in India and China.

In answer to this, Neapolitans—almost anyone on the street—will tell you that the first pizzeria opened in 1830 under the Port'Alba, one of the portals to the oldest part of the city, just behind Piazza Dante, exactly as the sign outside the still thriving Port'Alba Restaurant and Pizzeria so proudly boasts. This is arguable, but even if it was true, saying that the first pizzeria opened in 1830 begs the question of when the first pizza was made. I think because most Neapolitans would never consider baking pizza at home, and haven't for more than 150 years, since the first pizzerias opened, they don't realize it was around for much longer than that.

According to Professor Carlo Mangoni, who teaches nutrition at the Second University of Naples, and who recently got a $30,000 grant to study pizza and devise criteria for *la vera pizza napoletana* (the true Neapolitan pizza), the tomato sauce met the bread in about 1760. (Others speculate even earlier.) Ferdinand, King of Naples, who had famously vulgar tastes and habits and liked nothing better than to carouse with his most common subjects, had ascended to the throne only a year before. Once he had eaten this new bread dressed with tomatoes, olive oil, garlic, and oregano—the original pizza, now called pizza alla marinara—he wanted it served at court. His queen, Maria Carolina, on the other hand, was a Hapsburg princess with fine manners. She refused to have such vulgar food served at her table, but she needed to acquiesce to the king in some way. Her answer was to have an outdoor pizza oven built at the palace in Capodimonte. Thus she started a court fashion. Other nobles and courtiers followed suit, building outdoor pizza ovens at their own palaces. Pizza parties became the stylish way to entertain. These were the years that the English cried, "See Naples and die," meaning Naples was "the living end," and there are several reports from English travelers about these pizza parties.

By the beginning of the nineteenth century, there were apparently other varieties of pizza being made besides the marinara, and when the Port'Alba pizzeria opened in 1830, a new wave of fashionability started. Men of letters and philosophy, politicians, and artists frequented Port'Alba. Eventually, the rich, then the bourgeoisie followed. It became a "rite of the aristocracy," as one writer put it, to indulge in a pizza after the opera at San Carlo.

Things haven't changed in Naples. After the Christmas performance of a local amateur chorus I attended because one of the singers is a friend, she introduced me to her other friends—the Barone or Conte this, the Marchese that. Perhaps there was a Principessa, too. After all the introductions, some hand kissing, and polite small talk, someone asked, "Will you be joining us for pizza?"

The first major transformation of the Neapolitan pizza took place with the introduction of mozzarella to the pie. Most pizza historians agree that this happened before 1889, but it was in that year that the pizza with mozzarella gained its station of glory. Italy had been unified under the Savoy kings for twenty-eight years when, it is said, Queen Margherita, wife of Umberto I, voiced interest in the famous Neapolitan pizza on a visit to the city. It was a totally foreign food to this Piedmontese royal. Just as you might call for takeout today, the queen called Raffaele Esposito, the owner of Pizzeria di Pietro, what is now called Pizzeria Brandi, not far from the royal palace and the San Carlo opera house. In honor of the queen, and to show respect for the United Kingdom of Italy, Esposito embellished the classic pizza alla marinara with a few slices of mozzarella and whole leaves of basil—the *tricolore*, the red, white, and green of the Italian flag.

The new pizza caused a sensation. Esposito was a clever marketer and he publicized the letter the queen sent to him, thanking him and expressing her pleasure. The letter is today reproduced on the Pizzeria Brandi's many advertising posters. (The current owner, Eduardo Pagnani, is as brilliant a marketer as Esposito.) And the story goes, not only did everyday Neapolitans start eating the Margherita, but important people flocked to the Pizzeria di Pietro. Waiters at Brandi love to tell tourists the story of when Marchese Guglielmo Marconi came to try it. It was right after Marconi had patented his wireless telegraph in 1896. "Marconi said he liked the pizza," the waiters say. "But he complained that he had trouble eating the stringy cheese. To which his waiter responded, 'Perhaps Marchese Marconi should have invented wireless mozzarella.'"

Staff lunch at Pizzeria Brandi, where pizza Margherita was created.

Despite the joke, a good Neapolitan pizza isn't all that stringy. How could it be? It doesn't have much mozzarella. What little the eight-, nine-, or at most ten-inch pie does have is buffalo mozzarella, which has more than double the fat content of cow milk cheese, making it a better melter. Buffalo mozzarella gives off its milky liquid, however, and that, along with juicy chopped tomatoes, makes Neapolitan pizza Margherita softer than outsiders expect it to be. It's a thin-crusted pizza, but not a crisp-crusted pizza. All the better to fold it in half and eat it *a libretto* (like a little book), as one sees people do on the street.

A true Neapolitan pizza has a scant topping. On a Margherita, which is still the most popular, it's an accident if you get more than a single torn leaf of basil. Yet, like everywhere else in the world these days, Naples has its faddish pizza toppings. It has gotten to the point (lemon cream and amaretti!) where Neapolitans are arguing publicly about what can be legitimately called Neapolitan pizza. A movement headed by Professor Mangoni and a group of chefs and restaurateurs who call themselves the Association for True Neapolitan Pizza are attempting to have the government create a DOC, or area of origin guaranteed, for Neapolitan pizza. In other words, the pie would have to meet stringent standards in order to be called pizza napoletana, as wines and some other foods (such as Parmigiano-Reggiano and prosciutto di Parma) must meet criteria to be called what they are. One of those criteria is tomatoes, says Professor Mangoni. Without tomatoes, the pizza could be from anywhere, he argues. And the cheese must be mozzarella di bufala campana, buffalo cheese from one of Campania's two producing areas, in Salerno and Caserta. The professor also frowns on using oregano if the pizza has basil—"Abominable!"—an opinion I've heard elsewhere but not so strongly put.

MARGHERITA BIANCA	MARGHERITA A FILETTO	BOSCAIOLA	ANTIPASTO
RUCOLA - SCAGLIE PARMIGIANO PROSCIUTTO CRUDO		CARNE TRITATA PISELLI PANNA - FUNGHI	PROSCIUTTO CRUDO PROVOLONE SOTTACETI
L. 9.000	L. 6.000	L. 7.000	L. 7.000

PORCHETTA	PORCHETTA CON FRIARIELLI O FUNGHI	MARGHERITA CON WURSTEL	MARGHERITA BIANCA
			RUCOLA - SCAGLIE PARMIGIANO
L. 5.000	L. 7.000	L. 6.000	L. 7.000

PIZZA AI 4 FORMAGGI
GORGONZOLA - SORESINA ROMANO - PARMIGIANO
L. 8.000

Menu placards hanging on the wall are typical in pizzerias.

If pizza itself isn't always what it used to be, at least many of Naples's pizzerias are. A number date back to the nineteenth century and still have white marble walls, white marble floors, white marble-topped tables, and a white marble work bench for the *pizzaiolo*, the man who makes the dough, shapes it, and dresses it. On his bench is an array of bowls holding his ingredients—chopped tomatoes, herbs, fried vegetables, mushrooms, anchovies, olives—and his traditional copper and brass oil can, the *agliara* in dialect, *oliera* in Italian. It's the same can on every bench, in every pizzeria. With a tapering minaret cover, a brass star on its copper body, and a long, graceful spout, it looks slightly Turkish and is wielded with a flourish so only a fine "string" gilds the surface of the pie.

Another *pizzaiolo* mans the oven, a tiled, beehive dome fired by wood. He slides the raw pie off a wooden peel into the chamber, lets it bake a few minutes, then rotates it so every side is exposed evenly to the intense heat. The whole process takes less than eight minutes. Working with several pies at once, he needs the timing and agility of a juggler.

PIZZA NAPOLETANA

NEAPOLITAN PIZZA

YOU CAN'T MAKE THE best pizza at home, but you can make very, very good pizza, and whatever it may objectively lack is made up for by the pleasure and satisfaction of producing it yourself. It's easy, but it takes practice, particularly the stretching of the dough. At first, you won't be able to make an even circle. After a while, you may still form only amoeba-shaped pies. It doesn't matter. What counts is the taste of the dough and the finesse of the topping.

Neapolitans don't burden their pizzas with heavy toppings. For a pizza Margherita, still the most popular, the tomatoes are barely cooked, if cooked at all; the mozzarella is applied sparingly, and there's no more than a torn leaf or two of basil. Pizza alla marinara, the simplest and oldest type, is topped by only crushed tomatoes, a drizzle of olive oil, a light scattering of chopped garlic, and a couple of pinches of oregano.

In Naples now, the trendiest pizza is with prosciutto and what everyone calls "wild" rucola, which is actually a cultivated variety, but a tiny and very peppery green like the true wild kind. The base of the pizza is a marinara. The greens and the ham are draped on the moment it comes out of the oven, while the pizza still carries the heat to make them both slightly limp.

In Salerno right now, cherry tomatoes are replacing plum tomatoes for the trendy pizza, which is also strewn with whole leaves of rucola (arugula).

Quattro stagioni (four seasons), the pizza divided into quadrants and each filled differently, was the rage twenty years ago. I have one Neapolitan recipe that calls for mussels and clams in two of the quarters, olives and anchovies in a third, and artichokes preserved under oil for the fourth. Today quattro stagioni is more likely to be all vegetables, and because many pizzerias don't use prime-quality artichokes, mushrooms, etc., it's not the pizza of choice for knowing Neapolitans.

Pizza bianca can be several different things. In the old days, it was the dough spread with rendered lard and sprinkled with grated pecorino. Today, it is more likely to be mozzarella, basil, olive oil, and Parmigiano, or shavings of Parmigiano and leaves of rucola. It can also be prosciutto and rucola. *Bianca* doesn't mean pure white. It means no red.

Quattro formaggi (four cheeses) is not a traditional Neapolitan pizza, but it is popular. Like the quattro stagioni, the pie is divided into quarters. In this case, each one is topped with a different cheese. Mozzarella and gorgonzola are always two of them, and one of the others is likely to be Parmigiano. The fourth is up for grabs, but it's usually something foreign, like Swiss cheese.

Following is the basic dough for any pizza you make.

Makes 4 9- to 10-inch pizzas

1 envelope dried yeast (2½ teaspoons)

1 cup warm water

4 cups unbleached all-purpose flour

¾ teaspoon salt

½ cup warm water

1.   In a 2-cup glass measure, with a table fork, dissolve the yeast in the 1 cup of warm water. Stir in ½ cup of the flour, cover with a clean dishtowel and let it stand until the mixture foams up to about double—to 2 cups—about 30 minutes.

2.   In a large bowl, combine 3½ cups of the flour with the salt. Stir in the yeast mixture and the remaining ½ cup of warm water. Stir until the dough masses together. Gather the dough into a ball and turn it out onto a lightly floured work surface. Knead, folding and turning the dough onto itself, then pushing it away from you with the heel of your hand, about 10 to 12 minutes, adding, little by little, just enough flour to keep the dough from sticking. Be careful not to add too much flour or too much at one time. When you have finished, the dough should not stick to the board; it should be smooth, silken, slightly damp on the surface, and very elastic. Dust the dough lightly all over with flour and place in a bowl to rise, covered with a clean dishtowel, for about 1 hour, or until it has slightly more than doubled in bulk.

3.   While the dough is rising, and at least 30 minutes before baking, place an oven rack on the lowest level, preferably holding a pizza stone, and preheat the oven to 500 degrees.

4.   Punch down the dough and divide into 4 parts. Alternately, if you intend to use only a portion of the dough immediately, form each fourth into a smooth ball and let those to be used immediately rise on a floured board, a couple of inches apart, covered with a dishtowel. Refrigerate or freeze the remaining balls in plastic bags.

5. To form the dough into a pizza, flatten the ball of dough into a thick disk. On a lightly floured board, rotating the disk as you go, flatten the center of the pizza with your fingertips or heel of your hand. When a ridge of dough starts appearing on the perimeter of the disk, lift the dough up with both hands, and holding on to the ridge, let gravity and the weight of the dough stretch the circle. Keep turning the dough to get a relatively even 10-inch circle. Keep pulling the ridge slightly so the circle gets larger. Be careful not to make the center too thin or the ridge more than ½ inch deep. At some point the pizza will become too flimsy to handle. Now spread the formed pizza dough onto a large baking sheet or wooden peel that has been lightly dusted with flour.

6. Top as desired.

7. Bake for 6 to 8 minutes depending on your oven and on how well done you like pizza. The edge should be tinged with brown.

Note: Simple herb and olive oil toppings require less cooking time than tomato or other heavier/moister toppings.

IL CORNICIONE

Il cornicione (the big frame) is what Neapolitans call the puffed-up ring of unsauced dough around the seasoned center of a pizza. To a tourist, an amazing sight in the pizzerias is watching the many Neapolitans who carve up a pizza with knife and fork as delicately as they do a fine fish with bones, eating only the inside seasoned area, never cutting into the crust, never touching it, leaving the frame intact on their plates.

PIZZA ALLA MARINARA

THIS IS THE ORIGINAL cheeseless Neapolitan pizza, still second in popularity to the Margherita.

Makes 1 pizza

Dough for 1 pizza (page 71)

3 to 5 canned plum tomatoes, very well drained, seeded, and crushed or chopped into pieces no bigger than ½ inch

½ teaspoon finely minced garlic

Salt to taste (about ¼ teaspoon)

¾ teaspoon dried oregano

1½ to 2 tablespoons extra-virgin olive oil

1. At least 30 minutes before baking, place an oven rack on the lowest level, preferably holding a pizza stone, and preheat the oven to 500 degrees.

2. Shape the dough into a pizza following the preceding directions.

3. On the top (except on the ridge), evenly scatter, sprinkle, or drizzle on all the remaining ingredients in the order given.

4. Bake for 7 to 8 minutes, until the ridge is tinged with brown.

5. Serve immediately.

Pizza Margherita

Makes 1 pizza

Dough for 1 pizza (page 71)

3 to 5 canned plum tomatoes, well drained and seeded,
haphazardly cut or chopped into ½-inch or so pieces

½ teaspoon finely minced garlic

Salt to taste (about ¼ teaspoon)

1½ to 2 ounces mozzarella, sliced or coarsely shredded

2 tablespoons extra-virgin olive oil

1 or 2 basil leaves, torn

Follow the recipe for Pizza alla Marinara (opposite), eliminating the oregano and
adding the cheese and basil.

Pizza di Patate e Cipolle

Pizza with Potatoes and Onions

THIS IS NOT A POPULAR topping everywhere, but it is sort of "the thing" at Da Peppina di Renato, one of Ischia's most stylish restaurants. It is amazingly satisfying, especially with fresh rosemary.

Makes 1 pizza

Dough for 1 pizza (page 71)

1 small, waxy potato, boiled until tender, peeled and sliced

2 or 3 slices red onion, separated into rings

Salt

Extra-virgin olive oil

Optional: Fresh rosemary

(continued)

1. At least 30 minutes before baking, place an oven rack on the lowest level, preferably holding a pizza stone, and preheat the oven to 500 degrees.

2. Shape the dough into a pizza following the directions on page 73.

3. On the top, except on the ridge, arrange the potatoes without overlapping them. Scatter some rings of red onion over the potato, then sprinkle with salt to taste, a tablespoon or so of olive oil, then, if desired, some fresh rosemary leaves.

4. Bake for 7 to 8 minutes, until the ridge is tinged with brown.

5. Serve immediately.

CALZONE

PIZZA RIPIENA

STUFFED PIZZA

———

TRAVELERS DISAPPOINTED by the softness of Neapolitan pizza should try stuffed pizza, what Neapolitans might call calzone but more frequently refer to as pizza ripiena. Unless it is an original creation of the pizzeria, it never has tomatoes. It's baked with ricotta and either diced or whole thin slices of cooked ham—not prosciutto, although no one would flinch if it was.

Makes 1 calzone

Dough for 1 pizza (page 71)

⅓ cup ricotta

2 tablespoons diced cooked ham

1. At least 30 minutes before baking, place an oven rack on the lowest level, preferably holding a pizza stone, and preheat the oven to 500 degrees.

2. Stretch the dough as for a pizza, except do not make the center as thin or the edge as thick. Try for a fairly evenly thick disk.

3. Put a mound of the cheese on half the dough, toward the center, dot with ham, then drape the other half of the circle over the filling, matching the edges of the halves.

4. Pinch together the edges of the dough, then roll the edge slightly and pinch again to make a secure seal.

5. Bake the calzone for about 8 minutes, or until puffed and lightly browned.

PIZZA RUSTICA

SAVORY EASTER RICOTTA PIE

PIZZA RUSTICA, AN OPEN, lattice-topped or fully enclosed pastry filled with ricotta, diced cheeses, and various preserved pork products, is also called pizza ripiena (stuffed pie) or, in dialect, pizza chiena—from which comes the frequently used Italian-American name pizza gain. This particular pizza rustica is, in fact, a recipe from Italian-American friends Alison Alifano and her father, Vitale (Al), whose ancestors came from Alife, on the border of Caserta and Benevento provinces. Somehow, her family has managed to pass this on for four generations just the way it is still made today in that part of Campania, including using the spicy dried sausage that Alife is famous for and that we call pepperoni. This rich, thick version is a traditional feast food for Easter, but squares of pizza rustica with a much shallower filling, cut from a big pan, or fashioned into individual pies, are these days, in any season, also a common snack item in bars and takeout shops. The Alifano family makes theirs on Good Friday and eats it on Easter Sunday. It's also traditional for a picnic on Easter Monday.

Makes 2 10-inch pies

(continued)

1¼ teaspoons dried yeast

½ cup warm water

3 cups unbleached all-purpose flour

1 tablespoon sugar

1½ teaspoons salt

2 tablespoons lard

3 eggs, lightly beaten

For the filling:

3 ounces soppressata, cut into ⅛-inch dice

3 ounces prosciutto, cut into ⅛-inch dice

3 ounces cooked ham, cut into ⅛-inch dice

3 sweet Italian sausages, boiled, skinned, and finely chopped
(reserve the sausage cooking water)

8 ounces whole milk mozzarella, cut into ¼-inch dice

2 ounces dried sausage with hot pepper (pepperoni),
peeled and cut into ⅛-inch dice

3 eggs, lightly beaten

3¼ cups whole milk ricotta

½ cup freshly grated Parmigiano-Reggiano or pecorino,
or a combination

¾ cup finely cut parsley

4 hard-cooked eggs: 2 coarsely chopped, 2 sliced

1 teaspoon freshly ground black pepper

Plus:

1 egg, lightly beaten, as a wash

To make the pastry:

1.   In a small bowl or cup, dissolve the yeast in the water. Set aside.

2.   In a large bowl, stir together the flour, sugar, and salt. Pinch the lard into the flour to distribute it evenly. With a wooden spoon, stir in the eggs and dissolved yeast until a dough forms. Still in the bowl, knead the dough, sprinkling lightly with flour to make it less sticky.

3.　　Turn the dough out onto a floured board and continue to knead, adding flour a little at a time, even by the teaspoonful, until the dough is very smooth and silky, about 8 minutes. Dust lightly with flour, place in a bowl, cover with a clean dish-towel, and let the dough rise until doubled in bulk, at least an hour. Punch down and let rise a second time.

To make the filling:

4.　　In a large bowl, combine all the ingredients, except the 2 sliced eggs and the egg wash, and blend very well, stirring in about ½ cup of the sausage boiling water. It's a thick filling.

To assemble and bake:

5.　　Preheat the oven to 375 degrees.

6.　　Punch down the dough and divide into four equal pieces, to make top and bottom crusts for two 10-inch, preferably glass pie plates.

7.　　On a lightly floured board, roll out a quarter of the dough into a 14- to 15-inch circle. (It is a very elastic dough and this takes some effort.) It should be thin and large enough to fit the bottom and sides of the pie plate. Carefully drape the dough into the dish.

8.　　Fill with half the filling. Top with slices of 1 hard-cooked egg.

9.　　Roll out another quarter of dough to an 11-inch circle, large enough to cover the pie plate. Cut off the excess dough, then roll the edges of the top and bottom crusts together, pinching well to seal. Cut four slits in the center of the top crust, then brush with beaten egg.

10.　Make a second pie with the remaining pastry, filling, and sliced hard-cooked egg.

11.　Bake for 50 minutes to an hour. After 30 minutes, if the top is browning well, cover it with foil, shiny side out, to prevent it from burning. Let cool on a rack for 10 minutes, then remove from the pie plate and cool to room temperature. The pie may be eaten soon after it cools completely, but it can be kept, well-wrapped, in the refrigerator. It should keep well for several days.

Pizza di Scarola

Escarole Pie

Scarola . . . has the taste of something vital and warm-blooded; for me scarola
pizzas are the very best in the world. And most Neapolitans would loudly agree.

—Sophia Loren, *In the Kitchen with Love*

This is one of those dishes that Neapolitans wax poetic about. Usually, they go way beyond Sophia Loren's rather restrained "vital," "warm-blooded," and "best." No wonder. It has so many things they like in one place. It's a dough container holding bitter greens seasoned with the Neapolitan works, the "condiments" they hold most dear—Gaeta olives, anchovies, capers, garlic, hot pepper, raisins, and pine nuts.

When it is made with an extremely rich butter pastry crust, it is a refined delectable, a *Monzù* creation that you should not deny yourself. Neapolitans never do, especially around Christmas, when a version of it is on many overladen holiday tables. It is also a perfect first course for an elaborate winter dinner—to be followed by a pasta, fish or meat, side dishes, etc. It also can be the main course of a light supper or lunch.

With a change to the bread dough used for Neapolitan pizza, the dish completely turns character. It's now a rustic pie, perhaps elevated to feast level by its lavish use of the seasonings, and the kind of pizza or calzone di scarola that they make in pizzerias. It is a somewhat stylish pizza or calzone these days, too, as the vegetable filling is deemed so much more healthful than the traditional ricotta and ham. Or at least that is what I was once told by a beautiful woman sitting next to me in a pizzeria, relishing a calzone di scarola with knife and fork.

Serves 6 to 8

1 recipe pizza dough (page 71) or the following short pastry

For the short pastry:

8 tablespoons (1 stick) butter, cut into ½-inch cubes and rechilled

1¼ cups all-purpose flour

½ teaspoon salt

2 egg yolks, beaten lightly

3 to 4 tablespoons ice water

For the filling:

2 heads escarole (about 2 pounds)

¼ cup extra-virgin olive oil

1 tablespoon finely minced garlic

⅛ teaspoon hot red pepper flakes, or more to taste

2 tablespoons pine nuts

⅓ cup pitted Gaeta olives, each cut into several pieces

2 tablespoons salted capers, thoroughly washed

6 or 7 salted anchovies, washed and filleted, or 14 anchovy fillets in oil

2 tablespoons raisins

For the egg wash:

1 egg yolk beaten with 1 tablespoon water

1. Prepare the pizza dough and let it rise, or make a short pastry.

To make short pastry:

In a bowl, combine the flour and the cubes of butter and, using a pastry blender or 2
table knives, cut the butter into the flour until the pieces are the size of peas. Alternately, grate the butter on the coarse side of a box grater, tossing the butter in the
flour as you go. Sprinkle on the salt. Add the egg yolks and about 2 tablespoons of
the water. With a table fork, gingerly mix the liquid into the flour mixture, adding
additional water as needed to make a dough that will gather into a ball. Place the
dough on a lightly floured work surface and knead just a few times. Flatten the pastry into 2 disks, then wrap them in plastic and refrigerate for at least 30 minutes, to
relax the gluten and chill the dough slightly. (If the dough is made ahead and refrigerated for many hours or a few days, bring it back to a pliable temperature.)

To prepare the filling:

2. Prepare the escarole according to the recipe on page 340, with the following
changes: Cut the escarole fine; use a large, wide pan; leave out the salt; and add the
pine nuts, olives, capers, anchovies, and raisins after the escarole has cooked covered
for 3 or 4 minutes. Then, cook uncovered for the remaining cooking time, stirring
the escarole frequently until the vegetable is tender and almost all its juices have
evaporated, about 15 minutes. Cool before using.

(continued)

To assemble and bake with pizza dough:

3.   At least 30 minutes before baking, place an oven rack on the lowest level, preferably holding a pizza stone, and preheat the oven to 400 degrees.

4.   There are several ways to form the pizza, but the easiest is to make 2 calzone-shaped breads. After the dough has doubled in bulk, turn it out of the bowl and cut it in half. On a lightly floured board, slap and stretch each piece of dough in a circle, as you would for pizza, but do not leave a thick edge and do not make the center extremely thin. You should be able to get the dough to form a circle of about 12 inches.

5.   Place half the filling on half of the stretched-out disk of dough and fold the other half of the dough over the filling. Pinch the edges closed, then roll the edge to make a secure seal and give the pie a frame of doughy crust.

6.   Working gingerly, first releasing the pie from the work surface by lifting it on all sides, transfer the pizza to a baking sheet. Brush the top with olive oil.

7.   Bake for about 15 minutes, until nicely browned.

8.   Let rest and cool for 5 minutes before serving. If preparing ahead, wrap the calzone in a clean dishtowel as soon as it comes from the oven.

To assemble and bake with short pastry:

9.   Preheat the oven to 375 degrees.

10. On a lightly floured work surface, roll out the pastry disks to make 2 10-inch rounds. Place one on a baking sheet.

11. Spread the escarole mixture evenly over the pastry, leaving a ½-inch rim exposed.

12. Place the dough for the top over the filling and, with your fingers, press and seal the edge of the bottom pastry to the top, trimming off any excess that might make an edge too thick. Roll the edges together.

13. Brush the top of the pizza with egg wash. With a sharp knife, make 3 or 4 steam vents in the top crust, trying to be decorative.

14. Bake on the bottom shelf of the oven for 30 to 35 minutes, or until the top is a dark golden brown. Place on a rack to cool slightly.

15. Serve warm or at room temperature.

SAVORY BREADS

RICH, EGGY, YEAST BREADS with preserved pork products and/or cheese mixed into the dough may not be uniquely Neapolitan, but it is the Baroque Neapolitan culture that brought them to their heights of opulence. These, along with the extravagant pastry drums of pasta and fillings called timballi or timpani, seem to have been one of the specialties the *Monzù* chefs got competitive about. In trying to top one another, they turned what were essentially country breads into opulent presentation pieces. The one that is made most today is tortano, and though it is relatively simple compared to some of the historic ones, it's the thing most likely to be cited if a Campanian thinks you have any doubt about the greatness, nobility, and inventiveness of her cuisine. "You think Neapolitan cooking is all about tomato sauce and spaghetti with clams? Well, we have tortano!" That's how they challenge the foreigners' stereotype of their cooking.

Tortano is a snack, a hospitality bread, an antipasto. In the nineteenth century and into the twentieth, it was sold on the street in the morning when men were on their way to work. Casatiello is the Easter version of tortano—the same bread but with a streak of sweetness or at least eggs tied to its body with crosses of dough.

TORTANO OR CASATIELLO

THIS IS A RECIPE YOU can alter, depending on what pork product and cheese is available. Instead of salami, try prosciutto, or a mix of the two, or a melange of mortadella, salami, dried hot-pepper sausage . . . whatever you like. It's not unheard of to use Swiss Emmenthaler or Gruyère or Dutch Gouda instead of provolone. And smoked mozzarella is excellent, too. Do not, however, substitute solid white shortening for lard. The pork fat is much too important a flavor, and far healthier.

Makes 1 large horseshoe-shaped loaf, or 2 rings baked in 10-inch tube pans

(continued)

For the dough:

2 envelopes dry yeast (5 teaspoons)

½ cup warm water

5 cups unbleached all-purpose flour

½ teaspoon salt

2 ounces cold lard, cut into 4 chunks of about a tablespoon each

About 1¼ cups water

For the filling:

4 ounces lard, at room temperature

¼ cup grated Parmigiano-Reggiano

3 tablespoons grated pecorino

1 tablespoon freshly ground black pepper

From ⅔ to ¾ cup salami, measured after being cut into ⅛-inch dice

¾ cup provolone, measured after being cut into ⅛-inch dice

For casatiello:

6 uncooked eggs in their shells

1.   In a small bowl or a glass measuring cup, dissolve the yeast in the ½ cup warm water.

2.   On a large wooden board or work surface, make a mound of the flour and mix in the salt with your hand. Distribute the pieces of cold lard over the flour and rub them into the flour. Sprinkle the dissolved yeast over the flour and begin kneading, adding ¼ cup warm water at a time. At first, use a dough scraper to make sure the bits that stick to the board get kneaded into the mass that is forming. Be careful not to add too much water at one time. The dough should just barely be sticking to the board when you have finished kneading, after 8 to 10 minutes. You can dust the board with a tiny bit more flour as you knead, if the dough seems too sticky, but that means you've probably added too much water. In the end, the dough will be smooth, silken, slightly damp on the surface, and very elastic.

3.   Form the dough into a ball, dust it with flour, and place in a large bowl. Cover the bowl with a clean kitchen towel and let the dough rise until doubled in bulk, about 1½ hours.

4.   Meanwhile, assemble the filling ingredients and grease and flour a baking sheet or 2 tube pans.

5.   When the dough has risen, punch it down and turn it onto a floured board. Roll it out into a rectangle about ½ inch thick, about 32 inches long, and about 11 inches wide.

6.   Using your hand, spread the room-temperature lard evenly over the whole surface of the dough. Sprinkle evenly with the remaining filling ingredients.

7.   Roll up the dough jelly-roll fashion, starting with the long side. (If you are making casatiello, cut off an end of the roll, about 4 inches long. Roll it into a ball, set it aside in a bowl, and cover it with a kitchen towel.) Pinch the ends of the roll closed, then bend the roll into a ring or horseshoe shape. You could also cut the roll in half and bake it as 2 long loaves, but the traditional shape is round. Campanians have large aluminum ring molds made just for it. To fit a tortano into an American 10-inch tube pan, either halve the recipe or cut the roll in half and bake each half in a tube pan.

8.   To form a casatiello, punch down the reserved ball of dough after forming the main loaf, but before it rises again. Divide the ball in half. Roll the dough into two 24-inch ropes. Cut each rope into six 4-inch lengths. Arrange the eggs at regular intervals on top of the unrisen bread and fasten each to the body of the bread with dough ropes: Crisscross the dough over each, forming an "X" over the eggs, and pinch the ends of the dough ropes into the body of the bread to secure them.

9.   Place the shaped bread on the prepared baking sheet. Cover with a cloth and let it rise until doubled, an hour or more.

10. Preheat the oven to 350 degrees for tortano, 200 degrees for casatiello.

11. For tortano, bake for 1 hour or until light brown. For casatiello, place in the 200-degree oven, then immediately raise the temperature to 350. Bake for 1 hour.

12. Do not slice the bread until it has fully cooled. The eggs are edible, but more symbolic than delicious.

Pizza alla Campofranco

Prosciutto Brioche with Cheese and Tomato Sauce

This is the most often quoted *Monzù* brioche recipe, and it is not really a pizza at all but a horizontally split prosciutto brioche that is filled and topped with pizza Margherita ingredients—tomatoes, mozzarella, and basil. It seems rich, but it is amazingly light. It could substitute for pasta on a formal menu. It could even be an antipasto. It's also a great party or buffet dish, and with a salad it's an impressive luncheon or light supper entree. The baking instructions are strange, but they are correct. It does go into a cold oven. And as a convenience for parties, you should know it reheats very well, wrapped in aluminum foil.

Serves 6

For the brioche:

1 envelope dried yeast (2½ teaspoons)

¼ cup warm water

4 cups flour

3 eggs

2 tablespoons freshly grated Parmigiano-Reggiano

6 tablespoons butter, melted

4 ounces prosciutto, finely chopped

For the filling and topping:

10 ounces fresh or up to several-days-old mozzarella

2 cups Sugo di Pomodoro (see page 46)

3 tablespoons freshly grated Parmigiano-Reggiano

½ cup finely cut basil

(The oven is not preheated for this recipe.)

To make the brioche:

1. In a small cup, dissolve the yeast in the water.

2. In the bowl of a stand-up electric mixer with the dough hook, combine the remaining brioche ingredients. Pour in the dissolved yeast. Work the dough starting on low speed, then raising to medium when the ingredients are blended. At this point, you must judge if you need a little more warm water or flour to make a firm dough. Work the dough at medium until it detaches from the sides of the bowl and becomes a cohesive mass.

3. Turn the dough out onto a lightly floured board and knead vigorously, turning the dough over on itself and slapping it firmly on the board. Knead for about 5 minutes. You should have an elastic dough that does not stick to the board, but has a smooth, slightly damp surface.

4. Roll or pat the dough into a 10-inch disk. Place it in a buttered and floured 10-inch springform pan. Cover with a clean dishtowel and let rise until doubled in bulk, about 2 hours.

5. Place in a cold oven and turn the heat to 350 degrees. Bake for 20 minutes, or until the top is well browned.

6. Remove from the oven and let cool slightly. Remove the springform ring and bottom, then slide the hot brioche onto a baking sheet. Let cool until just tepid.

7. Preheat the oven to 400 degrees.

8. With a long-bladed serrated-edge bread knife, cut the brioche horizontally to form 2 layers. On the bottom layer, arrange about ⅔ of the mozzarella, to cover the surface well. Spoon on about ½ cup of tomato sauce, placing the sauce on the cheese slices. Sprinkle with grated cheese, then half the basil. Place the top of the brioche over the filling and arrange the remaining mozzarella over the very top. Sprinkle with the remaining basil, then spoon on another ½ cup of sauce, again placing it on the mozzarella slices.

9. Bake a second time for about 12 minutes, or until the cheese in the center seems melted.

10. Serve immediately.

TARALLI

One might say taralli are the breadsticks of Campania, but that would be underestimating their importance and their place. Neapolitans used to say that the only thing that went with a tarallo, a ring of crisp, larded or oil-shortened bread dough, was a glass of the sulfuric waters from a particular fountain at Santa Lucia, or a glass of wine or beer. When the beach at Mergellina was deeper, before the urban renewal that followed the Second World War, it was the custom of Neapolitans from the stifling, poorer quarters to sit at a table on the beach, enjoy the breeze, the people-watching, a glass of something, and almond-studded taralli. In those days, they were supposedly made by the fishermen's wives.

Today, vending carts line the bayside street along the marina and sell these crunchy, addictive treats along with potato chips, torrone and other candy, and roasted corn on the cob in the summer. Neapolitans, who are always remembering how it was, as if it used to be better, complain that the taralli "culture" is no more, but the taralli themselves go on.

There are other types of taralli, too. They are particularly popular in Caserta. *Tarallifici* (taralli bakeries) produce many different flavors of taralli—garlic, hot pepper, fennel; they even make them with sun-dried tomatoes.

TARALLI CON MANDORLE

BREAD RINGS WITH ALMONDS AND BLACK PEPPER

MERGELLINA IS THE SMALL boat basin and the upper middle-class neighborhood around it at the north end of the bay in Naples. There are grand nineteenth-century apartment buildings (*palazzi*) on the city side, facing the bay, while on the wide street along the water, where mainly young people (these days) promenade and hang out at night, vendors sell these hot rings of crisped and larded dough studded with almonds. You can make these with olive oil if you like—my taralli mentor, Michelle Scicolone, does, substituting ounce for ounce in her book *A Fresh Taste of Italy* (Broadway Books, 1997)—but lard taralli are traditional and have a flakier, crisper texture. Eat them as a snack with a glass of wine.

Makes 32

3½ cups unbleached all-purpose flour

1 envelope dried yeast (2½ teaspoons)

1 cup warm water

4 ounces lard, cut into approximately ½-inch chunks

2 teaspoons freshly ground black pepper

2 teaspoons salt

1 cup very coarsely chopped almonds or hazelnuts, still in their skins

1. In the bowl of a stand-up electric mixer with a dough hook (or the large bowl of a food processor fitted with the metal or plastic blade), combine the flour, the yeast dissolved in the warm water, the chunks of lard, the black pepper, and the salt. Process until the mixture gathers into a dough of medium consistency that is just dry enough not to stick to the bowl. If necessary, add more flour by the tablespoonful.

2. Turn the dough out onto a lightly floured board and knead in the nuts. Continue to knead until you have a smooth and elastic dough, about 8 minutes.

(continued)

3.   Place the dough in a very lightly oiled bowl. Cover with a clean dishtowel and let the dough rise until it doubles in bulk, at least 1 hour, but it could be longer.

4.   Punch down the dough and divide it in half. Then divide each piece in half again, then each piece in half again. You now have 8 pieces of dough. Take 1 piece to work with and leave the remaining pieces of dough on the lightly floured work surface, covered with a towel, until ready to form.

To form and bake the taralli:

5.   Preheat the oven to 350 degrees.

6.   Divide each piece (eighth) of dough into quarters. Roll out each to a rope of about 12 inches long and ¼ inch in diameter. Fold the rope in half to form a 6-inch-long double strand. Twist the strands together 3 times, turning from both ends of the double rope. Now pinch together the ends of the twisted ropes and place each on an (ungreased) baking sheet. (You will need 2 sheets to hold all the taralli.) Do not let rise; work quickly forming taralli.

7.   As soon as they have all been formed, bake for 1 hour. Turn off the oven and let the taralli cool in the closed oven for at least another hour, or until they are fully cooled.

8.   Eat warm or at room temperature. Store in a tin. (They may be gently reheated.)

MINESTRA
E ZUPPA

MINESTRA IS A DIFFICULT WORD and concept to define in English. While it can be what we call soup, it isn't necessarily soup. In Campania, it is almost always thick with stuff, even when it has sippable broth, and it is often a dry dish, as pasta and beans are most of the time. To confuse matters, zuppa isn't necessarily soup as we know it, or as Neapolitans themselves might define it. By definition, zuppa should be a sop; in other words a food cooked in or giving off some liquid that can, upon serving, be drawn up by a piece of bread, either dried or fried. Without the bread, it would be a minestra. But sometimes zuppa is a vegetable soup with no bread. In that case it would most likely have beans or potatoes, making it identical to what is legitimately called a minestra.

That said, there is one thing that is certain and easy to understand about the dishes in this chapter: They take the place of pasta in the menu, wherever that may be.

Meat and poultry broths were always a luxury in the impoverished Neapolitan kitchen, so minestre are rarely based on them. Still, broth, the result of a bollito misto (boiled dinner) perhaps, might be served for Christmas or a special meal, and, as is the case the world over, broth is considered a restorative for the sick, the old, or children, especially pampered sons.

The more usual Neapolitan minestre and zuppe are the living and loved relics and mainstays of *la cucina povera*, the simple kitchen of old. They are made by letting pasta or bread absorb the liquid that results from cooking—in *water*—the beans, vegetables, fish, or seafood that is in season and integral to the dish.

On the other hand, in a typical Neapolitan "there are no rules here" way, the most historically important and uniquely Neapolitan minestra, minestra maritata, is a rich pork broth "married" to lean green vegetables. (You guess which is the bride, which the groom.) It's a soup in every sense of the English word, with broth that can be sipped and poured. But then, it's brimming with greens and with bits of the rich pork that created the broth.

Also contradicting the rule of the Neapolitan minestra being dryish or completely dry is the homey habit of turning vegetable dishes into minestra, "stretching" them, as Italian recipes say, with water—nothing more if you are a traditional or a natural foods cook—or with bouillon from a cube. Many Italian home cooks like using bouillon cubes as a seasoning, to add a little oomph (not to mention salt) to a simple soup or sauce.

In organizing this book, I had trouble placing the most important group of Campanian minestre, the pasta and legume and pasta and vegetable combinations. These have sustained the region from the 1600s when pasta's popularity began to

HOT PEPPER OIL (OLIO DI PEPERONCINO)

Olive oil seasoned with hot pepper is a standard dressing for pasta and beans, or chickpeas or lentils. In a restaurant, it might be offered or you may have to ask. The more humble the restaurant, the more likely it is to be brought to the table without request. In many homes, the pepper oil automatically goes on the table with the pasta e fagioli.

The best way to make pepper oil is to break whole small dried chilies into olive oil, seeds and all, and let them infuse the oil with their sting. It really doesn't matter what kind of hot pepper you use, and hot red pepper flakes depending on their quality, can work well, too. In either case, it usually takes only hours before the oil is peppery enough to use. The proportions are not important. Although the heat can never really be too strong—one just uses less if it is impossibly incendiary—if, after twenty-four hours, the oil seems too aggressive, it can be tamed by adding more olive oil.

I use only extra-virgin olive oil for mine, but the infused oil will not last as long as unflavored oil. For some reason, the olive oil acquires a greasy heaviness after a month or so. For this reason, some cooks recommend a mixture of half olive oil and half light vegetable oil—what Italians call "seed" oil because it usually is extracted from sunflower seeds. It does keep longer but, I think, lacks an important nuance. It's individual choice and how long it takes to consume the oil.

soar. Various pastas, both dry and fresh, with and without eggs, are cooked with fresh and dried beans, and with some vegetables. Are they pasta dishes or are they minestre? Campanians find no need to categorize pasta e fagioli, or pasta e patate, or pasta e zucca. One might as well call them "food."

MINESTRA WITH PASTA

NO ONE IN CAMPANIA would call himself Campanian. Napoletano, Salernitano, Avellinese, yes, sometimes, but never Campano. People identify with a smaller place, their city of Naples (more likely their neighborhood in Naples), Salerno, Caserta, etc., or their tiny *paese*, their town and its countryside. Their provincial border is the outer limit of a particular culture that, no matter how worldly they've become, they can define by certain different customs. Pasta and beans is one of them.

Only a doctoral candidate would catalog all the ways to make pasta and beans.

Spaghetti, or vermicelli, as Neapolitans prefer to call it, is never broken when eaten with sauce, but it is frequently snapped into pieces for using in minestre, to cook along with beans, lentils, or in broth. Wrap no more than a quarter of a pound at a time in a clean kitchen towel; break it at no more than three-inch intervals. Capellini, or angel hair, is never used with a sauce in Campania; it is so thin it clumps up. It is, however, an excellent pasta for minestre.

Pasta e fagioli requires very few ingredients, and there are only so many ways to put them together, but, as contemporary Neapolitan food essayist Mario Stefanile explains, each product and method presents a choice, multiplying the possibilities exponentially. Pork fat or olive oil? Brown the garlic or not? Brothy or dry? Cook the pasta with the beans or apart? And what about the kind of pasta? The type of bean?

Where one province or zone or town or family uses olive oil, another uses rendered lard, another diced pork fat, another pancetta, another cotica (pig skin), or the creamy layer of fat and the flavorful skin trimmed from prosciutto. Some use a combination of fats. The choices have always been made based on availability and a taste acquired from the familiarity of what was available, according to location and economic means. But these days, when everything is available to everyone in Campania, no matter how remote the place or humble the circumstances, tradition is often abandoned in favor of olive oil, which most everyone recognizes as the healthiest choice. Still, there are holdouts who would argue that although olive oil may make a more "digestible" dish, it's hard to resist the siren call of some kind of pork fat.

Bianco or *rosato*, white or pink, is another consideration. Should the dish be made with no tomato or a small amount of tomato to make it pink? What kind of tomato? Fresh, canned or jarred pelati, puree, or tomato paste? Only when it is more brothy than stiff, which, in fact, is the minority of pasta e fagioli in Campania, does it have so much tomato that it appears *rosso*, red.

And what kind of beans? In the hills of Benevento and Avellino, the Monte Alburni and Cilento, where superior cannellini and chickpeas are grown, they use their local product. But try to find them in a store! One has to know a farmer, or a restaurant that knows a farmer, or grow them yourself. So store-bought dried cannellini are the basic bean of Campania. Cranberry beans, called borlotti when they are dried, spollichini when they are fresh, are also popular. Pinto beans, called fagioli messicani, are fashionable among younger cooks.

The pasta? It's incredibly confusing. There are many different pastas used with beans, chickpeas and lentils, but in different places there are also different names for the same pasta, and the same names for different pastas.

In the seaside stretch from Naples, around the Sorrento peninsula, and to the city of Salerno, dried macaroni products are preferred and large tubes used to be considered the ultimate because the beans get trapped in the tubes. These days, mixed shapes of pasta, bought together as pasta mista or pasta mischiata, seem at least equally popular, maybe more so.

North of Naples, in the province of Caserta, where pasta and beans may be somewhat more brothy, or at least looser than elsewhere in Campania, the traditional bean and chickpea pasta is a three-inch-long, flat egg noodle called laganelle. In Frasso Telesino, beyond the Benevento wine capital of Solopaca, the name for this same pasta has been transformed into laine. Elsewhere in the area, it's lavanelle. The name descends from the ancient Roman pasta, a fresh pasta or crêpelike dough called lagana, also laganum and lasanum, and supposedly from the Greek word *lasanon*, for a certain kind of pot.

Meanwhile, for chickpeas, they make lagane in Salerno's Monti Alburni, but there it's a trapezoid-shaped fresh pasta without eggs. And they also make a fresh flour and water pasta called tagliatelle for cannellini beans. It has little relation to the fine egg pasta of Emilia Romagna. These tagliatelle are thick and chewy and only four to five inches long—a relative of the Casertan laganelle.

Fusilli, which gets its name from being shaped on a metal rod—as, in English, the fuselage of a rifle—is also common in the mountain areas of Salerno province—the Monti Alburni and Cilento—mainly sauced with ragù, but also with beans. Fusilli can be a two- to six-inch-long, half-inch-wide ribbon of dough shaped into a tube around the rod, leaving the length open, like an incompletely formed tubular macaroni, or it can be a slightly narrower ribbon wound around the rod, giving it the spiral form we are more familiar with from factory-made fusilli, but with a flattened noodle.

Although pasta and beans at one time may have been the sustenance of the poor, today it is a beloved mainstay of the middle class, too. Every doctor, lawyer, and bureaucrat of Vomero, every businessman and career woman in Posillipo, every shopkeeper in Amalfi, every winemaker in Benevento, and every buffalo breeder in Caserta and Salerno can name his favorite form of the dish. It is delicious, filling, comforting, nowadays recognized as healthful and nutritious, and laced with the nostalgia of their history.

Pasta e Fagioli

Pasta and Beans

This is sublime comfort food and the style of pasta and beans that you are most likely to find on a family table or in a cantina or trattoria in Naples or Salerno. The pasta is never al dente, but soft from having absorbed the beans' seasoned juices, and some of the beans are allowed or encouraged to fall apart so they bind the whole beans and the pasta together. No one in Campania eats al dente pasta with beans, and certainly no one considers a firm bean to be worth eating, so it's a rather solid, substantial dish, made "dry," not soupy or saucy. In the old days, it was even heavier because the pasta would be cooked together with the beans from the raw state, not merely for the last few minutes.

A small amount of tomato gives this style of pasta and beans a pretty blush, and although the dish should be well seasoned while on the stove, a jar of hot pepper oil or the best-quality extra-virgin olive oil is almost always passed or offered to drizzle on top, further enhancing the dish's visual appeal—not that it is a gorgeous dish. The pastas specified are in order of their general desirability to Neapolitans, whose first choice would traditionally be large tubes that catch the beans.

Serves 4

¼ cup extra-virgin olive oil

2 large cloves garlic, finely minced

⅛ teaspoon hot red pepper flakes

3 canned and peeled plum tomatoes

½ teaspoon salt

2½ to 3 cups cooked cannellini beans,
with enough of their cooking liquid to barely cover them

6 ounces large tubular pasta, such as zitoni or rigatoni, or a wide, flat pasta,
such as mafaldine (manfrede in Neapolitan) or fettuccia riccia, or pasta mista
(mischiata), or ziti, penne, or ditali

Hot pepper oil (page 93)

1. In a 2½- to 3-quart saucepan or stovetop casserole, combine the olive oil, the garlic, and the hot pepper flakes over medium-low heat. Let the garlic sizzle gently in the oil.

2. As soon as the garlic begins to color, cut in or crush the tomatoes directly into the pot. (You can chop the tomatoes apart, then put them in the pot, but the Neapolitan home way is to roughly cut them directly into the pot, or crush each tomato by squeezing it in your hand and letting the pieces fall into the pot.)

3. Add salt, and with a wooden spoon, crush or break up the larger pieces of tomato. Increase the heat slightly and sizzle the tomato in the oil for about 5 minutes, stirring once or twice.

4. Stir in the beans and their liquid. Bring to a boil, stirring frequently, then adjust the heat so the beans simmer gently for 5 minutes. This is to let the beans absorb the flavor of the sauce and cook a little further.

5. While the beans simmer, crush some of them against the side of the pot. Taste for salt and add as necessary.

6. Remove from the heat until the pasta is cooked.

7. Cook the pasta in plenty of boiling salted water until just done or slightly underdone. Drain the pasta, saving ½ cup of the cooking water in case you need it later.

8. Stir the cooked pasta into the beans and return to medium heat. Let simmer gently for 1 or 2 minutes or longer, until the pasta is a little past al dente. If the pasta was slightly undercooked to start, you may need to add a spoonful or more of pasta cooking water to finish its cooking with the beans.

9. When the pasta is cooked, remove from the heat, cover the pot, and let stand for 5 to 10 minutes. Serve hot.

To reheat: Pasta and beans can be reheated in a covered casserole in the oven or in a microwave oven.

VARIATIONS:

Various herbs might be used to flavor the dish. Add a couple of bay leaves and/or sprigs of rosemary to the pot of simmering beans, or cook one, the other, or both in the oil with the garlic. Sage is also an excellent seasoning for beans, but it is not a favored Campanian combination.

Cubes or slices of potato are also sometimes cooked along with the pasta, then combined with the beans.

Pasta e Lenticchie

Pasta and Lentils

Carlo Mastroberardino, of Avellino's Mastroberardino Wines, says that when he was a boy, his mother made this dish so often, he can barely look at lentils anymore. Despite his personal protest, it is one of the most beloved and typical dishes of Campania, where, based in Atripalda (province of Avellino), the Mastroberardino family has been making wine since the 1500s. Carlo, who in his early thirties gained control of the company with his father, Antonio, says his mother, an elementary school teacher, always made it on Fridays when he and his brother were growing up, using a pasta mischiata (or pasta mista) of the different shapes of macaroni left in the boxes and bags in her pantry. Capellini, also known as capelli d'angelo (angel's hair), broken into 2- or 3- or 4-inch lengths, is another possibility and one many people prefer, if only because the very thin pasta cooks so quickly. Be warned: This is not soup. It should be very thick and it is eaten with a fork.

Serves 4

5 cups water

¾ cup lentils

2 large cloves garlic, crushed

3 tablespoons extra-virgin olive oil

1 cup chopped canned plum tomatoes, with some juice

2 teaspoons salt

¼ teaspoon hot red pepper flakes

½ pound vermicelli or capellini, or small tubular pasta, or pasta mista

2 rounded tablespoons finely cut or snipped parsley

Optional: Extra-virgin olive oil and hot red pepper flakes
or hot pepper oil (page 93) for garnish

1. In a medium saucepan, bring the water to a rolling boil, add the lentils, and cook, covered over medium-high heat, until nearly but not entirely tender, about 20 minutes.

2.   Add the garlic, the olive oil, the tomatoes, the salt, and the pepper. Reduce the heat, cover, and continue to simmer briskly for another 10 minutes, stirring a few times, or until the lentils are fully tender.

3.   If using capellini, break it into 2- to 4-inch pieces and add them to the lentils. Cook, covered, at a steady simmer, stirring several times and scraping the bottom of the pot when you do. Cook until the pasta is just done, stirring more frequently as it gets closer to that point. If using a small tubular pasta or pasta mista, cook the pasta at least halfway in plenty of salted boiling water. Drain the pasta, add it to the lentils, and simmer to finish cooking the pasta.

4.   When either pasta is cooked to taste, remove the pot from the heat, stir in the parsley, cover the pot, and let stand about 5 minutes before serving.

5.   Serve hot, passing hot pepper oil or the best-quality extra-virgin olive oil for drizzling on top.

VARIATION:

For Lenticchie e scarola, lentils with escarole, leave out the pasta and in its place add from ½- to 1-pound head of escarole, chopped or shredded. This will have a soupier consistency.

PASTA CON CECI

PASTA WITH CHICKPEAS

LAMPI E TUONI

THUNDER AND LIGHTNING

ONE OF THE VERY FEW TIMES, possibly the only time, a Campanian will brown garlic into crunchy golden bits, is to season pasta and beans or pasta and chickpeas. In the mountainous regions, where food is, in general, heartier and heavier to match the more rugged climate, this technique is more typical than on the coast, on the plains, or in the cities. At the tiny, humble trattoria called Da Pasquale in the Cilento hills of southern Campania, it is amazing how different the food is from that a few kilometers down on the neighboring Sele plain. Besides putting a lot of garlic in almost every-thing, the Cilentani frequently serve polenta as a winter minestra, seasoned with hot peppers, or fried onions, or bits of pork crackling—cicoli. Polenta is not a dish of the plains of Campania. Fresh fusilli made from flour and water and only sometimes a tiny measure of egg is favored over factory macaroni in the Cilento, and the ragù is often made with goat or lamb, instead of beef and/or pork. Superior, vibrant-tasting chickpeas and beans are grown in the Cilento, and the nubbins of toasted garlic sea-soning them and the fusilli or other flour-water pasta don't seem nearly as assertive as when blander legumes are used. Still, browned garlic adds a welcome punch to even our commercial chickpeas and factory pasta.

Serves 4

1 cup chickpeas

1½ teaspoons salt

2 quarts cold water

¼ cup olive oil

3 cloves garlic, cut into ⅛-inch mince

⅛ teaspoon hot red pepper flakes

1 teaspoon salt

12 ounces macaroni (ditali, small penne, fusilli . . .)

Optional: Hot pepper oil (page 93)

1. In a medium pot, combine the (unsoaked) chickpeas, the 1½ teaspoons salt, and the cold water. Bring to a boil on high heat. Lower the heat and simmer gently, partially covered, until the chickpeas are very tender and beginning to burst out of their skins, 2½ to 3 hours. Make sure the chickpeas are always covered with water, which may mean adding a little more as they cook.

2. In a 4- to 6-quart pot, over medium heat, combine the olive oil, the garlic, and the hot pepper flakes. Cook, stirring the garlic frequently, until it is golden. Remove from the heat.

3. Drain the chickpeas and measure the chickpea cooking liquid. Add enough water to make 4 cups. Add the chickpeas and this liquid to the sautéed garlic. Bring to a boil over high heat.

4. Add the additional teaspoon of salt and the macaroni. Stir well, then partially cover and reduce the heat to medium high. Stir occasionally at first, then more frequently as the pasta cooks and the liquid reduces. Just before the pasta is done, you will need to stir the pot almost constantly to prevent sticking.

5. Serve immediately, very hot, and while there is still a bit of liquid that has not been absorbed by the pasta. Pass extra-virgin olive oil or hot pepper oil to drizzle on top.

COTICA

Cotica is pig skin, which, when cooked a long time, becomes soft and almost gelatinous. A piece of cotica often gives body and savor to a pot of beans for pasta e fagioli. In old times, if you had it you used it. Today, when cooks try to use less pork fat and more olive oil, you might have to go to Grandma's or an old-time restaurant to get beans made with cotica. It is still widely used for ragù, however, giving the sauce a particularly rich, velvety texture. For ragù, the cotica is rolled, like braciole, with a filling of raisins, pine nuts, garlic, and parsley, and it cooks for several hours with the other meat or meats, becoming a soft and sensual extra goody that is cut in thin slices so everyone can get a tiny piece.

Pasta e Fagioli all'Ischitana

Pasta and Fresh Cranberry Beans, Ischia Style

THIS RECIPE IS MOST like the pasta fazool that Italian-Americans make, which is to say a more brothy dish than the dry pasta e fagioli that is typical in Campania. It is from Anna Gosetti della Salda, founder of *La cucina italiana*, Italy's most popular food magazine, and the author of the highly regarded *Le ricette regionali italiane* (Regional Italian Recipes), a compendium of the country's leading regional dishes. Gosetti keeps a summer home in Lacco Ameno, on Ischia, and perhaps that is why she makes it only with fresh cranberry beans—locally called spollichini—which are in season from August through the end of October, when she is in residence there. Of course, during fresh bean season, tomatoes are at their peak, too, so she uses the locally grown perini—pear-shaped tomatoes. During the winter, however, the recipe is excellent made with dried cranberry beans (borlotti, in Italian) or any other meaty beans, such as cannellini or soldier beans, and canned tomatoes.

Serves 4

2 to 2½ cups shelled, fresh cranberry beans (about 2 pounds in the pod)

1½ pounds fresh plum tomatoes, diced, or 1 28-ounce can pelati, coarsely chopped, with their juices

¼ cup basil leaves, torn into small pieces

½ cup finely chopped celery

1 teaspoon finely chopped garlic

2 ounces prosciutto fat, pancetta, or unsmoked American bacon, chopped almost to a paste

2 tablespoons extra-virgin olive oil

¼ teaspoon hot red pepper flakes

4 teaspoons salt

½ pound pasta mista or tubular macaroni, such as ditali, or medium shells

Grated Parmigiano-Reggiano

1. In a 4- to 6-quart pot, combine the beans, the tomatoes, the basil, the celery, the garlic, and 2 quarts of water. Bring to a boil over high heat. Reduce heat, cover, and simmer briskly for 30 minutes, until the beans seem about half-cooked.

2. Add the pork fat, the olive oil, the hot pepper, and the salt. Simmer, still covered, another 20 minutes.

3. Add the pasta and bring to a full boil. Cook until the pasta is not quite tender enough to eat. Cover the pot and let stand at least 5 minutes before serving.

4. Serve hot. Pass the grated cheese.

Note: The pasta and beans can be reheated, but it will be at its brothiest and the pasta at its firmest when first prepared. When reheating, if you want to restore the soup to a more liquid consistency, add a little water, then reseason if necessary with hot pepper and salt. The pasta will be soft, but pasta e fagioli is one of the few dishes in which Campanians appreciate very soft pasta.

SOFFRITTO

*S*offritto in Campania is not the minced and sautéed vegetable mix that is used as a basis for sauces and stews. And it is not for everyone, here or in Campania. Yet, as one of the nostalgic remnants of dire poverty, Campanian soffritto, stewed offal that is either a soup base or a pasta sauce, is one of the most honored of all Campanian dishes. At one time, it must have kept a lot of people alive. It consists of finely chopped lungs, trachea, heart, spleen, and sometimes liver, except that liver would have been considered too precious to put in the soffritto in the old days. The organ meats are boiled for hours, then cooked further hours with lard, or lard and oil, tomato or dried sweet red pepper paste, white wine, rosemary, and bay leaf. The result is dark red and very dense. When cool, it solidifies and can be kept as a preserve. Nowadays butchers sell it. For zuppa di soffritto, the mixture is reheated with water to thin it out, then poured over dried or toasted bread. For a macaroni sauce, it's thinned with some of the pasta cooking water.

PASTA E PISELLI

PASTA WITH PEAS

PASTA AND PEAS IS a dish made all over Campania; I venture to say all over Italy. Nowhere had I read or heard that it was a specialty of Capri, however, until I started poking into the island's kitchens. Almost invariably, the Capresi will tell you that pasta and peas is one of their specialties. As usual, everyone makes it differently—some with prosciutto, some with prosciutto fat only, some with pancetta, some with oil, some with butter. Some pound or chop the pork fat into a paste; some cut it into tiny cubes. Old-fashioned cooks in some parts of Campania still use lard, and one cook on Capri even told me that pasta and peas was best made with egg pasta, such as tagliarini, although almost everyone, everywhere, thinks short tubes are best, in particular the flat-ended ditali or diagonally cut pennette. The peas and diced prosciutto or pancetta catch easily in these, but the longer ziti or penne are good, too, as are small shells.

I use butter with prosciutto and olive oil with pancetta and prefer the former combination over the later, but this is all a matter of taste.

Serves 4 to 6

12 ounces to 1 pound short tubular pasta, such as ditali or pennette

4 ounces prosciutto or pancetta, cut into ¼-inch dice (about ⅔ cup)

4 tablespoons butter or extra-virgin olive oil

½ cup finely chopped onion

1 10-ounce package frozen small peas, defrosted

½ teaspoon black pepper

¼ cup finely cut parsley or mint

½ cup grated Parmigiano-Reggiano

Grated Parmigiano-Reggiano for the table

1. Cook the pasta in plenty of salted water until it is not quite cooked enough to your taste.

2. In a 10-inch skillet, combine the prosciutto or pancetta with the butter or olive oil, and the onion. Place over medium heat and cook, tossing occasionally, for about 10 minutes, until the onion is tender and, if using the pancetta, it has rendered some of its fat. Add the peas and mix well. Cook another 30 seconds, then remove the pan from the heat until the pasta is cooked.

3. Scoop off 2 cups of pasta cooking water, then drain the pasta.

4. Scrape the pea mixture into the pasta cooking pot. Add 1½ cups of the reserved pasta cooking water, and the macaroni. Stir over high heat for 2 or 3 minutes, until the pasta has finished cooking and there is still some liquid in the bottom of the pot. If you like a soupier mixture, add more pasta cooking water. Remove the pot from the heat and stir in the parsley or mint and the grated cheese. Cover the pot and let stand a couple of minutes before serving.

5. Serve hot. Pass the grated cheese.

VARIATIONS:

Instead of serving the peas with pasta, you can make them into a zuppa di piselli: After the peas have cooked with the pork and fat, add 2 cups of water and simmer for 2 or 3 minutes, until just done. Pour over freselle or pane biscottato, or serve with fried croutons.

For pasta e fave, instead of peas use 2 cups of the smallest and youngest fava beans. These don't really need to be peeled because their skins are not mature enough to be bitter, although it is usually better to do so.

PASTA E PATATE

PASTA WITH POTATOES

To an American, the idea of potatoes with pasta seems redundant, and possibly much too heavy. To a Campanian, it is like manna from heaven. I'll never forget calling my friend Ida Cerbone in the middle of August at her home in Pignataro Interamna, just a few kilometers north of the Campanian border near Cassino. Trying to live vicariously, I asked Ida, "What are you making for lunch today?" "Pasta e patate." "In the middle of August?" I was amazed. "If you love pasta and potatoes the way I do," said Ida, "you'd know there is no season for it."

Serves 6

3 to 4 ounces pancetta, cut into ⅛-inch dice (about ½ cup), or 3 to 4 ounces
unsmoked or smoked American bacon, cut into ⅛-inch crosswise pieces,
or an approximately 2-by-4-inch piece of prosciutto skin, left whole

2 tablespoons extra-virgin olive oil

1 medium onion, finely chopped (about 1 cup)

1 rib celery, finely chopped (⅓ to ½ cup)

1 carrot, finely chopped (⅓ to ½ cup)

½ cup peeled Italian tomatoes, drained and crushed

¼ teaspoon hot red pepper flakes

1¼ pounds potatoes, peeled and cut into ½- to ¾-inch dice
or ¼- to ½-inch slices (about 3 cups)

1 Parmigiano-Reggiano rind about 2 by 3 inches
(about 4 ounces), washed and scraped

3 to 4 teaspoons salt

½ pound pasta mista, ziti, penne,
or other medium-size tubular pasta,
or gemelli

1. In a 4- to 6-quart heavy-bottomed pot, combine the pancetta or bacon and the olive oil over medium heat and fry the pancetta until it starts to crisp. (If using prosciutto skin, add it later and use the olive oil to cook the vegetables.)

2. Stir in the onion, celery, and carrot (and the olive oil if using prosciutto skin instead of bacon). Continue to cook over medium heat, stirring a few times, until the onion is translucent, about 5 minutes.

3. Stir in the tomatoes and hot pepper and continue to cook, stirring frequently to prevent sticking, for about 4 minutes.

4. Add the potatoes and cheese rind, and the prosciutto skin if using. Stir well and cook about 4 more minutes, stirring occasionally, again to prevent sticking.

5. Add 1½ quarts water and the salt. Cover, increase heat to high and bring to a boil, then reduce heat and simmer, still covered, for 20 minutes. The strength and thickness of the soup depend on the amount of water you add at this point. Without any additional water, you'll have just enough liquid to cover all the ingredients when they are fully cooked, but you can add as much as 2 cups more water to make it soupier.

6. With the liquid at a full, rolling boil, add the pasta. While the pasta cooks at a steady boil, stir regularly to prevent sticking. When the pasta is cooked, but not quite as tender as you'd like, remove the pot from the heat.

7. Remove the prosciutto rind and cheese rind and keep the pot covered while cutting the cheese rind into ½-inch or smaller pieces. If desired, mince the prosciutto rind, too, or discard it. Stir these pieces into the pot, then let the minestra stand, covered, for about 10 minutes before serving.

8. Serve hot or warm.

PASTA E ZUCCA

PASTA WITH PUMPKIN OR SQUASH

———

PUMPKIN IN ITALY IS NO more flavorful than a jack-o'-lantern in the States, and without the sugar and spice that can make ours nice, the Italian squash makes for a pretty bland dish, especially when combined with pasta. Pasta e zucca is, however, one of the staples of the Neapolitan fall table, one of those dishes people eagerly await to come into season, and you'll see how it can grow on you, especially when made with sweet American squash or one of our flavorful pie pumpkins. It is, after all, aside from comforting and delicious with a generous sprinkling of grated cheese and black pepper, a healthful, easy, and very quickly prepared dish.

Serves 6

2 pounds butternut or acorn squash, or pie
(sometimes called cheese) pumpkin

⅓ cup extra-virgin olive oil

2 large cloves garlic, smashed

⅛ to ¼ teaspoon red pepper flakes

2 teaspoons salt, or to taste

½ pound spaghetti, broken into 1½-inch or slightly longer lengths,
or pasta mista, tubetti, ditali, or ditalini

⅓ cup finely cut parsley

Grated Parmigiano-Reggiano

1.   For easiest peeling and dicing, cut the squash crosswise into ¾-inch slices. Peel the slices and discard the seeds and fibrous interior. Now cut the squash into ¾-inch cubes. If using pumpkin, cut it into wedges, discard the seeds, then peel the wedges and cube the pulp.

2.   In a 3-quart saucepan, over low heat, combine the oil and garlic and cook the garlic until it is soft and barely coloring on both sides, pressing it into the oil a few times to release its flavor. Remove the garlic.

3.   Add the cubed squash or pumpkin and the red pepper. Sprinkle with ½ teaspoon of the salt. Increase the heat to medium-high and sauté the squash until it is soft and beginning to brown, about 15 minutes. If using pumpkin, it will take about 25 minutes to get to the same semicooked state.

4.   Add 5 to 6 cups of water and a teaspoon of the salt. Raise the heat, cover the pot, and bring to a rolling boil.

5.   Stir in the pasta, re-cover the pot, and when the water returns to a boil, uncover and cook the pasta until cooked to your taste. While the pasta cooks, stir it frequently and mash some of the squash cubes with the back of a wooden spoon to thicken the dish. Taste for salt and correct if necessary. Correct the consistency, if desired, by adding more water. It can be soupy, thick, or almost dry, depending on your taste.

6.   Stir in the chopped parsley and serve hot. Pass the Parmigiano.

Note: Although the pasta will get softer and the liquid will become entirely absorbed if the dish is left to sit and cool, or leftovers are refrigerated, it is nevertheless delicious reheated. A microwave does the job very well; just be careful to reheat on high for only a few seconds at a time, then stir, then heat further.

Variation:

For minestra di zucca e spollichini, a soup of squash and fresh cranberry beans, add 2 to 2½ cups shelled cranberry beans (2 pounds in the pod) with the water, which should be reduced to 1 quart. Leave out the pasta and simmer until the beans are thoroughly tender and the squash is falling apart, 30 to 40 minutes. Thicken the soup by smashing some of the squash against the side of the pot with a wooden spoon.

Minestra with Broth

Minestra Maritata

Il mangiar quotidiano del ver napoletano.
(The daily food of the true Neapolitan.)

—Giambattista del Tufo, *Ritratto di Napoli*
(Portrait of Naples), 1588

"A mythic soup of ancient tradition," says Nello Oliviero, the late Neapolitan food essayist, not exaggerating for once in his book *Storie e curiosità del mangiar napoletano* (Neapolitan Food Stories and Curiosities). He then waxes on and on in the most purple Neapolitan prose ("The historic residue of an epoch at its sunset . . ."), finally explaining, as anyone in Campania knows, that "the name comes from the marriage of vegetables and meat."

But let's let Oliviero continue. He expresses the metaphor of the dish so well and in such a classically male-chauvinist Neapolitan way: "Parts of the pig make up the husband [and] by law of contrast the fat pig takes as a wife the lean vegetables. . . . [It takes] time, competence, patience and money [to make a great marriage]. The vegetables must be selected for variety and picked over, washed many times. The husband is put on to bubble in his broth, which must be skimmed, defatted, strained and, at the end, clarified, so that it becomes limpid and of an amber hue. It is in this broth that the vegetables become tender."

The soup has nothing to do with real weddings. At least it never has. But I witnessed an interesting minestra maritata ceremony at an elaborate wedding I attended in the tiny, rural town of Piedimonte Matese, near the Molise border in the province of Caserta. The catering hall was called La Tour d'Argent, which should tell you everything about its pretensions. After several hours of eating about eight courses, the first one of which, La Fantasia dello Chef, was ten courses in itself, the band played a fanfare, everyone was asked to return to his table from his wanderings around the dining room, and a cadre of young, uniformed waiters rolled out a vast cauldron of the soup. It was big enough to boil a large human. And in this hall with the grand French name, at this fancy dinner where no luxury food went unserved, la maritata was given a fanfare and an ovation.

The following recipe, one of the many that I could have offered, is adapted from *La cucina napoletana in cento ricette tradizionali* (Neapolitan Cooking in 100 Traditional Recipes), by Maria Giovanna Fasulo Rak, an archivist and book restorer at the National Library (Biblioteca Nazionale), in Rome, who is from an old Neapolitan family. I've substituted kale for the large, dark, blue-green leaves of Campania's broccoli di foglia (also called broccoli di Natale because it is a winter crop). Otherwise, I've kept to Rak's very traditional formula. Note the lack of tomatoes. This recipe predates the tomato, and the advent of pasta as a main source of calories. It's from the period when Campanians were still known as *mangiafoglie* (leaf eaters).

Serves 12

For the broth:

1 pound well-trimmed rib end pork loin (country ribs), in 2 pieces

½ pound salami, in one piece

¼ pound pancetta, in one piece

½ pound fresh Italian sausages

4 ounces prosciutto skin, some fat attached

½ pound soppressata, in one piece

Fresh herbs tied together in a small bouquet—a large branch of rosemary,
a large sprig of sage, a few sprigs of thyme, and about 20 sprigs of parsley

The vegetables:

1 bunch kale (about 1 pound)

1 bunch broccoli rabe (about 1 pound)

1 head escarole (about 1 pound), root end removed and coarsely chopped

1 head curly chicory (about 1 pound), root end removed
and coarsely chopped

½ large head (1¼ to 1½ pounds) Savoy cabbage, coarsely chopped

Plus:

An approximately 4-by-4-inch rind of Parmigiano-Reggiano
or dried caciocavallo, scrubbed

¼ teaspoon hot red pepper flakes, or to taste

Salt to taste

Freshly ground black pepper to taste

Freshly grated pecorino or Parmigiano-Reggiano or a mixture of both

(continued)

To make the broth:

1.   In an 8-quart pot, combine all the meats with the herb bouquet. Cover with 5 quarts of water. Do not add salt. Cover and bring to a simmer. Uncover, adjust the heat so the liquid simmers very gently for about 3 hours, skimming if any scum rises. Add water as necessary to keep the meats covered with liquid.

2.   Discard the herbs. Remove the meats. Place them in a bowl and moisten with a few spoons of broth. Refrigerate until you are ready to complete the soup. Cool the broth. Strain it, then chill it so the fat can be easily removed. You should have about 3½ quarts.

To prepare the vegetables:

3.   Use only the leafy tops of the kale and broccoli rabe, discarding the stems. Coarsely chop the vegetables.

4.   Bring an 8-quart pot of salted water to a boil. Blanch each vegetable, except the cabbage, for 5 minutes, removing each with a slotted spoon, but reusing the water. Combine the vegetables and the raw cabbage. Discard the cooking liquid.

To finish the soup:

5.   In the same 8-quart pot, bring the meat broth back to a simmer, then add all the vegetables, the cheese rind, and the hot pepper. Simmer gently for about 30 minutes.

6.   Cut the meats into bite-size pieces, discarding the fat. Stir them into the soup and continue to simmer 10 minutes longer. Correct the seasoning with salt and freshly ground black pepper.

7.   Turn off the heat and let the soup rest for 20 minutes before serving it. (If desired, remove the cheese rind, cut it into tiny pieces, then put the pieces in the soup. Otherwise, remove the rind and discard it.)

8.   Serve hot with grated pecorino or Parmigiano-Reggiano or a combination.

VARIATION:

If you prefer, you can substitute beef short ribs or shank, or chicken legs, thighs, backs, and/or wings for the fresh pork, and you can substitute ¼ pound diced fatty prosciutto instead of the prosciutto skin. The variety and amount of green vegetables may be changed according to availability and taste, too.

MINESTRA VERDE DI NETTA BOTTONE

A MODERN MARITATA

IT WAS—NO EXAGGERATION—the coldest day in Ravello in thirty-two years. The wind blew so hard that in order to walk anywhere in this famous medieval town on the hill above Amalfi we had to hold on to the stone walls that line the narrow streets. The cyclamens that the town authorities had put in the many public planters were frozen, stiffened into a kind of rigor mortis that would, when the temperature rose above freezing the next day, become a black death. We somehow made it in one well-chilled piece to the best restaurant in Ravello, a particularly hospitable trattoria owned by a family that takes pains to grow most of its produce and buys the rest of its ingredients from local sources. The weather naturally made the fire in Cumpà Cosimo's dining room hearth even more appealing, and this soup, brought to us in deep brown crocks almost as soon as we were seated, was even more welcome than on a more typical Amalfi Coast night. Chef-owner Netta Bottone, who is actually quite worldly but likes to present herself in the restaurant as a simple provincial lady, even to wearing frilly, kitschy aprons from the 1950s, does not call it maritata. She is too respectful of tradition. Her soup is lighter than minestra maritata because it is made with only fresh pork and no preserved pork products, and it does have tomatoes.

Serves at least 8

For the broth:

1 to 1½ pounds meaty pork spare ribs or other fresh pork

1 rib celery, finely chopped

1 large onion, finely chopped (about 1½ cups)

5 canned plum tomatoes, coarsely chopped or crushed in your hand

¼ teaspoon red pepper flakes

2 teaspoons salt

The vegetables:

1 head (about 1 pound) curly endive (sometimes called chicory)

½ medium head Savoy cabbage (about 1 pound), cored, halved, and cut into ¼-inch-wide shreds

1 bunch kale (about 1 pound), tough stems discarded, coarsely chopped

½ pound all-purpose or boiling potatoes, peeled and cut into ½-inch cubes

(continued)

1. In a large soup pot, combine the pork and 4 quarts of water. Bring to a boil, lower the heat to a gentle simmer, then skim the surface until the scum stops coming to the top, about 10 minutes.

2. Add the celery, the onion, and the tomatoes. Season with hot red pepper and the salt. Simmer briskly, partially covered, for about 1½ hours.

3. Meanwhile, wash the chicory well, cut the leaves cross-wise into thirds or quarters, depending on the size of the greens, then cook for 3 minutes in salted boiling water, timing from when the water returns to a boil. Drain.

4. When the broth is ready, skim fat from the surface if necessary (there is usually very little fat, but if there is a lot, you may want to chill the broth to facilitate removing it). Remove the meat from the broth, strip the meat off the bones, then chop or tear it into bite-size pieces.

5. To the broth, add all the greens, the potatoes, and the bits of meat. Simmer briskly together, partially covered, for about 1½ hours, or until the vegetables are very thoroughly cooked. The soup is very thick with greens—vegetables with broth rather than broth with vegetables.

6. Serve hot. The soup reheats very well and may be kept refrigerated for up to a week.

Zuppa di Santé

Health Soup

Santé is not Italian, but from the French word for health, indicating, to a Neapolitan, that this soup is not only good for you, but perhaps a dish with fancy origins. It's the chicken broth on both counts. A precious thing in the traditional Campanian kitchen, chicken broth was food of the rich, which often took on a French accent. In less affluent households, broth was either for guests, for celebratory meals, or for children, the elderly, and the infirm, as a restorative. The protein additions of meatballs and beaten eggs and cheese to form a stracciatella, or egg drops, makes it even more "healthy" in the Campanian mind—a digestible meal in a bowl, to be sure—and, of course, the leafy vegetable does add vitamins and minerals. With all that, it is a soup eaten for pleasure these days. It goes down all too easily for something so medicinal. And it is not always based on chicken broth. A good vegetable broth will do—a place to use leftover tomato juices from canned tomatoes—which makes it feasible for any day.

Serves 6 to 8

3 quarts light chicken broth or the following vegetable-and-bouillon broth

For the vegetable broth:

1 28-ounce can peeled tomatoes (not drained)

1 large or 2 medium-size carrots, scrubbed

1 large onion, quartered

About 15 sprigs parsley, with their stems (or ¼ cup whole leaves)

Optional: 2 chicken or vegetable bouillon cubes

3 quarts water

Plus:

2 pounds chicory (sometimes called curly endive) or escarole

For the meatballs:

½ pound ground lean beef

1 egg

4 tablespoons grated Parmigiano-Reggiano

3 tablespoons dry bread crumbs

¼ teaspoon freshly ground black pepper

½ teaspoon salt

Optional (for the stracciatella):

3 eggs

½ cup grated Parmigiano-Reggiano

(continued)

Use chicken broth, or:

To make a vegetable broth:

1. In a 4- to 6-quart pot, combine the vegetables, the parsley, the bouillon, and the water. Boil together, covered, for about 1½ hours. Strain the broth and return it to the pot. (Or, to additionally flavor a light chicken broth, you may want to boil it, covered, for about 20 minutes with several chopped, canned, plum tomatoes or about ½ cup canned crushed tomatoes. There is no need to strain out any bits of tomato.)

To prepare the chicory:

2. Wash it well, then cut it crosswise into 2- to 3-inch lengths.

3. Bring a large pot of salted water to a rolling boil. Add the chicory and boil for 3 minutes, timing from when the water returns to a boil. Drain in a colander, discarding the water.

To make the meatballs:

4. In a mixing bowl, combine all the ingredients and, with a table fork, blend them together until well mixed. Between your palms, form meatballs the size of cherries: You should get 40 to 50.

To make the soup:

5. Bring the chicken or vegetable broth to a boil. Add the blanched chicory and simmer, covered, for 15 minutes.

6. Drop the meatballs into the soup and boil, uncovered, over high heat, for 6 to 7 minutes.

To make a stracciatella (egg drops):

7. While the meatballs are cooking, in a small bowl, beat the eggs and cheese together with a fork.

8. When the meatballs are cooked, slowly drizzle the egg and cheese mixture into the boiling soup, pushing the mixture into the greens and the greens down into the simmering soup. Boil 2 more minutes.

9. Serve very hot. (The soup reheats perfectly.)

Minestra with Vegetables

Zuppa di Fagioli e Scarola

Bean and Escarole Soup

THIS IS EASILY a meal unto itself.

Serves 8

1 pound cannellini beans

2½ quarts water

1 teaspoon salt

1 large bunch escarole or chicory (about 1 pound)

¼ cup extra-virgin olive oil

1 tablespoon finely minced garlic

3 or 4 canned peeled plum tomatoes

1 large rib celery, finely minced

½ cup finely cut parsley

¼ teaspoon hot red pepper flakes

Optional: Hot pepper oil (page 93) and either freselle or pane biscottato

1. In a 4- to 5-quart saucepan or stovetop casserole, combine the beans with 10 cups of water. Add the salt and bring to a boil, then adjust the heat so the beans simmer gently, partially covered, for 1 hour or longer, or until fully tender. (Or use four 19-ounce cans of cannellini.)

2. Meanwhile, wash the greens and cut into inch-wide crosswise pieces.

3. Bring a 4- to 5-quart pot of salted water to a rolling boil. Plunge in the greens, and when the water returns to a boil, let them boil for 5 minutes or until just tender. Drain and set aside.

4. When the beans are tender, add the olive oil, the garlic, the tomatoes, chopped or crushed into the pot with your hand; the celery, parsley, and hot pepper. Simmer another 15 minutes.

5. Add the greens and simmer another 5 minutes.

6. Serve hot and pass a cruet of extra-virgin olive oil or hot pepper oil. It can also be served over freselle or dry-toasted bread.

MINESTRA (ZUPPA) DI FAVE FRESCHE

STEWED FAVA BEANS

THIS IS CONSIDERED A very special soup in some households. I think it's mainly because shelling fava beans can be such tedious work that making this soup becomes an act of love. The beans pop easily out of their fleshy pods, but then each bean must be individually shelled. Not only is the skin of the bean bitter, but it turns an ugly gray-brown when cooked. Skinned fava, on the other hand, are more sweet than bitter and a pleasant, although not pretty, gray-green when cooked more than a few minutes, as they are here. I find my fingernails are the best tool for breaking the skin near the dark "eye" of the bean, the place where it is easiest to begin, but a very small paring knife can be helpful, too.

With the amount of water indicated here, you will get a mess of beans, more stew than soup. It is perfectly acceptable, however, to stretch the dish with water to make it more brothy.

Serves at least 6

1 tablespoon extra-virgin olive oil

2 to 3 ounces pancetta or unsmoked American bacon, finely minced,
or fatty prosciutto, minced or cut into matchstick pieces

1 medium onion, cut in half through the root end, then very thinly sliced

4 cups shelled and skinned fava beans
(4 pounds or more in the pod; see note)

2½ to 3 cups water

½ teaspoon salt

⅛ teaspoon red pepper flakes or ¼ teaspoon freshly ground black pepper,
or to taste

Freshly grated pecorino cheese

1.   In a 2- to 3-quart saucepan, combine the olive oil, pancetta, bacon, or prosciutto, and the onion. Place over low heat and let the fat render from the pork product of choice—about 20 minutes. Nothing should brown yet.

2.   Increase the heat and cook more briskly, stirring often with a wooden spoon, until the onion begins to color. Be careful not to let anything stick to the bottom of the pan and brown too much.

3.   Stir in the fava beans and, stirring often, let them cook over medium-low heat for about 10 minutes. At this point, they will be a vibrant green that will, unfortunately, not last for long.

4.   Add enough water to just cover the beans. Add the salt and the pepper of choice, then let the beans simmer gently for about another 10 minutes. The length of time you cook the beans depends on their size and tenderness, and your taste for tenderness. To some, the less cooked, greener beans are preferred. Others, like myself, prefer to accept the drabber color that they take on when they develop, in just a few minutes, a more complex flavor from cooking longer with the pork and onion. At this point—or if reheating the beans—you may want to add a little more water to extend the broth.

5.   Serve hot in pasta bowls. The beans can be eaten, like a soup, with a spoon. Pass the grated pecorino. For a heavier zuppa, either place a well-toasted piece of fresh bread at the bottom of the bowl, top with fried croutons, or pour each portion over a ring of freselle or a slice of pane biscottato (see page 2).

Note: The yield on fava beans can vary dramatically. Sometimes 4 pounds of pods will give 2 to 3 cups of beans, sometimes as much as 4 cups.

Minestra di Zucchine Cacio e Uova

Zucchini Soup with Cheese and Eggs

The one restaurant I know in Naples that makes this soup—a fancy and famous restaurant that in fact does not make it well—serves it mainly to a clientele of businessmen who must miss home very badly. You may find minestra di zucchine in a working man's cantina, or in a true mom-and-pop trattoria, but it is almost strictly a home dish, a cherished everyday/anyday kind of recipe. Indeed, it is among the pantheon of dishes that frequently symbolizes the old country to Neapolitan-Americans, although it never made it onto the menus of their restaurants, either. It's deemed too humble to be interesting to anyone but another nostalgic Neapolitan.

It is easy, fast, comforting, and restorative, and needs to be eaten the moment after it comes off the fire. Some people prefer the egg and cheese enrichment to curdle into dumplinglike balls, in a way like stracciatella, but I think it is much more delicious to the uninitiated if the eggs and cheese thicken the broth without scrambling. This consistency requires more care, but it's worth it. (See Tubetti Cacio e Uova, page 137, for more on cacio e uova.)

Serves 4 to 6

1 medium onion, finely sliced or diced

2 tablespoons extra-virgin olive oil

2 pounds zucchini (preferably small ones), scrubbed,
ends cut off, cut into ½-inch pieces

½ teaspoon salt

Water (2½ to 3 cups)

3 eggs

1 cup grated Parmigiano-Reggiano or pecorino, or, preferably, a combination

2 rounded tablespoons finely cut parsley or basil

Freshly ground black pepper

1.   In a 2- to 3-quart saucepan, over medium heat, combine the onion and oil and sauté until the onion is well wilted, but not browning, about 5 minutes.

2.   Add the zucchini and stir well. Continue to cook, uncovered, tossing the zucchini regularly, for 3 or 4 minutes. Do not let it brown, either. Add the salt and enough water to barely cover the zucchini. Cover and simmer briskly for 8 to 10 minutes. The zucchini should be very tender but not falling apart. Occasionally it takes longer than 10 minutes.

3.   While the zucchini cooks, in a small bowl, beat the eggs, the grated cheese, and the herb together.

4.   When the zucchini is cooked, remove the pot from the heat and stir about ½ cup of the zucchini broth into the eggs, a few tablespoons at a time. Still off the heat, stir the egg mixture into the soup. Return to the lowest possible heat and stir a minute or so, until the soup has thickened slightly. Try not to let it curdle, but if it does, know that some people actually prefer it that way.

5.   Check for salt and add freshly grated pepper or pass the pepper mill at the table. Serve very hot.

VARIATION:

For a more old-fashioned taste, instead of using all olive oil, use 2 tablespoons of finely diced pancetta, or unsmoked American bacon, or prosciutto fat, plus 1 tablespoon of olive oil. Before adding the onion, over low heat, render some of the pork fat in the oil.

To turn this into a vegetable side dish in which the zucchini is enrobed in a rich egg and cheese sauce, use only 1 cup of water to cook the zucchini.

Minestra di Stagione

Spring Soup

THIS POTFUL OF SPRING flavors is more stew than soup, as so many Campanian vegetable minestre are. It's not meant to be followed by an important main course. At most, a cheese dish or a frittata, then fresh fruit, would round out the everyday meal at which it would be served.

Serves 8

2 tablespoons extra-virgin olive oil

3 ounces pancetta or unsmoked American bacon, finely diced

5 or 6 small spring onions, finely sliced, or 3 bunches scallions,
much of the green removed, chopped (about 2 cups of either)

3 pounds fresh fava beans, shelled and skinned (about 2 cups)

3 cups shelled fresh peas or 2 10-ounce boxes frozen peas

6 large artichokes, cleaned down to the bases, the bases cut into ⅛-inch-thick
slices and kept green by immersing in acidulated water

1½ teaspoons salt

1 cup water

1 pound new potatoes, cut into ½-inch cubes

8 large leaves basil, torn into small pieces (about ½ cup loosely packed)

4 to 5 cups water

Freshly grated Parmigiano-Reggiano, pecorino, or a combination

1. In a 5-quart or larger pot, combine the olive oil, the pancetta, and the sliced onions or scallions. Place over medium heat and cook, stirring frequently, until the onions are golden. about 15 minutes.

2. Add the favas, reduce the heat slightly, cover, and continue to cook gently for 10 minutes, stirring occasionally.

3. Add the peas, the sliced artichoke bottoms, the salt, and 1 cup of water. Cook gently, covered, 10 minutes longer, still stirring occasionally.

4.   Add the potatoes, the basil, and enough water or broth to barely cover all the vegetables, 4 to 5 cups. Cover and raise the heat to bring the soup to a boil, then adjust the heat so the soup will simmer gently, partially covered. Cook until the vegetables are very tender, from 30 to 45 minutes.

5.   Taste for salt, adding more if necessary, and serve hot. Pass the pepper mill and grated cheese, although I find the cheese detracts from the sweet flavors of the vegetables. Others find it not only pleasing, but essential.

MINESTRA WITH BREAD

PANCOTTO DI BROCCOLI DI RAPE CON SALSICCE

PANE DURO CON BROCCOLI

SAUSAGE WITH COOKED BREAD AND BROCCOLI RABE

THIS WAS CONTRIBUTED by Renato Angelillo of Naples to the loose-leaf cookbook published by the Naples daily newspaper, *Il Mattino,* and called *L'antica cucina della Campania* (The Old Cooking of Campania). Signor Angelillo calls his recipe pancotto and says it is "a traditional recipe of Battipaglia," but, strangely, my friends in Battipaglia, which is a center of mozzarella production in Salerno, all call it pane duro. Pancotto, which is essentially the same as Tuscan pappa, is the name used more in Benevento, where they are also fond of this dish and other minestre based on soaked bread, such as bread with white beans and bread cooked with tomato sauce.

Serves 6 as a one-dish meal, 8 to 10 as a first course

(continued)

1¾ to 2 pounds sweet or hot Italian sausage (8 to 10 links)

1½ cups water

2 tablespoons extra-virgin olive oil

2 bunches broccoli rabe (about 2 pounds)

1 or 2 large cloves garlic, slightly smashed

Big pinch hot pepper (if not using hot sausage)

2 quarts of pieces and slices of completely dried-out bread,
crusts removed only if it's not too difficult to do so, or 2 quarts of broken
freselle or pane biscottato (see page 2)

4 to 5 cups cold water

Optional: Hot pepper oil (page 93) or extra-virgin olive oil

1. Pierce each sausage 2 or 3 times with the point of a sharp knife.

2. In a 10-inch skillet, sauté pan, or stovetop casserole, combine the sausage, the water, and the olive oil. The water should come about halfway up the sides of the sausage.

3. Cook the sausage over high heat until the water has evaporated, then lower the heat and brown the sausage all over in the fat remaining in the pan. The whole process should take 30 to 40 minutes. (Be careful: At the point the water has almost evaporated, the fat will begin to spatter.)

4. While the sausage is boiling, prepare the broccoli rabe: Trim off the heavy stems and wilted leaves, then plunge the broccoli into a large pot of boiling, salted water. Cover, return to a boil, and cook the broccoli, uncovered, for 5 minutes from the time the water returns to a boil, about 8 minutes altogether. Drain the broccoli.

5. Remove the browned sausage and set aside. Do not clean the pan or discard the fat in it. In the same pan, over medium-low heat, cook the garlic with the hot pepper, if using, until the garlic begins to color, pressing it down several times to release its flavor. Remove the garlic, if desired.

6. Add the blanched broccoli rabe to the pan and cook over medium heat, turning it and pushing it around the pan constantly, for about 5 minutes. At the same time, deglaze the pan by scraping it with a wooden spoon. The moisture of the broccoli will do the deglazing.

7. In a large pot, combine the stale bread and 4 cups of the water. Let the bread soak a few minutes, stirring it a few times, then start breaking it up with a wooden spoon. Place over medium-low heat and continue to use the spoon to break up the bread until it has disintegrated into a pap. It may be necessary to add more water; do so a little at a time. After a few minutes, it will probably be necessary to concentrate on a difficult few chunks of bread that don't disintegrate, especially those that have crusts attached. Be careful not to scorch the bread.

8. When the bread is a fluffy pap and heated through, add the broccoli rabe and continue to stir over medium-low heat until the mixture is fairly homogenous.

9. The pancotto can be served immediately or reheated later. To serve, place a portion of the bread in a shallow pasta bowl and top with whole or sliced sausage. To reheat, pack the pancotto into a shallow baking dish, cover with foil, and place in a preheated 350-degree oven for 10 minutes. Garnish with sausage reheated for 2 or 3 minutes, also in foil, in the same oven. Or cut the sausage in fourths lengthwise, then crosswise every ½ inch to form diced sausage. Mix the sausage pieces into the pancotto and reheat in a 350-degree oven.

10. Serve hot with condiment-quality extra-virgin olive oil or hot pepper oil to drizzle over the top of each portion.

PASTA

*T*his macarone is to be eaten looking skywards, where the taste of the macarone brings about ecstasy, with a thought to God for his divine providence.

—Bartolomeo Nardini, a Frenchman (obviously of Italian descent) describing his Neapolitan experience in the early nineteenth century, quoted in *Partenope in cucina* (Parthenope in the Kitchen)

*E*verything you see, I owe to spaghetti.

—Sophia Loren, actress born in Pozzuoli

NEAPOLITANS ARE VERY SERIOUS when they say that pasta is the only food that human beings can eat every day. And every day they go about proving it. It is for good reason they are called macaroni eaters (*mangiamaccheroni*) by other Italians. It is meant disparagingly, but, actually, dried pasta and the infinite ways in which Neapolitans dress it best exemplify their cunning for turning hardship and necessity into pleasure. Dried pasta is simply Naples's greatest contribution to the world.

Forget Marco Polo. Forget China. Pastalike foods have been created by peoples all over the world for precisely the same reason: the need to preserve grain against the vagaries of nature, weather, politics, and economics. The grain itself is subject to oxidation (rancidity), fungi, molds, insect infestation, animal pests, and unimaginable microorganisms. Prehistoric man learned that toasting the grain reduced some of the problems somewhat. Eventually, he learned that grinding and boiling the toasted grain staved off the problems for a little longer, and that the ensuing gruel—polenta, the ancient Roman migliaccio—whatever it is called wherever it is made—was more digestible than the whole grain. The moist gruel was still subject to spoilage, though. Dry it. Bake it. Now came bread, certainly starting as unleavened

Pasta is usually eaten as a first course in Italy, followed by a second course. But even when pasta is the only course, Italians eat a much smaller amount than is served in North America these days. The average Italian portion is about three ounces, which computes to twelve ounces to serve four. That is the portion size recommended in these recipes. Italians do not use as much sauce as we do, either. Sauce is meant to season pasta, and a light coating of every strand is all that they usually desire. Indeed, in Campania, many pasta dishes do not have sauce at all. The pasta is instead impregnated with the flavor of the sauce by being cooked briefly with it. In those cases, the pasta is slightly under-cooked so that it will still be al dente when it finishes this second cooking, and there may be only enough liquid left in the pan to lightly gloss the pasta or to put an extra spoonful on top of the pasta as a garnish.

flat bread similar to that still made by the Bedouins. And probably pasta. Instead of baking the pancake of gruel on a hot rock, you tossed the dough into boiling water. Some people may have even discovered that they could dry the dough for a second round of storage.

Among the many material proofs that there was pasta in Italy before Marco Polo is a fourth-century B.C. Etruscan tomb in Cerveteri, just north of Rome, that contains pasta-making implements similar to those used today. The ancient Romans made a fresh noodle called lagane, a name still used in Campania for a fresh, short ribbon eaten mainly with beans and chickpeas. The Roman word is also the root of "lasagne."

There are many fresh pastas made in Campania, but the advent and advancement of dried pasta as we know it today is a development particular to Naples. It was the mid-sixteenth century, but the same story as in ancient times: a need to store grain. Under the mismanagement of the ruling Spanish viceroys and local barons, the outlying provinces of Naples became subject to famines. Country people flooded the city. Supplies of grain became more taxed by the demand. By the turn of the sixteenth century, Naples was the second most populous city in Europe, after Paris. Grain shortages became more frequent.

Dried pasta was already well known. It may have been introduced from Sicily, where the first written mention of macaroni was dated 1126 in Arabic. The word "macaroni" is probably from Arabic. Naturally, not to be outdone by the Sicilians, some Neapolitans also like to lay claim to an early acquaintance with macaroni. In a story meant to be culturally self-deprecating, making fun of the Neapolitans' tendency to be boastful about everything Neapolitan, Matilde Serao (1856–1927), the revered Neapolitan journalist, essayist, novelist, and founder of *Il Mattino*, the Neapolitan daily newspaper, tells the legend of a magician: In 1220, this conjurer, who lived like a hermit in the Vico dei Cortellari, a street in Naples, emerged from his cave and announced that he had invented macaroni. The only problem is, by the time he came out, everyone was eating it already.

Everyone wasn't really eating macaroni until the seventeenth century, by which time Neapolitans were feeling it prudent to keep macaroni at hand against the threat of famine, plague, or an eruption of Vesuvius. In 1631, there was a huge eruption, and some historians consider that a turning point for pasta. To quote contemporary Neapolitan food writer Stefano Milioni, pasta became "the symbol of a nation not for its gastronomic merits, not because it was a fashionable food able to deal out pleasures, but only for its skill in fighting hunger and lack of resources."

Until the beginning of the eighteenth century, dried pasta was essentially the food of the poor. Its consumption on the street—eaten with the hands and dressed only with cheese—is depicted in innumerable watercolors, etchings, and paintings. These pictures are often said to be from the late nineteenth century and are used as proof that spaghetti with tomato sauce was not yet a food of the people. Those later pictures, however, were depicting old times as souvenirs for tourists. By the middle of the nineteenth century, tomato sauce was well established and eaten by everyone.

Spaghetti drying on the streets of early-twentieth-century Naples.

Now, while all of the region enjoys a bowl of spaghetti with tomato sauce or ziti with ragù, one can, in fact, divide the region into three pasta zones. (1) The cities of Naples and Salerno definitely favor factory-

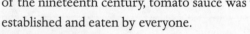
FOOD SAFETY, EIGHTEENTH-CENTURY NEAPOLITAN-STYLE
When macaroni was cooked and eaten on the streets of Naples, the plates were sanitized by being dipped into the boiling pasta water.

FERDINAND AND THE FORK

Catherine de Medici is duly credited with introducing the three-pronged fork to the refined table. Until the Florentine aristocrat, who married King Henry II of France in 1533, did so, there was only a two-pronged fork in general use, and it was for holding meat, to transfer it from platter to an individual plate, and to hold the meat down while it was being carved.

In the early part of Ferdinand IV's reign, in the 1770s, about the same time his queen Maria Carolina was refining Neapolitan cooking, making it more French and more court-worthy (see pages xl–xli), Ferdinand, a notoriously gross fellow who identified with the commonest of his subjects (for which they naturally loved him), decided that macaroni, the food that sustained his subjects, should be eaten every day at court.

As the first Neapolitan-born king, and a supporter of all things Neapolitan, the king loved his macaroni and spaghetti, or vermicelli as Neapolitans still prefer to call the long strands. However, at the time, Neapolitans were eating vermicelli with their hands, drawing the pasta above their tilted heads and letting it fall into their mouths. Such table manners were disdained by Maria Carolina, a refined Hapsburg princess. To placate her, Ferdinand asked, or rather demanded, that his chief steward, Giovanni Spadaccino, develop an eating implement that could manage to get the pasta to his mouth without such sloppiness. Hence, the four-pronged table fork on which long pasta could easily be twirled.

This may be mere legend, however, because there is another story involving pasta, Ferdinand, and Spadaccino. In this version, it was not the four-tined fork for eating pasta that Spadaccino invented, but a timballetto di maccheroni, which in its day was called sformato Ferdinandaio (Ferdinand's mold). The pasta was mezzanelli—a strand as long as spaghetti but with a hole in the center, in essence large bucatini—and it was baked in round dishes, then unmolded, making it easy to eat with a fork. It is said that the dish was welcomed with great enthusiasm by the court, and the diners amused themselves by piercing the pasta with forks. The pasta would jump around still, leaving stains of sauce on the tablecloths and on their clothes, but no one seemed to mind.

made dried pasta. (2) Along the Caserta coast north of Naples and the Salerno coast south of Naples, fresh pasta usually has eggs. (3) In the mountainous areas, the fresh pasta is usually made from only flour and water or with very few eggs.

There are also pastas that are particular to a place. In Amalfi, scialatielli (page 155) is a fresh pasta made with milk instead of water, and with grated cheese and either basil or parsley in the dough. Parsley goes in when the sauce is seafood, basil when the sauce is eggplant or zucchini. Scialatielli are very fashionable all over Campania now because so many chefs are from Amalfi.

In Capri, the ravioli the locals are so proud of is an eggless pasta filled with caciotta, a basket cheese that comes fresh or salted and slightly aged, and dried marjoram, which grows wild on the island. In the summer it is sauced with a simple fresh tomato sauce, in the winter with ragù.

In Avellino, they make a flour and water pasta that is shaped like a condom, a sort of very large orecchietta, with the center portion very thin and a ridge or frame of thicker dough. It's called gnocchi di Avellino, although it is not a dumpling at all.

Potato gnocchi are a dish of Sorrento, usually baked with tomato sauce and mozzarella. However, gnocchi to most Campanians means strangoloprieti, chewy strands that "strangled the priest" because he was either too greedy or the pasta is so chewy, depending on which story one subscribes to.

Following are the main pasta shapes of the region.

PASTA VENDOR

Il maccarunaro was the street vendor who cooked and sold all kinds of pasta. When they came on the scene, making pasta available to the poorest of the poor, they changed the Neapolitans from "leaf eaters" to "pasta eaters." In those days, instead of asking for "al dente," one yelled, in dialect, *"Vierdi, vierdi!"* ("Green, green!"), the Neapolitans' (literally) colorful way of saying they wanted it freshly boiled and still firm.

Neapolitan Pasta Shapes

DRY PASTA

SPAGHETTI (LITTLE STRANDS OR STRINGS) OR VERMICELLI (LITTLE WORMS)

Neapolitans do use the word "spaghetti," but they prefer the word "vermicelli." The big pasta companies accommodate their preference by using local parlance on their packages of pasta sold in the city. Depending on the manufacturer, vermicelli can be thicker or thinner, but it is never thinner than our thin spaghetti (or spaghettini) and rarely as thick as our regular spaghetti. Vermicelli is good with tomato sauce or ragù, of course, and any seasoning that doesn't have large pieces in it. Large bits of food do not integrate with long strands of pasta. The point is to have every mouthful have every flavor in it.

ZITI

We know ziti as a flat-cut tube about one-quarter inch in diameter (when still dried) and two inches or so long. It is actually a long tubular pasta, one that is the length of or longer than spaghetti. The reason many pasta manufacturers refer to their ziti as "cut ziti" is that these long tubes have been cut to the size sold. In the old days (and some people still do this), the ziti was broken into short lengths by the cook. Uncut ziti was and still is used for baked macaroni dishes, but when the shape is used with sauce it is always cut or broken. It is the classic pasta for ragù ('e zite cu' rragù in Salernitan dialect), for Genovese (pages 57–64), and for baked dishes, such as ziti alla Sorrentina (the original baked ziti, page 190). Uncut ziti is occasionally available in specialty food stores.

LINGUINE (LITTLE TONGUES)

Neapolitans are happy to eat seafood with spaghetti (and several other pastas), but mostly they prefer linguine. It "catches the flavor" better, they say. Indeed, the famous spaghetti and clam dish of Naples is often called linguine pe' vongole in Neapolitan dialect (page 146), even when prepared with spaghetti.

BUCATINI AND PERCIATELLI

Bucatini is thin spaghetti-length macaroni pierced with a small hole. It is the finest tubular pasta. Perciatelli is Neapolitan dialect for the same pasta. (It derives from the dialect verb *perciare*—to make a hole.) Some manufacturers use both names, however, making one slightly finer than the other. It is used with piquant sauces, such as puttanesca (page 164), in baked pastas, and with ricotta and tomato sauce (page 159).

TUBETTONI (LARGE TUBES) There are many names for large tubes. Tubettoni is generic for all of them. The largest are called paccheri (also spelled paccari), and Campanians love them the most. I sometimes think they love saying the name as much as they love eating them. Paccheri are so big that they flop closed when cooked, and the name is supposedly onomatopoeic for the slapping sound they make as you eat them. Large tubes are used with beans, so the beans get trapped in the pasta. Paccheri are also a classic pasta for a dressing of ricotta and tomato sauce (page 159). They have other uses, too, including, on occasion, being filled and baked. Pastas labeled paccheri are available in the United States, at specialty markets, but the ones I've purchased imported from Puglia are not as long or large as the Neapolitan version. Use instead pastas labeled manicotti or cannelloni, preferably without ridges. They are essentially the same as paccheri. Since paccheri break in the plate and become a somewhat flat noodle, another good substitute is lasagne broken into two- to three-inch lengths.

TUBETTI (LITTLE TUBES) AND DITALI (THIMBLES) Small tubes are dressed with creamy sauces and sauces with peas or small beans. Campanians love peas caught inside pasta tubes. It's again that idea that every flavor in the dish should be in every mouthful.

CAPELLI D'ANGELO OR CAPELLINI (ANGEL HAIR OR FINE HAIR) The finest of all strand pastas is used mainly in broth and often with lentils.

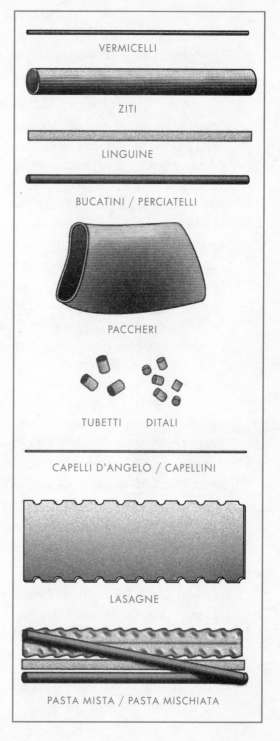

VERMICELLI

ZITI

LINGUINE

BUCATINI / PERCIATELLI

PACCHERI

TUBETTI   DITALI

CAPELLI D'ANGELO / CAPELLINI

LASAGNE

PASTA MISTA / PASTA MISCHIATA

LASAGNE (FLAT STRIPS) This wide pasta is used, as it is in North America, for baked dishes. The most famous Neapolitan version is the rich, pre-Lenten, cheese-and-meat-filled Lasagne di Carnevale (page 206), which is the prototype for Italian-American lasagne.

PASTA MISTA, PASTA MISCHIATA (ASSORTED PASTA SHAPES AND PIECES) Until packaged pasta became widely available after World War I, macaroni products were bought loose at the local grocer. He'd pack them into cones of dark blue paper (hence the color of so much of today's pasta packaging), weighing out individual orders. Eventually, the grocer would be left with bits and pieces and odd lots of pasta that he would combine and sell at a bargain rate. These leftovers were called minuzzaglia or munnezzaglia. Today, they are sold in bags and boxes as pasta mista or pasta mischiata. The packages usually contain a mix of tubular shapes—ditali, penne, cavatappi (corkscrews), plus broken laganelle, a long, ripple-edged ribbon pasta that is also called mafaldine in Naples, and broken spaghetti or capellini. They do not all cook at the same time, but that, in fact, is a point in its favor. Pasta mista provides several textures to play against the creamy beans and lentils. It also provides interest to the simplest minestre—pasta and potatoes (page 106), pasta and pumpkin (page 108), etc.—those dishes of *la cucina povera* on which Campanians still dote.

FRESH PASTA

RAVIOLI In Campania, round, ricotta-filled ravioli are the standard, often without even a speck of parsley in the filling, as they often have elsewhere. Sometimes the pasta has eggs; more often it is a surprisingly tender fresh flour and water pasta. The trick to its tenderness—along with a skill that takes time to acquire—is using boiling water. Ricotta ravioli are most often served with tomato sauce (in summer) or ragù (in cold months), but they can also be dressed with sautéed porcini and other delicacies, including black truffle butter. On Capri, they have particular ravioli (see page 131).

FUSILLI (SPIRALS) Factory-made spirals, as are sold in North America, are available to Campanians, too. But when they say fusilli, they mean a fresh flour and water pasta that is formed on a metal rod (*fuso* means spindle). (See pasta and beans, page 96.) Fusilli with ragù are considered "the living end," but the pasta is also served with beans and with Genovese.

COOKING PASTA AND PASTA COOKING WATER

The rule of thumb for cooking pasta is to use one quart of water for every 100 grams (three and a half ounces) of pasta. Therefore, for twelve ounces of pasta, four portions, you should use between four and five quarts of water; for one pound of pasta, five to six quarts is best. Salt—no less than a teaspoon per quart of water—should be added when the water comes to a boil, at which point the water will momentarily stop boiling. When it returns to a boil, add the pasta and cover the pot so the water returns to a boil quickly. When it does, uncover the pot, stir the pasta to make sure it is not sticking to itself or the pot, and, keeping the pot uncovered and the water at a rolling boil, stir the pasta a few more times while it is boiling.

The starchy, salted water that results from cooking pasta can be an invaluable ingredient. It can be a thinning agent, or, because it is starchy, it can be a thickener. Campanian cooks—actually cooks all over Italy—use spoons of it to loosen a tight sauce, to stretch a sauce, or sometimes as a major ingredient in a sauce, giving it a creaminess it would otherwise not have.

It has been written elsewhere that this is a technique of restaurant chefs and should be avoided by home cooks because it tends to obscure the brightness of fresh ingredients, but I've seen many home cooks use their precious pasta cooking water to great advantage. I do it myself, and I have never noticed any dulling of flavors. Indeed, there is an old Neapolitan habit of not draining pasta in a colander at all, but lifting it out of the pot with a fork, leaving the pasta a bit more drippy than if it had been well drained. This is depicted in paintings and engravings of the late eighteenth and early nineteenth centuries. In the earliest days of pasta eating, before tomato sauce existed or was common, when hot spaghetti was sold from street stands and carts, its clinging moisture would essentially form a sauce with the grated cheese that was its only condiment.

Nowadays, whenever I am in doubt about the consistency of a pasta sauce, I scoop out a cup of pasta cooking water before draining the pasta, keeping it on the side just in case it's needed. Many recipes in this chapter suggest you do the same.

Always try to serve pasta in warmed bowls.

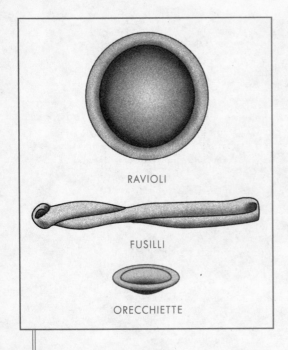

RAVIOLI

FUSILLI

ORECCHIETTE

ORECCHIETTE (LITTLE EARS) Small "ears" of fresh flour and water pasta, inch-wide cupped disks formed with the thumb, are made most notably in Avellino, and may originally be a pasta of neighboring Puglia, but they are popular all over the south of Italy and are usually served with vegetables, broccoli rabe being by far the most popular (see page 168).

LAGANE, LAGANELLE, LAVANELLE, LAINE These are the various names for a short, fresh ribbon made from flour and water. They are used exclusively with beans and chick peas (see page 95).

CAVATELLI These curled nubbins of dough—not unlike gnocchi—are, in Campania, eaten mainly in Benevento. When well made they are seductively tender. As with ravioli, the secret to their tenderness is using boiling water to moisten the flour, plus considerable skill. Fortunately, good cavatelli can be purchased frozen in many American markets.

Pasta with Eggs

Tubetti Cacio e Uova

Tubular Macaroni with Cheese and Egg

Cacio e uova, beaten eggs with grated cheese, is one of the oldest ways of dressing pasta. It predates the rise of the tomato in the eighteenth century, and points to the wide and easy availability of eggs and cheese in the old days and how they were used in small quantity to add protein to a largely vegetable diet. The magic of eggs thickening and cheese melting from the heat of the food forms a sauce or, more precisely, a creamy flavor coating.

Pasta cacio e uova is in truth seldom made these days, but the egg and cheese amalgam still plays its part in Campania's zucchini soup, Minestra di Zucchine Cacio e Uova (page 120), and in the lamb stew with peas prepared for Easter (page 289). Stracciatella, the cheese and egg mixture that is curdled into broth (as in Zuppa di Santé, page 114) is also a form of cacio e uova. I think of this as the Campanian version of the classic Abruzzese carbonara, and like carbonara it is eaten with a copious amount of freshly ground black pepper.

Serves 4 to 6

1 pound short, tubular macaroni, such as ziti or penne;
smaller tubes such as ditali or pennette, or perciatelli or mezzanelli,
broken into 2- to 3-inch lengths

3 tablespoons butter, extra-virgin olive oil, or lard

3 eggs

1 teaspoon freshly ground black pepper

¾ cup loosely packed parsley or basil leaves, finely cut

¾ cup freshly grated pecorino

¾ cup freshly grated Parmigiano-Reggiano

1. Cook the macaroni in plenty of well-salted boiling water.

2. Meanwhile, place the fat of choice in the bowl in which you will toss the pasta. Put the bowl in a 200-degree oven.

(continued)

3. In another bowl, beat the eggs with a fork, then beat in the pepper and parsley or basil.

4. Drain the pasta.

5. Remove the hot bowl from the oven—carefully with pot holders—and immediately pour the macaroni into the heated fat. Toss to coat the macaroni with fat, then pour in the egg mixture and continue tossing until lightly blended and the eggs have thickened slightly. They should not curdle, but if they do the dish will still be delicious, if not as attractive or as smooth on the tongue.

6. Add the grated cheeses and toss again to mix thoroughly. Work quickly so the pasta doesn't cool too much.

7. Serve immediately, and pass the pepper mill for those who like a more piquant dish or appreciate the aroma of freshly grated pepper.

[Macaroni] is a healthy food, which easily fills you up, inexpensive, and the Neapolitan gets more benefit from it than from polenta. The wealthy dress macaroni in a variety of ways, but the Neapolitan eats it most often just with simple white cheese. To the side of the large and steaming pot of macaroni (caldaia maccaronese) is a wide plate or basin (scafarea) filled with a new Egyptian pyramid—of white cheese, decorated with black stripes of pepper and often topped with a tomato or red flower.

—C. T. Dalbono, *Usi e costumi di Napoli* (Neapolitan Ways and Customs), a collection of essays published in 1866

'O Vermiciello, 'O Puvuriello

Spaghetti ro Puveriello / Spaghetti alla "Puverielle"

Poor Man's Spaghetti

Spaghetti con L'uovo Fritto alla Salernitana

Spaghetti with Fried Eggs, Salerno-Style

Neapolitans revere and romanticize the food of their poverty, as the musical dialect names of this dish reveal. It is, after all, clever cooking that got them through natural disasters, political and criminal oppressions, the overcrowding and dangers of the inner cities. In some cases, a dish called by one of the above names is the same as cacio e uova, eggs and cheese beaten together, which, when tossed with hot pasta and oil or lard or butter, or heated gently with the pasta, form a creamy sauce (see preceding recipe). Using exactly the same ingredients but a different cooking technique, this has a totally different effect. Soft clouds of gently fried egg white mingle with spaghetti coated with the yolks, grated cheese, plenty of black pepper, and, if you wish, a hint of garlic. I particularly like the version without cheese, but with garlic, and with a little lard, if not all lard. Here is hard evidence of how, in poorer days, eggs were a main source of protein in the Campanian diet, one of the reasons there aren't many recipes for the chickens that lay them.

For each person:

3 to 4 ounces thin spaghetti

2 tablespoons extra-virgin olive oil or lard

1 large clove garlic, lightly smashed

1 teaspoon lard (if not using all lard)

2 eggs

Freshly ground black pepper

Optional: Grated Parmigiano-Reggiano or pecorino cheese

1. Cook the spaghetti in well-salted boiling water until al dente.

2. Meanwhile, in a small skillet, over medium-low heat, combine the oil and the garlic. Cook the garlic, pressing it into the oil a couple of times to release its flavor, until it barely begins to color on both sides. Remove the garlic. Add the teaspoon of lard now if you aren't cooking entirely with lard.

(continued)

3. Break the eggs into the pan and cook gently, lowering the heat if necessary, so that when the spaghetti is cooked, the egg whites will be set and the yolks still runny.

4. Drain the spaghetti well and toss well with the eggs and all the fat in the pan, breaking up the whites as you do. Season generously with freshly ground black pepper and eat immediately, with grated cheese if desired.

SPAGHETTI DI ETTORE

SPAGHETTI WITH FRIED EGGS AND ROASTED PEPPERS

THIS IS THE SENSATIONAL creation of Cecilia Bellelli Baratta, owner of Tenuta Seliano in Paestum, a working farm that takes in guests as part of Italy's Agri-Tourism system. It is less than a mile away from Paestum's Greek temples and museum. Cecilia often prepares this for her guests because it is always a huge success, but it started as a family dish, a favorite of her now-adult son, Barone Ettore Bellelli, who runs the family's water buffalo operation. It's an elaboration on spaghetti with fried eggs (see preceding recipe), in essence combining that dish with a gratin of roasted red peppers (see page 346). Incidentally, Cecilia, who does indeed do some of the cooking at Seliano, is hardly a simple farm woman. She is a highly educated and cultured businesswoman who speaks several languages, is an art and antique collector (her guest rooms in elegantly converted former farm buildings benefit from that hobby), and a breeder of thoroughbred horses. It was for horse breeding that her late husband's ancestor, the first Barone Bellelli, earned his title from Joachim Murat, Napoleon's brother-in-law, who was installed as King of Naples from 1808 to 1815, during Napoleon's brief rule. Murat's faded, framed proclamation hangs in Cecilia's huge wood-beamed dining room, formerly stables.

Serves 4

2 red bell peppers

1 tablespoon salted capers, thoroughly rinsed, coarsely chopped if large

1 or 2 large cloves garlic, finely chopped (or more to taste)

¼ cup finely cut parsley

Salt

Freshly ground black pepper

3 rounded tablespoons fresh or dried bread crumbs

5 tablespoons extra-virgin olive oil

12 ounces spaghetti, linguine, or bucatini

2 eggs

Optional: Freshly grated Parmigiano-Reggiano or pecorino, or a combination

1. Roast, peel, and clean the peppers according to the directions on page 344. Cut them into ¼-inch-wide, lengthwise strips.

2. In a small baking dish, combine the pepper strips, the capers, the garlic, and the parsley. Season with salt and freshly ground pepper. Sprinkle bread crumbs on top. Set aside until you are ready to finish the dish. This can be done as far ahead as the morning for the evening.

3. When ready to assemble the dish, put water to boil for the pasta. Just before placing the pasta in the salted water, drizzle the pepper mixture with 2 tablespoons of the olive oil, then place it in a preheated 350-degree oven for 10 minutes.

4. While the pasta is boiling and the peppers are baking, fry the eggs over medium heat, in 2 or 3 tablespoons of olive oil, sunny-side up, until the whites are set and the yolks are still runny.

5. Drain the pasta and pour it into a large (preferably heated) serving bowl. Using 2 forks, toss in the baked peppers and the fried eggs, using some or all of the egg-cooking olive oil, too. As you toss, break the whites into pieces and let the yolks act as sauce—they will spread over the pasta and cook further from the heat of it.

6. Check for salt and pepper and serve immediately with or without grated Parmigiano or pecorino cheese.

Pasta with Fish*

Spaghetti con Acciughe

'E Vermicielle C'alice Salate

Spaghetti with Anchovies

So much depends on the fine points for this dish to be right. First, its appeal depends mainly on the quality of the anchovies and the olive oil, but there's much more to it than that. It's not as nearly foolproof as aglio-olio, with which it competes in popularity in Campania, because there's an extra ingredient to showcase and balance. In the province of Salerno, where anchovies are still preserved under salt or salt water in crockery, everyone understands these fine points, although, of course, not everyone agrees on what they are.

Much is made of cooking the anchovies at nearly the same moment that the spaghetti is done, a sort of acrobatic feat that can turn balletic with practice. The theory is, the anchovies are losing fragrance with every passing second. So you must time their sizzle, smashing, and dissolution in oil—a 15- to 20-second operation that requires full attention—about the same time that you should be draining the spaghetti. As for garlic, too much obscures the sweet-salty sea-breeze perfume of a Salernitan anchovy, so more than a hint is too much. On the other hand, if the anchovies aren't the absolute best, a little more garlic may be in order. Use your taste and judgment, as you must to make a grand success of it.

Serves 2 or 3

½ pound spaghetti

6 tablespoons extra-virgin olive oil

1 or 2 cloves garlic, lightly smashed

Big pinch hot red pepper flakes, or to taste

6 whole salted anchovies, thoroughly rinsed and filleted, or 12 oil-packed
anchovy fillets, rinsed

4 or 5 tablespoons fine, dry bread crumbs

* (See also Fish and Seafood chapter, page 226)

1.   Cook the spaghetti in plenty of well-salted boiling water.

2.   Meanwhile, in an 8-inch skillet, over low heat, warm the olive oil, the garlic, and the hot pepper together, pressing the garlic into the oil a couple of times to release its flavor. Cook until the garlic is soft and barely colored on both sides, then remove.

3.   Seconds before the spaghetti is ready to be drained, add the anchovies to the hot oil and smash them into the oil, using a table fork or the back of a wooden spoon. They will dissolve quickly. Raise the heat slightly if necessary.

4.   Drain the spaghetti and turn it into the skillet with the anchovy oil. Toss well until all the strands have been seasoned with the anchovy sauce.

5.   Fork the spaghetti into warmed individual bowls or a large serving bowl. Toss the bread crumbs in the oil left in the pan, sprinkle them on the spaghetti, and eat immediately. (Cheese is totally inappropriate.)

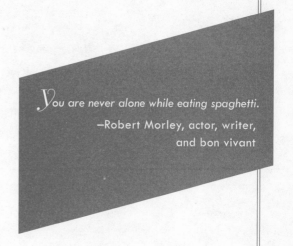

You are never alone while eating spaghetti.
—Robert Morley, actor, writer,
and bon vivant

Linguine all'Amalfitana

Linguine with Walnuts and Anchovies

AFTER A MORNING OF cooking with the chefs at La Palumba, the famous luxury hotel in Ravello, learning some of the local dishes as well as a couple of the hotel's signature dishes, I turned to Giuseppe Cretella, a young cook who was born and still lives down the hill, in Amalfi. "You're hanging out with your buddies and suddenly you're all hungry. What would you make?" I asked. Without hesitating, he shot back with this recipe that takes less time to cook than the pasta. In fact, the pasta briefly finishes cooking in the sauce, which is made up of the seasonings and some of the pasta cooking water. This last step is all-important because not only does the pasta cooking water reduce the need for a large amount of oil to lubricate the pasta, but it carries the flavors of the anchovies, garlic, and walnuts into each strand. In the end, the pasta will be beige, full of flavor, but without any liquid sauce.

Serves 2 or 3

½ pound linguine

3 tablespoons extra-virgin olive oil

3 large cloves garlic, lightly smashed

⅓ to ½ cup shelled walnuts, coarsely chopped (pieces no bigger than ¼ inch, but not too many that are much smaller)

⅛ teaspoon hot red pepper flakes, or more to taste

4 whole salted anchovies, thoroughly rinsed and filleted, or 8 oil-packed anchovy fillets, rinsed

1. Cook the linguine in plenty of well-salted boiling water.

2. Meanwhile, in a deep 10-inch skillet or sauté pan, over low heat, combine the oil and garlic, cooking the garlic until it is soft and barely colors on both sides, smashing it into the oil a few times to release its flavor.

3. When the garlic is just beginning to color on one side, add the nuts and the pepper flakes. Remove the garlic as it is done on the other side, and continue frying the walnuts and pepper another minute or so.

4. Increase the heat to medium, add the anchovies, and smash them into the oil with a wooden spoon. As soon as they dissolve—which is almost immediately—scoop out ½ cup of the pasta cooking water and add it to the pan. Remove the sauce from the heat until the pasta is cooked.

5. When the pasta is still a little undercooked—about 2 minutes less time than usual—drain it, then turn it into the pan with the sauce. Cook the linguine in the sauce, stirring and tossing constantly, until all the liquid has been absorbed and the pasta is tender enough to eat.

6. Serve immediately, making sure each plate has about the same amount of walnuts, and a few on top.

LINGUINE, SPAGHETTI O VERMICELLI ALLE VONGOLE

PASTA WITH CLAM SAUCE

---

*Pasta with clams or mussels should be avoided if you are in the city or inland.
. . . If you are eating outside, on a terrace by the sea or under a pergola filtering
the bright sun, and a soft wind rumples your hair and caresses your cheeks; if
there is an immaculate tablecloth with blindingly shiny cutlery and sparkling
glasses giving off blue and green highlights; and if you hear the sea with its soft,
muffled recurrent murmuring stretching out beneath you; if the faraway sails
contrast with the expanse of water and your nostrils breathe in the pungent
saltiness, and if you are surrounded by the joy of waiters rushing about, of
laughter and toasts; if a sweet nostalgic Neapolitan tune is being played on a
mandolin and a voice sings: "Vicino 'o mare facimmo 'ammore . . . [Near the sea
we'll make love . . .]," only then can you fully savor pasta with clams.*

—JEANNE CAROLA FRANCESCONI,
LA CUCINA NAPOLETANA (NEAPOLITAN COOKING)

THIS IS, AFTER SPAGHETTI with tomato sauce, the most popular pasta dish of the
region, and despite Francesconi's warning, it is deeply appreciated everywhere—in
restaurants in the country, far from the sea, at home, and in trattorias along the dark narrow streets of Naples's old quarters. Campanians will wax rhapsodic about ragù, Genovese, fresh tomato sauce as it tastes on Ferragosto, at the peak of tomato season, but
they eat pasta with clams whenever possible. Yes, they appreciate it more by the seaside,
but they make it from the hills of Avellino to the cliffs of the Cilento. When I asked a
chef in the interior how it was that pasta and clams was so popular in his restaurant, he
explained that the Autostrada now connects every corner of Campania with a fish market—either the huge one in Pozzuoli, the famous suburb of Naples, now said to be the
most important fish market in southern Italy or the smaller market in Salerno.

The particular clams of Naples, vongole veraci, tiny, striped-shelled bivalves, are
not available in the United States, but an excellent facsimile of the Neapolitan sauce
can be made with the tiny Manila clams you can now find in American markets. East
Coast Littleneck clams will do, but including their larger shells with the pasta makes
for a very clumsy dish.

Whichever clams you use, you should be aware that different batches of clams give off dramatically different amounts of liquid. If you happen to have some that don't express much liquid when cooked, cook the pasta all the way and do not finish its cooking in the clam juices, as the recipe instructs. Just dress the pasta with the clams and their juices. As a last resort, you can add more olive oil or a little bit of pasta cooking water.

Serves 3 or 4

1 recipe Sautè di Vongole (page 236)

3 tablespoons extra-virgin olive oil

12 ounces thin or regular linguine or spaghetti

1. Prepare the clams according to the recipe, but use an additional 3 tablespoons of olive oil and do not stir in the parsley. When the clams have opened, remove them and set aside in a bowl, covered to keep them warm. You may want to remove some of the clams from their shells, reserving a few for garnish. Or you might serve all the clams in their shells.

2. Cook the pasta very al dente—a full minute less than fully cooked—drain it, then turn it into the pan with clam juices. Toss and cook over medium heat until the pasta is done to taste. It will absorb most of the clam juices. Toss with the parsley. If using shelled clams, toss them in along with the parsley.

3. Portion the pasta into hot bowls and top with the clams in their shells. Serve immediately.

VARIATION:

Rosa Mazzella, whose linguine alle vongole is gorgeous, was the first of several Neapolitans to tell me that "tomatoes carry flavor," by way of explaining why she puts a couple of diced cherry tomatoes in hers. It gives the clam juices a rosé color, and sometimes the dish will even be referred to as linguine alle vongole rosé. For what it is worth, back in the more scientifically analytical United States, I learned that tomatoes are naturally high in glutamates (as in monosodium glutamate) and probably do enhance other flavors. For the above proportions, add at most 2 or 3 diced ripe cherry tomatoes.

It is very fashionable to toss fried zucchini rounds with the pasta and use a few to garnish the bowl.

RAGÙ D'ASTICE

LOBSTER RAGÙ FOR FUSILLI OR PACCHERI

THE MAIN INGREDIENT HERE is a luxurious lobster, but the recipe is an exercise in Neapolitan frugality. Rita De Rosa, who raised her sons in the Vomero, a solidly middle-class section of Naples, but now cooks in her sons' restaurant in New York, makes one lobster serve four. The shell flavors the sweet cherry tomato sauce. The meat is sautéed and served on top of the sauced pasta. It's a great dish and an easy recipe, except that some patience is required if you want to salvage every bit of flavor from that lobster shell.

Serves 3 or 4

1 1½-pound lobster

3 tablespoons very finely minced celery (½ large rib)

3 tablespoons very finely minced carrot (1 small)

¼ cup very finely minced onion (½ small)

2 tablespoons extra-virgin olive oil

3 tablespoons red wine

1 pint cherry tomatoes (about 20), cut in half

1 tablespoon tomato paste dissolved in ¼ cup water

Pinch hot red pepper flakes

8 ounces long fusilli or paccheri (or other very large tubular pasta)

2 tablespoons extra-virgin olive oil

Optional: 1 tablespoon finely cut parsley

1.   Split the lobster in half and crack the claws and the joint below the claws (or have your fish merchant do this if you are cooking the lobster within a few hours of purchase). With a boning knife or other narrow-bladed knife, detach the body meat from the shell. Then, using a teaspoon, scrape out every last bit of lobster meat. Do the same with the claws. Cut the large pieces of lobster into sizable bite-size pieces—to be used as garnish—and store the lobster meat in a bowl, in the refrigerator, until ready to cook, which will be just before serving.

2.   In a medium saucepan, combine the minced vegetables and oil. Place over medium heat, and as soon as the vegetables begin to sizzle, reduce the heat so they cook very slowly. Add all the lobster shells, broken up if necessary to fit into the pot. Cook the vegetables and lobster shells over low heat, stirring occasionally and scraping the vegetables down so they remain on the bottom of the pan, until the vegetables are very, very tender—practically dissolved, but not browned, about 20 minutes.

3.   Add the wine and cook until nearly evaporated.

4.   Add the cherry tomatoes, the tomato paste dissolved in water, and the pepper flakes. (The sauce will likely not need salt because lobster is salty.) Cook over medium-low heat, stirring occasionally, until the tomatoes have become a sauce, about 20 minutes.

5.   Remove the lobster shells, scraping any sauce out of them and into the pot, and set the shells aside to cool. Pass the sauce through a food mill, then return the sauce to the saucepan.

6.   When the lobster shells have cooled enough to handle, break up the legs and squeeze out the tiny bits of sweet leg meat. Scrape any last bit of meat or sauce from the shells before discarding them. The sauce can be made ahead to this point. Keep refrigerated if holding more than an hour or so.

7.   Cook the pasta in plenty of salted, boiling water.

8.   While the pasta is cooking, heat the remaining 2 tablespoons of oil in a small skillet and sauté the reserved lobster meat until just cooked through, no more than a couple of minutes. Just before the pasta is tender enough to eat, drain it and finish cooking it for a minute or so in the hot sauce.

9.   Serve the pasta in heated bowls, topped with the sautéed lobster meat and, if desired, a sprinkling of finely cut parsley.

SPAGHETTI CON TONNO SOTT'OLIO

SPAGHETTI WITH CANNED TUNA

IN AGROPOLI, A THRIVING resort town at the southern end of the coast south of Salerno, near the beaches on which the Allies landed to liberate Naples in 1943, you can still buy home-canned tuna. There is a long tradition of preserving tuna in olive oil along the Campanian coast, yet these days good canned or jarred tuna is expensive all over Italy, and I find it is being used sparingly. We are lucky to have a constant and relatively inexpensive supply in North America, canned tuna being the best-selling fish in the United States. Try to find solid, light tuna packed in olive oil. Two domestic brands, Bumble Bee (in the green, white, and red-striped can) and Progresso, are excellent. Genova brand is a good, widely available Italian import that is about the same price and quality as the rather pricey Progresso. With the exception of aglio-olio, nothing could be easier and quicker than this recipe. I proportioned it for two because I think that's as many as can be satisfied by a single six-ounce can of tuna.

Serves 2

6 ounces spaghetti, linguine, or tubular macaroni

1 6-ounce can tuna fish packed in olive oil, drained,
but reserving 2 to 3 tablespoons of the oil from the can

2 large cloves garlic, finely minced

Pinch of hot red pepper flakes

2 tablespoons finely cut parsley

1 tablespoon extra-virgin olive oil

1.   Cook the pasta in plenty of salted, boiling water.

2.   While the pasta cooks, in a 7- or 8-inch skillet, combine the olive oil from the tuna can with the garlic and the hot pepper. Place over low heat. Cook the garlic until it is soft and barely begins to color, pressing it into the oil a few times to release its flavor. Remove the garlic.

3.   Using a table fork, break the tuna into the skillet and stir it into the oil, making sure not to make it mushy.

4. Drain the pasta, reserving ½ cup of the pasta cooking water.

5. Toss the pasta in the skillet with the parsley and the tuna and oil, adding a few tablespoons or more of the pasta cooking water and a tablespoon of uncooked extra-virgin olive oil.

6. Serve immediately.

VERMICELLI ALLA CAMPOLATTARO

SPAGHETTI WITH CANNED TUNA AND ANCHOVY SAUCE

DON EMILIO CAPOMAZZA, Marchese di Campolattaro, lived in the second half of the nineteenth century, and to quote Jeanne Carola Francesconi, "He was a versatile and cultured gentleman, of great charm [she uses the French word *charme*] and was a fascinating conversationalist. He was Mayor of Naples and a member of parliament, but he did not disdain the cultivation of the most prosaic of the arts: He created three famous pasta recipes that were named for him."

Of course, Don Emilio had a *Monzù* chef who prepared this dish for him and his guests, but it was not uncommon to direct your *Monzù* to create recipes for you, or, at least, to have his dishes named for you, his patron. This is the most approachable and oft-quoted of the "three famous pasta recipes" named for Campolattaro. It is totally contemporary in taste, absolutely delicious, and can be served as a family dish or as the first course for a more formal meal.

Serves 5 or 6

(continued)

4 whole salted anchovies, thoroughly rinsed and filleted, or 8 oil-packed
anchovy fillets, rinsed

1 6-ounce can tuna packed in olive oil, drained

1 13½-ounce can beef broth, with enough water to make 2 cups

½ teaspoon freshly ground black pepper

¼ teaspoon hot red pepper flakes

1 pound spaghetti

4 tablespoons sweet butter

2 tablespoons extra-virgin olive oil

2 tablespoons finely chopped parsley

1. In a blender, puree the anchovies and the tuna with ½ cup of the broth.

2. In a 10- to 12-inch skillet, combine the puree with the rest of the broth, the black pepper, and the hot red pepper. Bring the mixture to a boil over high heat. Cook briskly until the sauce reduces slightly, about 5 minutes, stirring frequently at the beginning, constantly at the end. Set aside.

3. Cook the pasta in plenty of salted, boiling water until not quite done to taste. Drain the pasta, then return it to the pot.

4. Toss the pasta with the butter, the oil, and the parsley. Pour the prepared sauce over the pasta and toss well over medium-high heat for a few minutes to finish the pasta's cooking and to let the pasta absorb the flavor of the sauce.

5. Serve immediately. (Cheese is not appropriate.)

PACCHERI MARE DA GEMMA

DA GEMMA'S LARGE MACARONI TUBES WITH FISH SAUCE

THIS DISH IS OFTEN described by travel writers and noted in travel guides. It is easy to make, delicious, and altogether justifiably famous, but I think it gained its fame mainly because it is the signature dish of Trattoria Da Gemma, the restaurant directly across the piazza from the colorfully decorated Arab-Norman style Duomo in Amalfi, a major tourist destination. You can eat it while looking out windows facing the exotic-looking cathedral, an architectural reminder of the foreign occupations this region has suffered, or on a second-floor terrace in the warm weather. Untold numbers of travelers must go home with memories of this lovely dish, which is just as delicious without the view.

Serves 6

3 tablespoons extra-virgin olive oil

2 large cloves garlic, lightly smashed

2 pints cherry tomatoes, washed and halved

⅛ teaspoon hot red pepper flakes

½ cup loosely packed, finely cut parsley

½ teaspoon salt

½ pound monkfish, cut into ½-inch cubes or pieces

½ pound rock shrimp

½ pound calamari, cut into ¼-inch-wide rings, tentacles cut into small pieces

1½ pounds paccheri or other large tubes, such as cannelloni, manicotti,
or large rigatoni, or freshly made scialatielli (page 155)

¼ cup finely cut parsley

1. In a 10-inch sauté pan or stovetop casserole with a cover, combine the olive oil and garlic and place over medium-low heat. Cook, pressing the garlic into the oil a few times to release its flavor, until the garlic is soft and barely begins to color on both sides. Remove the garlic.

(continued)

2. Immediately add the tomatoes and cover the pan. Increase the heat to medium and let the tomatoes cook for 5 minutes, until they start to fall apart and become a sauce. Stir in the hot pepper flakes, the parsley, and the salt.

3. Add the monkfish and continue to cook, uncovered, for about 3 minutes, until the sauce returns to the simmer and the monkfish is just cooked.

4. Add the shrimp and calamari and again cook, still uncovered, until the sauce returns to a simmer and the shrimp have turned opaque, about another 3 minutes or so. Set aside until the pasta is cooked.

5. Cook the pasta al dente in plenty of salted, boiling water. Drain well.

6. Turn the paccheri into the sauce, add the remaining parsley, and heat the pasta and sauce together for about a minute.

7. Serve immediately.

Note: If using scialatielli, cook the pasta for 2 minutes in plenty of salted, boiling water. Drain well, then turn them into the sauce. Heat the pasta and sauce together for a couple of minutes, turning the pasta in the sauce constantly.

Guai e maccarune se magnano caude.
(Problems and macaroni have to be resolved ("eaten") immediately ("while still hot").

—Old Neapolitan proverb

SCIALATIELLI

SCIALATIELLI HAVE GOTTEN so popular in Campania that some people outside its hometown of Amalfi think the pasta is theirs. The reason is that many of the region's restaurant chefs are from Amalfi—Amalfitani chefs are considered, along with the Abruzzesi, to be the tops in Italy—and the chefs have had a huge success with this unusual, old-time pasta. Call it a novelty. Call it trendy. It is a very easy pasta to make at home with an electric mixer and hand-cranked pasta machine, and it has a very satisfying chewiness and unusual flavor. I think it is best described as a cross between pasta and gnocchi.

The liquid in the dough is milk and eggs, and the pasta is flavored not only with grated cheese, but also with either parsley or basil, depending on the sauce you serve on it. Parsley goes with zucchini and seafood, basil with eggplant. Amalfitani chefs have told me that in the old days—before the pasta was known outside their coast and only home cooks in Amalfi and Atrani made it—it was mostly served with either zucchini sautéed with onion and moistened with pasta cooking water, or eggplant fried with garlic and then moistened. Nowadays, one is most likely to be offered scialatielli with a seafood sauce—a luxurious and fashionable dressing for what is now considered a special pasta.

Serves 6, with seafood sauce (or eggplant sauce or zucchini sauce)

3 cups plus 6 tablespoons all-purpose flour

⅛ teaspoon salt

1 whole egg

1 egg yolk

¾ cup plus 3 tablespoons whole milk

½ cup loosely packed, freshly grated Parmigiano-Reggiano

¼ cup finely cut parsley or basil

3 tablespoons extra-virgin olive oil

1 recipe sauce from Paccheri Mare Da Gemma (see page 153)
or an eggplant or zucchini sauce as described above

(continued)

1.   In the bowl of a standing electric mixer, combine all the ingredients except the sauce. Using the dough hook, and starting on low speed, work the ingredients together until they begin to hold together. Stop the mixer, scrape down the bowl, then increase the speed slightly and continue to mix another minute. The dough should now gather into a ball when you press it together. (This can be done by hand.)

2.   Tear off pieces about the size of a baseball. Keep the remaining dough wrapped in a clean dishtowel. Press the dough ball into a flat piece, then put it through the thickest setting of a hand-cranked pasta machine. Pass the dough through the rollers. Fold it in thirds, as you would a letter, then pass it through the machine again. When the dough comes out without tearing or ragged edges, it has been kneaded enough. You may need to run the pasta through the machine 1 or 2 more times.

3.   Now run the dough through the next thinner setting, so that you end up with a strip of dough from 3 to 4 inches wide. Lay the strip of dough in front of you horizontally on a cutting board and, with a sharp knife, cut it into $1/8$- to $1/4$-inch-wide pieces. Separate the pieces of cut dough and lay them out on a kitchen towel. Cover with another kitchen towel while continuing to roll out the remaining dough.

4.   To cook the pasta, bring a large pot of water to a rolling boil. Salt it well, then cook the pasta for 2 minutes. It will float to the top of the water after about a minute. Count another minute to 75 seconds after that.

5.   Heat whichever sauce you are using in a wide pan large enough to hold all the pasta. Toss the pasta in the sauce (with some pasta cooking water if using fried vegetables) and heat them together for another 2 minutes or so. Serve immediately.

Pasta with Tomatoes

Bucatini alla Caruso

Caruso was in New York from 1903–1920 and in Brooklyn restaurants he used to prepare dishes for himself and friends such as "bucatini alla Caruso," sautéing garlic in oil, adding fresh chopped tomatoes, basil, parsley, a pinch of hot red pepper and surrounding the dish with disks of fried zucchini.

—Maria Giovanna Fasulo Rak, *La cucina napoletana in cento ricette tradizionali* (Neapolitan Cooking in 100 Traditional Recipes)

Enrico Caruso was more sensitive about his fame as a cook than as an insuperable tenor. Endowed with a magnificent appetite he would often descend into the Neapolitan restaurants of Brooklyn to give account of his culinary abilities, encouraged by an endless stream of admirers. In this way, Don Enrico was famous for his "bucatini alla Caruso," a dish which sent Americans and Italo-Americans wild. The recipe, however, does not offer anything particularly new: Fry the garlic gently in oil, add fresh tomatoes broken up by hand, basil, parsley, and a little chili. The bucatini, mixed in with this sauce, were then studded by small disks of courgettes [zucchini]. A modest recipe, but the "bucatini alla Caruso," and the popularity of their inventor, helped spread Neapolitan cookery and open up the American market to pasta.

—Noura Korsch, "Good Living with Maccheroni," in *Partenope in cucina* (Parthenope in the Kitchen)

Enrico Caruso was discovered when he sang in Neapolitan restaurants. I've read that he was a singing waiter. That's a misconception. He was a troubadour, a singer who went from restaurant to restaurant, working for tips. There are still many in Naples. They are called posteggiatori, and they stop in at Masaniello, a modest but terrific restaurant on the Riviera di Chiaia, near Naples's most fashionable shopping area, at Trattoria Dante e Beatrice, a bastion of old-fashioned Neapolitan food in the Piazza Dante, another central location, and many other restaurants. There is also a pizzeria called Cantanapoli on Via Chiatamone, behind the big hotels that line the sea drive, where the gimmick (besides waiters in the dress of nineteenth-century *lazzaroni*, or commoners) is live performances by Neapolitan singers.

Naples was an international music capital from the early eighteenth century until before World War II. The city's composers wrote some of the best-known popular songs of their day. Still today, although the big recording studios are in Milan, much of the Italian musical talent comes from or has been nurtured in Naples.

Caruso has another pasta dish named after him, but it is not an authentic Neapolitan recipe. The great one must have adored chicken livers, and so there are a number of versions of spaghetti alla Caruso that are composed of tomato sauce reduced with beef stock, thyme, and bay leaf, then blended with sautéed chicken livers and mushrooms. Louis Diat, the French chef who was ensconced at New York's Ritz Hotel during Caruso's day, claims to have created it. Diat also invented vichyssoise (named for his hometown, Vichy) during the same era.

Serves 4

¼ cup extra-virgin olive oil

2 medium zucchini, well scrubbed, cut into ¼-inch-thick rounds and dried

12 ounces bucatini (also called perciatelli)

2 to 2½ cups tomato sauce made with garlic, a good pinch of hot pepper,
and parsley instead of basil (pages 46, 48, or 50)

Freshly grated pecorino or ricotta salata

1. In a medium skillet, heat the olive oil until a slice of zucchini will sizzle in it immediately. Fry the zucchini slices several at a time until browned on both sides. As they are done, remove them to a plate. (Do not put them on absorbent paper. The oil adds to the dish.)

2. Cook the pasta in plenty of salted, boiling water.

3. Heat the tomato sauce.

4. Drain the pasta and turn it into a serving bowl, preferably warmed. Toss the pasta with 1½ cups of the tomato sauce and half the fried zucchini.

5. Serve each portion topped with the remaining zucchini slices and a spoon of sauce. Pass the grated cheese.

Maccheroni con Ricotta e Salsa di Pomodoro

Macaroni with Ricotta and Tomato Sauce

———

One stifling summer day in New York, I was having coffee with an acquaintance from Sant'Agata sui Due Golfi, a town in the hills above Sorrento where one can glimpse the bays of both Naples and Salerno. I asked her, so hot I could barely think about eating, "If you were home right now, what would you be cooking?" Her instant answer, as I now know many Campanians would agree, was this dish of pasta dressed with ricotta, tomato sauce, grated cheese, and basil. Indeed, paccheri with ricotta and tomato sauce surprisingly tops the list of most essential and particularly Neapolitan dishes given to me by Naples's foremost cooking teacher and caterer, Michi Ambrosi.

Michi and so many other Neapolitans love paccheri and how the huge tubes flop closed, trapping sauce and solids. They are fun to eat. But this is one of those cases when if Neapolitans are not near the pasta they love, they love the pasta they're near. Creamy ricotta and fresh tomato sauce is always welcome on ziti, penne, perciatelli, or mezzanelli. Spaghetti is too thin.

Serves 4 to 6

2 cups tomato sauce with basil (pages 46 and 48)

1 cup whole milk ricotta

½ cup freshly grated Parmigiano-Reggiano or pecorino, or a combination

1 pound paccheri or other large tubular pasta, or perciatelli (bucatini) or mezzanelli, or lasagne broken into 2- to 3-inch lengths

Freshly ground black pepper

A few leaves of finely cut or torn fresh basil

Freshly grated Parmigiano-Reggiano or pecorino, or a combination

1. Prepare the tomato sauce. Or reheat. Keep it hot, but not simmering.

2. Put the pasta water to boil.

3. In a pasta serving bowl, combine the ricotta and the grated cheese. Work them together with a spoon or fork until well blended.

(continued)

4. Cook the pasta in plenty of salted, boiling water until al dente. **Before draining** it, scoop out about ½ cup of the pasta cooking water.

5. Pour about ½ of the hot tomato sauce into the cheese mixture in the bowl. Stir well. Add the drained, hot pasta to the sauce, then black pepper to taste. Toss well, adding hot pasta cooking water by the tablespoon if a looser, creamier texture is desired (the sauce tends to thicken as it cools in the plate, so 2 or 3 tablespoons are usually a good idea.)

6. Serve immediately, preferably in hot bowls, each portion topped with a little more tomato sauce and with additional basil, if desired. Pass grated cheese and the pepper mill.

SPAGHETTI SCIUÈ SCIUÈ ALLA CAPRESE

SPAGHETTI IN A HURRY

TECHNICALLY, THE DELIGHTFUL-SOUNDING dialect expression *sciuè sciuè* (shoe-ay, shoe-ay), meaning "hurry, hurry," can be used for any tomato sauce that cooks while the pasta boils. "There are basically two types of Neapolitan tomato sauce, ragù and sciuè sciuè," says chef Bruno De Rosa, who was trained at the Naples Istituto Alberghiero, the culinary public school in Naples, and now heads the kitchen at Pierino, his family's restaurant in New York. "We cook tomatoes a long time with meat, or very quickly to retain their freshness."

On Capri, however, sciuè sciuè is usually more specific. It's more than simply a quickly made sauce. The expression is most often applied to a sauce of cherry tomatoes, which grow profusely on the island and which have been a staple of the Campanian kitchen for centuries. In the last decade, they have also become an extremely stylish ingredient all over the region and increasingly north of Rome, too.

The following sciuè sciuè is unusually heavy on the garlic and basil. I learned it from Beppe Desiderio, a native of Capri who now lives in New York, with a cooking hint or two from his cousin Anna Maria Desiderio, who heads the kitchen at her family's restaurant, Da Giorgio, off the main piazza of Capri. Combining an abundant amount of basil and a little oregano is not original with Beppe, though. Virtually the same recipe (but with less garlic) is served at Le Sirenuse in Positano, one of the best hotels of the Amalfi Coast, where it is, in fact, a signature dish called Pasta Don

Camillo, after the founder of the hotel, Don Camillo Sersale, whose nephew, Antonio, is now the director. Don Camillo, a man of considerable girth, is known for his love of pasta, and this is one of his favorites.

Serves 4

12 ounces spaghetti

3 to 4 tablespoons extra-virgin olive oil

3 cloves garlic, lightly smashed

⅛ to ¼ teaspoon red pepper flakes

1 pound (about a pint) ripe cherry tomatoes, cut in half in any direction, or in quarters if they are large

½ teaspoon salt, or to taste

3 cups loosely packed basil leaves, finely cut

½ teaspoon (or a little more) dried oregano

Freshly grated Parmigiano-Reggiano

1. Cook the spaghetti in plenty of salted, boiling water.

2. Meanwhile, in a 9- to 10-inch skillet, combine the oil, the garlic, and the hot pepper. Cook over low heat until the garlic is soft and barely begins to color on both sides, pressing it into the oil a few times to release its flavor. Remove the garlic or not, according to taste.

3. Increase the heat to medium-high, immediately add the tomatoes and the salt, and cover the pan (to prevent spattering, as well as to retain the tomatoes' moisture). Cook, covered, stirring a couple of times but not mashing the tomatoes, until they become saucy, about 2 minutes.

4. Lower the heat and let the sauce simmer gently, still covered. After 4 to 6 minutes, stir in about ¼ of the basil. Cook 2 more minutes, then remove from the heat if the pasta is not yet done.

5. Drain the spaghetti and put it back in the pot in which it cooked. Toss with the remaining basil, the oregano, and about ⅓ of the sauce.

6. Serve immediately, topping each bowl of spaghetti with a portion of the remaining sauce.

7. Pass the cheese.

PACCHERI DEL CARDINALE

THE CARDINAL'S PACCHERI

M. Aulissin, a highly trained lawyer from Naples, and a delightful amateur
violincellist, dined one day at my home and eating something which pleased him
especially, said to me, "Questo è un vero boccone di cardinale!"
["This is truly a mouthful for a cardinal."]

"Why," I asked him in the same language,
"don't you say as we do in France: fit for a king?"

"Monsieur," the amateur replied, "we Italians feel that kings cannot possibly
be gourmands, because their meals are too short and too solemn; but cardinals?
Eh?!!" And he chuckled in his own well-known little way."

—JEAN ANTHELME BRILLAT-SAVARIN, *THE PHYSIOLOGY OF TASTE*
(1825; TRANSLATED BY M.F.K. FISHER, 1949)

A FRIEND, RECALLING HAVING eaten this dish at my table, remembered it as sporting lobster, which it doesn't. That's how sumptuous an impression it makes. The recipe was created by Franco Santasilia, Marchese di Torpino, whose family has always had a *Monzù* and who published this recipe in his *La cucina aristocratica napoletana* (The Cooking of the Neapolitan Nobility).

Santasilia says, "You want the truth? I developed the following recipe to bring back to life the pleasure I felt as a child when [our family's] *Monzù* Guglielmo served us pink paccheri. *Monzù* Guglielmo didn't stay with us long. He went through our family's kitchen in the 1940s like a meteor, but still leaving exquisite memories of his elaborations. The thing that I liked best was furtively dragging the paccheri (how big they seemed to me) through the sauce to collect as much as possible. The goodness of each pacchero was directly proportional to the intensity of my father's glare. He disapproved of us playing with our food like that."

The tomato sauce, made with butter and broth (*Monzù* hallmarks) and aerated by whipped cream, is a rich mouthful, and you, too, will want to wipe up every last bit on the plate.

Serves 8

2 28-ounce cans plum tomatoes, drained of can juice
and pureed through a vegetable mill

1 cup strong beef broth (canned is acceptable)

2 medium bay leaves

½ teaspoon dried thyme

½ teaspoon hot red pepper flakes

1½ pounds paccheri (cannelloni or manicotti are the substitutes)

6 tablespoons butter

1 cup heavy cream, whipped until stiff (unsweetened, of course)

1 cup grated Parmigiano-Reggiano

Grated Parmigiano-Reggiano

Salt to taste

1. In a 2½- to 3-quart saucepan, combine the tomato puree, the broth, the bay leaves, the thyme, and the red pepper. Simmer gently over medium-low heat, stirring occasionally, for 40 to 45 minutes, until the sauce is reduced by more than half. Make sure to scrape the sides of the pot regularly with a wooden spoon. You should have 2¼ cups.

2. Cook the pasta al dente in plenty of boiling, salted water.

3. Don't finish the sauce until the pasta is 2 minutes away from being cooked. Make sure the tomato sauce is hot (it will require reheating if prepared ahead). Take it off the heat. Stir in the butter, then gently stir in the stiffly whipped cream and finally the grated cheese and salt to taste.

4. Drain the pasta very well (large tubes tend to retain water) and return it to its cooking pot. Pour the sauce over the pasta, and toss for 30 seconds before serving.

5. Serve immediately with more grated Parmigiano.

SPAGHETTI PUTTANESCA

As for the etymology [of *puttanesca*], the imagination of many academics has had to work overtime in an attempt to get to the correct interpretation. Some say that the name arose, at the beginning of this century, from the owner of a brothel in the Spanish Quarter who used to feed his guests on this dish that did not require a particularly complex or lengthy preparation. Others refer to the undergarments of the young ladies who, in order to catch their customers' eyes and lure them into their clutches, would try wearing anything, including garish colors and promising transparent clothes. This multicolored array has been compared to the sauce: the green of parsley, the red of tomatoes, the purple of olives, the gray of capers and the garnet red of chili. Others say that it was the imagination of a "ragazza di vita" [girl in "the life"], Yvette la Francese [Yvette the French girl] who based it on one of Provençal origins. The girl was probably not only endowed with imagination, but also a sense of humor and caustic wit to commemorate the oldest profession in a recipe.

—Nello Oliviero, "A tavola con la sirena"
(At Table with the Siren) in *Partenope in cucina* (Parthenope in the Kitchen)

[Puttanesca] used to be called marinara, but right after World War II, in Ischia, the painter Eduardo Colucci—for what reason it is not known—changed the name. Colucci lived for his friends during the summers at Punta Mulino, at the time one of the most picturesque places on the island. He had a tiny country cottage—one room, a very small kitchen and a terrace with an olive tree growing in the middle. Besides his close friends, he entertained on this terrace a hugely varied group of famous Italians and foreigners. After serving a chilled local wine, he would put together an informal supper based on this pasta which was his specialty.

—Jeanne Carola Francesconi, *La cucina napoletana* (Neapolitan Cooking)

And there are plenty of other stories about how or why what might be called marinara is also called puttanesca: That the sauce is so quickly made it can be whipped up between tricks. (You could say that about most Campanian pasta sauces.) That its aroma is so seductive it entices tricks off the street. (Ditto.) How about my friend's mother's theory? It isn't the sauce of a whore. It's the dish of a "lady" who comes home from her afternoon trysts in need of a quick dish to put on the table for her husband.

Francesconi's story, from the book many consider the bible of the Neapolitan kitchen, has specifics, though, and her story may be the true one. "No one ever heard of puttanesca until 1950," says Franco Santasilia di Torpino, whose aristocratic Neapolitan family has always had (and still has) a *Monzù* cook. "My parents were friends of Colucci and I remember them laughing about the name when they first heard it." Santasilia was also a friend of Francesconi, who died in 1996, and he says her research is impeccable. Another source in Naples, also from an aristocratic family, confided that from her parents she had the impression that Colucci, a flamboyant man, was jokingly referring to himself when he called his dish puttanesca.

What is certain is that the word "puttanesca," though hardly verboten in Naples, where prostitution is a more honored profession than in most places, is rarely used on Neapolitan restaurant menus. Most people say they are making marinara, not puttanesca. Then there are some who might say that all of the above is not even true, and that puttanesca and marinara are *not* the same. And thus the polemics of the Neapolitan table run on.

The recipe Francesconi presents as the original has triple the garlic, double the olives, and three times the anchovies of the marinara recipe (page 166). All the other ingredients are the same. A lighter version of puttanesca can be found in the recipe for bucatini with roasted red peppers (page 174).

SPAGHETTI MARINARA ALLA CECILIA

THIS CAN BE CONFUSING. Marinara means so many things in Italy. In Campania, however, it is not a simple sauce of tomatoes, onion or garlic, and oil. In Naples and its surrounding provinces, that is called tomato sauce, sugo di pomodoro. In Campania, marinara means a tomato sauce with fish, usually anchovies. If that sauce also has olives and capers, as it most often does, it might also be called puttanesca, but that depends on who's doing the calling. Sometimes distinctions are made between these two sauces that only a Neapolitan can detect, and some people say there is no difference, that marinara and puttanesca are the same.

This version, as prepared by Cecilia Bellelli Baratta in my American kitchen one afternoon, also includes a bit of canned tuna, underscoring its marinara-ness. When she asked her friend, Onofrio Piccirillo, a distinguished Casertan water buffalo breeder and typically critical Italian eater, what he thought, he tasted, contemplated, then pronounced: "Not enough anchovy." As you can see, however, marinara is a powerfully flavored sauce, and Cecilia's is very well balanced. Add a larger amount of anchovy only if you want that flavor to stand out, as Onofrio does. With the lesser amount of anchovy, even anchovy haters won't detect their presence, and anchovy is a necessary undertone. Don't leave it out.

Serves 4 or 5

1 pound spaghetti or linguine

For the sauce:

½ cup extra-virgin olive oil

1 clove garlic, lightly smashed

1 or 2 whole salted anchovies, thoroughly rinsed and filleted,
or 2 to 4 oil-packed anchovy fillets, rinsed, or to taste

1 28-ounce can peeled plum tomatoes

½ 6-ounce can light tuna in olive oil

5 pitted Gaeta or round Greek olives, each one cut into at least 6 pieces

4 to 5 large sprigs parsley, with tender stems, finely cut

½ teaspoon hot pepper oil (or to taste) (page 93),
or ¼ teaspoon hot red pepper flakes (or to taste)

¼ cup salted capers, thoroughly rinsed

Bread crumbs browned in olive oil

1. Cook the spaghetti or linguine very al dente in plenty of salted, boiling water.

2. Meanwhile, in a deep 10-inch skillet or sauté pan, over medium-low heat, combine the oil and the garlic. Cook the garlic, pressing it into the oil a couple of times to release its flavor, until it barely begins to color on both sides. Remove the garlic.

3. Immediately add the anchovy fillets, increase the heat to medium, and with a wooden spoon, mash them into the oil. They will melt quickly. Add the tomatoes with all their juice. Using the side of the wooden spoon, break and mash the tomatoes into a coarse sauce. Stir in the remaining ingredients and simmer over medium-high heat, without stirring again, for 5 to 8 minutes, until the oil separates a bit from the tomato. Taste and season with salt, if needed, and with more hot pepper oil or hot pepper, as desired.

4. Drain the pasta and pour it into the sauce. Toss over medium heat for a minute or so, until the pasta is cooked to taste.

5. Serve immediately, either plain or sprinkled with bread crumbs fried in olive oil. Do not add cheese.

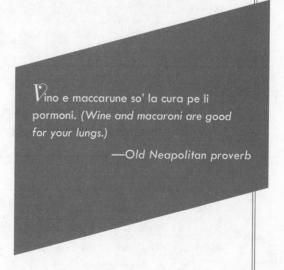

Vino e maccarune so' la cura pe li pormoni. (Wine and macaroni are good for your lungs.)

—Old Neapolitan proverb

Pasta with Vegetables

Orecchiette con Broccoli di Rapa

Orecchiette with Broccoli Rabe

THIS RANKS UP THERE along with pasta and beans, and pasta and potatoes in the pantheon of Campanian comfort dishes, particularly in Avellino and Benevento . . . well, actually all over southern Italy. Now it is popular in the United States and Canada, too, but rarely made with the finesse of the genuine article. In this traditional version, the broccoli rabe is tamed by blanching, then cooked as usual with olive oil, garlic, and hot red pepper, while the pasta cooks in the bitter vegetable water. The pasta—orecchiette, the thumb-fashioned flour and water disks said to look like piglet's ears—gain minimal bitterness, but the broccoli water somehow does add more depth to the dish. At the end, if you want a near broccoli cream, or to return some of the broccoli's bitter oomph, stir in a few spoons of the cooking water.

Serves 6

2 recipes broccoli di rapa affogati (page 316)

1 pound orecchiette

Freshly grated pecorino

1.   Prepare 2 bunches of broccoli rabe according to the recipe, but reserve the vegetable blanching water and cook the broccoli so that it falls almost into a cream.

2.   Cook the orecchiette in the water reserved from blanching the broccoli.

3.   When the pasta is almost al dente, scoop out about 1 cup of the pasta cooking water. Drain the pasta. Turn the pasta into the pan with the broccoli (or combine the pasta and broccoli in the pot used to cook the pasta), and toss well, thinning out the sauce slightly, if necessary and desired, with a few spoons of pasta cooking water.

4.   Serve very hot with grated pecorino.

VARIATION:

In Avellino and Benevento, this pasta is also frequently served with sliced or crumbled sautéed or grilled sausage mixed with the broccoli. Use ½ to ¾ pound for 6 servings.

Spaghetti o Maccheroni con Verza

Spaghetti or Macaroni with Cabbage

THIS IS SUCH A SIMPLE and useful dish, with meat and vegetable in one bowl. It's perfect for cold-weather family meals. It's amazing what a small amount of sausage will do to add flavor and substance. And, like almost nothing other than tomato sauce, it works well with almost any dried pasta.

Serves 5 or 6

3 tablespoons extra-virgin olive oil

2 cloves garlic, lightly smashed

½ pound sweet Italian sausage, removed from its casing

½ medium head green or Savoy cabbage (about 1 pound),
cored and very thinly sliced

1 tablespoon tomato paste

½ cup water

1 pound spaghetti or macaroni

Grated Parmigiano-Reggiano or pecorino, or a combination

1.   In a 2- to 3-quart saucepan or casserole, over medium-low heat, combine the oil and the garlic. Cook the garlic, pressing it into the oil a couple of times to release its flavor, until it barely begins to color on both sides. Remove the garlic.

2.   Add the sausage, raise the heat slightly, and, with the edge of a wooden spoon, break up the meat into small pieces. This gets easier as the meat cooks. Continue to cook and break up the meat until it begins to brown, in 3 or 4 minutes.

3.   Add the cabbage and mix well. Cook, uncovered, about 3 minutes, mixing occasionally. The cabbage should be wilted. (It will probably not be necessary to add salt or pepper because the sausage is well seasoned.)

4.   Dissolve the tomato paste in the water and add it to the cabbage. Mix well, cover, and cook gently for 15 minutes, until the cabbage is tender.

5.   Cook the spaghetti until al dente in plenty of boiling, salted water.

6.   Toss the pasta with the sauce and serve immediately. Pass the grated cheese.

Spaghetti con Melanzane e Mozzarella

Aumme Aumme

Spaghetti with Eggplant and Mozzarella

On Capri, they call this aumme aumme, dialect for "hush, hush," a common dialect expression, although no one can explain why it is used for this pasta. Instead of mozzarella, a large amount of grated cheese may be used, but either way the pasta gets stringy with cheese, which is as it is supposed to be.

Serves 4

1 pound eggplant, peeled or unpeeled, as desired, cut into ½-inch cubes

Salt

Oil for frying

2 large cloves garlic, lightly smashed

½ teaspoon hot red pepper flakes

1 pint (1 pound) cherry tomatoes, cut in halves or quarters

12 to 14 ounces spaghetti

2 tablespoons finely cut basil or parsley

8 ounces fresh or several-days-old mozzarella, cut into ¼-inch cubes,
or 1 cup grated pecorino or ricotta salata

1. Salt the eggplant and let it drain in a colander for 30 minutes or longer. Dry it well with paper towels, pressing the eggplant to remove moisture.

2. In a skillet, heat about ½ inch of oil and fry the eggplant until it is soft and lightly browned. Remove the eggplant with a slotted spoon and drain on absorbent paper.

3. Pour out (and discard) all but about 2 tablespoons of the frying oil. Add the garlic and the pepper flakes and place over low heat. Cook the garlic, pressing it into the oil a couple of times to release its flavor, until it barely begins to color on both sides. Remove the garlic.

4. Add the tomatoes, immediately cover the pan, increase the heat to medium-high, and cook the tomatoes until they fall apart and become saucy, about 8 minutes.

5. Meanwhile, cook the spaghetti until al dente in plenty of salted boiling water.

6. Just before the pasta is done, add the eggplant cubes to the tomato sauce, lower the heat, and cook gently, still covered, for another minute or so.

7. Drain the spaghetti and turn it into a well-warmed serving bowl. Add the egg-plant and tomato sauce, plus the finely cut herb. Toss well. Add the mozzarella or other cheese and toss again.

8. Serve immediately, passing grated pecorino or ricotta salata.

CREMA DI FUNGHI

MUSHROOM CREAM SAUCE

I FIRST ENCOUNTERED THIS rich and silken sauce at Cumpà Cosimo, Netta Bottone's restaurant in Ravello, but a puree of mushrooms like this has become fashionable in the region. Netta calls her sauce a "cream" even though it has no dairy products, but I've eaten other versions that are, indeed, enriched with a little cream. In either case, it is elegantly smooth and an appropriate pasta sauce for a fancy dinner party—or just when you want to pamper yourself with something smooth and lush. Netta serves it as part of her famous pasta mista, an array of four or five pastas, all different shapes, colors, and flavors. The day I tried the mista it was orecchiette with pesto, crespolini filled with ricotta (page 194), handmade fusilli with ragù, and this sauce on a minuscule twist she calls riccioline. I found the same pasta at a nearby grocery labeled sfiziusielli. I was told they are a shape particular to the province of Salerno, and as anyone can tell by looking, related to fusilli. Ditali is a good shape for this sauce, too, especially if you make the variation with peas, which always benefit from being caught in a tube. I think it also works well on farfalle and gemelli and other fanciful, sculptural shapes. Thin spaghetti would not be out of line, either.

Serves 6

¼ cup extra-virgin olive oil

3 large cloves garlic, lightly smashed

1½ pounds white mushrooms, wiped clean and sliced

¾ teaspoon salt

Optional: 2 tablespoons Marsala

¾ cup hot pasta cooking water

3 tablespoons freshly grated Parmigiano-Reggiano

Optional: 2 to 3 tablespoons heavy cream

½ teaspoon freshly ground black pepper

1 heaping tablespoon finely cut parsley

1 pound small macaroni, such as ditali or small shells, or a fanciful shape,
such as farfalle or gemelli

Grated Parmigiano-Reggiano

1. In a 10-inch skillet, combine the olive oil and garlic over medium-low heat and, pressing the garlic into the oil a couple of times to release its flavor, cook until the garlic is soft and lightly golden on both sides. Remove and discard the garlic.

2. Increase the heat to medium and add the mushrooms. Cook, tossing almost constantly, until they give off their liquid. Add the salt and Marsala. Raise the heat to high and continue cooking, still mixing almost constantly, until all the liquid has evaporated. Measure out ¾ cup of the mushrooms and set aside.

3. Place the remaining mushrooms in the jar of a blender. Have the grated cheese, the cream, the pepper, and the parsley ready at hand to finish the sauce.

4. Cook the pasta until al dente in plenty of salted water, and just before draining it, scoop out a cup of the pasta boiling water. Drain the pasta.

5. Pour ¾ cup of the pasta water into the jar of the blender with the mushrooms and process the mushrooms into a smooth cream. Add the grated cheese. Process another couple of seconds to blend. If the sauce is too thick, add a little more pasta cooking water. Finally, whirl in the cream and the black pepper. Taste for salt.

6. Toss the pasta with the mushroom cream sauce and the parsley. Garnish each serving with 2 tablespoons of the reserved sliced mushrooms.

7. Serve immediately in heated bowls with extra grated cheese.

BUCATINI CON PEPERONI ARROSTITI

BUCATINI WITH ROASTED PEPPERS

THERE ARE THREE WAYS to present this dish, meaning there are three ways you can put together bucatini (perciatelli), the spaghetti-length macaroni with the tiny hole, roasted sweet peppers, and a sauce that is essentially a variety of puttanesca or marinara. Two of the three presentations are traditional and take some patience and skill. One of these is the *Monzù*-style timballo or drum of roasted peppers, possibly of alternating colors, filled with sauced pasta. The other is whole peppers baked with a pasta stuffing. The third way, the easy way, is to simply toss everything together. It doesn't look impressive but it tastes fantastic.

Impressive is definitely the word for the timballo made by Francesca Pasca di Magliano for me at GiòSole, her home and Agri-Tourism farm in Capua. She managed to turn the ingredients into a free-standing red and orange striped dome. Not only that, with the aid of a few bread crumbs, the construction could be cut into neat wedges without the pasta falling into a heap on our plates. I have yet to be so lucky.

I have had better success stuffing whole roasted peppers, although you must have the type of pepper with a flat (not pointy) bottom, and you'll find that even they are slippery things that sometimes resist standing straight up unless the baking dish is exactly the right size. The stuffed vegetable is the more classic, home presentation. Finally—and I have several times resorted to this final "serving suggestion" out of frustration at trying one of the others—you can simply toss everything together in a bowl. It's the beloved medley of flavors that is really important—although appearances do count quite a lot in Naples and on the more sophisticated tables of the provinces. Macaroni with roasted peppers, capers, olives, garlic, anchovies, tomatoes, parsley, oregano, hot pepper—who could ask for more?

Serves 8

8 large red peppers, a type with flat bottoms that can stand on their own
if making the stuffed version; 4 peppers if tossing with pasta

For the sauce:

¼ cup salted capers, thoroughly rinsed

¼ cup not too coarsely chopped, pitted Gaeta olives

1 large clove garlic, finely minced

¼ cup extra-virgin olive oil

3 whole salted anchovies, thoroughly rinsed and filleted, or 6 oil-packed anchovy fillets, rinsed

1½ cups well-drained peeled plum tomatoes, coarsely chopped or crushed, plus a few tablespoons of juice held in reserve

½ cup finely cut parsley

2 teaspoons dried oregano

¼ teaspoon hot red pepper flakes

12 ounces bucatini (also called perciatelli), or, if making stuffed peppers, ditali, pennette, or other small, tubular macaroni

Plus:

2 or 3 teaspoons extra-virgin olive oil

2 tablespoons water

Optional (for a pepper dome): 3 tablespoons dry bread crumbs

1. If making stuffed peppers, you will need a baking dish that holds the peppers snugly. Before roasting the peppers, place them in the dish or pan you plan to use to see if they fit. Keep in mind that they will fill out a bit more when stuffed. A 9- to 10-inch-diameter and 3½-inch-high or slightly shallower casserole dish works very well.

If making a timballo, you will need a dome-shaped receptacle that can go in the oven. A large stainless-steel mixing bowl will work. I once successfully used an enameled cast-iron paella pan with a nonstick interior. In either case, you need to line the pan first with aluminum foil, then oil the foil.

2. Roast and peel the peppers according to the directions on page 344.

Alternately, you can roast the peppers directly on the oven rack in a preheated 400-degree oven for 15 minutes, until the skin puffs out and begins to blacken, then put them in the closed pot or bag.

If you are making stuffed peppers, you will need the tops later, so cut about ¾ inch off the stem end and set aside. leaving you with pepper cavities for stuffing. If making a timballo, the peppers need to be cut into wedges or other shapes that will attractively line the mold you are using. If making a tossed pasta, cut the peppers into ½-inch dice or into ¼-inch-wide strips.

To make the sauce:

3. Finely chop the capers and olives and mix with the garlic.

(continued)

4.   In a small saucepan, heat the oil over medium heat, then add the caper-olive-garlic mixture and let sizzle for 2 minutes, stirring occasionally. Add the anchovies and, with a wooden spoon, mash them into the caper-olive mixture. They should dissolve very quickly. Stir in the tomatoes (and any pepper liquid that you've managed to save) and simmer over medium-low heat until the sauce is thick and the oil has started to separate, about 10 minutes. If the sauce gets too dry or thick, add a little tomato liquid. Stir in the parsley, oregano, and hot pepper.

To prepare the pasta:

5.   Cook the pasta in plenty of salted, boiling water, until quite al dente for the further baked dishes, or ready to eat for the tossed dish. Drain well.

6.   In a large bowl, toss the sauce and pasta together well, adding the bread crumbs if making a timballo. If making the tossed dish, add the diced or sliced peppers and toss again. Serve immediately.

To assemble and bake:

7.   Preheat the oven to 375 degrees.

8.   To make stuffed peppers, pat the outside of the peppers dry and fill each one with the pasta mixture, being careful not to overfill. Place the filled peppers in the baking dish, standing them up the best you can, leaning one against the other if necessary. Drizzle each with a scant ½ teaspoon of olive oil and put on the reserved pepper tops. (Can be prepared several hours ahead to this point. Do not refrigerate.) Add 2 tablespoons of water to the dish, sprinkling it around, not on, the peppers.

If making a timballo, after having decoratively lined the mold with peppers cut to fit, fill the mold with the pasta, previously tossed with the bread crumbs. Place another sheet of aluminum foil over the top.

9.   Bake for 40 minutes. Let the timballo stand in its mold for 5 minutes before turning it out onto a serving platter. Can be served warm.

TWO CENTS PLAIN, NEAPOLITAN-STYLE

*I*n the second half of the nineteenth century, *roie allattante* was the name for the simplest dish of macaroni, sold both on the street and in the pubs. For two cents—*roie* derives from *due* (two)—you got a portion of cooked vermicelli dressed with a pinch of grated pecorino. It was therefore as white as milk—*allattante*, deriving from the word "latte" (milk). Even today, when Neapolitans eat spaghetti with only cheese, as they might do when they are eating bland because they are ill or have a digestion problem, they are eating "spaghetti col due."

The sign of a *maccarunaro*, the logo of the macaroni cook, was a big stick crossing a huge white cauldron of boiling water, and hanging from the stick were limp vermicelli, a plate of grated cheese in a cone shape and decorated with carnations, peppercorns on strings, and a big pot of cooked tomatoes. So there was choice.

For three cents, you could get tre Garibaldi—a plate of vermicelli with tomato sauce. Garibaldi because it was patriotic, but also referring to the covering tomato sauce. Garibaldi's followers wore and were called Red Shirts. The word *tre* may be a pun, too. It means "three" and refers to the extra penny paid for the tomato sauce, but, says journalist and food historian Alberto Consiglio in *Cento ricette di maccheroni* (100 Macaroni Recipes), it could also be a corruption of the ancient word for vermicelli, which was *trii*.

FRITTATA DI SCAMMARO

FASTING DAY EGGLESS SPAGHETTI OMELET

THIS IS CALLED A FRITTATA but it is not made with eggs. It is a cake of fried spaghetti seasoned with the usual and much-beloved Neapolitan condiments of garlic, olives, anchovies, capers, hot pepper, and parsley. It merely resembles a frittata. As admired as this dish is, I know busy Neapolitan families in which no one has time to nurse the pancake to its requisite crispness, which is why faces often light up particularly bright when frittata di scammaro is brought to the table or served as a snack.

Scammaro refers to days of fasting, and this is one of the so-called lean dishes. (*Cammaro* is an antique dialect word for a day when meat *could* be eaten. Adding the prefix "s" to the word is, in Italian, negating the action—as we use "un" in English.) While it contains no meat or dairy, it does have a significant olive oil content. Fortunately or unfortunately, I have found no way of being meager with the oil and turning out a pancake as crisp on the surface as it must be to be delectable. It takes time to accomplish, too—an hour of nearly constant attention.

Serves 4 as a pasta or main course, 6 to 8 as an antipasto

12 ounces thin spaghetti

¼ cup plus 2 tablespoons extra-virgin olive oil

2 large cloves garlic, finely chopped

½ cup Gaeta olives, pitted and finely chopped

3 whole salted anchovies, thoroughly rinsed and filleted, or 6 oil-packed
anchovy fillets, rinsed

2 tablespoons salted capers, thoroughly rinsed, chopped if large

¼ teaspoon (or less to taste) hot red pepper flakes

1 rounded tablespoon finely cut parsley

1. Cook the spaghetti until al dente in plenty of salted, boiling water. Drain well.

2. In a 10-inch skillet (a nonstick omelet pan or cast-iron skillet is perfect), over medium-low heat, combine the ¼ cup oil and the garlic. Cook the garlic a minute or so, but before it begins to color, add the olives, the anchovies, the capers, the pepper, and the parsley and mix well. Increase the heat very slightly and cook for 3 to 5 minutes, mashing the anchovies into the oil until they dissolve. Transfer the mixture to a large bowl. Add the spaghetti and toss well to distribute the seasonings throughout.

3.   Add 2 tablespoons more olive oil to the same skillet (1 tablespoon if using a nonstick skillet). Place over medium heat, then return the dressed spaghetti to the pan, distributing it evenly and pressing it down a little. Cook, continuing to press down occasionally with a wooden spoon or spatula, until the bottom and sides of the frittata are well browned, about 30 minutes. To get the bottom and sides of the frittata evenly crisped and browned, rotate the pan over the heat, tipping and holding it so that the outside edge of the pan can also benefit from direct heat. (This can be done with an electric burner, as well as gas.) Also, as the frittata fries, rotate a knife around the edge to prevent it from sticking to the pan, and shake the pan occasionally so the bottom doesn't stick. (Do this with a nonstick pan as well.)

4.   When the bottom and sides of the frittata have browned, slide it onto a large dinner plate or platter, then flip it back into the pan with the uncooked side down, adding a little more oil to the pan if it seems necessary.

5.   Cook the second side like the first, also paying attention to the edges if they didn't seem brown enough when you flipped the frittata. When all sides have browned well, turn the frittata onto absorbent paper. Pat the top with paper, too.

6.   Serve hot, warm, or at room temperature, cut into wedges (scissors work best), as an antipasto, first course, or second course.

SPAGHETTI ALLA PASQUALE

AFTER MANY COURSES, including two kinds of pasta, two main courses, a slew of both simple and elaborate vegetable dishes, fruit, dessert, and liqueurs, plus a heated discussion among the women of the family about how to prepare each—as if they had not all learned from the same grandmother—Pasquale Amore, the patriarch of his extended and very worldly family in the deep countryside of Frasso Telesino, at the foot of the Taburno mountain in the province of Benevento, took the chair across from me at the table and finally piped up: "You've got to put my recipe in your book, too." Even though Gianna, his wife, is a working woman, an English teacher, Pasquale is not, as you might imagine, a man who usually needs to prepare his own meals. Like most Italian men, however, he can at least make himself a plate of pasta when necessary. Pasquale's concoction, the ultimate in bachelor cooking, is absolutely delicious, but it is more than that. Pasquale has had coronary bypass surgery, and his dish fits his new, contemporary way of eating. It is vegetarian and relatively low in fat. You could say it is a sort of finto Genovese, a meatless, quick-cooked imitation of the meat-flavored, long-cooked, onion-based Genovese.

Serves 6

1 large or 2 medium onions

1 medium or 2 small carrots

2 large ribs of celery

¼ cup extra-virgin olive oil

¾ cup water

1 14-ounce can peeled Italian tomatoes or 1½ cups with juice,
roughly chopped

½ cube vegetable or chicken bouillon (or amount for 1 cup broth,
as given on package)

½ teaspoon salt (or to taste)

1 pound spaghetti or macaroni

¼ cup freshly grated Parmigiano-Reggiano or pecorino cheese

Freshly ground black pepper

Freshly grated Parmigiano-Reggiano or pecorino

1. In a food processor, chop the onions very finely, almost into a puree. You should have about 1½ cups. Process the carrot and celery the same way. You should have about ½ cup each.

2. In a 2- to 3-quart saucepan, combine the vegetables with the oil and water. Place over medium-high heat and simmer briskly, stirring occasionally, for 15 to 20 minutes, until the mixture is dry.

3. Meanwhile, bring the water for the pasta to a boil.

4. When you stir the sauce and the liquid no longer puddles in the wake of the spoon, add the tomatoes and the bouillon cube. With the side of a wooden spoon, break up the tomatoes a little more, then continue to simmer briskly while the pasta cooks.

5. Salt the pasta water and cook the spaghetti or macaroni al dente.

6. Just before the pasta has finished cooking, spoon 2 or 3 tablespoons of the foamy pasta water into the sauce to loosen it up slightly. Taste for salt and add it according to taste.

7. Drain the pasta, turn it into a bowl, and dress with about ⅔ of the sauce, ¼ cup freshly grated cheese, and a generous amount of freshly ground pepper. Toss well.

8. Top each portion with a spoonful of the remaining sauce and perhaps another dose of freshly ground pepper. Sprinkle with a little more grated cheese or pass additional grated cheese. Pass the pepper mill, too.

BAKED PASTA

TIMBALLO DI TAGLIOLINI

PASTRY DRUM WITH FINE EGG PASTA

THERE ARE FIFTEEN RECIPES called timballo or timpano in Jeanne Carola Francesconi's *La cucina napoletana* (Neapolitan Cooking), which is often called the bible of Neapolitan cooking. Both words mean the same thing—a drum, as in the timpani of a symphony orchestra. A few years ago, in a movie called *Big Night*, the preparation of a timballo di maccheroni was featured and made a big impression on audiences. Recipes for timballi ran in newspaper food sections, and suddenly the dish came to the attention of Americans.

Timballo or timpano—the words are used interchangeably, but timballo is more popular—are from the aristocratic *Monzù* tradition, but they are still made today—not necessarily much by home cooks, but certainly by caterers and shops that make such elaborate dishes to take away. At L.U.I.S.E., the tavola calda on the Piazza dei Martiri, at the heart of Naples's fancy Chiaia shopping section, you can usually buy some kind of timballo by the slice and eat it at the counter for lunch. Pasta of some kind, ragù, sausage, tiny meatballs, salami, prosciutto, porcini, green peas, cheeses, hard-cooked eggs, chicken livers—in short, all the ingredients that might go into an elaborate baked pasta—can also be layered in a sweetened pastry crust and baked into a free-standing drum. It makes quite a visual sensation on the dinner table and is extremely delicious, too.

This particular timballo uses egg pasta instead of macaroni, is based on a ground meat ragù (ragù di macinata is how they refer to such a sauce in Campania), not a classic Neapolitan ragù, and contains white sauce. I ignorantly considered that these touches might have been borrowed from Emilia-Romagna, but when I remarked about that possibility to a Neapolitan friend, she got in a huff. "You think only the Bolognese know how to make egg pasta and white sauce?"

Serves 8 as a main course or the first course of an elaborate menu

For the timballo pastry:

3 cups cake flour

½ teaspoon salt

2 tablespoons sugar

8 tablespoons (1 stick) cold butter

1 large egg

5 to 6 tablespoons milk

For the ground meat ragù (about 4½ cups):

1 cup finely chopped onion

1 cup chopped carrot

1 cup chopped celery (including a few leaves)

3 tablespoons extra-virgin olive oil

1 pound ground beef (85 percent lean)

3 tablespoons dry Marsala or tawny port

¼ cup dry white wine

2 28-ounce cans peeled plum tomatoes, drained of can juices

1 teaspoon salt

For the white sauce:

2 tablespoons butter

2 tablespoons flour

1½ cups milk

¼ teaspoon salt

Several gratings of nutmeg

⅛ teaspoon freshly ground black pepper

Plus:

1 10-ounce package frozen small peas, defrosted

1 tablespoon butter

8- or 8¾-ounce package of dried egg tagliolini or tagliarini (also called fine fettuccine), or other long egg pasta no more than ¼-inch wide)

1 cup grated Parmigiano-Reggiano

1 egg, beaten, for the egg wash

To make the pastry:

1.   Combine the dry ingredients in the bowl of a food processor fitted with a metal blade, then add the butter cut into 1-inch pieces. Pulse the flour mixture and butter together until the mixture resembles coarse meal. In a small bowl, beat together the egg and the lesser amount of milk, then pour it into the work bowl. Pulse a dozen or so times to mix thoroughly, then let the motor run a few seconds, until the dough gathers into a ball. If the dough seems dry and doesn't quite hold together, add a little more milk. Remove the dough from the food processor bowl and place it on a board. Knead it a few times. Let it rest under a kitchen towel. Divide the dough into 2 portions, one about ¾ of the dough for the bottom of the drum, the remaining ¼ for the top crust. Form two 1-inch-thick disks, wrap them in plastic, and refrigerate (to rest) for at least 30 minutes. (If refrigerated longer, return to room temperature before rolling.)

To make the ragù:

2.   In a 3-quart saucepan or casserole, combine the onion, carrot, celery, and olive oil. Set over medium heat and cook, stirring frequently, until the vegetables are soft and beginning to brown, about 20 minutes. Add the chopped beef and stir well to mix with the vegetables. Continue cooking over medium heat until the meat has lost all its raw color and has started to brown, about 20 minutes. Add the Marsala and the white wine. Let cook another 3 minutes. Add the pureed canned tomatoes and salt. Simmer very gently, uncovered, for 1½ to 2 hours, stirring every 15 minutes or so and making sure to scrape down the sides of the pan every time you stir. When finished, the meat should still be covered with sauce. Add water a little at a time, if necessary. Allow the sauce to cool, then skim off any fat that has risen to the surface. The sauce can be made ahead, cooled, and refrigerated until the timballo will be assembled, but make sure to cool it to room temperature, without stirring, before refrigerating. That allows more fat to separate and rise to the top.

3.   Just before assembling the timballo, with the sauce skimmed and just warm, pour the sauce into a strainer and strain the meat out of the sauce. Reserve the meat and sauce separately. You should have a little more than 1 cup of sauce without meat.

To make the white sauce:

4.   In a small saucepan over medium heat, melt the butter. Stir in the flour and cook for about 2 minutes. Pour in the milk and stir vigorously to combine. Stirring constantly, cook until sauce simmers and thickens, about 5 minutes. Season with salt, nutmeg, and pepper. Cover and set aside.

To prepare the peas:

5.   Place the peas in a skillet with 1 tablespoon butter. Cook, stirring occasionally, over medium-high heat, until heated through, about 2 minutes. Cover and set aside.

To assemble and bake the timballo:

6.   Butter a 9-inch springform pan. Preheat the oven to 425 degrees.

7.   On a lightly floured board, roll out the larger disk of dough into a circle at least 16 inches in diameter—large enough to cover the bottom and sides of the 9-inch pan. Then roll out the small disk into a circle at least 11 inches across.

8.   Gently drape the larger circle of dough over the springform and carefully fit it into the pan. Let the excess dough hang over the edge of the pan. Set aside covered with a dishtowel to prevent drying.

9.   Boil the pasta in salted water until not quite done. Drain, then toss in a bowl with the strained sauce, mixing well.

10.   Make a layer of half the pasta on the bottom of the pastry-lined pan. Make a layer of half the meat. Make a layer of half the white sauce, then half the peas, then half the grated cheese. Repeat with a layer of pasta, meat, white sauce, peas and cheese. (If there is some sauce left in the pasta bowl, mix it back into the remaining meat for the last layer of meat.)

11.   Cover with the top crust and cut the pastry to shape. Brush the edge of the circle with the beaten egg and pinch together. Use the remaining egg wash to brush on the top pastry. Cut 2 or 3 slits in the pastry.

12.   Place the timballo in the next-to-the-lowest rack for about an hour, until the pastry is well browned. If necessary, after 20 to 30 minutes, drape a piece of aluminum foil over the top to prevent it from browning too much. Remove the foil for the last 5 to 10 minutes of baking to make sure the top is well browned. When done, the pastry will have pulled away from the sides of the pan slightly.

13.   Let the timballo cool for at least 10 minutes and up to 30 minutes, then remove the springform ring and slide the timballo onto a serving platter. Serve hot.

Timballo di Maccheroni

Pastry Drum with Macaroni

THIS IS MY OWN CONTEMPORARY interpretation of the dish, and it is not nearly as elaborate or heavy as most of the recipes in Francesconi. Instead of making meatballs separately, for instance, I use the meat from the ragù, shredded very well. Instead of fresh sausage, I use salami. Because the dish can be made in stages over a couple of days, it doesn't have to consume the good part of a day to prepare. And because it can stand composed but unbaked for several hours, it makes a great showpiece for a party. At a grand dinner, a timballo would be served instead of pasta, but this and the preceding recipe are rich enough to stand as a main course—preceded by vegetable antipasti and followed by a salad.

Serves 8 to 10

1 recipe Neapolitan ragù (page 53) (1 quart of sauce and the meat)

1 recipe pastry for timballo (page 182)

1 tablespoon butter

1 10-ounce box of frozen peas, defrosted

1 pound ziti or small rigatoni

1 cup freshly grated Parmigiano-Reggiano

Salt and freshly ground black pepper

3 ounces of salami or prosciutto, sliced paper-thin, finely minced (¾ cup)

12 ounces mozzarella, cut into ¼-inch-thick slices

1 egg, beaten, for the egg wash

1. Make the ragù, and when it has finished cooking, let it cool and remove the meat. You should have 4 cups of ragù. Shred the meat finely with your fingers, discarding any membrane or gristle you run across. Stir ½ cup sauce into the shredded meat.

2. Make pastry and refrigerate.

3. In a skillet, heat the butter and sauté the peas until just cooked, about 2 minutes.

4.   Cook the pasta until very al dente in plenty of salted, boiling water and drain well.

5.   Turn the pasta into a mixing bowl and stir in 1½ cups of the sauce. A tablespoon at a time, toss the pasta with ½ cup of the Parmigiano. Season with salt and freshly ground black pepper.

6.   Roll out the pastry according to directions on page 185, making the bottom round slightly larger, and fit it into a well-buttered 10-inch springform pan.

7.   Distribute all the meat in an even layer on the bottom of the pastry-lined pan. Sprinkle on half the dried salami. Scatter on half the peas. Make a layer with half the macaroni. Arrange all the mozzarella over the pasta. Scatter on the remaining peas, then macaroni. Sprinkle on the remaining Parmigiano.

8.   Roll out the top pastry, cover, and crimp the edges of the timballo (page 185).

9.   Preheat the oven to 425 degrees.

10.   Bake on the next-to-the-lowest rack for 1 hour. If necessary after 20 to 30 minutes, drape a piece of aluminum foil over the top to prevent it from browning too much. Remove the foil for the last 5 to 10 minutes of baking to make sure the top is well browned. When done, the pastry will have pulled away from the sides of the pan slightly.

11.   Let cool 10 minutes in the pan, then release the ring and slide the timballo onto a serving platter. Serve hot with the remaining ragù to spoon over each portion as it is served.

PASTIERA RUSTICA DI TAGLIOLINI

SAVORY PASTA AND CHEESE PIE

A LOOSE-LEAF COLLECTION of recipes called *L'antica cucina della Campania* (The Old Cooking of Campania), published by *Il Mattino*, the daily newspaper of Naples, with contributions from readers chosen by a panel of important gastronomes, provides insight into what Campanians lived on before World War II and what they consider their comfort food today: pasta and pork products.

This recipe was contributed by Emilia Orilio, who lives in a suburb of Naples. Incredibly rich, aromatic, and savory, easy to prepare, and perfect for parties and buffets, it can be made ahead and served at room temperature or served gloriously hot from the oven.

Pastiera is the name of the sweet pie of ricotta and whole-wheat berries (page 412). The Orilio family is not the only one, however, to apply it to baked pasta, with cheese and salami. The word *rustica* does not mean rustic, by the way. It means "savory" in the sense of the opposite of sweet. For example, pizza rustica is a savory pie, while pizza dolce, the opposite, is a dessert pie. Anything seasoned with diced salami, sausage, prosciutto, cheeses, etc., is usually called *rustica*.

Serves 8 to 10

1 pound dried narrow egg pasta: tagliolini, tagliarini, tagliatelle,
or, if those are not available, fettuccine

4 tablespoons butter (½ stick), cut into 6 to 8 pieces

2 cups cold milk

4 large eggs, beaten to mix well

⅔ cup loosely packed, freshly grated Parmigiano-Reggiano (about 2 ounces)

⅔ cup loosely packed, freshly grated pecorino (about 2 ounces)

½ teaspoon freshly ground black pepper

2 tablespoons butter or lard (for greasing pan)

4 ounces provolone, cut in ¼-inch dice (about ¾ cup)

4 ounces pancetta, cut in ⅛-inch dice (about ¾ cup)

4 ounces soppressata, cut in ¼-inch dice (about ¾ cup)

1.   Preheat the oven to 350 degrees.

2.   Cook the pasta in boiling, salted water, until slightly underdone, usually about 3 minutes.

3.   Drain the pasta well and place it in a large bowl. Toss with the butter. Pour in the milk. Toss and stir well; let stand, tossing every 5 to 10 minutes, until the pasta absorbs all except perhaps a tablespoon or so of the milk—this can take as long as 30 minutes.

4.   While the pasta is standing, in another bowl, beat the eggs with the grated cheeses and pepper. With 2 tablespoons of butter or lard, grease a baking pan or a shallow casserole of at least 4-quart capacity.

5.   When the pasta has absorbed the milk, add the egg mixture, then the provolone, pancetta, and soppressata. Mix well. Pour into the greased baking pan.

6.   Bake for about 50 minutes, or until the top has browned lightly.

7.   Let rest 10 to 20 minutes before serving, or serve warm instead of hot, or at room temperature.

Note: Cut into individual portions, the pastiera reheats very well in a microwave. Just be careful not to overheat it. Bring it just to a warm serving temperature.

Ziti alla Sorrentina

Baked Ziti

THE FOLLOWING RECIPE MAY not look much different from one for baked ziti you'd see in a shelter magazine, or the one you were passed down from your immigrant grandmother or neighbor, but it's much lighter than the usual Italian-American standard. In fact, it's a good example of how some of the finesse of the Neapolitan kitchen has been lost on this side of the ocean.

Serves 6 to 8 as a pasta course, 4 to 6 as a main course

1 pound ziti

1 cup whole milk ricotta

2½ to 3 cups ragù or tomato sauce (pages 46, 50, 53, or 56)

8 ounces mozzarella, thinly sliced

1 cup grated Parmigiano-Reggiano or pecorino cheese, or a combination

About 10 basil leaves, torn into small pieces

1. Preheat the oven to 350 degrees.

2. Cook the ziti in boiling salted water until it is almost tender enough to eat, about 2 minutes less than usual.

3. Meanwhile, in a large bowl, blend 2 tablespoons of the ragù or tomato sauce into the ricotta.

4. Spread about ¾ cup of the ragù or tomato sauce on the bottom of a 9- by 13- by 2-inch baking dish or a round or oval dish of similar capacity (about 3½ quarts).

5. When the ziti is done, drain it well, then toss it with the ricotta.

6. Spread half the pasta in the baking dish. Evenly spoon over it ¾ cup more ragù or tomato sauce. Cover with the sliced mozzarella, the basil, and ½ cup of the Parmigiano. Top with the rest of the pasta, 1 cup more ragù or tomato sauce, and the remaining ½ cup grated cheese.

7. Bake for about 45 minutes, or until bubbling.

8. Let the casserole cool for 10 minutes before cutting it into portions. Serve hot.

Millerighi Imbottiti al Ragù

Baked Stuffed Tubes with Ragù

The efficiency and refinement of this recipe is impressive. It seems ordinary, but the ragù that results from cooking sausage with white wine, onion, and diluted tomato paste is exceptionally velvety and intense in flavor. The efficiency is that the meat used to flavor the ragù is afterward chopped and used in the ricotta filling. The recipe is from Lejla Mancusi Sorrentino, a Neapolitan cooking teacher and cookbook author, and shows what a fine hand can do with simple ingredients.

What are sold in North America as ridged manicotti are the closest I've found to millerighi. Any large tube that is stuffable will do, and jumbo shells work well, too. But the smaller the pasta, the higher the ratio of pasta to filling and the heavier the dish. Therefore, with smaller pasta, you should get a greater number of servings.

Serves 6 to 8; makes 12 manicotti, or 32 jumbo shells

For the ragù:

12 ounces sweet Italian sausage

½ cup finely diced onion

½ cup dry white wine

2½ cups water

¼ cup tomato paste

¼ teaspoon salt

⅛ teaspoon freshly ground black pepper

1 cup loosely packed fresh basil leaves

For the filling:

15 ounces (1 container) ricotta

4 ounces mozzarella, cut into ¼-inch cubes

2 tablespoons freshly grated Parmigiano-Reggiano

½ teaspoon salt or to taste

¼ teaspoon freshly ground black pepper

Plus:

¾ cup freshly grated Parmigiano-Reggiano

8 to 12 ounces pasta (see above)

(continued)

To prepare the ragù:

1.   With the point of a knife, prick each sausage 2 or 3 times. In a 2½- to 3-quart saucepan or stovetop casserole, over medium-low heat, combine the onion and the sausages. Cover the pot and, stirring a couple of times with a wooden spoon, cook until some liquid and fat begins to collect at the bottom of the pan, about 10 minutes.

2.   Uncover the pot and raise the heat slightly. Cook, stirring frequently, until most of the onions are deep brown and beginning to stick to the pot, about 30 minutes. (The sausages will not brown much.) Before any onions burn, add the wine and stir well, scraping the bottom of the pot to deglaze it. Let the wine simmer briskly and nearly evaporate, stirring a few times, about 5 minutes.

3.   Stir in the water, the tomato paste, and the salt and pepper. Cover the pan, increase the heat to medium, and bring the liquid to a gentle simmer. Keeping the pan covered, adjust the heat so the liquid simmers very gently for 1½ hours.

4.   Uncover the pan, raise the heat slightly, and let the ragù simmer a little more rapidly so the sauce thickens and reduces a little, about 20 minutes. Add the basil and continue to simmer gently for another 10 minutes. Let cool slightly.

5.   Remove the sausages and set aside. Strain the sauce, pressing the basil leaves and any solid onion with the back of a wooden spoon against the strainer to retrieve every last bit of sauce. Discard the basil. You should have 1⅔ to 2 cups of thin ragù.

To make the filling:

6.   In a bowl, combine the ricotta, the mozzarella, and 2 tablespoons of Parmigiano.

7.   Leaving the casings on, finely chop the sausages from the ragù. Add the sausage meat, salt, and pepper to the cheeses. Mix very well.

To assemble and bake the dish:

8.   Preheat the oven to 350 degrees.

9.   Cook the pasta very al dente in plenty of boiling, salted water.

10. Drain the pasta and place it in a bowl of very cold water. Let the pasta cool. Drain the pasta again and arrange it on a kitchen towel. If holding it a while, cover it with a damp towel until you are ready to fill it. (The pasta can be cooked while the ragù is cooking.)

11. Spread 3 tablespoons of ragù over the bottom of a minimum 9- by 13-inch baking pan.

12. Fill each large tube of pasta with ¼ to ⅓ cup of filling, or each jumbo shell with about 1 tablespoon of filling. If using shells, close the shells around the filling. Place the pasta in the dish as each is filled.

13. Spoon on the remaining ragù, coating the pasta well and letting the sauce drip into the pan. Sprinkle evenly and thoroughly with the ¾ cup of Parmigiano, which will seem like a lot.

14. Bake for about 20 minutes, or until an "inviting golden crust" has formed. Serve immediately.

VARIATION:

This is a good recipe to transform into Rotoli di Melanzane (also called Involtini di Melanzane), or Eggplant Rollatini, as we say in Italian-American: Use the same filling and sauce inside fried (unbreaded) slices of eggplant cut the long way. Use only ¼ cup Parmigiano on top. Bake as above.

The juice and fried onion that result from cooking the sausage (before the tomato paste and water are added) is itself an extraordinarily delicious and intense pasta sauce, with the bonus of cooked sausage as a second course. The sauce would be called sugo di salsicce, and because there is very little of it in the pan, add the almost but not quite fully cooked spaghetti or macaroni to the pan with the sauce, perhaps with a few spoons of pasta cooking water, and turn the pasta in the sauce, over low heat, to finish its cooking and absorb some flavor from the sausage sauce.

NETTA BOTTONE'S
CRESPOLINI DI RAVELLO
CHEESE-FILLED ROLLED CRÊPES

CRESPOLINI, MEANING LITTLE crêpes, are a specialty of Ravello, the most romantic town of the Amalfi Coast. (Greta Garbo and Stravinsky famously "disappeared" at Ravello's Villa Cimbrone in 1939—there's a marker outside the villa that says so.) They are served in a curious, particular way. After the crêpes are filled, they are cut in half on the diagonal, then baked standing up, diagonal cut end up, and served in that position, their tops gilded with white sauce and cheese. This is the version of the traditional cheese- and salami-filled crespolini that Netta Bottone has made famous at Cumpà Cosimo, her restaurant in Ravello, the best in town. The crêpes are also made with a spinach filling and a veal filling. I'm told those are adaptations of the traditional recipe by the fancy hotel dining rooms of the area.

Makes 12 6- to 7-inch crêpes or 8 larger crêpes, serving 8 as a pasta course

For the crespolini batter:

1 cup milk

¾ cup all-purpose flour

1 egg

1 egg yolk

2 tablespoons melted butter

¼ teaspoon salt

Butter or oil for the pan

For the filling:

½ cup mozzarella, cut into ¼-inch dice

½ cup provolone, cut into ¼-inch dice

½ cup Gruyère, cut into ¼-inch dice

½ cup Fontina, cut into ¼-inch dice

1 cup ricotta

⅔ cup salami, cut into ¼-inch dice

For the white sauce:

1 tablespoon butter

1 tablespoon flour

¾ cup milk

¼ teaspoon freshly ground nutmeg

¼ teaspoon salt

To make the crêpes:

1. In a mixing bowl, using a fork or whisk, or in a blender, or using an electric mixing machine, combine the crespolini ingredients and blend together very well, until smooth. The batter will be the consistency of heavy cream.

2. Pour the batter through a strainer into a clean mixing bowl to remove any possible lumps. Let the batter rest at room temperature for at least 30 minutes. Batter can be prepared in advance and refrigerated, covered.

3. Use a 6- to 7-inch skillet to make 12 crêpes. (If all you have is a minimum 8-inch skillet, count on only 8 or 9 crespolini.) Heat the pan over medium-high heat, then grease it lightly by wiping it with a paper towel dipped in vegetable oil or butter.

4. Pour 3 tablespoons of batter, scooped up in a ¼-cup measure, into the center of the hot pan and swirl the batter around so that it covers the bottom entirely and evenly. If any holes are left, maneuver the pan so that wet drops will fill them, or spoon a tiny bit more batter into each one. When the edges are golden brown, in about 40 seconds, turn the crêpe over and cook 30 seconds longer. Slip onto a plate.

(You may or may not need to grease the pan after the first crêpe. Don't be dismayed if the first crêpe is not perfect. Add water by the tablespoon if the batter is too thick to spread evenly. It is highly unlikely that it will be too thin, but in that case beat in more flour by the teaspoon or tablespoon. Adjust the heat as necessary. If the heat is too high, the crêpe will be scorched in the center and not evenly cooked to the edges. It's better for the heat to be too low.)

5. As the crêpes are done, turn them out onto a clean, cotton dishtowel. As they cool, they can be stacked. Keep covered with a dishtowel. If not stuffing the crêpes within a few hours, put a piece of wax paper between each crêpe, then wrap the stack in aluminum foil and keep refrigerated.

(continued)

To make the filling:

6. In a mixing bowl, combine all the ingredients.

To make the white sauce:

7. In a small saucepan, melt the butter over medium-low heat, blend in the flour, and let the mixture bubble for about 2 minutes, stirring frequently. Add the milk all at once, stirring or whisking vigorously. Bring the sauce to a boil, stirring or whisking constantly. Let simmer 1 minute. Season with nutmeg and salt.

To assemble and bake:

8. Preheat the oven to 400 degrees.

9. Place the crêpes on your work surface with the pale sides facing up. Make a log of about 2 tablespoons of filling in the middle of each crêpe. Roll it up, starting by turning the bottom half of the crêpe over the filling.

10. With a very sharp knife, cut each rolled crêpe in half diagonally. To prevent the filling from melting out of the crêpe while baking, tuck the uncut edges in and under the filling.

11. Stand the crêpes up, diagonally cut side up, in a lightly buttered 1-quart soufflé dish or other high-sided baking dish. (Although not the authentic presentation, the crêpes can also be arranged on their sides in a baking pan.)

12. Drizzle the white sauce over the crespolini, getting most on the filling but letting some drizzle over the side.

13. Bake for 20 minutes. Serve immediately.

SARTÙ
RICE IN A MOLD

Take rice away from a Chinaman and he'll die, take it away from a Lombard and
he'll become melancholy, take it away from a Neapolitan and he'll never notice.

—NELLO OLIVIERO, *STORIE E CURIOSITÀ DEL MANGIAR NAPOLETANO*
(NEAPOLITAN FOOD STORIES AND CURIOSITIES)

THIS IS THE GRAND EXCEPTION to Nello Oliviero's observation. Although Campanians are now loving to eat seafood risottos (mainly in restaurants), and the fry shops all
carry rice balls (page 29), Neapolitans are absolutely boastful about sartù, a molded
case of rice filled with delicacies: porcini, chicken livers, and marble-sized meatballs to name just a few. The speculation is that the word "sartù"
comes from the French *surtout*, which literally
means "above all." Sartù is conspicuously of
noble birth, definitely a dish from the Bourbon court of the late eighteenth century.
This is an old and elaborate recipe. More
contemporary ones might start with a risotto
into which are mixed all or some of the "filling" ingredients.

Serves at least 8

(continued)

TIP ON RECONSTITUTING DRY PORCINI

Use hot water, not boiling water, to
reconstitute dried porcini. And never let
them soak longer than 20 minutes or so,
unless the recipe calls for the soaking liquid
as well. Much of the mushrooms' flavor will
transfer to the water if the water is too hot
or the soaking too long. If not using the
mushroom soaking water in the same
recipe, keep it in the freezer to add to
stews, sauces, and soups.

For the "case" of cooked rice:

2½ teaspoons salt

3 cups Arborio rice

⅓ cup ragù (page 53)

¾ cup grated Parmigiano-Reggiano

3 eggs, lightly beaten

For the filling:

1 ounce dried porcini mushrooms

2 tablespoons extra-virgin olive oil

½ cup finely chopped onion

¼ to ½ pound chicken livers, cut into roughly ½-inch pieces

2 tablespoons ragù

15 cooked, ½-inch-diameter meatballs,
made with 4 ounces chopped beef (page 269)

2 cooked (boiled or broiled) fresh pork sausage,
cut into ¼-inch-thick slices

1 10-ounce package frozen small peas, defrosted

1 tablespoon butter or finely minced pancetta

⅛ teaspoon salt

3 tablespoons butter

⅔ cup bread crumbs

4 ounces prosciutto, finely chopped or cut into fine, thin strips

3 hard-cooked eggs, halved lengthwise

6 ounces mozzarella, cut into ½-inch dice

Also:

2 to 3 cups ragù (page 53)

Optional: Freshly grated Parmigiano-Reggiano

To prepare the rice "case":

1. In a 4-quart saucepan, bring 2½ quarts of water to a rolling boil. Add the salt and the rice and simmer briskly, uncovered, until the rice is cooked slightly firm, about 15 minutes.

2.   When the rice is done, drain it in a colander or strainer, then put it in a large mixing bowl.

3.   Stir in the ragù, then the grated cheese a few tablespoons at a time. After the rice has cooled a few minutes, stir in the eggs.

4.   Set the rice aside, covered, while you prepare the filling.

To prepare the filling:

5.   In a bowl, reconstitute the porcini in enough hot, not boiling, tap water just to cover. Cover the bowl, and after 15 minutes, drain the porcini in a fine strainer and reserve the liquid. Coarsely chop the porcini. Strain the mushroom liquid through a coffee filter or strainer lined with cheesecloth. Reserve the liquid.

6.   In a 7- or 8-inch skillet, heat the olive oil over medium heat and sauté the onion until it starts to color.

7.   Add the porcini and toss them with the onion a few seconds.

8.   Add the chicken livers and sauté until they've lost their pink color, about 3 minutes.

9.   Add the 2 tablespoons of ragù and the reserved porcini liquid. Cook, stirring occasionally, for about 6 minutes, or until the livers are just cooked and the liquid is reduced to a syrup.

10.   Scrape the livers and their sauce into a medium-size mixing bowl. Add the prepared meatballs and the sliced sausage. Set aside.

11.   In a small skillet, over medium-high heat, sauté the peas in 1 tablespoon of the butter or in the pancetta (after having rendered its fat for several minutes in the same skillet). Cook until heated through, about 2 minutes.

12.   Stir in the salt and set aside.

To build the rice case:

13.   Grease a 9-inch springform pan with 1 tablespoon of the remaining 3 tablespoons butter. Coat the bottom and sides generously with bread crumbs, setting aside ⅓ cup for the top.

14. Set aside about ¼ of the rice mixture for the top, then line the pan with the remaining rice. To do this and keep the crumb lining intact, place large spoonfuls of the rice in the bottom of the pan, then pat them together to form a base ¾ inch thick. Now build a wall of rice on the sides of the pan, using the same method. Make sure to make the wall a little thicker where the sides meet the bottom.

To fill and bake the rice case:

15. Preheat the oven to 400 degrees.

16. Make layers, starting with the prosciutto, then the peas, then the halves of hard-cooked eggs arranged like the spokes of a wheel, then the meat mixture, spreading it to fill the space evenly. Finally, scatter on the cubes of mozzarella.

17. Top the mold with a layer of rice and smooth it with a spatula, making sure the edge is compacted with the wall of rice and the filling is entirely encased in rice.

18. Sprinkle the top with bread crumbs and dot with the remaining 2 tablespoons of butter.

19. Bake until the top is nicely browned, about 1 hour.

20. Let the sartù cool on a rack for 10 to 15 minutes before opening the springform and sliding the sartù onto a serving dish.

21. Cut in wedges, sauce with ragù, and serve hot.

22. Pass grated cheese, if desired.

MARIA RUSSO'S TAGLIATELLE ALLA BOSCAIOLA

Baked Pasta Woodsman-Style, with Meat Sauce and Mushrooms

WHEN MARIA RUSSO OF Castel Volturno, in Caserta, makes this, she somehow gets the white sauce to seep into the serving cuts she makes before putting the dish in the oven. It makes portioning the casserole easier. The trick has yet to work totally for me. Nevertheless, it's a wonderful baked pasta, perfect for big family meals, buffets, and parties.
Serves 8

For the ground meat ragù:

2 tablespoons extra-virgin olive oil

1 small onion, cut into dice no larger than ¼ inch (about ⅔ cup)

1 pound ground beef (no leaner than 85 percent)

1 28-ounce can peeled Italian tomatoes, with their juices, finely chopped

¾ teaspoon salt

Pinch hot red pepper flakes

For the white sauce:

4 tablespoons butter

6 tablespoons flour

3½ cups milk

1¼ teaspoons salt

¼ teaspoon freshly grated nutmeg

Plus:

1 ounce pancetta or unsmoked bacon, finely chopped, or 1 tablespoon butter

1 10-ounce package frozen peas, defrosted

2 tablespoons extra-virgin olive oil

2 cloves garlic, lightly smashed

10 ounces mushrooms, wiped clean and thinly sliced

⅓ cup dried porcini, reconstituted

1½ teaspoons dried oregano

1 teaspoon salt

12 ounces tagliatelle

8 ounces mozzarella, cut in ½-inch cubes

½ cup grated Parmigiano-Reggiano

To prepare the ragù:

1. In a 2- to 3-quart saucepan or stovetop casserole, over medium heat, warm the oil and sauté the onions until they are golden, about 8 minutes.

2. Add the meat and cook until it's brown and starting to crisp.

3. Stir in the tomatoes, the salt, and the hot pepper.

(continued)

4. Bring to a simmer, then adjust the heat so that the sauce simmers very gently, uncovered, for 1½ hours. Stir occasionally, making sure to scrape down any sauce on the sides of the pot. (A flame tamer helps.)

5. When the ragù is ready and while it is still hot, pour it into a strainer placed over a deep bowl and let the liquid drip through.

To prepare the white sauce:

6. In a 2- to 3-quart saucepan, melt the butter over medium-low heat and stir in the flour. Cook for 2 to 3 minutes, stirring a few times.

7. Pour in the milk and stir or whisk vigorously. Stirring constantly, cook over medium heat until the sauce begins to simmer and has thickened, about 5 minutes. Season with salt and nutmeg. Cover and set aside.

8. In a medium skillet, over low heat, render the pancetta, or over medium heat, melt the butter. Add the peas and cook over medium heat until the peas are heated through, about 2 minutes. Turn into a bowl and set aside.

9. In the same skillet used to cook the peas, heat the olive oil over medium heat with the crushed garlic. When the garlic is golden on both sides, remove it and add the sliced mushrooms, the reconstituted porcini, the oregano, and the salt. Cook over medium heat until the mushroom liquid is exuded then evaporates. Set aside.

10. Cook the pasta in plenty of salted boiling water. Drain it and place it in a bowl with the liquid strained from the ragù. Mix well.

To assemble and bake:

11. Preheat the oven to 400 degrees.

12. Evenly spread about ⅓ of the pasta on the bottom of an oiled 9- by 13-inch baking dish. Then add a layer each of half the peas, half the mushrooms, half the meat from the ragù, half the mozzarella, and ⅓ of the Parmigiano. Make the layers as even as possible.

13. Repeat the layers, ending with the last ⅓ of pasta, then a final sprinkling of the remaining Parmigiano.

14. Using a sharp serrated knife, cut the uncooked casserole into 8 portions. Pour on the white sauce. Recut the portions after you've poured on the white sauce.

15. Bake until lightly browned, 30 to 40 minutes. Let stand at room temperature for 10 to 15 minutes before serving the precut portions.

Lasagne Vico della Neve

Pizzeria Vico della Neve is in Salerno's medieval quarter, a maze of streets behind the city's main drag, Via Roma, which is itself steps away from the lush, palm-lined waterfront municipal park and the sea. It is Salerno's oldest restaurant, and it is lined with paintings and murals by local artists, all devoted customers, most of them long gone. The pizzeria continues to attract the city's artistic and intellectual community, who flock to its cramped room for the "antique flavor of Salerno," as one local put it.

All the food served at Vico della Neve comes from the pizza oven. I suppose the pasta e fagioli is boiled in the tiny back kitchen earlier in the day, but it is kept in a huge bowl on a long marble service counter and goes into the pizza oven to be reheated as it is ordered. The rest of the menu is set out on a group of small marble shelves in the dining room. Waiters scoop up portions of stuffed peppers, or ciambotta, or eggplant parmigiana out of large, beat-up, and blackened baking pans, then put them into smaller beat-up and blackened baking pans. The food then goes to the man at the pizza oven, who shuffles them in and out alongside the pizzas and calzones.

This is an old-fashioned sort of lasagne, a baked pasta that can also be made with tubes, such as ziti, rigatoni, or paccheri. It is replete with hard-cooked egg, mozzarella, salami, and a rich ragù, but everything is used parsimoniously.

Serves 8 to 10

(continued)

12 ounces curly-edged dried lasagne

6 hard-cooked eggs

8 to 10 ounces mozzarella, sliced about ¼ inch thick

¼ pound very thinly sliced soppressata

1 recipe Neapolitan ragù (page 53 or 56)
(4 cups of sauce, meat removed and set aside for another meal)

1½ cups loosely packed freshly grated Parmigiano-Reggiano

1.   In a large pot of salted boiling water, cook the lasagne 4 or 5 at a time, until al dente. As each batch is cooked, remove it with a slotted spoon and a helper spoon, or with tongs, and plunge the pasta into cold water to stop the cooking. When cool (and before the next batch is done), lift them out of the cold water and lay flat on a clean dishtowel. After cooling 2 batches in the cold water, you will have to change the water because it will get warm.

2.   Cut each hard-cooked egg into 6 slices. Cut the mozzarella slices into pieces about the size of the larger slices of egg. Cut the slices of soppressata into halves or quarters, depending on the diameter of the soppressata.

3.   Spread ½ cup of ragù on the bottom of a 9- by 13-inch baking pan. Arrange a layer of 5 or 6 lasagne over the ragù, running the pasta their full length in the pan and overlapping them by about an inch. Arrange about ⅓ of the egg slices on the lasagne, then intersperse about ⅓ of the pieces of mozzarella. Dot with 1 cup of ragù. Sprinkle with about ½ cup of the Parmigiano. Disperse about ⅓ of the soppressata.

4.   Repeat with a layer of pasta, this time running the pasta in the opposite direction, with the width of the pan. Cut 1 piece to size and use it as a guide for cutting the remaining slices necessary. Add another layer of egg, mozzarella, another cup of ragù, Parmigiano, and soppressata, as above.

5.   Repeat again, this time using up all the broken or odd shaped pieces, making a mosaic of slightly overlapping pieces. Repeat with the remaining egg, remaining mozzarella, all but ¼ cup of the remaining Parmigiano, and the remaining soppressata. Finish with a layer of perfect lasagne, running the pasta the length of the pan.

6.   Press down lightly on the top layer of pasta to get everything to spread and settle slightly. Spread on a final cup of ragù. Sprinkle with the final ¼ cup of Parmigiano. The lasagne can be prepared ahead to this point.

7.   Preheat the oven to 350 degrees. Bake the lasagne for 30 minutes if it is at room temperature, slightly longer if cool from refrigeration.

8.   Let cool for 10 minutes, then cut into portions and serve immediately.

LASAGNE DI CARNEVALE

CARNIVAL LASAGNE

THE SUMPTUOUS NEAPOLITAN LASAGNE, baked for carnival and brimming with all the meats and cheeses forbidden during Lent, is the prototype for the lasagne the whole world knows. Many Campanians themselves don't hold the dish in such high regard. Almost without fail, mention lasagne to a Neapolitan and he or she will tell you that "the really good lasagne is from Bologna." It seems contradictory to the local, usually prideful character to make such a claim, yet Campanians are all suckers for the creamy softness of white sauce (they love mayonnaise, too).

Serves 8

1½ pounds curly-edged dried lasagne

1½ recipes Neapolitan ragù (see page 53) made with 4 sweet Italian sausage
cooked with the sauce for the last hour (6 cups sauce, the meat removed
and set aside for another meal, the sausage sliced very thin
and reserved for the lasagne)

3 cups whole milk ricotta

¼ recipe Polpette, made without pine nuts and raisins,
shaped into marble-size balls (about 50 polpettine),
fried until brown (page 269)

1½ cups freshly grated Parmigiano-Reggiano

1 pound mozzarella, diced or shredded

1.　In a large pot of salted boiling water, cook the lasagne 4 or 5 at a time, until al dente, usually about 8 minutes. As each batch is cooked, remove it with a slotted spoon and a helper spoon, or with tongs, and plunge the pasta into a bowl or pan of cold water to stop the cooking. When cool (and before the next batch is done), lift them out of the cold water and lay flat on a clean dishtowel. After cooling 2 batches in the cold water, you will have to change the water, because it will get warm.

2.　Use a 10- by 14-inch lasagne or roasting pan (or a pan of similar volume). Start by spreading the pan with ¾ cup ragù. Then arrange a layer of pasta on top of the ragù, overlapping the pieces slightly and covering the bottom completely. Dab on ½ cup of ricotta, then, with the back of a spoon, spread the ricotta on the pasta.

Arrange about a third of the sausage slices over the ricotta, dot with half the polpettine, sprinkle with about ½ cup Parmigiano, and sprinkle with about a third of the mozzarella. Spoon on about ¾ cup more sauce.

3.   Arrange another layer of pasta, placing the pieces in the opposite direction from the previous. Dab and spread on more ricotta, then begin to be creative: You won't be able to use all the ingredients in all the layers. Two more can have sausage. One more can have tiny meatballs. Two more can have mozzarella. Some ricotta, sauce, and Parmigiano can go in every layer. Make sure to save close to 2 cups of ragù and ¼ cup grated cheese for the top. Altogether, there should be five pasta layers, then a generous covering of sauce. The lasagne can be prepared ahead to this point. Bring to room temperature before proceding.

4.   Preheat the oven to 350 degrees.

5.   Bake for 1 hour and 20 minutes, until bubbling at the edges.

6.   Let cool for 15 minutes before cutting and serving.

CHEESE
AND EGGS

CHEESE CAN BE and often is eaten at any meal and for every course in Campania. Antipasti are composed around it—fried pockets of cheese, fried sandwiches of cheese, whole mozzarella, mozzarella sliced or diced into a salad with tomatoes, ricotta rolled and spiraled into a frittata, to name just a few. Grating cheeses season minestre and pasta, vegetables and main courses. Other cheeses take a leading role in pasta sauces. Cheese can be a main course itself, or it can dress a main course of meat, vegetables, even fish sometimes. Cheese can be eaten at the end of a meal—as a cheese course or in a dessert. Cheese can be eaten apart from a formal meal—as a snack, or on pizza.

Campania has sheep, goats, cows, and water buffalo, all of which produce distinctive cheeses. The most important cheeses of Campania, however, are made from buffalo milk and cow milk and all by the same general method. In English we call these cheeses heated and drawn because the curd is first heated, then pulled or drawn to form a stringy mass—pasta filata—before the cheese is shaped and consumed, or shaped and aged, depending on the cheese. These cheeses are mozzarella, fior di latte, provola, provola affumicata or smoked provola, scamorza, caciocavallo, and provolone. There is also ricotta, which is the recooked whey resulting from the cheese making. It can be fresh or salted and dried, in which case it is called ricotta salata.

As for grating cheese, Campanians use Parmigiano-Reggiano, which is made in Emilia and not their region, and they use pecorino, sheep milk cheese, which may be made in Campania, but more likely comes from other southern Italian regions, or from Rome, Tuscany, or Sardinia—the same places from which we get our pecorino. Many towns in the mountainous areas of the region have some pecorino production, but it is strictly artisanal and the cheeses are not well distributed. As for goat cheeses, there are some made by farmers (more likely the farmers' wives), who usually preserve their logs of cheese under oil until they get incredibly sharp and funky.

CHEESES OF CAMPANIA

MOZZARELLA

Mozzarella is the most distinctive agricultural product of Campania. Italian law agrees with that. Only cheese made with buffalo milk can be called mozzarella, and only the broad, low plains of Caserta and Salerno, respectively the provinces north and south of Naples, support water buffalo. Small quantities of buffalo milk mozzarella are now also being produced in California, Venezuela, and Argentina, but nowhere else in Italy.

Cow milk cheese made by the same process should be called fior di latte, literally "flower of milk." In spite of its legal definition, however, the word "mozzarella" is often used outside Campania for either cheese. Nevertheless, an authentic cheese from Campania is labeled "Campano" on its outer paper wrapping.

The best-quality real thing is imported to North America, and in greater and greater quantity. Unfortunately, it is rarely in top condition. Mozzarella di bufala is very perishable and should be consumed the same day it is made. A Neapolitan wouldn't eat a day-old cheese. After that it goes into the pasta, or a casserole, or is fried like a meat cutlet. Yet producers like to say that it will keep for at least a week. Here, importers say it lands the day after it's made. The wholesalers say it's in the store the next day. My store says it came in this morning. It should work for cooking, but too often it has softened and soured. Producers say that larger balls will keep longer, and they hope one day they can develop a market for them so that it becomes economically feasible to export them. Mozzarella di bufala is an expensive cheese, even in Italy.

ALLA SORRENTINA

Baked dishes topped with tomato sauce and fior di latte (cow milk mozzarella) are usually called *alla Sorrentina*. Gnocchi alla Sorrentina are potato dumplings with tomato sauce and melted cheese, Saltimbocca alla Sorrentina (page 282) are veal cutlets baked with sauce and cheese, and Ziti alla Sorrentina (page 190) are what we call baked ziti. The name is from the peninsula that divides the Bay of Naples from the Bay of Salerno, not after the famous city on the peninsula. The city is known for romance, both bought and real, and for being the sentimental subject of the song *"Turna a' Surriento"* ("Return to Sorrento"), a sort of Italian-American anthem. In the old days, the peninsula was known for its fior di latte, because cows grazed there. Today, the curd for Sorrento cheese can come from anywhere.

The flavor and texture of buffalo mozzarella is very different from that of cow cheese. There are protein and fat structure differences in the milks, but the difference that has the most impact is the fat content. Cow milk has 4 percent fat or less, while buffalo milk has about 9 percent fat. The fresh buffalo milk cheese is springy, not rubbery, and has a sweet, slightly salty, clean, rich lactic flavor. It oozes whey when you cut into it. These qualities, or their lack, can be the subject of earnest table debates. Here's another subject of mozzarella connoisseurship: When it is right out of the vat, the center of the cheese is somewhat tough. In Naples, where the cheese can't possibly be as young as it is when bought on the spot it is made, I've heard people say the cheese should be "relaxed." On and around the farms where the milk is produced, no one complains when the cheese is "tight." What it shouldn't be is like cream cheese. In Naples, customers often

demand to see the container in which the cheese was shipped, if it isn't sold directly out of it. In the country, they know the hour it's made. Near the beaches of both plains—from Battipaglia down to Paestum, and from Formia south to Castel Volturno—there are cheese makers (*caseifici*) along the roads where day trippers buy cheese in the morning for their picnics by the sea.

The water buffalo that produce the milk for the cheese were introduced by the Lombards sometime during the seventh or eighth century, their period of occupation in the region. The first mentions of mozzarella, however, are from the 1400s. The breed is said to be a cross between Asian and African water buffalo. (How the Lombards brought such animals doesn't appear to be documented.) They love to wallow in mud, but they are not dirty animals, and they are considered much smarter, sweeter, and friendlier than cows.

The word "mozzarella" comes from the Italian verb *mozzare,* which means "to cut off" or "to take away" and refers to the way the cheese is shaped. After the milk is curdled with rennet, it is cut, then heated. The heated curd falls to the bottom of the vat, where it is stirred with a wooden paddle until it becomes stringy. This stringy mass is then worked with the hands in warm water until it is finally pulled by one operator as another holds on to the larger mass. It looks like a taffy pull. The cheese grabbed and pulled away is mozzarella.

Since prime specimens of buffalo mozzarella are so hard to find in our retail markets, I recommend eating and using cow milk mozzarella. Italian specialty stores in large cities can and do buy curd and make the cheese themselves, so it is possible to find it freshly made. As an alternative, try to find the Polly-O brand of mozzarella packed in brine and packaged in plastic tubs for supermarket sale. It is vastly better than the rubbery balls of cheese sold in the dairy case.

In Campania, mozzarella comes in large balls, in small balls called bocconcini (little mouthfuls), and in a braid form called a treccia. Bocconcini di Cardinale are small balls packed in thick buffalo cream, usually in a crock. For a special meal, they're served either as an antipasto or as a cheese course before dessert.

PROVOLA AND PROVOLA AFFUMICATA

Technically, provola should be a buffalo milk cheese, but these days cow milk and the more expensive buffalo milk are often mixed. Provola is, in essence, aged mozzarella. It is shaped into balls that have a topknot around which string can be tied for the hanging and aging, and it can be plain or smoked. It is eaten as a table cheese. It can be grilled (page 214). It can be fried (page 216) or cooked in sauce (page 215). It can be used in baked pastas and timballi (pages 182–207), and gattò (page 353). A good substitute is domestically made scamorza, mild provolone, or Gouda, or, for the smoked provola, a firm smoked mozzarella or smoked Gouda.

FIOR DI LATTE

The cow milk equivalent of mozzarella.

SCAMORZA

Scamorza is the cow milk equivalent of provola—basically, a several-weeks-old fior di latte. It can also be plain or smoked. There are locally made domestic versions available. A decent substitute is Gouda.

BURRINI

As the name indicates, these are buttery cheeses. They have an outer layer of mild provolone (really more like scamorza) and an inner core of butter. They are made small because the butter is perishable. They are a table cheese, usually reserved for a cheese course.

RICOTTA

Ricotta means recooked, and this slightly sweet, high-moisture cheese is made from the recooked whey that results from cheese production—whether cow milk, buffalo milk, or sheep milk. Every last bit of protein is coagulated, and the resulting product is drained. Unfortunately, in the United States, we use whole milk to make ricotta, and our cheese, while delicious, does not taste the same or behave the same way when it is cooked. U.S. ricotta can be made to work in Italian recipes, and the recipes in this book have been written using it. But the real thing is being made at the same stores that make mozzarella, and it is also being imported from Italy, mainly from Rome, where the ricotta is made from sheep milk. I urge you to find some, if only for the taste experience.

RICOTTA SALATA

Ricotta salata is well drained, compressed, and lightly salted ricotta, usually sheep milk ricotta that comes from Lazio. It is eaten as table cheese, and is used for grating over dishes made with fresh flour and water pastas, such as fusilli or strangolapreti.

CACIOCAVALLO

Caciocavallo means horse cheese either because it looks like saddlebags or because it used to be hung over wooden horses to age, or both, depending on which story you believe. In any case, caciocavallo is a softball-size or larger cow milk cheese with a topknot around which string can be tied: Two hang and age together, giving the impression of saddlebags hanging over the horse, or perhaps it is the wooden horse that makes them look like saddlebags. It is another cheese made like mozzarella—the curds are cooked, then stretched like taffy before being kneaded into shape—but denser, and it can be aged for several months or longer. It is eaten as a table cheese when young and when well aged, but it is also used as a grating cheese when it attains the texture of an old cheddar. Caciocavallo silano, which is made in the southernmost end of the province of Salerno, across the border from Basilicata, is considered the best.

PROVOLONE

To oversimplify, provolone is a well-aged caciocavallo, but larger, denser, and more often shaped like a sausage rather than a ball. Most of the provolone consumed in Campania comes from Calabria, but some is made in the region. It is used as a table cheese and in the same baked dishes as provola.

SCAMORZA ALLA GRIGLIA

GRILLED SCAMORZA

GRILLED CHEESE, SCAMORZA or provola—plain or smoked—is to some Campanians as good as, if not better than, grilled meat. Certainly, the custom of including a slice of cheese on a mixed grill with lamb chops, sausage, and, say, a piece of liver, is putting it on the same level. Grilled cheese, a golden crust outside, melting and oozy inside, can be a second course on its own, too—with a salad or a vegetable, after a plate of pasta or a bowl of soup. It's a good antipasto or snack, too.

Until I tried this in a nonstick skillet, I worried how I was going to give directions for cooking the cheese. When made in a steel, iron, or aluminum pan, as it is in Italy, the cheese can be extremely difficult to turn and remove from the pan without breaking its gorgeous crust, the best part.

½-inch-thick slices of scamorza or firm, smoked mozzarella

1. Place a nonstick skillet over high heat and heat the pan until a drop of water will dance on the surface and evaporate almost immediately.

2. Place the cheese slices in the pan and cook, still over high heat, until you see, first, a little fat oozing around the edges, then see the edge turning brown. Peek under the cheese to see if the underside has browned. Turn the cheese over when it does. Cook the second side as you did the first. The result should be a slice of cheese that is well crusted on both sides, but not melted, just soft and oozy. Serve immediately.

Scamorza alla Pizzaiola

Scamorza in the Style of the Pizzamaker

THIS IS ONE OF THOSE homey, nothing, but wonderfully satisfying dishes that can be whipped up in minutes and is practically worshipped for its humble comfort. If you have leftover tomato sauce in the refrigerator or a favorite commercial product in the pantry, you can use that instead of a freshly made pizzaiola. Almost any mild cheese that melts well—such as Gouda or Fontina—can be used instead of scamorza, even a smoked cheese. The proportions depend on what you have on hand. Make sure to serve good bread with this.

Serves 2

2 cups well-drained, canned peeled plum tomatoes,
coarsely chopped or crushed, as desired

2 tablespoons extra-virgin olive oil

1 teaspoon finely minced garlic

½ teaspoon dried oregano

⅛ to ½ teaspoon salt (depending on saltiness of tomatoes,
canned needing less than fresh)

Pinch hot red pepper flakes

4 ¼-inch-thick slices scamorza or several-days-old mozzarella

Bread, toasts, or fried bread slices

1.   In an 8-inch skillet, combine the tomatoes, the olive oil, the garlic, the oregano, and the salt and pepper flakes. Place over medium-high heat and cook, uncovered, for 5 minutes, stirring several times. Lower the heat so the sauce barely simmers.

2.   Arrange the cheese slices on the bubbling sauce so they do not touch. Cover the skillet and simmer a minute or so, until the cheese is soft but not runny.

3.   Use a wide, flat spatula to scoop up some sauce with a slice of cheese and serve immediately on a plate with bread on the side, or serve on a slice of toasted or fried bread.

Mozzarella Milanese

Mozzarella in the style of a Milanese Veal Chop

When the mozzarella is first-rate and the "cutlets" are freshly fried, these have very little relation to the fried mozzarella sticks sold in American chain restaurants. They are, however, the prototype—a slice of cheese dipped in flour, egg, and bread crumbs, then pan-fried, in the way a veal chop would be prepared in Milan, or, for that matter, how schnitzel is made in Vienna. These are morsels to make when the refrigerator holds some several-days-old but still good mozzarella begging to be cooked. The "cutlets" make a fine main course for a midweek meal. Just add a salad or a vegetable—and of course a little pasta first. They must be eaten within seconds after they come out of the oil.

Serves 2 or 3

½ cup all-purpose flour

2 eggs, lightly beaten with a big pinch of salt

¾ cup fine, dry bread crumbs

10 ounces mozzarella (preferably lightly salted), at least 1 day old and cold, direct from the refrigerator, cut into 6 approximately ½-inch-thick slices

Extra-virgin olive oil for frying

1. Place the flour, the beaten eggs, and the bread crumbs in separate flat plates. Arrange them in front of you, in a work space next to the stove.

2. Dredge the slices of mozzarella in the flour, coating thoroughly, but not heavily. Using a fork to hold the cheese, dip the slices into the egg, again coating well and paying special attention to the sides. Still using a fork to handle the cheese, dredge the slices in bread crumbs, piling crumbs on top and pressing them into the sides so they cover the cheese completely.

3. In a frying pan, heat ⅛ to ¼ inch of oil over high or medium-high heat.

4. Just before you place each slice in the hot oil, dip it again in egg. (If you run short of egg, add a teaspoon or so of water.) Fry the cheese slices in hot oil for 1 minute per side.

5. Serve immediately.

INSALATA CAPRESE

MOZZARELLA AND TOMATO SALAD, CAPRI-STYLE

———

THE CAPRESI ASSUME THAT this salad, now known all over the world, has been made on their island for at least 100 years. But according to the monograph *Addio cicerchia* (Goodbye Chickpeas), a history of Capri's cooking by Marino Barendson, a Neapolitan food writer and resident of Capri, it wasn't until the early 1930s, at Ristorante Luigi ai Faraglioni, that it got its name.

As most of the world knows it today, the salad is a plate of sliced tomatoes alternated with sliced mozzarella, garnished with basil, and dressed with olive oil, salt, and pepper, but never vinegar. On Capri and in Naples today, it may be different from the traditional. It is, for example, considered very of-the-moment to strew the salad with the tiny leaves of supposedly but not really "wild" rucola (arugula) instead of the basil. Or the salad may be made with a few pinches of oregano in addition to the basil, especially on Capri, where everyone loves the island's particularly sweet wild oregano.

Barendson points out that the recipe has gone through many changes. At one time, for instance, the tomatoes were chopped, lightly salted, and drained, then seasoned with oil, garlic, salt, and pepper, and finally tossed with diced mozzarella and a few leaves of basil. At La Capannina, one of Capri's fanciest restaurants, insalata caprese is a halved tomato with the mozzarella and basil tucked in to make it look like a flower. It looks like a contemporary presentation befitting an international restaurant, but it is, says Barendson, another old way of arranging the salad.

The tomato that is preferred for insalata caprese is a large, round type called cuore di bue, beef heart, also called the Sorrento tomato. It is approximately the same as an American beefsteak tomato. And on Capri and the Sorrento peninsula, but not necessarily in Naples or elsewhere in the region, the cheese is always cow milk mozzarella—fior di latte—and not buffalo cheese. Sorrento is Capri's closest mainland port, and it is known for fior di latte.

Spiedini Napoletani

Neapolitan Skewers

Fried, Battered, Skewered Mozzarella Sandwiches

Mozzarella in carozza, literally mozzarella in a cart—a slice of mozzarella carried by two slices of bread dipped in flour and egg and fried—is much more popular than this skewered seven-layer version, a crisply fried cylinder of melted mozzarella and soft bread. The classic, square, flat, fried sandwich is served everywhere from proper restaurants to snack shops. Truth be told, it is often indigestible. This method and presentation is not only lighter and more refined, but easier to make, and actually impressive to serve with a small salad of sharp greens, as a first course for a formal dinner, or main course for a light meal.

Serves 4 as an antipasto or snack, 2 as a light main course

7 slices thin-sliced, firm, packaged white bread, several days or more old

½ pound mozzarella, cut into ¼-inch-thick slices

½ cup milk

1 cup all-purpose flour

2 eggs

1 tablespoon water

Peanut oil for frying

1. Using a 1½-inch diameter biscuit or cookie cutter, stamp out 3 rounds from each slice of bread. Do not include any crust. You will have 21 rounds.

2. Using the same cutter or tool, stamp out 16 1½-inch rounds of cheese.

3. Stack a round of bread, then one of cheese, another of bread, another of cheese, etc., until you have used 5 rounds of bread and 4 of cheese. Push a flat, 6-inch skewer or trussing pin through the stack to hold it together. Set aside on a plate until ready to fry. Repeat with the remaining bread and cheese. You will end up with 1 extra round of bread.

4.   Pour the milk into a shallow bowl. Spread the flour on a plate. In another shallow bowl, beat the eggs with the tablespoon of water.

5.   In a skillet large enough to hold the 4 rolls, heat ¼ inch oil. Use the extra slice of bread to test the heat. A bit of bread should sizzle immediately and brown in less than a minute.

6.   Holding on to the ends of the skewer, carefully roll the cylinder quickly through the milk. Use the skewers only as a guide so they don't rotate. You do not want the bread to become saturated, only moistened. Roll the cylinder through the flour, covering completely, so the cheese won't ooze out during frying. Finally, roll the cylinder through the beaten egg, also making sure to coat thoroughly.

7.   Fry the skewers, using tongs to turn them after the first side has browned.

8.   Serve immediately, sprinkled with a little salt if desired.

Eggs

Uova in Purgatorio
Uova 'mpriatorio

Eggs in Purgatory

Eggs Poached in Tomato Sauce

EGGS SIMMERED in a little tomato sauce. That's all this is, but I think it exemplifies the Neapolitan genius for making something out of nothing.

Serves 2 or 3

1 small onion, cut in half, then finely sliced or chopped

2 or 3 tablespoons extra-virgin olive oil

Pinch hot red pepper flakes, or more to taste

2 cups tomato puree, canned crushed tomatoes,
or chopped and drained canned tomatoes

¼ teaspoon dried marjoram

Salt

4 to 6 eggs

Grated cheese

1. In a 9- or 10-inch skillet, combine the onion, the olive oil, and the hot pepper and cook over medium heat until the onion is lightly golden, about 6 minutes.

2. Add the tomato puree, dried marjoram, and a big pinch of salt to start. Simmer for 5 or 6 minutes, until the sauce has concentrated a little. You can set the pan aside now (at room temperature or in the refrigerator) if you are not cooking the eggs until later.

3. Before cooking the eggs, bring the sauce back to a simmer, taste and add more salt if necessary, then break the eggs into the bubbling sauce. Cover and cook until the eggs are done to taste, meaning with fully set whites and runny yolks, or until the yolks are set further or completely.

4. Serve with grated Parmigiano-Reggiano, a pecorino, or ricotta salata.

Frittata

Flat Omelet

NEAPOLITANS CLAIM TO HAVE invented the frittata. Someone told me, "All the eggs we don't put in our pasta, we put into frittatas." It was just a joke, but Neapolitans do love frittatas. Their pasta frittata has to be the favorite (see page 178), but plain and elaborate frittatas are eaten in wedges as an antipasto or in large portions as a light main course. One of my favorites was one I saw in Avellino, at Ristorante La Taverna Do'Scuorzo. It was a thin frittata like this, spread with ricotta and rolled up jelly-roll fashion, so when the log was cut into slices, it revealed a spiral of yellow egg and white ricotta. American ricotta is too loose to use for this, but if you can find the firmer imported type, it's worth a try for a special meal. It looks good on a buffet table.

This is the most basic frittata. To make a vegetable frittata, sauté or steam the vegetable first, then add it to the eggs before turning it all into the pan. Add diced ham, salami, sausage, any good melting cheese, or fresh herbs. Neapolitans do not make thick frittatas, except for the frittata with pasta. Keep this in mind as you invent your own.

Serves 2 as a light main course

4 eggs

¼ teaspoon salt

⅛ teaspoon freshly ground black pepper

¼ cup grated Parmigiano

1 tablespoon extra-virgin olive oil

1. In a mixing bowl, beat the eggs with the salt and pepper until light and well mixed. Beat in the cheese.

2. In a 6- to 8-inch nonstick skillet, heat the oil over medium heat. When the oil is hot, give the eggs a final stir and pour them into the pan. Immediately reduce the heat to low. Cook until the bottom is well set, usually about 5 minutes.

3. With the aid of a metal spatula, slide the frittata out of the skillet onto a plate. Hold the skillet over the frittata and reverse the plate and the skillet so the frittata falls back in the skillet uncooked-side down. Cook about a minute until set.

4. Serve hot, warm, or at room temperature.

FRITTATA DI SPAGHETTI

FRITTATA NAPOLETANA

SPAGHETTI OMELET

I've heard Italians from other regions make jokes about how Neapolitans love their frittatas of pasta—"those poor people whose cuisine is so limited and who eat so much pasta they even put it in their omelets." It's a point not well taken in Naples, where the pasta frittata is instead considered a stroke of Neapolitan genius: "We clever people who can take just a few eggs, some bits of cheese, and leftover spaghetti and make such a glorious dish." Once you have made a spaghetti frittata, you will definitely side with the Neapolitans and make the dish a part of your life, too.

Serves 4 as a main dish, about 8 as an antipasto

6 to 8 ounces linguine, spaghetti, or other pasta, cooked and sauced or not sauced, left over or freshly cooked, at room temperature

4 eggs, lightly beaten

Freshly ground black pepper to taste

¼ cup freshly grated Parmigiano-Reggiano or pecorino, or a combination of both (or more to taste)

1 tablespoon extra-virgin olive oil

Optional: 5 ounces scamorza or several-days-old mozzarella, sliced

1.　In a large mixing bowl, combine the pasta, the beaten eggs, the black pepper, and the grated cheese. Mix well.

2.　In a 9- to 10-inch nonstick skillet, heat the oil over medium heat and swirl it around to make it coat the bottom of the pan.

3.　Add half the pasta and spread it evenly in the pan. Place the sliced cheese on top (if using), but don't put any cheese within ½ inch of the edge. Add the remaining pasta and spread it to make sure it covers the bottom pasta layer and the sliced cheese. Cook over medium heat for 5 minutes to 8 minutes, or until the bottom browns.

4.　Place a plate on top of the pan and reverse the frittata so it falls onto the plate. Slip the frittata back into the skillet and cook the other side for another 5 to 8 minutes, until it browns.

5. Serve hot, warm, or at room temperature.

VARIATIONS:

Instead of scamorza or mozzarella, you can use any good melting cheese, such as Gouda, Fontina, Gruyère, or Swiss (Emmenthaler).

In addition to, or instead of, the melting cheese, sprinkle a few extra tablespoons of grated cheese between the layers of pasta.

Add diced salami or diced, thinly sliced ham with the cheese.

FRITTATINE IMBOTTITE
FILLED OMELET ROLLS

CANNELLONI FINTI
FAKE CANNELLONI

THESE ARE LITTLE EGG pancakes filled with ricotta, ham, and melting cheese, then baked in a casserole with tomato sauce. They are similar to cannelloni, except with a much easier to prepare omelet shell instead of a fresh pasta. Neapolitans love the idea of fake anything. It's a sly joke, a way to make light and the most of the meager food before them. They have many dishes that are said to be in imitation of something else—for instance, pizza finta (page 19), a pizza made on toast, finto Genovese (page 180), an onion pasta sauce made without the usual meat, and my favorite, patate con l'agnello scappato, which is, "potatoes with the lamb that got away," and in reality is merely potatoes roasted with the rosemary one would use for lamb.

Makes 8 rolls, serving 4 as a first course or light main course

(continued)

For the sauce:

1 28-ounce can peeled plum tomatoes, well drained and chopped (2 cups)

1 small onion, finely diced (½ cup)

2 tablespoons finely cut basil or parsley

2 tablespoons extra-virgin olive oil

½ teaspoon salt

⅛ teaspoon freshly ground black pepper

For the filling:

1 cup whole milk ricotta

3 tablespoons freshly grated Parmigiano-Reggiano

2 ounces sliced cooked (boiled) ham, cut in ¼-inch dice

4 ounces mozzarella or Bel Paese, cut in ¼-inch dice (about ¾ cup)

2 tablespoons finely chopped parsley or basil

For the frittatine:

2 teaspoons flour

½ cup milk

6 eggs

2 tablespoons grated Parmigiano-Reggiano

¼ teaspoon salt

¼ teaspoon freshly ground black pepper

For frying:

1 tablespoon butter

Optional: 2 tablespoons freshly grated Parmigiano-Reggiano for topping

To make the sauce:

1. In a large skillet, over medium-high heat, combine the tomatoes, onion, parsley, oil, salt, and pepper. Simmer 15 minutes, stirring occasionally, during which time the tomato water will have evaporated but the onions will remain slightly crunchy. Alternatively, sauté the onions in oil until tender but not browned, then continue to make a sauce.

To make the filling:

2.   Blend all the ingredients together in a small bowl.

To prepare the frittatine:

3.   Put the flour into a bowl and gradually add the milk, stirring well with a fork. Still using the fork, beat in the eggs, cheese, salt, and pepper, mixing thoroughly.

4.   In a 6-inch skillet, over medium-high heat, melt ½ teaspoon of the butter. Pour in ¼ cup of the egg mixture and cook until the top is just firm. Slip the frittatina onto a countertop or large work surface. The first will probably not turn out perfectly— adjust the temperature and the amount of butter and batter so the rest will be easier. Continue with the rest of the batter. You should end up with 8 or 9 frittatine.

To assemble and bake:

5.   Preheat the oven to 375 degrees.

6.   Spread about 2 tablespoons of the filling on the more raw-looking, top side of each frittatina. Roll them up cannelloni style. Arrange in an 8- or 9-inch square baking pan, or other equivalent-size baking pan. Spoon the tomato sauce over the frittatine to cover completely. If desired, sprinkle with the 2 tablespoons of grated Parmigiano.

7.   Bake for about 20 minutes. Serve hot.

FISH AND SEAFOOD

HERE'S A RELATIVELY NEW Neapolitan legend:

On September 9, 1943, Naples and Salerno became the first Italian cities to surrender to the Allies, or as Napoletani and Salernitani like to think of it, the first to throw the Germans out. On this momentous and joyous occasion, the local powers-that-be wanted to fête the Allied generals. But how could they have a banquet when there was no food in Naples? Women and children were selling themselves for an egg. The aristocracy were living in empty palazzi, having sold all their furniture and possessions to buy food. What could the city fathers possibly offer the victorious and welcome Allied generals? They decided to see what they could find at the municipal aquarium. All that was left was a manatee. So the generals, unbeknownst to them, dined on manatee. When word got out on the street that the politicians had served the manatee to the generals, and gotten away with it, no one was shocked. Neapolitans had done and eaten stranger things. The only question was, "How did they prepare the manatee?" "Why aglio-olio, of course, with a little parsley."

Garlic, olive oil, parsley: There's not much more one needs to know about cooking seafood and fish Neapolitan style, except to add a tomato now and then.

"When the fish is good, you don't want to do much to it. And when the fish isn't good, you don't want to eat it," said Antonio Sersale of Le Sirenuse in Positano, one of the grand hotels of the Amalfi Coast, explaining the Campanian philosophy on fish. Not doing much to it means that, if the fish is large, it is baked, grilled, or steamed in a parchment package (*in cartoccio*) with garlic, olive oil, and parsley. And if the fish is small, then it is deep-fried or simmered in water flavored with garlic, olive oil, parsley and a little bit of tomato (*all'acqua pazza*). Bivalves—clams and mussels—are always steamed in their own juices—usually with garlic, olive oil, and parsley, and only sometimes tomato. Crustaceans such as shrimp and scampi are grilled or they're cooked into a sauce with garlic, olive oil, parsley, and tomato. Octopus are cooked in their own juices—with garlic, olive oil, parsley, and sometimes tomato. Squid and cuttlefish are either deep-fried or grilled, or sautéed with garlic, olive oil, and parsley, or stewed with garlic, olive oil, parsley, and tomato. And so it goes. The fin fish are mostly cooked whole. The rest are almost always served in their shells—unless it's a particularly elegant occasion.

Excellent fish and shellfish are not hard to find in Campania, either. It's expensive, but people who have the money are willing to pay the price. The fish stores in Naples spill onto the street with an astounding array of trays filled with every creature that lives on and around the sea rocks, with several kinds of clams, with mussels, oysters, octopus, a baffling variety of shrimp and other crustaceans, with squid and cuttlefish in various sizes, and with a rainbow of small fish and baby fish and all their fully grown relatives.

The Tyrrhenian Sea is much more bountiful than the Ligurian Sea to its north, and Neapolitans and all those Campanians who live along the shore have always exploited the waters and especially the sea rocks. Traditionally, however, few could afford the glorious white-fleshed fin fish of the area, the gilthead bream (orata), white bream (sarago), small bass (spigola), and red mullet (triglie). The average man had to make the most of the lesser fish, the so-called pesce azzurro, blue fish, the gray-blue skinned, oily, and darker-fleshed fish such as anchovies (alici), sardines (sarde), and mackerel (sgombro), along with the clams, mussels, cockles, periwinkles, and snails. The aristocracy ate white-fleshed fish and oysters. For hundreds of years, all of these were highly taxed. The crafty Neapolitans had to work around the law to meet their voracious appetite for seafood, creating a network of black market seafood sellers supplied by the street urchins (*scugnizzi*) who scavenged the beaches "dressed only in salt water and seaweed," as one writer put it. Perhaps that is why even today Neapolitans, careful food shoppers in general, are particularly wary at the fish market. They invariably sniff the wares, prod them, examine them, and look them in the eye before they buy.

With superhighways connecting every corner of the region, fresh fish and seafood are available all over now. It wasn't so long ago, however, that those in the land-locked provinces of Benevento and Avellino, and Neapolitans who couldn't afford fresh fish, who were many, ate mainly preserved fish—salted anchovies, salt cod, and the air-dried cod called stockfish (stocco). The anchovies come from local waters. The cod has been imported from the North Sea countries at least since the Middle Ages. This could be another Neapolitan tall tale, but I've been told that there's a town in Finland whose entire economy continues to be based solely on supplying Naples with salt cod. Salt cod (baccalà) is one of those tastes from *la cucina povera* that persists despite the easier availability of fresh fish, and there are innumerable ways of preparing it. It's more expensive than it used to be, but it is a ritual during the Christmas season. Signs outside fish markets everywhere announce their special price for baccalà, fish that's already been washed of its salt in special tanks with running water. Stockfish is another story. Air drying produces a product with a strong taste and aroma, and while many Neapolitans like to wax nostalgic about it, not many people have a taste for it anymore.

PESCE ALL'ACQUA PAZZA

FISH IN CRAZY WATER

THERE ARE SEVERAL EXPLANATIONS for the name of this, the most popular way of cooking whole, small fish in Campania. The one that sounds most likely and that I like best is that "crazy water" refers to the sea water used by fishermen of yore to cook their catch while out at sea. Can't you see some fisherman yelling at another, pinching his fingers together and jabbing the air in front of his face, the way Neapolitans do when they're skeptical, "What! Are you crazy? You're going to cook dinner in sea water?!" Indeed, when people are lost at sea and get crazy with thirst, if they drink sea water they can die.

Another far less probable interpretation of the name has it that the "crazy" refers to the spiciness of the broth from the addition of red pepper. But not everyone uses red pepper, and even if they do, it's not likely to be so much that it makes the dish crazy hot. In any case, the dish seems to predate the introduction of chili peppers (and tomatoes), which were first brought to Europe by Cortez's contingent in 1519 (Cortez himself stayed in Mexico to marry, murder, and plunder), and not used widely until well over a century later. The earliest and still most basic "crazy water" is nothing more than water, salt, garlic, parsley, and olive oil. Today, tomatoes are almost always added, either a few cherry tomatoes—fresh in season, otherwise canned, a product nearly unavailable in North America—or a diced or crushed, peeled plum tomato—again, either fresh or canned.

This is a method for cooking whole fish, not filleted fish, because only whole fish make a broth worth sipping or one flavorful enough to dress the fish well. There is, however, a nontraditional way of making a good acqua pazza with fish fillets. Get some fish heads and trimmings at the fish market, optimally those removed to make the fillets you are cooking (do not use salmon trimmings). Cook these with the flavorings to give the "crazy water" some body and flavor, then remove the fish trimmings before adding the fillets. You'll get the same good broth as you would if you'd cooked a whole fish, but you won't have to look at the head on your plate or deal with the bones.

Serves 2 to 4

(continued)

2 cups water

½ teaspoon coarse sea salt

1 to 2 tablespoons extra-virgin olive oil

1 or 2 large cloves garlic, sliced thickly or lightly smashed

2 to 4 whole sprigs parsley, with stems

1 small whole red or green chili pepper, or a pinch of red pepper flakes,
or a few drops of hot pepper oil

Optional: ½ to 1 canned plum tomato, sliced or coarsely chopped,
or 3 to 4 cherry tomatoes, halved, or 1 rounded teaspoon tomato paste

2 to 3 pounds small, whole fish, such as whiting, mackerel,
Spanish mackerel, black bass (sometimes called sea bass), or red mullet

1. In a skillet or sauté pan large enough to hold the fish in 1 layer, combine the water, salt, oil, garlic, parsley, pepper, and optional tomato product. Bring to a boil and let boil 5 minutes.

2. Add the fish, reduce the heat, and cook gently until done to taste, from 3 to 5 minutes for a fillet, up to 10 or 12 minutes for a whole small fish. If the fish is not covered by the crazy water, which whole fish probably will not be, turn the fish once to cook both sides.

3. Remove fish to a serving platter or individual plates or shallow bowls. Pour on the broth. If desired, for a stronger but lesser amount of broth (this is not a sauce, but a true broth), reduce the liquid over high heat before pouring it on the fish.

VARIATION:

White wine can be substituted for up to ½ of the water.

For the last 3 to 4 minutes, add a few of the smallest clams you can find.

Bocconcini di Rana Pescatrice alla Mediterranea

Chunks of Monkfish, Mediterranean-Style

THE NAME OF THIS DISH, although not the actual recipe, comes from the 1997 kitchen calendar given out by the Centro Ittico Costiera Amalfitana (CICO), one of the best fish markets on the Amalfi Coast, with joint wholesale-retail stores in Positano and Amalfi. Braising firm, meaty fish in a tomato and wine base is, as the Amalfitani fishmongers obviously know, a standard technique around the European Mediterranean. Indeed, my own first experience cooking fish this way was with an almost identical Niçoise recipe made with onions instead of garlic, basil instead of parsley, and embellished with that region's tiny olives. In Sardinia, the tomato sauce may be flavored with saffron and mint. Around the Amalfi Coast, people add pitted Gaeta olives, or a few anchovies, and/or some capers. In the CICO recipe, brandy is used instead of white wine, reflecting the fact that the fish company supplies some of the most elegant hotel kitchens on the peninsula.

Serves 4

2 tablespoons tomato paste

¼ cup dry white wine or dry vermouth

2 tablespoons extra-virgin olive oil

2 or 3 cloves garlic, lightly smashed

1½ to 2 pounds monkfish fillets, membrane removed
and cut into 1½-inch chunks

1 to 1½ cups coarsely chopped fresh plum or salad tomatoes (do not juice)
or canned plum tomatoes, drained before measuring
and coarsely chopped or crushed

Pinch of hot red pepper flakes (or more to taste)

½ to 1 teaspoon salt (depending on tomatoes and taste)

1 rounded tablespoon finely cut parsley

1.   In a small cup or bowl, dissolve the tomato paste in the wine, using a table fork to blend. Set aside.

(continued)

2.   In a deep, 10-inch skillet, sauté pan, or stovetop casserole, over low heat, combine the oil and garlic and cook until the garlic is soft and barely begins to color on both sides, pressing the garlic into the oil a couple of times to release its flavor. Remove the garlic.

3.   Still over medium-low heat, add the fish chunks. Turn the fish over in the oil to firm it up on all sides. The surfaces will become opaque. Do not cook it further.

4.   Add the wine and tomato paste mixture to the pan. Increase the heat to medium and let the liquid simmer a minute or so to evaporate the alcohol.

5.   Stir in the tomatoes, the hot pepper, the salt, and half the parsley. Turn the fish in the sauce, then adjust the heat so the fish simmers very, very gently, uncovered, for 8 to 10 minutes, stirring and turning the fish a couple of times. If the fish cooks to your taste before the tomatoes coalesce into a sauce, remove the fish chunks with a slotted spoon and set aside on a serving dish. Increase the heat under the pan and simmer the sauce briskly until it reduces to your taste. On the other hand, if the sauce becomes too thick, add water by a tablespoonful at a time until it returns to a consistency you like.

6.   Just before serving, stir in the remaining parsley, taste for seasoning, and correct salt and pepper as necessary.

7.   Serve the fish in the sauce, either hot or at room temperature.

Variations:

Along with the tomatoes, add 6 to 8 pitted and coarsely chopped Gaeta olives and / or up to a tablespoon of capers (coarsely chopped if large).

For a little anchovy flavor, melt up to 4 anchovy fillets in the olive oil after removing the garlic, then proceed as directed.

As instructed on the CICO calendar, you can use brandy instead of white wine.

Substitute tuna or swordfish for the monkfish, following the recipe but cooking these fish slightly less, 5 or 6 minutes instead of 10. (Tuna is particularly good served at room temperature the day after it is prepared. Of course, it should be refrigerated until about an hour before serving time.)

Just before the fish is cooked, you can add about ½ pound of shelled, small shrimp, or a couple of clams or mussels per person. The shrimp take about 3 minutes to cook in the sauce, adding almost no liquid to it. Clams or mussels take 2 or 3 minutes to open and do express liquid into the sauce. In that case, you want to remove the fish and shellfish with a slotted spoon and reduce the sauce slightly before recombining the fish with the sauce.

PESCE CON OLIVE, CAPPERI, E LIMONE
FISH FILLETS WITH OLIVES, CAPERS, AND LEMON

THIS METHOD OF COOKING fish is from *Menu napoletani* (Neapolitan Menus) by Lejla Mancusi Sorrentino and Germana Militerni Nardone, a book of contemporary recipes with introductory historical musings, all organized by the season. In this recipe, apparently created by one of the authors or one of their sophisticated friends, you are, in a way, poaching fish fillets in olives, capers, olive oil, and lemon juice. The low heat gives the fish a velvety texture. The condiments enliven even the blandest white fish fillet, such as flounder, sole, catfish, or tilapia, and are also a good match for dark-fleshed fish, such as mackerel and our North Atlantic bluefish. The olives will end up sticking to the fish, which is how it should be. I have also tried the recipe with chicken cutlets with great success.

Serves 2 or 3

2 tablespoons extra-virgin olive oil

1 tablespoon salted capers, thoroughly rinsed and chopped coarsely if large

4 ounces green olives (preferably large Sicilian type, about ¾ cup), pitted and finely chopped

Juice of 1 lemon

1 pound fish fillets (any kind)

1 rounded tablespoon finely cut parsley

(continued)

1.   Mix together the olive oil, capers, olives, and lemon juice in a 10-inch skillet. Place over low heat and let the mixture warm slowly until it begins to sizzle gently. (If, after 10 minutes, the mixture has not heated enough to sizzle, raise the heat slightly.)

2.   Arrange the fish fillets in 1 layer over the olives. If there is more fish than will fit in 1 layer, cook the fish in 2 batches. Depending on the thickness of the fillets, cook the fish from 1 to 2 minutes on the first side, then turn the fish and cook another minute or so. If cooking the fish in 2 batches, make sure to leave behind enough of the olives and pan juices to cook the second batch.

3.   Sprinkle the fish with parsley and serve hot or at room temperature.

VARIATION:

To prepare chicken in this manner, use plump chicken breast halves, not ones that have been butterflied or pounded out. Follow the directions above, but expect chicken breasts to cook about 4 minutes on the first side and about 3 minutes on the second. They will not brown, but should be coated with chopped olives, at least on the first side. Serve olive-side up for looks.

GAMBERONI AL LIMONE

JUMBO SHRIMP WITH LEMON

By THE TIME THIS DISH is finished, the chunks of lemon pulp will have turned into a sauce lightly thickened by the flour that otherwise will have formed a nice crust on the shrimp. If such huge shrimp are not available, you can use the same recipe for smaller shrimp, but be sure to remove them as soon as they are cooked and give the sauce a little more time on its own to reduce to a syrupy consistency.

Serves 4

2 lemons

½ cup flour

8 jumbo shrimp (about 1 pound)

3 tablespoons extra-virgin olive oil

Salt

2 tablespoons finely cut parsley

Because the shrimp cook so quickly, all the ingredients must be ready and at hand.

1.   Prepare the lemons: With a sharp knife, cut about ¼ inch off the ends of 1 lemon. Stand the lemon up on a cut end, then cut down, removing the peel and white pith in strips. Make sure to trim off all the white pith. Discard the peel and pith. Cut the lemon lengthwise in quarters, remove the pits, then cut it crosswise into pieces no larger than ½ inch. Set the lemon cubes aside. Juice the other lemon.

2.   Place the flour on a plate or piece of wax paper.

3.   Try to buy shrimp still in their shells, the heads removed. With a very sharp (preferably serrated) knife, cut the shrimp lengthwise through the underside of the shell, but still leaving the top side of the shell and the tail intact and attached—in other words, butterfly the shrimp.

4.   In a 10-inch skillet, heat the oil over medium heat until hot enough for the first shrimp to sizzle slightly as soon as it is put in the pan. As you are about to put each shrimp in the pan, cut-side down, season its open side lightly with salt, then dust it with flour. Fry about 1 minute. Turn the shrimp shell-side down and fry another minute, or until the shells have turned red and the shrimp seem almost but not quite done. Turn the shrimp cut-side down again, then add the lemon juice, the cubes of lemon, the water, salt, and the parsley. Swirl and stir the liquid and lemon pieces in the pan for about 15 seconds, then remove the shrimp to plates and give the juice in the pan a final stir.

5.   Pour the sauce over the shrimp and serve immediately on warm plates.

Sautè (Sotè) di Vongole o Cozze

Sauté of Clams or Mussels

———

There is no simpler or more basic way to cook clams or mussels in Campania. As is, with no further embellishment and in a smallish portion, this is a very popular restaurant antipasto—a few clams to nibble while figuring out what else to eat. Poured on dried or toasted bread, it becomes zuppa di vongole, a course that could replace pasta before a main course or could be a main course itself. On pasta, it becomes linguine alle vongole, which, after fresh tomato sauce, is the second most popular way of eating pasta in Campania.

Serves 3 or 4

3 tablespoons extra-virgin olive oil

2 large cloves garlic, lightly smashed, or cut in half, or thickly sliced

⅛ teaspoon or more hot red pepper flakes,
or a piece of a whole, fresh hot pepper

3 to 4 pounds clams or mussels, cleaned well

3 tablespoons finely cut parsley

1. In a 12-inch or larger sauté pan, or a large, deep pot, over medium-low heat, combine the oil, the garlic, and the hot pepper. If using smashed or halved garlic, cook until it barely begins to color, pressing it into the oil a few times to release its flavor, then either remove it or not, depending on your taste. If using sliced garlic, there's no need to press it into the oil.

2. Add the clams or mussels, cover the pan, then shake it a few times. Increase the heat to medium-high to high and cook, shaking the pan another once or twice, until the bivalves open—usually no more than 2 minutes for mussels or manila clams, often even less, and usually 3 to 4 minutes for Littleneck clams. If using both, put the clams in the pan first, then add the mussels after about 2 minutes.

3. When the shellfish have opened, stir in the parsley and serve immediately.

Variation:

This recipe is the base for making Linguine alle Vongole (page 146) and the following Zuppa di Vongole o Cozze al Pomodoro.

Zuppa di Vongole o Cozze al Pomodoro

Clam or Mussel Soup with Tomatoes

THIS IS, IN ESSENCE, the sauce of linguine with red clam (or mussel) sauce, but instead of putting it on pasta, which more often takes a white clam sauce these days, it is served, as zuppe always are, on dried or toasted bread. It is a filling dish and one of those minestre/zuppe that can be considered a main course. If you serve it in place of pasta, follow it with the clear flavor of barely adorned broiled, roasted, or grilled fish, or a fish cooked in parchment.

Serves 4

¼ cup extra-virgin olive oil

2 large cloves garlic, lightly smashed, or cut in half, or thickly sliced

⅛ teaspoon or more hot red pepper flakes,
or a piece of a whole, fresh hot pepper

1 14-ounce can peeled plum tomatoes, coarsely chopped (1½ to 2 cups)

3 to 4 pounds clams and/or mussels

⅓ cup finely cut parsley

Salt

4 freselle (page 257) or 2 cups fried croutons (page 242)

1. In a large pot with a cover, over medium-low heat, combine the oil, the garlic, and the hot pepper. Cook the garlic, pressing it into the oil a couple of times to release its flavor, until it barely begins to color on both sides. Remove the garlic or not, as desired.

2. Add the tomatoes with their juice and bring to a simmer. Add the clams or mussels, cover the pot, and cook until they open, about 2 minutes for mussels, somewhat longer for clams. Stir the sauce, then taste it. If you'd like it stronger or thicker, remove the mussels with a slotted spoon or skimmer and cover them to keep them warm, then reduce the sauce over high heat. Stir in the parsley. Taste for salt and adjust if necessary.

(continued)

3. Serve the mussels and their sauce, in or out of the shell, over freselle, or with fried croutons. If serving the clams or mussels out of their shells, they will cool while you're shelling them, so reheat them for a minute in simmering sauce.

VARIATION:

For Linguine alle Vongole al Pomodoro, instead of serving this as a zuppa, on dried bread or with crostini, use it to sauce 1 pound of linguine.

COZZE IMPEPATE
'MPEPATELLA DI COZZE

PEPPERED MUSSELS

There is a specialty known as "'mpepatella di cozze," that is truly a dish to be savored by the seashore as the fishermen handle their nets. Like very black bunches of corymbs, the mussels arrive from Fusaro; are cleaned again and again in sea water and rubbed one against the other until they become resplendent, as if they were basalt polished to a fine finish. They are then placed in a clay dish and ladle after ladle of boiling sea water is poured over the mussels until the valves open into a wide yawn revealing the very irritated and slightly clotted interior. Freshly ground pepper is then ground in abundance over the mussels. Gingerly, because they are almost too hot to touch, bring the mussels to your mouth and gently pull away the salty, pimento-colored meat with your lips.

MARIO STEFANILE, NEAPOLITAN GASTRONOME AND WRITER, IN *PARTENOPE IN CUCINA* (PARTHENOPE IN THE KITCHEN)

MUSSELS AND FRESHLY GROUND black pepper have a remarkable synergy. They bring out the best in each other—the mussels' sweetness and the pepper's fragrance—and cancel out the worst in each other—the mussels' bitter edge and the pepper's harshness. So although there are only two ingredients in this recipe—not counting the bread that sops up those mingled flavors and the lemon you may or may not want to squeeze over them—the whole is truly much greater than its parts.

For each person:

**1 fresella, slice of pane biscottato, or slice of toasted
or dried and toasted bread**

1 pound mussels

Freshly ground black pepper

Lemon wedges

1. Have soup bowls ready, each one with a fresella or piece of toasted bread in the bottom.

2. Clean the mussels well and place them, still wet from their washing, in a large pot with a cover. Place over high heat and steam the mussels open, usually no more than 2 minutes. As soon as the mussels have opened, uncover the pot and grind a copious amount of black pepper over them, right in the pot.

3. Divide the mussels among the bowls, then divide the liquid among the bowls.

4. Serve immediately, with wedges of lemon to squeeze on as desired.

COZZE AL GRATIN

BAKED MUSSELS

COZZE ARRIGANATE

MUSSELS OREGANATA

THIS IS THE RECIPE FROM which Italian-American "baked clams" or "clams oreganata" are derived. It's a much lighter treatment than most Italian-American recipes and is a heavenly antipasto. Campanians might use clams instead of mussels, too, but mussels are a far more plentiful and inexpensive bivalve than clams in Campania, and the local clams are mostly too tiny for this treatment. One of the great things about baked mussels is that, although it takes time to prepare them, the work can all be done ahead. They just go under the broiler for a few minutes at the last minute.

Makes 30 to 35 pieces, serving 4 to 6 as an antipasto

2 pounds mussels (30 to 35), debearded if necessary and very well scrubbed

For the topping:

½ cup dried bread crumbs

3 tablespoons extra-virgin olive oil

1 to 2 tablespoons of the mussel broth (from steaming)

1 generous tablespoon very finely minced garlic

½ teaspoon salt

½ teaspoon freshly ground black pepper

½ teaspoon oregano

1. In a large, covered pan, steam the mussels open without adding any liquid or seasonings. It usually takes less than 2 minutes over medium-high heat. Let the mussels cool, then remove them from their shells, reserving the shells. Reserve the broth separately.

2. Place 2 or 3 mussel meats in each shell half, depending on the size of the shell, and arrange the shells in a single layer in a shallow, broiler-proof pan.

3. In a small bowl, using a fork, blend together the bread crumbs and the other topping ingredients, using just enough mussel broth to moisten the crumbs very slightly.

4. Using a teaspoon, cover the mussels in each shell half with crumbs, packing them slightly so they are not loose. The recipe can be prepared in advance up to this point but no more than a few hours ahead. Refrigerate then return to near room temperature.

5. Just before you are ready to serve the mussels, place the pan under the broiler, about 4 inches from the heat source, and broil until the tops have browned, 1 to 2 minutes. Watch carefully so the mussel topping does not burn. Serve immediately.

Zuppa di Frutti di Mare con Cannellini alla Antonio Evangelista

Shellfish Soup with White Beans

COMBINING SEAFOOD AND BEANS, a fruit of the sea with a fruit of the mountains, is a popular idea in Campania. Squid, cuttlefish, octopus, clams, mussels, snails, and cockles are mixed and matched with cannellini, chickpeas, pinto beans, and cranberry beans—in hot dishes and cold. A mix of shelled creatures gathered from seaside rocks is especially popular on the Salerno coast, where a menu listing might call a dish made with them *allo scoglio* or *di scoglio, scoglio* being the word for a seaside rock. And when the sea creatures are coupled with beans, I've seen it called *di scoglio e monte*, referring to the mountains behind the shore where particularly good chickpeas and cannellini thrive.

Antonio and Gina Evangelista

At Sordella 1919, a restaurant that is not near the sea but in Cervaro, just outside of Cassino (politically in the region of Lazio, but in ancient times Campania felix, at the north end of the Caserta plain), chef-owner Antonio Evangelista is breaking culinary ground with this dish, as he is by serving grated cheese with some fish-sauced pastas. That's being done now, too, as some people say it was in their great-grandparents' time.

Serves 6 to 8 as an antipasto, 4 as a minestra

(continued)

For the fried croutons:

Olive oil for frying

4 cups ½-inch bread cubes

For the zuppa:

1 recipe Sautè di Vongole o Cozze (see page 236)
(you can use clams or mussels or both)

¼ cup extra-virgin olive oil

2 large cloves garlic, lightly smashed, or cut in half, or thickly sliced

¼ teaspoon or more hot red pepper flakes,
or a piece of a whole, fresh hot pepper

2 pints (2 pounds) cherry tomatoes, cut into halves or quarters,
depending on size

3 cups fully cooked, drained cannellini beans (they may be canned)

¼ to ¾ teaspoon salt

¼ cup finely cut parsley

To fry the croutons:

1. Heat at least ¼ inch olive oil in a medium-size skillet. Add the bread cubes and, tossing constantly, fry until they turn a nutty brown. Immediately and quickly remove the cubes with a slotted spoon or skimmer and let them drain on absorbent paper or a draining rack. The croutons can be prepared as much as several days ahead. Keep them in a tin, then reheat on a baking sheet in a 350-degree oven. Be careful not to let them darken or burn too much.

To make the zuppa:

2. Prepare the Sautè di Vongole o Cozze. Remove the shellfish meats from their shells and place them in a bowl until you are ready to add them to the soup at the end of cooking. If preparing the soup ahead, strain the broth over the shellfish and cover until ready to complete the dish. Otherwise, you can keep the shellfish meats in a bowl and leave the broth in the sauté pan.

3. In a 3-quart saucepan or stovetop casserole, over medium-low heat, combine the oil, garlic, and hot pepper. Cook the garlic, pressing it into the oil a couple of times to release its flavor, until it barely begins to color on both sides. Remove the garlic or not, depending on your taste.

4. Add all the tomatoes, cover immediately, and let simmer briskly for about 8 minutes, until the tomatoes fall apart and become saucy. About halfway through the cooking, stir the tomatoes and smash the bigger pieces with your wooden spoon.

5. Add the mussel broth and continue to simmer, now uncovered, for about 2 minutes.

6. Add the cannellini beans, which will stop the simmering, and let them heat through, at most at a very gentle simmer, another minute or so. You do not want the beans to become too mushy. Taste for seasoning, and add salt if necessary.

7. Add the clams and heat through.

8. Stir in the parsley and serve very hot, garnished with fried croutons.

VARIATION:

At Taberna la Rustica da Peppe in Casagiove, which is, literally, one block beyond the Caserta city limits, Giuseppe Canganiello, one of the region's growing cadre of young, contemporary-minded chefs, cooks Seppie con Fagioli Messicani, cuttlefish stewed in pinto beans. It is so similar to the above recipe, you can make it using the same outline: Unfortunately for home cooks, cuttlefish, which are the cephalopod with all the black ink, are nearly impossible to buy in North America. If you can find them, use them; otherwise the dish is also delicious with squid. Make the cherry tomato sauce as described. Add 1 pound of cuttlefish, sliced thin, or calamari cut into thin rings, the tentacles cut in halves or quarters. Simmer the seafood in the sauce, covered, until tender, about 30 minutes. Add 3 cups of precooked pinto beans, heat through, then serve as above with fried crostini.

Giuseppe Canganiello

Sautè di Cozze con Purè di Ceci

Sautéed Mussels with Chickpea Cream

ONE DOESN'T EXPECT TO see a wealth of seafood in a restaurant kitchen in the town of Avellino, set in a lush interior valley surrounded by hills of hazelnut trees. Chef Antonio Rosolio of Ristorante La Taverna Do' Scuorzo (since 1821) explains that nowadays, with the Autostrada making the fish market in Pozzuoli less than a two-hour drive (closer to an hour and fifteen minutes the way he drives), fresh fish is a luxury that the Avellinese can now afford. After centuries of impoverishment and natural disasters, the latest of which were the monstrous earthquakes of 1981, the city and the zone in general have been rebuilt and are achieving newfound affluence from modern agriculture, winemaking, and light industry.

Chef Rosolio claims to have learned most of what he knows about cooking from his mother, who helps out in the restaurant by cleaning vegetables and making "suggestions" to her son, but this is his own elegant and very satisfying creation, following the current trend of combining seafood and legumes. It can be served in a small portion as a first course, or in a larger portion as a second course.

Serves 4 as a first course

¼ cup extra-virgin olive oil

4 cloves garlic, lightly smashed

⅛ teaspoon hot red pepper flakes or a piece of fresh hot pepper

3 pounds mussels, debearded and well scrubbed

3½ cups cooked chickpeas, drained (reserve ¼ cup cooking liquid)

Whole leaves of parsley, for garnish

Hot pepper oil (page 93)

1. In a deep, 10- to 12-inch skillet or sauté pan, over medium-low heat, combine the oil, the garlic, and the hot pepper. Cook the garlic, pressing it into the oil a couple of times to release its flavor, until it is soft and barely begins to color on both sides. Remove the garlic.

2. Add the mussels, cover the pan, increase the heat to medium high, and shake the pan well. Let the mussels steam open, usually no longer than 2 minutes.

3. Remove the mussels with a slotted spoon and place them in a large covered pot, with about ½ cup of their steaming juices, to keep them warm over the lowest possible heat.

4. Put the chickpeas in a blender with ¼ cup of their cooking liquid and ½ cup of the hot mussel broth. Process to a very smooth puree about the consistency of sour cream, adding a spoon or so more of mussel broth if necessary.

5. Divide the chickpea puree among 4 heated bowls. Top with the steamed mussels. Divide any remaining mussel juices evenly among the bowls. Garnish with whole leaves of parsley, which are meant to be eaten.

6. Serve immediately, if desired with hot pepper oil to drizzle over the mussels and chickpea puree.

SAUTÈ DI CALAMARI

SAUTÉED SQUID

AT FIRST WE THOUGHT it was the magic of the moment and the place that made the calamari taste as good as they did. It was a brilliant early September afternoon, about three o'clock. We had just arrived in Casamicciola Terme, on Ischia, by ferry from Naples, had checked into the Hotel Paradiso, luxuriated for a few moments on our terraces on a hill facing Vesuvius across the Bay of Naples, and were now worried that no one would feed us at this late hour.

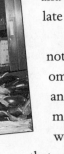

Angela De Siano of the restaurant 'O Padrone on Ischia.

We headed for 'O Padrone d'o Mare, which was not only the closest restaurant on my list but also a recommendation of Anna Gosetti della Salda, the founder and retired publisher of *La cucina italiana*, Italy's foremost food magazine. We figured dropping her name would assure us of a meal from the De Siano family that owns 'O Padrone—sister Angela and brothers Franco, Gennaro, Salvatore, and Ciro.

At 'O Padrone, we sat on the protected terrace; with the island of Procida, and Vesuvius as a backdrop; the sandy beach, a few colorful dinghies, and the often pictured "mushroom" rock at our feet. The restaurant's pet turtle was shuffling on the floor, making the rounds of the tables, we supposed hunting for fallen scraps. Almost as soon as we were seated, we were presented with a basket of the housemade pizza bread and a small dish with rings of calamari. We took a bite and looked at each other. Our eyes bugged. Coming from New York, where fried calamari is as common as potato chips and the best you can say about it is that it's tender and not greasy, this was amazing calamari. The best and freshest taste of the sea. Naturally, there was nothing to it—rings and tentacles of fresh squid sautéed in good olive oil, garlic, and hot pepper.

Serves 4 as an antipasto, 2 or 3 as a main course

1 pound already cleaned, fresh calamari (about 1¼ pounds uncleaned)
(see box)

2 tablespoons extra-virgin olive oil

2 large cloves garlic, lightly smashed

⅛ to ¼ teaspoon hot red pepper flakes

Salt, if necessary

1. With a dull table knife, scrape off the speckled outer membrane of the calamari if this has not already been done. Slice the calamari crosswise into approximately ¼-inch rounds and the tentacles in half or quarters, depending on the size of the calamari.

2. In a 10-inch skillet, combine the oil, the garlic, and the hot pepper. Set over low heat and cook the garlic until it is soft and barely begins to color on all sides, pressing it into the oil a few times to release its flavor. Remove the garlic.

3. Increase the heat to high and immediately add the calamari. Toss constantly over high heat for 1 to 2 minutes, or until just cooked through. If the fish cooks longer it will toughen. Taste the calamari after about a minute.

Note: You may end up with a lot of juice, depending on the calamari. I like to mop up the juices with bread, but if you care to, or if you are going to use the sauté of calamari for a gratin (recipe follows), remove the calamari with a slotted spoon, and reduce the juices over high heat for a minute or so, until they become syrupy.

CALAMARI

*I*t is possible to get fresh squid in North American markets, although frozen will do for stewing or frying. Frozen squid are invariably cleaned already, but fresh are not, and cleaning them is a tedious, sloppy job. If possible, have it done for you at the fish market. If the squid are being sold as cleaned, but still have their speckled outer membrane, as is often the case, this "fell" is easily removed by scraping a table knife (not a sharp knife) across the cavities. Nothing has to be removed from the tentacles, which are, incidentally, more tender than the cavities, but they can be cut in halves or quarters, grouping a couple or a few tentacles together, depending on their size. Always keep squid well chilled. If they are very fresh when bought, they should hold for two days in the refrigerator, placed (in a plastic bag) on top of a bed of ice (which I put in a roasting pan). Just before cooking the squid, rinse them under cold water to remove any specks of hard cartilage.

CALAMARI AL GRATIN

CALAMARI AL PANGRATTATO

Baked Squid

SAUTÉED SQUID IS EASILY turned into this delectable dish, a casserole of squid topped with piquantly seasoned bread crumbs browned under the broiler. In small portions, it makes a good antipasto, and an especially convenient one because the base of sautéed squid can be prepared ahead, and simply heated at the last moment with its mantle of crumbs.

Serves 4 as an antipasto, 2 or 3 as a main course

1 recipe Sautè di Calamari (page 246)

1 rounded tablespoon salted capers, thoroughly rinsed

1 rounded tablespoon minced, pitted Gaeta olives

½ teaspoon dried oregano

2 tablespoons extra-virgin olive oil

¼ cup dried bread crumbs

1.   Prepare the sauté of calamari.

2.   Off the heat, toss in the capers, the olives, and the oregano. With a slotted spoon, remove the cooked calamari and arrange them in a shallow, 10-inch round or similarly sized oval or rectangular, broiler-proof pan—a gratin dish.

3.   Over high heat, reduce the juices until they are syrupy and pour them evenly over the calamari, scraping out the skillet to get every last drop.

4.   In a small bowl or cup, stir the olive oil into the bread crumbs. Sprinkle the oiled crumbs evenly over the calamari. They should not cover the calamari, but every bite should have a little crunch.

5.   Place the pan under a broiler, about 4 inches from the heat source, until the bread crumbs brown lightly, about 2 minutes.

6.   Serve immediately.

CALAMARI IN CASSUOLA

CALAMARI IN UMIDO

SQUID STEWED WITH TOMATOES

THE DARKER FLAVORS OF both squid and tomatoes emerge when they are stewed together with garlic, hot pepper, and oregano. And they are as devilishly seductive as any moonlit night on Capri. Besides, stewing squid is the only no-fail way of cooking it. If it's still tough, add a little more water to the sauce and stew it some more. Squid gets tough almost immediately, then after long cooking it becomes tender again. If you cook it much too long, it can get cooked out and dry, but it never gets tough a second time.

Serves about 6 as an antipasto, 4 as a main course

3 tablespoons extra-virgin olive oil

2 large cloves garlic, lightly smashed

¼ teaspoon or more hot red pepper flakes
or a piece of fresh or dried hot pepper

1 14-ounce can peeled plum tomatoes,
with their juices (1½ to 2 cups)

¼ teaspoon dried oregano

2 pounds already cleaned, fresh calamari (about 2½ pounds, uncleaned),
cut into ¼-inch rounds, tentacles cut in halves or quarters

¼ cup finely cut parsley

Optional: freselle (see page 257)

1. In a 2½- to 3-quart saucepan or stovetop casserole, over low heat, combine the olive oil, the garlic, and the hot pepper. Cook until the garlic is soft and beginning to color on all sides, pressing the garlic into the oil a few times to release its flavor. Remove the garlic.

2. Add the tomatoes and the oregano and, with a wooden spoon, break up and coarsely crush the tomatoes. Increase the heat to medium high and simmer briskly, uncovered, for 5 minutes.

(continued)

3. Stir the calamari into the sauce and continue to simmer steadily, uncovered, for about 30 minutes, or until the sauce has thickened and the calamari are tender. Some calamari may take longer to cook, in which case you may need to add a tablespoon or as many as a few tablespoons of water so the sauce doesn't become too reduced.

4. Add the parsley and cook another 15 seconds.

5. Serve very hot, as is, with bread, or over freselle.

VARIATION:

For Calamari Napoletani, a less generic, more strictly Neapolitan and complexly flavored dish, add 4 teaspoons raisins, 4 teaspoons pine nuts, and about 10 pitted, coarsely chopped Gaeta olives for the last 10 minutes of cooking. Use the parsley, too.

CALAMARI RIPIENI O IMBOTTITI

STUFFED SQUID

HERE AGAIN IS A NEAPOLITAN recipe—like sugo alla Genovese or braciole al ragù or salsicce al pomodoro . . . oh, so many things—that creates two courses. The squid, stuffed mainly with their own tentacles and some shrimp, easily stand alone as a second course, leaving most of the now sea-scented sauce to dress a bowl of pasta as a first course. If you want to eat the squid together with the sauce, make sure to serve plenty of bread for mopping it up.

Long-cooked squid reheat surprisingly well. In fact, I think this dish, although delicious when just made, is even better reheated the day after. To reheat, place the squid and either all the sauce or a tablespoon of sauce per squid in an oven-proof casserole. Cover with foil and let heat through in a 350-degree oven for ten to fifteen minutes. The squid should be warmed through, not piping hot, and the sauce should be very hot. If using the sauce on pasta, place the remaining sauce in a pan large enough to hold twelve ounces of cooked pasta and reheat the sauce. When the pasta is al dente, drain it and pour it into the pan with the sauce. Let heat together for a couple of minutes, then serve immediately.

Serves 4 as a main course, 8 as an antipasto

8 medium cleaned squid (about 1½ pounds)

For the filling:

2 tablespoons extra-virgin olive oil

1 large clove garlic, lightly smashed

⅛ teaspoon hot red pepper flakes

¼ pound small shrimp, shelled and cut into ½-inch pieces

¼ cup loosely packed finely cut parsley

¼ cup dry bread crumbs

1 tablespoon salted capers, thoroughly rinsed, chopped if large

¼ cup Gaeta olives, pitted and coarsely chopped

For the sauce:

2 tablespoon extra-virgin olive oil

1 large clove garlic, lightly smashed

1 28-ounce can peeled plum tomatoes, with all their juice

½ teaspoon salt

Pinch hot red pepper flakes

1 tablespoon finely cut parsley

1. Rinse the squid cavities and set aside. Rinse the squid tentacles and chop finely.

2. In an 8-inch skillet, combine the olive oil, the garlic, and the hot pepper over medium-low heat and cook the garlic, pressing it into the oil a couple of times, until it begins to color. Remove the garlic.

3. Immediately add the chopped tentacles and the shrimp. Sauté over medium heat, tossing constantly, until the shrimp turn pink and the squid has given off its juices. This should take less than 1 minute.

4. Remove the pan from the heat, add the remaining filling ingredients, and mix well until the bread crumbs have absorbed all the liquid in the pan.

5. Stuff the squid cavities with this filling and, using sturdy toothpicks or short trussing skewers, close up the open end. You should be able to get almost ¼ cup of filling into each cavity, but you may have a little filling left over (delicious as the chef's share). Set the stuffed squid aside while you start the sauce.

(continued)

6. In a 10-inch sauté pan or stovetop casserole, combine the olive oil and garlic over medium-low heat. Cook the garlic, pressing it into the oil a couple of times, until it begins to color. Remove the garlic.

7. Add the whole can of tomatoes, and with a fork or the side of a wooden spoon, break up and crush the tomatoes to a coarse puree. Add the salt, a pinch of hot red pepper flakes, and the parsley. Let simmer gently but steadily for 10 minutes, stirring a few times.

8. Add the stuffed squid. They will not be covered in sauce. Baste them with sauce. Bring the tomato sauce to a gentle but steady simmer. Simmer the squid for 10 minutes, then turn them.

9. Simmer the squid for 20 to 25 minutes longer, until the cavities are tender and the tomatoes have reduced to a fairly thick sauce.

10. Serve hot or warm.

VARIATIONS:

In Naples, many cooks might add a few raisins and pine nuts to the sauce or to the filling.

A more standard recipe for stuffed calamari would use as a filling soaked and squeezed-out mollica di pane (the doughy part of day-old bread), the same condiments, plus finely chopped garlic, and only the chopped tentacles; no shrimp.

CAPITONE FOR CHRISTMAS

Large eels called capitoni are a traditional dish for Christmas Eve dinner—La Vigilia di Natale (the Christmas Vigil). The usual way to prepare them is fried, but some families stew them in tomato sauce. Either way, the eels are cut into serving lengths of no more than five inches, then rubbed and kneaded with salt and lemon to "freshen" them. After sitting a few hours in water acidulated with lemon juice, they are either floured and fried or simmered in sauce. Because eel have dark, oily flesh, the sauce may well be pizzaiola-style, denoting more garlic than a typical tomato sauce and a good dose of oregano. It takes about thirty minutes to cook eel in tomato sauce.

CALAMARI FRITTI

FRIED SQUID

UPON RETURNING FROM A TRIP to Campania, one of the first things that struck me back in New York was a restaurant review that complimented the calamari for being tender and cleanly fried. "What about the taste?!" I thought for an instant, forgetting that "tender" and "cleanly fried" were indeed our highest compliment. Good, fresh squid do have a refreshing, subtle, sea-breeze flavor that frying frames, and it's a shame to cover it up with a heavy, highly seasoned breading or tomato dipping sauce. (Stewed squid is something else. In that case, the squid gives most of its flavor up to the tomatoes, and becomes more intense with the long cooking.)

That's not to say that all the calamari served in Campania is delicious. Much of it is frozen (which, by law, must be noted on a restaurant menu) and considered, as it is here, something mindless to nibble that one can only hope is "tender" and "cleanly fried." When it is fresh, however, a dusting of flour is all that's needed to give the squid rings and tentacles a crisp finish. Within a small range, you can adjust the amount of flour and consequential breading thickness to taste by how much excess flour you shake off.

To keep the squid tender, they must be cooked for the briefest time. That means the oil has to be very hot, just below smoking or at least 380 degrees—hotter than an electric deep-fat fryer can get. If the oil is at the right heat, the squid should brown very lightly in seventy-five to ninety seconds. Sprinkle them with salt, then serve them immediately, with lemon on the side for those who want to squeeze it on.

It is hard to say how much squid to prepare per person. All I can is that my friends and family can easily go through three-quarters of a pound each, which is also about the maximum amount I feel comfortable frying at one time, in about one and a half inches of oil, in a deep pot offering an eight-inch-diameter cooking surface on that oil. That means for four people, I fry three pounds of cleaned squid in four batches. Since the calamari fry up so quickly, I leave one batch to drain for a minute while frying a second batch, so about a pound and a half of squid can go on the table at a time.

(continued)

SCUNGILLI

The word "scungilli" is the Italian-American corruption of the Neapolitan dialect word for conch, which is *sconciglio*. In Italian the word for conch is *murice*, from the Latin *murex*.

Squid, rinsed and sliced into ¼-inch-thick rings,
tentacles cut in half or quarters

Flour

About 1 quart oil for deep-fat frying

Fine sea salt

Lemon wedges

1. Keep the squid very cold until the moment you flour it. If you are frying a large quantity and need to keep it by the stove to work with it, place it on ice in a glass or stainless-steel baking dish or bowl.

2. Pour plenty of flour into a large bowl.

3. Pour about 1 quart of oil into a 3- to 4-quart saucepan—enough oil to rise about 1½ inches, and place over medium-high. Heat the oil to 385 degrees. Just before it is ready to cook in, bubbles will begin forming on the bottom and rising to the top. Now is the time to start flouring the squid.

4. No more than ¾ pound at a time, toss the squid in the flour. If you want a lot of flour to cling to the squid, remove the excess flour by tossing the squid in your hands, using your open fingers as a sort of sieve. Or, for a finer coating, place the floured squid in a strainer and shake the squid up and down, of course holding it over the bowl with the flour to catch the excess.

5. Lift the squid with your fingertips, perhaps giving it another shake, then drop it in the hot oil. The oil will foam. It is from the excess flour, which will burn after several batches are fried, necessitating a change of oil. The temperature does have to be adjusted. Usually, as soon as a first large, cold batch of squid hits the oil, the temperature of the oil drops enough to make it right for the remainder of the frying time. But be aware that you will occasionally have to increase or decrease the flame, between and during frying batches, in the medium to high range.

6. Drain the fried squid on absorbent paper or a draining rack. Serve immediately, on a napkin or paper, sprinkled lightly with salt. Garnish with or pass lemon wedges.

POLIPO (PURPO) ALLA LUCIANA

OCTOPUS IN THE STYLE OF SANTA LUCIA

The octopus has got to cook in its own water.

—OLD PROVERB

THIS IS THE BASIC WAY of stewing octopus in Naples—with garlic, olive oil, tomatoes, hot pepper, and parsley—the likely seasonings. Luciana refers to Santa Lucia, the marina that is the subject of the sentimental Neapolitan song known the world over, but no fisherman has brought octopus into Santa Lucia in who knows how many years. Fishing boats no longer dock in what is now the very stately center of the city. Il Lungomare, the wide thoroughfare that curves along the bay and technically has different names along its route, goes right by Santa Lucia. And Naples's two grandest hotels—the Vesuvio and Santa Lucia—have been across the street for more than 100 years. The marina itself has become a cluster of restaurants and cafés.

In Naples, where octopus ranks as a food of the gods, there are rules and superstitions about cooking the cephalopod that no one dares break. Besides the old proverb about cooking it in its own juices—an expression also used figuratively to mean "You've made your bed, now sleep in it"—there is the one about the cork. You must cook octopus with a wine cork, they say, or it won't become tender. I've been in the kitchens of hyper-educated lawyers and college professors, worldly people, not to mention experienced chefs, and they always have a cork bobbing around the pot with the octopus, even though they cannot explain what it does or if, indeed, it does anything. They just don't dare not put in a cork. I do dare to cook octopus without a cork, and I've never had any problem getting it tender.

Tenderness is an overriding issue with octopus, but I've found that it is more the octopus than the cook that makes the difference between creamily tender and eternally chewy. Neapolitan cooks will swear that only their small, double-suckered octopus are even worth cooking, but I've cooked nearly 2-pound frozen octopus from the Philippines that, although they are not as superb tasting or buttery as Tyrrhenian octopus fresh from the sea, are very delicious and tenderize after about an hour of cooking or a little longer. (If pressed, experienced octopus cooks will admit that if you just keep on cooking, eventually the octopus gets tender, no matter where it is from.)

The juice of the octopus is where most of the flavor is. Hence the rule about cooking it in its own water, which really means don't add water because the octopus creates plenty of its own flavorful broth as soon as hits the oil. The broth—and here's a myth that probably has some truth—is supposed to be restorative. It can make a man or woman virile, and in the old days, Naples prostitutes would gather at Santa Lucia early in the morning, as their busy evening ended and the fishermen were coming in with the day's catch, to sip octopus broth to revive their flagging energy.

You can serve this in a small portion as an antipasto or as a zuppa to take the place of pasta, or as a sauce for pasta, or as a main plate.

Serves 4 to 6 as a main course, at least 8 as an antipasto

⅓ cup extra-virgin olive oil

2 large cloves garlic, lightly smashed or cut in half

⅛ teaspoon hot red pepper flakes or a piece of fresh hot pepper

3 to 4 pounds octopus, rinsed

1 28-ounce can peeled plum tomatoes, well drained and chopped

Finely cut fresh parsley

1. In a 3- to 4-quart saucepan—or, preferably, a similarly sized earthenware casserole with a lid—combine the oil, garlic, and red pepper. Cook the garlic, pressing it into the oil a couple of times to release its flavor, until it barely begins to color on both sides. Remove the garlic.

2. Add the octopus and turn it in the oil. As soon as the octopus liquid accumulates, coming up a couple of inches, add the chopped tomatoes. Place a piece of foil over the pot, then the lid. Continue to cook at a brisk simmer, well covered, for 45 minutes to 75 minutes, or perhaps even a little longer. The timing depends on the octopus.

3. If the octopus are large, remove them from the sauce and cut them into manageable pieces. Serve hot with plenty of sauce and parsley sprinkled on the top. Pass bread to mop up the sauce or serve the octopus with fried croutons (page 242), or, for a zuppa, with a piece of dried, toasted bread or a fresella at the bottom of each bowl. You might also cut the octopus into small pieces, return it to the sauce, and dress macaroni with it—rigatoni or a very large tubelike paccheri (or cannelloni) is excellent.

ZUPPA DI PESCE

FISH SOUP

THERE ARE MANY FISH soups in Campania. It has, after all, the largest coastline of any mainland region of Italy, and from the north, around Gaeta, which is technically in Lazio but still spiritually part of Campania, to the south, in Agropoli and Sapri, there is a considerable difference in cooking styles. Take the bread sop essential to any zuppa. Near Gaeta and south to Naples, you are most likely to get fried croutons scattered on top of fish soup. In Sorrento and on the Amalfi Coast, you're most likely to get zuppa di pesce with freselle, the dried bread rings that are an old-time specialty of Castellammare di Stabia, the first town on the Sorrento peninsula as you come from Naples. South of the peninsula, along the Salerno coast, the bread addition might be freselle, too, but more likely pane biscottato, a rectangular instead of ring-shaped slice of white or whole-grain bread that has been dried and toasted. And it would come not in the soup, but in a basket on the side, so you can break it in yourself.

Not every zuppa di pesce starts with octopus and squid. Many contain only fin fish and bivalves and their sauce turns out lighter in color, lighter in body, and more purely fish and tomato flavored. I like this darker version, but if you'd like to create a lighter one, start with Zuppa di Vongole o Cozze al Pomodoro (page 237), using half clams, half mussels. Remove the shellfish, set them aside, then cook the various fin fish in the bivalves' juices. Add the clams and mussels back to the sauce (in their shells or not), reheat them briefly, and serve very hot.

Timing is the only difficult part of cooking an extraordinary fish soup. For that, you have to know your fish—how long each will take to get done—and that knowledge is gained only through familiarity and practice. This is a soup that you build by cooking the potentially toughest critters first—the octopus and squid—then adding the shorter-cooking fin fish, and finally the bivalves that need only brief steaming to open them. As each cooks up in the tomato-based sauce, it adds its flavor and some liquid to the soup. I add the small fish before the large one because I want a maximum amount of their flavor in the broth. They often fall apart in the process, flaking into the soup, which is fine as far as I'm concerned, but may not be to you. In that case, put them in after the large fish so they are more presentable and more . . . well, more fish. You should try to cook the larger fish—the presentation fish—so that it cooks just so and looks just so, adding the clams and mussels about 2 minutes before it is done. Or remove the whole fish to a platter and cover it to keep it warm for 2 minutes, while the bivalves steam open in the otherwise finished soup.

I like to serve each person a bowl of soup with octopus, squid, shellfish, and whatever flesh has flaked off the small fish—and of course croutons or dried bread—then place the presentation fish on a platter with some of the other seafood arrayed around it.

Serves 6 to 8 as a main course

1 recipe Polipo alla Luciana made with 3 pounds octopus (page 255)

½ pound cleaned calamari, cut into ¼-inch rings,
tentacles cut in halves or quarters

3 small whole white-fleshed fish, such as red mullet,
porgy, or whiting, weighing a total of about 1½ pounds

1 large white-fleshed fish, such as sea bass,
striped bass, red snapper, weighing about 2 pounds

1 pound mussels, cleaned

12 to 16 Littleneck or small cherrystone clams

Fresh parsley for garnish: whole leaves, torn leaves, or coarsely cut leaves

1. Prepare the octopus according to the recipe. Judging how long the octopus will take, add the calamari about 30 minutes before it will be done.

2. When the octopus is tender (the calamari may still be slightly chewy), transfer everything to a 12-inch-wide sauté pan. A paella pan is perfect.

3. Bring the broth back to a simmer and lay the small fish in the pan. Simmer gently until they are almost done.

4. Push the small fish to the sides of the pan. Place the large fish in the middle of the pan. There will not be enough liquid to cover it. Cook it gently on one side, basting a few times with the sauce around it. When almost done, use two spatulas or wooden spoons to turn the fish over. Continue cooking it gently.

5. When the large fish is almost cooked, add the shellfish and poke them down into the sauce. Simmer gently until they open, about 2 minutes. If necessary, remove the small and large fish from the pan when done, then steam the mussels and clams in the broth remaining.

6. Serve scattered with fresh parsley.

SOAKING SALT COD (BACCALÀ)

Salt cod is such a basic food in Campania that it is sold already soaked. The fish markets have special, shallow, stainless-steel display sinks plumbed with constantly running water to wash away the preservative salt, plump up the fish, and make it ready for the pot. Supermarkets sell the fish reconstituted in plastic packages. It's almost a convenience food, because once soaked, salt cod needs only to be fried, or a ten-minute boil in water, or a thirty-minute simmer with seasonings to turn it into a splendid dish.

In North America, we still buy salt cod in its preserved state and it must be soaked from twenty-four to thirty-six hours, sometimes even longer, in regular changes of cold water. Place the fish in a large bowl, cutting it as necessary to make it fit. Cover with very cold tap water and let it stand at room temperature. Change the water every couple of hours for the first six to eight hours, then change it every six to eight hours—whatever is convenient. It is not necessary to refrigerate the fish if very cold. Put a few ice cubes in the water if your kitchen is hot. The thinner cuts of the fish should be sufficiently desalted after twenty-four hours, the thicker sections may take thirty-six hours. To test for saltiness, cut off a small piece, boil it for ten minutes, then taste it. Once soaked, you can keep the salt cod in the refrigerator for several days, in a covered container or wrapped in plastic. Salt cod roughly doubles in weight after soaking.

Here, as in Campania, cod is sold with or without bones and with or without skin. Although it is more expensive, I buy skinless and boneless cod because boning and filleting can be troublesome. In the end, you don't save much by buying cod with skin and bones anyway, because of the waste.

The cod we get in North America usually comes from either Newfoundland or Nova Scotia, in Canada, or from Maine. It is sometimes available in supermarkets packed into small, quaint, slide-topped wooden boxes that hold roughly one pound of fish. Large, full-fish fillets can often be ordered from a specialty fish market. In Italy, most of the salt cod comes from Europe's North Atlantic waters. Salt cod used to be an inexpensive fish anywhere in the world, but now that the cod catch has dramatically diminished all over the world, the price here, as abroad, has soared. It may one day be a rare and luxurious delicacy.

BACCALÀ IN BIANCO

Salt Cod Salad

———

NEAPOLITAN BACCALÀ AFICIONADOS—purists, of course—say the boiled fish dressed with only lemon juice, the best olive oil, and parsley tastes best, *ottimo*. Some might even frown on the red onion, or disagree that any other ingredients, like olives or capers, could be "optional." Serve this as an antipasto, or part of a spread of cold salads in the summer.

Soaked, skinless and boneless salt cod, boiled for 10 minutes

Red or sweet onion

Whole or torn fresh parsley leaves

Extra-virgin olive oil

Lemon juice or white wine vinegar

Freshly ground black pepper, or hot red pepper flakes, or hot pepper oil

Optional ingredients:

Gaeta and/or Sicilian green olives, whole or pitted and cut into pieces

Salted capers, thoroughly rinsed

1.   There are no proportions given in this recipe because no proportions are necessary. At its most classic home form, it is a simple salad of boiled fish tossed with raw onion, parsley, olive oil, and lemon juice. (Instead of lemon juice, white wine vinegar is used, too.)

2.   Arrange the fish on a platter, broken or flaked into large pieces. Strew it with onion slices separated into rings and the parsley. Dress it with plenty of olive oil, then lemon juice.

3.   Or flake the fish and toss it with diced onion and parsley, plenty of oil, then lemon juice.

4.   Lemon wedges are sufficient garnish—to be used by those who like more.

5.   Hot pepper or pepper oil can be added when dressing the salad, but many Campanians prefer to grind fresh black pepper on their salad in front of them, to get the pleasure of the spice's aroma at its peak. Salt is not usually necessary because the fish can be salty, although sometimes a mild cod made milder from soaking and boiling does ask for a little salt.

Baccalà Fritto

Fried Salt Cod

It's hard to believe that something so simple can be so good. For those of us who like salt cod, this is like candy. Serve the cod with wedges of lemon, so everyone can season his portion to taste. As a further garnish-accompaniment, it's hard to beat fried sprigs of parsley and a green salad.

Soaked, skinless and boneless salt cod, cut into serving pieces

Oil for frying (preferably olive oil)

All-purpose flour

Whole springs of parsley, touch stems removed

Lemon wedges

1. It depends on the cod into what size pieces it should be cut. Cut pieces that are small enough to cook quickly, that will cook in about the same time if placed in the oil together, and that will look attractive on a plate together.

2. Heat about ½ inch of oil in a skillet, or use more oil in a deep-fat fryer.

3. While it is still moist (but not dripping wet), dredge the salt cod well in the flour. Shake off the excess, but don't worry if patches of the flour look thick.

4. When the oil is very hot, fry the cod without crowding the pan. Turn the pieces if frying in shallow oil.

5. Drain well—on a rack or on absorbent paper—and serve almost immediately, although the cod is still delicious at room temperature.

6. To fry the parsley, put it in the hot oil for just a few seconds, until it becomes crisp.

Variations:

One of the most popular ways of serving fried cod is in tomato sauce. It can be a simple pureed tomato sauce—made with fresh plum tomatoes in summer or canned tomatoes in winter, but these days the base may be cherry tomatoes instead. These days, too, the sauce may be merely poured over the fried pieces of fish, while the classic method is to simmer the fried fish in the sauce a few minutes.

(continued)

A more elaborate sauce is also made with the usual Neapolitan condiments: Add halved or coarsely chopped Gaeta olives, a few capers, and an anchovy or two that has been crushed so it melts in and disappears.

For Zuppa di Baccalà, make a tomato sauce with a minced onion or garlic, a minced rib of celery, and a 28-ounce can of peeled tomatoes, undrained and either pureed, chopped, or crushed, or 1½ pounds fresh tomatoes, peeled and chopped. Season the sauce with hot pepper, then dilute the sauce with 1 cup or a little more of water. Simmer the fried cod in the sauce for 5 minutes (or, if the cod is not fried, just soaked, for 10 minutes), then pour the cod and its sauce over freselle, or serve topped with fried crostini. To the tomato sauce, with the cod, you might also add the olives, capers, and anchovy.

Baccalà con Peperoni Arrostiti

Baccalà e Peperoni al Gratin

Casserole of Salt Cod and Roasted Peppers

SHREDS OF SLIGHTLY SALTY preserved cod—baccalà—and soft, sweet, oily strips of roasted red peppers—salty with sweet, chewy with tender. Garlic and parsley enliven the combination, while olive-oiled bread crumbs add slight crunch to the top of the dish and a soft, comforting texture to the rest. During the off season, when they come from Holland and other foreign locales, red peppers will probably not give off much liquid after they have been roasted. But when locally grown peppers are roasted, they'll most likely exude sweet, viscous juices as they stand. Do not discard this liquid. It adds delicious moisture to the dish. You may want, however, to add a tablespoon or two more of bread crumbs to absorb it. The finished dish should not have liquid at the bottom of the pan. Because this casserole can be prepared as much as a day ahead, then merely heated through—after which it can be served hot or at room temperature—it's an excellent choice for buffets, or for those summer days when you want to do most of your cooking in the cool of the morning. In many Neapolitan homes, a gratin of salt cod, with, but more likely without, peppers, but possibly with tomatoes, is part of the traditional Christmas Eve fish meal.

Serves about 4 as a main course, 6 to 8 as an antipasto

4 medium sweet red peppers, roasted, peeled, seeded,
and cut into ½-inch strips (see page 344)

1 pound boneless and skinless salt cod, soaked and boiled 10 minutes,
broken into pieces (page 258)

2 large cloves garlic, finely chopped (about 4 teaspoons)

¼ cup finely cut parsley

6 tablespoons fine, dry bread crumbs

¼ cup extra-virgin olive oil

Freshly ground black pepper

(continued)

1. Preheat the oven to 450 degrees.

2. Place the prepared roasted peppers in a shallow casserole that accommodates about a quart.

3. Break up the cooked salt cod into chunky pieces and flakes and add to the peppers. Do not mix yet.

4. Add the garlic, the parsley, the bread crumbs, the olive oil, and the black pepper. Toss well to mix. (May be made ahead to this point.)

4. Bake for about 8 minutes, until the bread crumbs on the surface brown lightly.

5. Serve immediately or at room temperature.

VARIATIONS:

For a different effect, toss in only about half the crumbs and sprinkle the remaining over the top.

For a different Baccalà al Gratin, toss the cod with 2 or 3 chunked-up canned, peeled tomatoes, a few salted capers (thoroughly rinsed and chopped coarsely if large), and a few cut-up, pitted Gaeta olives.

Baccalà "Arrecanato"

Casserole of Salt Cod and Potatoes

BENEVENTO IS OFTEN THE exception to the rule in Campania. It was ruled by the Germanic Lombards long after any other part of southern Italy was. It was never part of the Kingdom of Naples or the Kingdom of the Two Sicilies. It was still a papal state at the time of Italian unification. And, more to the culinary point, the Beneventani are more likely to combine garlic and onion in one dish when most Campanians would make a face of disgust at the mention of such a thing. Except for that touch, this could as easily be Neapolitan, or from Salerno.

Mussillo is the center cut of the cod, a thick and solid cut—you might say the tenderloin. North American cod bought in the approximately one-pound box usually provides such a piece; the thinner or scraggly pieces are generally trimmed off and sold as flaked cod.

Serves 4 as a main course, 6 to 8 as an antipasto

1 medium-large onion, thinly sliced

1 large clove garlic, thinly sliced

2 tablespoons extra-virgin olive oil

1 pound mussillo of salt cod (the thick "fillet" section), weighed after it has soaked for 36 hours (page 258), cut into ½-inch-thick slices (about ½ pound dry)

¾ pound all-purpose potatoes, peeled and sliced into ¼-inch-thick crosswise slices

2 canned peeled plum tomatoes, with their interior juices

12 Gaeta olives, pitted and halved

2 tablespoons salted capers, thoroughly rinsed

1 teaspoon dried oregano

½ cup water

1 tablespoon extra-virgin olive oil

(continued)

1.   In a deep 10-inch skillet, a sauté pan, or a shallow stovetop casserole, which should have a cover and, optimally, should be presentable enough to take to the table, sauté the onion and the garlic in the olive oil until the onion is golden, about 8 minutes. Remove and reserve about half the onion and garlic mixture.

2.   Arrange a layer of salt cod over the onions remaining in the pan, then make a layer of sliced potato. Spread around the reserved onion mixture. Cut or crush the tomatoes directly into the pan and spread them around. Spread around the olives, the capers, and the oregano. Pour the water over all, then drizzle with the additional tablespoon of olive oil.

3.   Cover and bring to a simmer over medium heat. Keep the heat adjusted so the dish simmers briskly for about 30 minutes. In the end, the potatoes should be tender and a flavorful broth will have developed.

4.   Let stand, covered, for 10 minutes, during which time the potatoes will become softer, absorbing some of the juices; the juices left in the pan, although reduced in volume, will become a rosy-colored sauce.

5.   For maximum visual effect, bring the pan to the table undisturbed and serve, hot or warm, directly from the pan. (The longer the dish sits and cools, the fewer but more viscous the juices, which is actually the way some people prefer it.)

MEAT AND POULTRY

Let's be honest. I must confess that Southern Italian meat has never been able to compete in terms of quality and tenderness with Northern Italian meat . . . Maybe because of this difference, Neapolitans have always found it necessary to season their meat, to cook it long, or to grind it.

—Jean Carola Francesconi,
La cucina napoletana (Neapolitan Cooking)

MEATBALLS, BRAISED MEAT ROLLS, meat pizzaiola (in the style of the pizza maker), fresh and preserved pork sausage, and two meat sauces, il ragù and la Genovese: These are the distinctive, traditional meat dishes of the Campanian kitchen, where meat is more often a flavoring than a focus.

Meat? In times past it was more often pork than beef, and even today in Campania, the beef edges toward older veal (vitellone), not the rich, red, fully grown, grain-fed beef we know. Veal itself is still a luxury, and although scaloppine are very popular all over Italy today, judging from the butcher shop displays and from how many times I've been served it as a guest, lamb is what Campanians think of these days when they want an impressive display of meat.

In the old days, chicken wasn't cooked much, either. Eggs were too precious a source of protein and too useful in the kitchen to kill the bird that laid them. For a feast, you might roast a chicken with rosemary, or boil one to have broth for a first course, the meat for a second. Today, chicken cacciatora, braised with white wine and tomatoes, is the most popular everyday chicken dish. And in Italy (not only Campania), as here, a free-range chicken (pollo ruspante) is highly prized. One might even take a Sunday trip to a rustic country restaurant to enjoy one grilled on a wood fire, basted with olive oil and rosemary. Rabbit is still more popular than chicken, although these days boneless breasts of chicken, chicken "cutlets" just like ours, are showcased in every butcher shop, along with premade hamburgers of every flavor description.

POLPETTE ALLA NAPOLETANA

NEAPOLITAN MEATBALLS

ALONG WITH PIZZA and spaghetti with tomato sauce, meatballs have to be the most internationally famous, even infamous specialty of Naples. Foreigners and Italians from other regions (who might as well be foreigners) have all complained that Neapolitan meatballs are too bready—too meager, too poor, too deceptive. "You call these *meat*balls?" It is, in fact, that high ratio of soaked, dried bread they complain about that makes Neapolitan meatballs so light, so crusty, so juicy, so really clever. They encapsulate the best of Naples, not only in their flavor but in how they make so much of so little.

Polpette alla napoletana deserve and get full attention in their homeland. They are never put on the same plate as spaghetti (they are in Puglia), although when made into marble-size balls Campanians do include them in the fillings of baked pastas, including their famous Lasagne di Carnevale (page 206), and timballi, the pastry drums filled with pasta and an array of other ingredients, and in sartù (page 197), their ornate rice cake. Mostly, however, meatballs are about one and a half inches in diameter and they are fried and eaten as a second course, without sauce but with a cooked vegetable. Or they are fried just to brown them, then simmered in a simple tomato sauce, in which case the sauce can also dress a first course of macaroni or spaghetti. Sometimes they aren't fried at all, but simply simmered in tomato sauce, in which case they would likely be made even breadier than these. Any way you cook them, however, Neapolitan meatballs are at their best when freshly made. These days, not everyone adds pine nuts and raisins to the meatballs—it's up to family tastes—but these embellishments make for a much more interesting dish, a Baroque touch from the Baroque city.

Makes 12 meatballs, serving 4 to 6

(continued)

3 cups dried crustless bread cut into 1½-inch cubes
before measuring

1¼ pounds ground beef (preferably 80 percent lean, not leaner)

3 eggs, beaten to mix well

2 large cloves garlic, finely minced

½ cup (loosely packed) grated pecorino cheese

¼ cup (loosely packed) finely cut parsley

⅓ cup pine nuts

⅓ cup raisins

1 teaspoon salt

½ teaspoon freshly ground black pepper

¼ cup vegetable oil

1 quart tomato sauce (page 46 or 50)

1. Soak the bread in cold water. Meanwhile, in a large mixing bowl, combine, but do not yet mix, the remaining ingredients, except the oil and tomato sauce.

2. Squeeze the bread by fistfuls to drain it, then break it up into the bowl. First with a fork, then with your hands, blend the mixture very well, squishing it in your hands to make sure the bread blends with the meat. Do not worry about handling the meat too much.

3. With your hands moistened in cold water, roll the mixture between your palms into 12 meatballs, each using about ⅓ cup of meat.

4. Heat the oil in a 10-inch skillet over medium to medium-high heat. When a drop of water sizzles immediately, it's hot enough for the meatballs. Gently place them in the pan and as soon as the first side looks brown, using a metal spatula, dislodge them and turn to another side. As the cooking side browns well, continue rotating the meatballs—I find a combination of a wooden spoon and a spatula/hamburger turner does the job best. After about 10 minutes the meatballs should be well browned but still slightly rare in the center.

5. If serving the meatballs without sauce, lower the heat slightly and continue to cook, rotating the meatballs regularly, for another 5 to 8 minutes. Serve immediately. If serving the meatballs with sauce, place them in the sauce now and simmer gently for 15 minutes. They may be held, but are best when served within an hour.

ITALIAN-AMERICAN MEATBALLS

*T*he practice of using moistened, dry bread dough as a filler for and, consequently, lightener of meatballs, is, unfortunately, something that seems to have been largely forgotten among Italian-Americans. When Neapolitan and other southern Italian immigrants arrived in the United States, the land of beef, they naturally used more meat and less bread. Beef was not only significantly less expensive and vastly more available in their prosperous new land, but they associated bready meatballs with their Italian poverty. Without the addition of bread, though, the meatballs became heavier. Eventually, the milk- or water-soaked soft interior dough of fresh bread (called mollica di pane) gave way altogether to the convenience of packaged toasted bread crumbs, often not even soaked, which made the meatballs heavier yet. Some Italian-Americans still do use mollica, however, and they are often considered the best meatball makers in their communities.

POLPETTE DI VITELLO IN SCIARPE DI MELANZANE

VEAL MEATBALLS IN EGGPLANT SCARVES

FIRST CAME A ZUCCHINI FRITTATA, then a Timballo di Peperoni (page 174), a red and orange sweet pepper–cased dome of puttanesca-dressed bucatini. Then came these meatballs—involtini di polpette, Francesca Pasca di Magliano called them. We were being served lunch on a balmy September afternoon, under a white tent, amid the orchards of the Masseria GiòSole, the fruit farm of Francesca and her husband, Sandro, in Capua. Besides being the full-time mother of two small children and two older stepchildren, and a part-time schoolteacher, Francesca produces and sells marmalades and jams from her farm's fruits, she has turned the large villa into an elegant Agri-Tourism inn that can sleep fourteen, and she runs the old tobacco barn and terraces around it as a catering facility. From an aristocratic Neapolitan family, and an active member of L'Accademia Italiana della Cucina, Francesca cooks with delight both the humble dishes of *la cucina povera*, the old peasant dishes, and with skill the *Monzù*-like presentation dishes created for the tables of the rich. This way of presenting meatballs is neither one nor the other, but appears to be the invention of a contemporary cook. Francesca says she's seen similar recipes in food magazines, and I found it in a recently written Neapolitan cookbook, where it was called by the fanciful name above—meatballs in eggplant scarves.

The meatballs, although made with veal instead of beef, and mint instead of parsley, are otherwise absolutely standard. The "scarves" are strips of fried eggplant that wrap each small meatball and hide the taste surprise of a whole leaf of mint or basil. They are mainly for a special menu and, as Francesca served them, an amusing and reasonably light meat course for following an elaborate pasta. Held together by a long toothpick, however, they are great for passing around at a cocktail party. Packed into a casserole and reheated with tomato sauce and a sprinkling of Parmigiano, they work as a buffet dish.

Makes about 45 small meatballs, serves 4 to 6 as a main course, 8 to 12 as an antipasto

For the eggplant:

2 pounds eggplant (approximately)

4 tablespoons kosher salt

¾ cup extra-virgin olive oil

For the meatballs:

1½ cups dried, crustless bread cut into 1½-inch cubes before measuring

1 cup cold water

1 pound ground veal

1 egg, beaten to mix well

1 teaspoon finely minced garlic

⅓ cup (loosely packed) grated pecorino or Parmigiano-Reggiano

3 tablespoons (loosely packed) finely cut parsley or mint

¼ cup pine nuts

¼ cup raisins

¾ teaspoon salt

¼ teaspoon freshly ground black pepper

¼ cup oil used for frying the eggplant

For the final assembly:

1½ cups loosely packed fresh mint leaves (or basil)

Optional: Tomato sauce (see page 46 or 50)

4 tablespoons grated Parmigiano-Reggiano

To prepare the eggplant:

1.   Wash the eggplants, but do not peel. Cut the eggplants the long way into slices ⅜ inch thick. Place the eggplant in a colander and toss with the salt. Place a weight on top. A plate with a couple of cans of tomatoes on it works well. Let the eggplant drain in the sink or over a bowl or tray for at least 30 minutes, turning the slices at least once.

Meanwhile, prepare the meatballs:

2.   Soak the bread in the cold water. In a large mixing bowl, combine, but do not yet mix, the remaining ingredients except for the frying oil. Squeeze the bread by fist-fuls to drain off the water, then break it up into the bowl. First with a fork, then with your hands, blend the mixture very well, squishing it in your hands to make sure the bread blends with the meat. Do not worry about handling the meat too much.

3.   With your hands moistened in cold water, roll the mixture between your palms into 45 meatballs, each about 1 inch in diameter. Set aside.

4.   Now fry the eggplant: Heat the oil in a 10-inch skillet, over medium heat, until it is hot enough to make a piece of bread sizzle rapidly as soon it hits the oil. While the oil is heating, thoroughly pat the eggplant slices dry. Fry the eggplant until golden on both sides.

5.   With a slotted spoon or skimmer, transfer the fried eggplant to absorbent paper to drain. Cut the slices into strips ¾ to 1 inch wide and 4½ to 5 inches long. Set aside.

6.   Now fry the meatballs: Heat ¼ cup of the oil used for frying the eggplant in a 10-inch skillet over medium to medium-high heat. When a drop of water sizzles immediately, it's hot enough for the meatballs. Gently place ½ the meatballs in the pan and as soon as the first side looks brown, using a metal spatula, dislodge them and turn to another side. Keep rotating the meatballs to brown them all over. A com-bination of a wooden spoon and a spatula/hamburger turner does the job best. After about 5 minutes, the meatballs should be well browned and cooked through. Drain on absorbent paper and continue frying the rest of the balls.

For the final assembly:

7.   Place about 2 mint leaves on each strip of eggplant, then wrap the eggplant and mint around a meatball. If you are finishing the meatballs with sauce and cheese, place each ball with eggplant strip up—not the open side—in a casserole. If you are serving them as finger food, place the balls on a baking sheet with a toothpick through each meatball to hold the eggplant in place.

8.   If serving the meatballs with sauce, spoon the sauce over the meatballs, then sprinkle with Parmigiano. Bake in a preheated 400-degree oven for 15 to 20 minutes. They may be held, but are best when served immediately or within an hour. If serving the meatballs as finger food, serve them, without sauce, within the hour or reheat in a preheated 400-degree oven for just 10 minutes.

VARIATIONS:

The eggplant can be grilled instead of fried.

Zucchini, fried or grilled, can be substituted for the eggplant. Use 7- to 8-inch-long zucchini, cut off the ends, then cut them lengthwise about ⅛ inch thick.

Polpette con Capperi e Limone

Veal Meatballs with Capers and Lemon

An invention of Cecilia Bellelli Baratta of Paestum, these are a refreshing change from the traditional meatball mixture, but do not serve them in or with tomato sauce. The flavors conflict. Serve them instead as is, as a second course.

Makes about 32 small meatballs, serves 4 to 6 as a main course, 8 as an antipasto

1 recipe Polpette di Vitello (page 271)

⅓ cup salted capers, thoroughly rinsed and coarsely chopped if they are large

3 tablespoons freshly squeezed lemon juice

Extra-virgin olive oil for frying

1. Follow the recipe for Polpette di Vitello, eliminating the raisins and pine nuts and adding the capers and lemon juice.

2. Shape meatballs to the size desired and fry in a pan skimmed with olive oil.

3. Serve hot or at room temperature.

Variation:

These are delicious wrapped in fried zucchini scarves with whole leaves of basil, mint, or parsley (as in the preceding recipe). Make the meatballs no bigger than an inch in diameter and choose zucchini that are between 7 and 8 inches long and about 1½ inches in diameter, so the strips will be long enough and wide enough to cover the meatballs. Do not top these with tomato sauce. Reheat in a covered casserole.

Polpettone alla Napoletana

Neapolitan Meatloaf

THE TRADITIONAL NEAPOLITAN meatloaf is, even if cylindrically shaped, really a large, stuffed meatball braised on top of the stove. It's tricky turning it and browning the large mass of bread-softened meat, and it requires constant attention, too. So these days, Neapolitan cooks are just as likely to bake their meatloaf in the oven as we are. Filled with unmistakably Neapolitan flavors, this classic version is a mosaic of herb-flecked ground meat with cubes of prosciutto, soppressata, and provolone, and a central, decorative core of hard-cooked egg. It's practically a terrine and both a special treat for the family and a great dinner party dish.

Serves 6

3 cups dried bread (crusts removed) that has been cut into 1½-inch cubes

2 pounds ground beef or any mixture of ground veal, pork, and beef

2 eggs, beaten to mix well

1 tablespoon finely minced garlic

1 cup loosely packed grated pecorino

½ cup loosely packed finely cut parsley

2 teaspoons salt

1 teaspoon freshly ground black pepper

2 to 3 ounces prosciutto, cut into ¼-inch dice

2 to 3 ounces soppressata, cut into ¼-inch dice

Optional: 2 to 3 ounces sharp provolone, cut into ¼-inch dice

3 whole hard-cooked eggs

Optional: 2 to 3 cups tomato sauce (see page 46 or 50)

1. Preheat the oven to 375 degrees.

2. Soak the bread in cold water.

3. Meanwhile, in a large mixing bowl, combine, but do not yet mix, the ground meat, the eggs, the garlic, the cheese, the parsley, the salt, and the pepper.

4. Squeeze the bread by fistfuls to drain it of water, then break the bread into the bowl. First with a fork, then with your hands, blend the mixture very well, squishing it in your hands to make sure the bread blends with the meat. Do not worry about handling the meat too much. Mix in the diced prosciutto and soppressata, and, if desired, the diced provolone. Make sure they are all distributed fairly evenly. Divide the mixture in half.

5. In a 9- by 13-inch baking pan, pat 1 portion of the meat into an approximately 10- by 6-inch rectangle about 1 inch thick. Arrange the hard-cooked eggs, end to end and close together, down the center of the meat. Top with the remaining meat, distributing it evenly, pressing the whole into a neat loaf shape, patting it out smooth, and pinching and smoothing together the seam between the top and the bottom. There will be cubes of cheese, salami, and prosciutto at the surface. Push these inside the loaf with a finger and patch the spots closed. (Note that even when you do this, some cubes of cheese near the surface will melt and erupt like Vesuvius.)

6. Bake for 1 hour. Let rest 10 minutes.

7. Serve immediately or at room temperature, with tomato sauce if desired.

BISTECCA (O CARNE) ALLA PIZZAIOLA

MEAT IN THE STYLE OF THE PIZZA MAKER

THIS IS THE ONE FAMOUS Neapolitan dish that is really hard to find made well in Naples—in restaurants, that is. Too often the meat is paper-thin slices of beef awash in greasy tomato sauce, or a thicker piece of meat that is tough even after having been braised for a half hour. I was embarrassed by this observation, thinking I must be prejudiced toward North America's much more tender, succulent meat, until I talked about the dish with Basilio Avitabile, the chef at La Cantinella, arguably Naples's foremost fancy restaurant.

Chef Avitabile left Naples as a teenager, found himself as a kitchen apprentice in London, and worked there through his twenties. A trip home and the love of a local girl has him back in Naples, in his mid-thirties, to raise a family. With a more worldly perspective than many other restaurant chefs in Naples, he is contemporizing his cooking as much as he can in a restaurant that is considered the last word in elegant traditionalism. He didn't need any prompting to point out that there's no reason carne alla pizzaiola can't be done with a great piece of beef.

What Americans call a minute steak is what Avitabile uses at La Cantinella—a half-inch-thick boneless slice of sirloin. Rib eye, also called a club steak in our markets, is an excellent choice, too. And fans of fillet should note that this is a great way to add flavor to that tenderest but least flavorful beef cut. I like a T-bone myself—which offers a piece of fillet along with a full sirloin strip— but a thick T-bone should be appreciated for its own sake. Use T-bones only if you find them or can get them cut no more than a half-inch thick. At the opposite end of the price and tenderness spectrum, what is called cubed steak in our markets makes a great pizzaiola and is really more in keeping with the intent of the dish—a tough piece of meat tenderized by cooking in the sauce, which in turn absorbs the meat's flavor. (Cubed steak is the name given inexpensive meat—usually chuck—that has been run through a tenderizing machine that punctures it and breaks its chewy fibers.)

Serves 4

4 tender steaks of your choice, each 1 portion (see above)
or 4 to 6 cubed steaks weighing a total of 1½ to 2 pounds

Salt

2 pounds fresh plum tomatoes, peeled and coarsely chopped,
or 1 28-ounce can peeled plum tomatoes, drained of the can juice

1 to 2 tablespoons extra-virgin olive oil

2 large cloves garlic, finely minced (about 2½ teaspoons)

⅛ teaspoon dried hot red pepper flakes

¾ teaspoon dried oregano or marjoram

½ to ¾ teaspoon salt

1. Sprinkle both sides of the steaks with salt.

2. In a large skillet, preheated over high heat, pan-broil the steaks, until the large ones are almost done to taste, or the small ones are well browned. If using large steaks, you probably will not be able to fit them all in the pan at once. Do a couple at a time, then remove them and set them aside while cooking the rest. The small steaks should fit comfortably in the pan side by side, but if they crowd the pan, do not brown them all at once. When all the steaks have been cooked, pour off any fat in the skillet.

3. Add all the remaining ingredients, stirring and scraping up any brown film or bits in the pan. Return the cubed steaks to the pan if you are using them and they were set aside. Bring to a simmer over high heat. If using cubed steaks, cover the pan and adjust the heat so the tomatoes simmer gently for about 40 minutes, or until the meat is tender. If cooking large steaks, adjust the heat so the tomatoes simmer briskly, uncovered, for 5 to 8 minutes, or until they get saucy and reduced. Return the large and/or tender steaks to the pan, all at once this time, even if they overlap. Turn them in the sauce, giving each a minute or so at the bottom of the pan.

4. Place each steak on a dinner plate and top with sauce, which should now be even thicker. If the sauce on the cubed steaks is not thick enough, uncover the pan at the end of the cooking time and let it reduce.

5. Serve hot.

BRACIOLE AL RAGÙ

Beef Rolls in Meat Sauce

———

In the past, southern Italians rarely had meat tender and juicy enough to dry roast, broil, or sauté. If you didn't grind it for sausage or meatballs, you braised it. The quintessential example of this is Bistecca alla Pizzaiola (see page 278), where the tough beef is braised and tenderized in the same sauce a pizza maker would use on his pies. Braciole is the other outstanding and distinctively Neapolitan dish that resulted from the need to tenderize and enhance the flavor of beef by cooking it in a flavored liquid. The liquid is tomato puree here, as with all Neapolitan ragùs, but it differs from ragù made for the sauce's sake in that the meat is meant to be enjoyed equally. For that reason, you don't want to cook all the flavor out of the meat or cook it so long that it becomes ropy.

Which cut of beef to use for braciole is a problem. In American supermarkets, thin slices of bottom round are usually sold as "beef for braciole." This is the same cut that is used in Italy, but I find, here as there, the meat is not marbled enough to provide a really succulent result. I much prefer chuck, and if you can get a butcher to make thin slices of chuck and pound them out slightly, you will have braciole as delicious as the ragù they make.

Serves 6

For braciole filling:

3 tablespoons pine nuts

¼ cup loosely packed, finely cut parsley

1 tablespoon finely minced garlic

¼ cup freshly grated Parmigiano-Reggiano

⅓ cup raisins

For the meat:

2½ pounds chuck or top round,
cut into 12 6- by 4- by ¼-inch-thick slices

Salt

For the ragù:

¼ cup extra-virgin olive oil

1 small or ½ medium onion, halved and thinly sliced (about ½ cup)

½ cup red wine

2 28-ounce cans Italian peeled tomatoes, crushed or run through a food mill

1 teaspoon salt

⅛ teaspoon hot red pepper flakes

1.   In a small bowl, mix all the filling ingredients together.

2.   Place the meat slices on a work surface and season lightly with salt. On the bottom half of each slice, place a scant tablespoon of the filling. Roll up each slice starting from the filled bottom half. Tie each slice with kitchen twine or secure with toothpicks.

3.   Place the braciole in a heavy-bottomed 6- to 7-quart pot or flame-proof casserole, along with the oil and the onion. Cook over medium-high heat, turning the rolls regularly with tongs, until the meat has lost its raw color and is starting to brown, about 10 minutes.

4.   Add the wine and continue cooking over medium-high heat for about 5 minutes longer, continuing to turn the rolls regularly. The liquid in the pan should mostly evaporate.

5.   Add the tomatoes, the salt, and the hot red pepper. Stir well, then bring to a gentle simmer. Cook over the lowest possible heat so that the sauce barely bubbles. Stirring often, cook uncovered for 1½ to 2 hours.

6.   Remove the braciole when tender. Either keep them warm in a covered dish, to serve as a second course, or cool and refrigerate for another meal. You may want to continue cooking the ragù over very low heat for another 30 minutes or so, until it reaches a good consistency.

VARIATION:

A combination of braciole and sausage is excellent. After the braciole have cooked in the tomatoes for about 30 minutes, add up to 1 pound (about 5 links) of sweet sausage, with fennel if desired. Remove the sausage with the braciole.

(continued)

MEAT AND POULTRY

To enhance the ragù even further, for the last 15 to 30 minutes that the ragù simmers, you can also finish meatballs that have already been browned. If you need that much meat, however, you will probably need more sauce for pasta, so increase the other ragù ingredients by half: 6 tablespoons of olive oil, ¾ cup onion, ¾ cup red wine, 3 28-ounce cans tomatoes, 1½ teaspoons of salt, and few more flakes of pepper.

SALTIMBOCCA (SCALOPPINE) ALLA SORRENTINA

VEAL SCALLOPS WITH TOMATO SAUCE, PROSCIUTTO, AND MOZZARELLA

I'VE BEEN TOLD THAT this dish, which in some form has been a popular item on Italian-American restaurant menus since World War II, is, in the Campanian scope of things, also a very recent creation. Perhaps, the speculation goes, it was introduced at one of the many luxury resort hotels in Sorrento, because the tender veal the dish requires was not available to the average Campanian cook until recently. Note that the ingredients are used in a more restrained way than they are in American restaurants, making these scaloppine a much lighter dish than you might expect.

Serves 3 or 4

1 pound thinly sliced leg of veal for scaloppine, 4 or 5 slices

1 or 2 tablespoons extra-virgin olive oil

Salt

2 ounces prosciutto, sliced paper-thin

4 ounces mozzarella, cut into quarter-size, ¼-inch-thick pieces

1 recipe Filetto di Pomodoro, prepared without garlic (see page 49)

A few tablespoons grated Parmigiano-Reggiano

1. Preheat the oven to 450 degrees.

2. Cut each slice of veal into 2 or 3 pieces, so that each piece is no more than about 3 inches square.

3. In a 10-inch skillet, heat the oil over medium-high heat, and when it is very hot, pat the veal pieces dry with a paper towel and add to the oil. Do not crowd the pan. Cook no more than 3 or 4 pieces at a time. Cook about 1 minute on each side, then transfer to a shallow baking dish or heat-proof platter. Season with salt.

4. Don't trim them of fat, but cut the slices of prosciutto to roughly fit the veal pieces (I use scissors for this). Tuck in the excess ham, including any fat, so none overlaps the veal. Top each meat slice with 2 or 3 quarter-size slices of mozzarella. The cheese should not entirely cover the meat. Spoon a heaping tablespoon of tomato sauce over each piece. Sprinkle lightly with grated Parmigiano.

5. Just before serving, bake the veal in a preheated 450-degree oven for 5 minutes. The mozzarella should melt, but not bubble. Serve immediately.

6. The dish can be prepared as far ahead as in the morning for the evening. In that case, assemble the meat, prosciutto, and mozzarella, cover with plastic, and refrigerate. Prepare the sauce and store separately. At least an hour before serving, bring the meat and sauce back to room temperature, then top the meat with sauce and bake, perhaps a minute or so longer than indicated if the dish is still cool. If preparing only an hour or so ahead, the dish can be completely assembled and left at room temperature.

WATER BUFFALO MEAT

Water buffalo breeders and growers in the mozzarella-producing areas of Caserta and Salerno do serve buffalo meat on their tables, and make cured sausages from it, too. However, the meat is not readily available in stores, and many contemporary Campanians think it is disgusting—too strong and, well, it's just the idea. But the meat of Campanian water buffalo, which have no relation to North American bison, can be delicious. It is only the fat on older animals that can have a bad odor and obnoxiously strong flavor. Young buffalo meat tastes much like beef, only deeper flavored. You might even say sweeter, as people say horsemeat is sweeter.

BRACIOLONI DI VITELLO
ALLA GENOVESE

VEAL ROLLS IN GENOVESE SAUCE

THIS IS A CONTEMPORARY recipe that appeals to the many Campanians looking to "lighten" their cooking. Using veal instead of beef certainly gives the onion sauce a more subtle meat flavor, but it is mainly what the onions do to the meat, not vice versa, that makes this recipe so appealing. The rolls, stuffed with strips of prosciutto, sticks of carrot, and whole sprigs of parsley, slice into beautiful pinwheel rounds and take on the sweet flavor of the sauce.

Serves 4, enough sauce for 12 ounces of pasta, plus meat for a second course

2 pounds veal shoulder roast, butterflied to make 2 flat pieces,
each pounded out to ¼ inch thickness, then cut into 4 ½-pound slices
about 4 inches by 7 to 8 inches long

For the filling:

1 ⅛-inch-thick, 3½- to 4-ounce slice of prosciutto

1 medium carrot

8 fine stems of parsley, left whole and long enough
to run the length of the veal

For the sauce:

2 tablespoons extra-virgin olive oil

4 pounds onions, cut into ¼-inch dice

½ cup finely minced carrot

¼ cup finely minced celery

½ teaspoon dried marjoram

1½ teaspoons salt

Plus:

½ cup dry white wine

1.   Have a butcher prepare the meat for you. Arrange the slices on your work surface so the top and bottom are the long sides.

2.   Cut the slice of prosciutto into 10 strips about the same length as the long side of the veal—no longer. Each veal slice gets 2 and you should have 2 left; reserve them.

3.   Scrape the carrot and cut it into 8 ¼-inch strips about the same length as the prosciutto. Place 2 strips of carrot and 2 strips of prosciutto on the lower third of each veal slice. Arrange the sprigs of parsley over the carrot and prosciutto.

4.   Roll the veal slices, starting from the bottom, enclosing the filling tightly. Tie with string or secure with toothpicks or flexible skewers.

5.   Dice the remaining 2 strips of prosciutto into ¼-inch cubes.

6.   In a 5-quart pot or stovetop casserole wide enough to hold the veal rolls on the bottom, heat the olive oil over medium-high heat and brown the veal rolls on all sides. After a few minutes, the veal will exude juices. Keep cooking. Reduce the heat slightly and keep turning the veal rolls regularly, until their juices have evaporated and meat has browned lightly, about 15 minutes altogether.

7.   As soon as the veal has browned, add the onions, the carrots, the celery, the marjoram, and the salt. Stir the onions down and under the veal so that the rolls are immersed in the onions, not at the bottom of the pot. Cover the pot and, still over medium heat, let the onions sweat until they become almost covered by their own liquid. This takes about 25 minutes. Check a few times to stir and make sure nothing is sticking.

8.   When the onion juices have risen, place the cover ajar and continue to simmer gently. After another 40 minutes (65 minutes total), check the veal to see if it is tender. When the veal rolls are done, remove them, scrape off the onions sticking to them, and keep them covered on a platter until ready to reheat.

9.   Continue to cook the onions, uncovered, for another 30 minutes, stirring vigorously and, during the last 15 minutes, frequently. The goal is to get the onions creamy.

10. Add the white wine, increase the heat, and boil, stirring frequently, for 10 to 20, even 30 minutes, depending on the onions, until the sauce is thick enough that when a spoon is pulled through it exposing the bottom of the pot, the bare space does not fill immediately with liquid.

11. Save some sauce for serving the veal. Serve the remaining sauce with ziti or penne, passing the pepper mill and grated Parmigiano and encouraging everyone to use an abundant amount of both.

Note: To reheat the veal rolls, put a few spoons of sauce on each and place, covered, in a 350-degree oven for 5 to 10 minutes. To serve the veal, put a few spoons of sauce on hot plates. Cut the veal rolls into 1-inch-thick slices and arrange them in a circle around the edge of the circle of sauce, overlapping it slightly.

AGNELLO O CAPRETTO AL FORNO

AGNELLO O CAPRETTO ARRIGANATA

BAKED LAMB OR GOAT

JUDGING BY HOW MANY times Campanian hosts served me lamb, goat, even buffalo prepared this way, I would say that this is what Campanians consider their most generous, sumptuous meat dish, their equivalent to our standing rib roast or tenderloin. Naturally, the pan provides enough flavorful dripping to dress pasta, too.

The first time I ate meat arriganata it happened to be a whole kid cut into pieces, and because I liked the idea of having different cuts of meat on the same platter, I devised the following recipe, using various cuts of lamb. More typically, a Campanian would use a leg or shoulder of lamb, making cuts in it every couple of inches, down to the bone, so the meat will cook more thoroughly and in less time. This is not a recipe for those who eat only rare meat—although some portion of a leg will be pink at the center following these directions. It is a perfect recipe, however, for meaty pork ribs or a braising cut of beef.

Serves 6

3½ pounds various chops and pieces of bone-in lamb (including rib chops, loin chops, shoulder chops, and steaks cut from the leg—anything except shanks—all cut about 1 inch thick)

Salt

Freshly ground black pepper

1 medium onion, halved through the root end and thinly sliced

1 rounded tablespoon dried oregano

4 or 5 3- to 4-inch sprigs of rosemary (don't use woody stems) broken into pieces

4 or 5 fresh or canned plum tomatoes, very coarsely chopped, or just cut into 6 or 8 pieces each

2 tablespoons extra-virgin olive oil

1. Preheat the oven to 400 degrees.

2. In a shallow, 10- to 12-inch round baking dish or equivalent-size roasting pan, arrange the meat and season on all sides with salt and pepper. Scatter on the sliced onion. Sprinkle evenly with oregano and rosemary. Place the tomato pieces on top of everything. Drizzle with olive oil.

3. Bake uncovered for 1½ hours, turning and rearranging the meat twice—after 30 minutes, then after 1 hour. When done, the meat will be very well cooked, even with some crispy edges, and the liquid that accumulated in the pan at the beginning will have mostly evaporated. The tomatoes, onions, and herbs will have formed a small amount of caramelized sauce.

4. Serve hot or warm, spooning a bit of the concentrated vegetable sauce over each serving or using it to season spaghetti or macaroni tossed in it (see page 288).

Variations:

The exact same method and seasonings can be used for a leg or shoulder of lamb, but make about 2-inch-deep cuts in the meat about every 2 inches before seasoning it. The meat closest to the bone should remain slightly pink using the above timing, or cook the leg for up to 30 minutes longer.

Costolette di Maiale Arriganata: This is also an excellent way to cook bone-in, rib-end pork loin cut into slices between the ribs—what we call "country-style" spare

*J*uices from a roasting or braising pan never go to waste in Campania. If they are not going to be used as a few spoonfuls of sauce to dress the meat, then they are used to dress a first course of pasta. The verb for flavoring the pasta with . . . whatever . . . is *insaporire,* to flavor. It is a very common practice to toss the pasta in the roasting pan and let it *insaporire,* absorb the flavors from the roast. For instance, after baking lamb or goat, if there is no liquid in the pan, just fat, pour off the excess fat, add a little water, and deglaze the pan on top of the stove, scraping up, with a wooden spoon, any brown film on the bottom of the pan. Now toss in the pasta, cooked until it is just a little too firm to eat, and finish cooking it, while you are flavoring it, by tossing it in the pan juices. Serve immediately with grated cheese.

ribs. Lower the heat to 350 degrees and cook 1 hour, then turn the meat and cook 30 minutes longer, or until very tender.

Bistecca Arriganata: A chuck steak cut 1 to 2 inches thick is also delicious cooked this way. Again, lower the heat to 350 degrees and turn the meat once, after about an hour, then continue cooking until the meat is very tender, about another 40 to 60 minutes, depending on the thickness.

Agnello al Forno con Patate: For the last 45 minutes of cooking, toss 2 pounds of potatoes, peeled and cut into ¾-inch cubes or ½-inch-thick slices, in the juices, fat, and vegetables in the pan. The potatoes will not get a crisp surface, although that is the goal of many cooks. I've read and tried several "tricks" for giving the potatoes a crust, but the only one that really works is to fry the potatoes separately, then toss them in the fat of the pan right before serving them.

Agnello Cacio e Uova

Lamb with a Cheese and Egg Sauce

Incorporating three signs of spring—lamb, eggs, and peas—this is a traditional dish for Easter, although in this day, when frozen peas are usually even better than fresh, there's no reason not to enjoy it anytime. Some versions of the recipe use lamb shoulder with the bone in, and this ragù-style braising is a good method for tenderizing that tough cut. As one might imagine, however, using the tender, boneless meat from the butt end of the leg makes for a more luxurious stew and, as an added bonus, it doesn't take as long to cook. Instead of peas, other spring vegetables are often used—tiny fava beans, asparagus cut into two-inch lengths, wedges or cubes of artichoke bottom, or tiny artichokes cut in halves or quarters.

Serves 4 to 6

2 to 2½ pounds butt-end leg of lamb,
cut into approximately 1½-inch, lean and well-trimmed pieces

1½ cups thinly sliced spring onions or scallions
(trimmed of all dark green and hollow stems)

2 tablespoons extra-virgin olive oil

½ teaspoon salt

½ cup dry white wine

1 10-ounce box frozen peas

3 eggs

½ cup (loosely packed) grated Parmigiano-Reggiano

½ cup (loosely packed) grated pecorino

Freshly ground black pepper

Juice of 1 lemon

Lemon wedges for garnish

1. In a 10- to 12-inch skillet, sauté pan, or shallow stovetop casserole, combine the lamb, onions, and oil. Place over medium to medium-high heat and cook, turning the lamb constantly, until it no longer has a raw color and meat juices are collecting in the pan, about 15 minutes.

(continued)

2. Season with salt and pour in the white wine. Continue cooking, uncovered, keeping the liquid at a slow but steady simmer and turning the meat regularly. Eventually, you will probably have to add water, a tablespoon or so at a time, to keep some liquid in the pan. At the end of about a total of 45 minutes cooking, the meat should be tender, still ever so slightly pink at the center, and there should be no more than a glaze of liquid at the bottom of the pan.

3. Stir in the peas, still frozen. Continue cooking gently for another 5 to 10 minutes, until the peas are cooked but still bright green. Again, add water by the tablespoon if necessary.

4. Meanwhile (or ahead of time), in a mixing bowl, beat the eggs with the cheese.

5. When the peas are cooked, remove the pot from the heat and immediately stir in the egg and cheese mixture. The eggs should set into a sauce—but not curdle—as soon as they combine with the hot meat and peas. If not, place over low heat and stir a few seconds until they do.

6. Season with freshly ground black pepper and the juice of 1 lemon and serve immediately.

SANT'ANTONIO ABATE—SAUSAGE AND POTATOES

There was a short time, beginning in 1799, when Neapolitans rejected San Gennaro. A Parthenopean Republic had been declared, formed under the influence of French Republicans and under the protection of French generals. It was the first Saturday in May, and the city was gathered at Santa Chiara to see San Gennaro's blood liquefy. It didn't. Hours went by, and no amount of reproach and abuse from his relatives made the saint's blood change. Instead of turning on their beloved saint, as usual, the relatives and the throng started turning on the French VIPs who were gathered with them. As the priest bent down to offer the vials for a French general to kiss, the general whispered, "Either the saint's blood liquefies in ten minutes or you're dead in fifteen."

To the horror of the believers, their saint caved in to the French. San Gennaro was a traitor, a collaborator. Some months later, when the short-lived Parthenopean Republic failed, San Gennaro's statue was torn from its chapel and Naples turned instead to Sant'Antonio Abate, who is regarded as the protector from fire and the protector of farm animals. Naples, as any congested city would be, was fearful of fire. And what people do not need protection for their farm animals? In those days, even in the narrow streets of Naples, people kept chickens and pigs at their front door. The reasoning also went that Vesuvius's eruptions could be construed as fire.

In 1804, the theory was tested. Vesuvius erupted and the lava flow threatened Naples as it had rarely done before. No amount of prayer to Sant'Antonio helped. His image was carried to the lava flow but the flow went unabated. It got as far as the city's outskirts when it came to a statue of San Gennaro. Legend has it that the saint's arm raised imperiously and the lava stopped at its marble feet.

Although San Gennaro was readopted, Sant'Antonio Abate's feast day, January 17, continues to be celebrated in Naples. Part of the tradition used to be to burn useless furniture on the street. Today, the horses are still blessed, along with their modern-day equivalent, the taxi cabs. In Benevento and in the piazzas of nearby towns, they used to set bonfires, too. Feeding the flames became a social occasion, and it was once the custom to wrap dried sausages in many layers of oiled paper and to put them in the diminishing embers of the fires. They would do that also with potatoes, and everybody in the piazza would eat, sharing potatoes and sausage. In Pago Veiano, they still follow this custom, and their parish priest goes around blessing the fires and, of course, tasting everyone's sausages.

SALSICCE

SAUSAGE

SUCCULENT, FRESH PORK SAUSAGE, seasoned with nothing more than salt, pepper, and perhaps some fennel seed, could well be the most popular meat of Campania. There are many flavor variations, although Campanians do not crave the variety that we do. Their ideal is not an exotic experience, but rather a sausage where the meat has been hand-diced and not ground, and the links virtually burst with juices when cut into. The two basic ways of cooking sausage are to grill them (on top of the stove, under a broiler or on a charcoal grill) until crusty and well browned, or to cook them in water, then brown them. To cook by this second method, pierce the sausage skins in a few places with the point of a knife and place the links in a skillet or sauté pan. Add enough water to come about half up the sides of the sausage. Place over high heat and boil the sausage, turning them a few times so they cook evenly, until all the water has evaporated. Lower the heat so the fat doesn't burn and continue cooking the sausage, turning them frequently, until browned all over. The brown film in the pan can be deglazed with water or white wine, and the small amount of sauce that results can be used to flavor spaghetti. Place al dente pasta in the skillet with the juices and toss to impregnate with flavor.

SALSICCE AL POMODORO

SAUSAGE IN TOMATO SAUCE

THE AROMA OF SAUSAGE simmering in tomatoes expresses Naples as well as any long-cooked ragù. Indeed, the ensuing sauce is often called ragù di salsicce. In this recipe, you produce just enough sauce for a first course of pasta—either spaghetti or ziti is perfect—with a beautiful bonus of meat for the second course. To make the most of the sauce, set aside only a spoonful to top each portion of sausage, then add the cooked pasta to the pot with the sauce, turning the pasta in the sauce until it is evenly dressed and has soaked up some of the sauce's savor.

Serves 4

> **1 to 1½ pounds fresh, sweet Italian sausage**
>
> **1 tablespoon extra-virgin olive oil**
>
> **1 28-ounce can Italian-style peeled tomatoes**
>
> **⅛ teaspoon or more hot red pepper flakes**

1. Divide the sausage into links, if necessary, and prick them in several places with the point of a sharp knife. Arrange the links in a deep 10-inch skillet or sauté pan and place over medium heat with the olive oil. Turn the sausage in the hot pan and, as some fat accumulates, increase the heat slightly and brown the sausage lightly all over. This takes about 10 minutes, adjusting the heat as necessary so the fat and the eventual brown film in the pan do not burn. Pour or spoon off all the fat in the pan.

2. Pass the tomatoes through a food mill directly into the pan with the sausage. Season with hot pepper flakes. Salt is generally not necessary because the sausages are well seasoned. Simmer gently for 30 to 35 minutes, until the sausages are cooked through and the sauce has thickened.

3. Use the sauce for spaghetti or ziti (there should be enough for 12 ounces) and pass the grated cheese. Serve the sausage as a separate course with broccoli, broccoli di rapa, spinach, or another green vegetable.

Costole di Maiale Beneventana

Pork Chops with Fennel, Benevento Style

———

The seeds of wild fennel, which grows so profusely in Campania that the feathery leafed plant lines many roads, are frequently used with pork and especially in sausage. Here fennel seeds flavor handsome chops and a brown pan sauce.

Serves 4

4 1-inch-thick pork chops

Salt

Freshly ground pepper

Flour

1 tablespoon extra-virgin olive oil

1½ teaspoons fennel seed

2 large cloves garlic, lightly smashed

½ cup dry white wine

½ cup water

½ beef bouillon cube

1.   Preheat the oven to 300 degrees.

2.   Pat the chops dry and season them with salt and pepper. Dredge the chops in flour, tapping off the excess.

3.   In a heavy skillet that's large enough to hold the chops in 1 layer without touching and that can be put in the oven (a 10- to 12-inch cast-iron pan is perfect), heat the oil to just below smoking. Add the chops and brown them on both sides, about 1 minute on each side.

4.   Remove from the heat and sprinkle ½ the fennel seeds on the chops. Turn the chops over and sprinkle the remaining fennel seeds on the second side.

5.   Place the chops in the preheated oven for 15 minutes, until just done.

6.   Remove the chops and set aside on a serving platter. Cover with foil or another plate placed upside down over them to keep them warm. Place the pan over medium heat and add the garlic. Cook until the garlic is just beginning to color. Add the white wine and water. With a wooden spoon, scrape up any browned bits in the pan.

7. Crumble the bouillon cube into the pan. Simmer, stirring constantly, until the liquid has reduced to about ½ cup. Discard the garlic and pour the sauce over the chops.

8. Serve immediately. (If the chops have cooled too much, reheat them by turning them in the simmering sauce for a minute or so.)

LA MAIALATA

After la maialata [the pig slaughter], we ate a dense soffritto perfumed with bay leaf and rosemary, served with slices of dark homemade bread, pan-fried sausages shiny with fat and golden, served with soft and crusty potatoes. Then the true delight was a big soup bowl of steamed macaroni with ragù, then spareribs, very tender and crunchy, and sausages with tomato and fried pickled peppers, giving a lashing to our stomach that allowed us to taste the extraordinary liver with the "rezza" [spleen] and fried blood. Were we done? No. A pizza di scarola appeared. No one would have touched it but for the explosion of enthusiasm of a fellow diner, who didn't want to disappoint the host. He tasted it and convinced us to follow suit. I'm ashamed to say this, but we had seconds. It was the perfection of perfections.

—Jeanne Carola Francesconi, La cucina napoletana (Neapolitan Cooking)

CICOLI E PAPACELLE CON PATATE

HASH OF PORK CRACKLING, PICKLED PEPPERS AND POTATOES

————

DURING THE THIRTY YEARS of my food writing career, and I am sure much longer than that, pork with vinegar peppers has consistently been a recipe sought by Italian Americans who remember their grandmothers making it. My friends in Campania wax nostalgic about it, too. One night, in the car, leaving a trattoria called Da Pasquale in Lauriana Cilento, Cecilia Bellelli Baratta was prompted into a Proustian reminiscence by the cicoli e papacelle we had just eaten, a hash of crackling pork, pickled peppers, and potatoes. "I thought it was okay," my non-Italian, American traveling companion said later of the hash, "but it wasn't *that* good." For Cecilia, however, the dish brought back memories of the annual pig slaughter (*la maialata*), when trimmings of pork not used for fresh meat, cured hams, sausage, and all the other salumi were rendered over an open fire, producing the copious amount of fat used for cooking and so much crisp crackling that it could be eaten for its own sake. You can make a reasonable facsimile of the hash using cubed pieces of fatty but meaty rib-end pork loin, which are called country ribs in our markets.

Serves 4 to 6

3 pounds boneless rib-end pork loin, trimmed of particularly large fat
deposits and cut into ½-inch cubes

Salt

1½ pounds all-purpose or boiling-type potatoes, peeled and cut into ½-inch
cubes

1 cup ½-inch diced sweet peppers preserved in vinegar

Optional: 1 or 2 small hot peppers, diced

1. Put the meat cubes in a 10- to 12-inch, heavy skillet (cast iron is perfect) and place over medium-low heat. Season with salt. Cook, tossing the meat occasionally, until a good layer of fat has been rendered and the meat is sizzling in it.

2. Continue cooking, raising the heat slightly, until the meat cubes are tender and crusty, about 45 minutes.

3. Add the potatoes, toss well in the fat and with the meat, and continue cooking until the potatoes are tender and a little crusty, at least another 15 minutes.

4. Add the diced vinegar peppers and optional hot peppers. Toss and cook another 5 minutes.

5. Serve hot.

Costole di Maiale con Peperoni sott'Aceto

Pork Chops with Vinegar Peppers

THIS IS A VERSION OF PORK and peppers made with substantial chops, which is another popular and much more contemporary way of handling the combination.

Serves 4

4 1-inch-thick pork chops from the rib end of the loin

Salt

2 cups sweet red vinegar peppers, measured after being cut into ¼-inch-wide strips

Optional: 1 or 2 large cloves garlic, each cut in a few pieces or sliced thickly

1. Preheat the oven to 300 degrees.

2. Salt the pork chops well.

3. On the stovetop, over the highest possible flame, heat a large, heavy skillet that can later go into the oven. Heat it until it is extremely hot. A black cast-iron or steel pan is perfect, and you'll know it is hot enough when a drop of water will dance on its surface and evaporate almost instantly. Add the pork chops and brown them well on both sides, 45 seconds to a minute on each side.

4. Remove the skillet from the heat and add the pepper strips and the optional garlic. Stir them around in any fat that has accumulated in the pan. Make sure that both the chops and the peppers are making contact with the surface of the skillet. Don't put peppers on top of the chops.

(continued)

5. Place the skillet in the oven for about 12 minutes, until the chops are just cooked—they should still have a trace of pink in the center. Arrange the chops on dinner plates, toss the peppers in the fat in the pan, then place some peppers over each chop.

6. Serve immediately. Pass the pepper mill.

VARIATION:

Instead of using all sweet peppers, use a mixture of sweet and hot peppers packed in vinegar.

POLLO ALLA CACCIATORA
CHICKEN HUNTER-STYLE

CACCIATORA, WHICH IN CAMPANIA is a strikingly simple dish of chicken braised in tomato sauce, is the most popular way of cooking chicken in the region and, strangely, in a place where no one agrees on anything, everyone uses rosemary as the herb and onion, not garlic, in the sauce.

Serves 4

3 tablespoons extra-virgin olive oil

1 3- to 3½-pound chicken, cut into 8 serving pieces
(2 wings, 2 legs, 2 thighs, and each breast cut in half crosswise)

1 medium onion, peeled, halved, and thinly sliced,
or 3 large cloves garlic, smashed

2 4- to 5-inch sprigs rosemary or 2 teaspoons dried rosemary

½ cup dry white wine

¾ teaspoon salt

Big pinch hot red pepper flakes

2 cups canned plum tomatoes, well drained and coarsely chopped

1. In a 10- to 12-inch sauté pan with cover, heat the oil over medium-high heat, and when it is hot, brown the chicken on the skin side first, then the underside. Do not crowd the pan. Brown the chicken in batches if necessary, setting aside the browned chicken on a plate until the rest is done.

2. When the last few pieces of chicken are almost browned and still in the pan, add the onion and rosemary sprigs (or dried rosemary) and sauté until the onion is tender.

3. Arrange all the browned chicken in the pan, skin side up, and add the white wine. Season with salt and hot red pepper flakes, then let the wine cook until it has almost entirely evaporated, just a couple of minutes. While it is reducing, turn the chicken in the liquid once or twice, but leave it skin side up at the end.

4. Add the tomatoes. Cover the pan, lower the heat, and let cook at a gentle simmer, without turning, for about 30 minutes, or until the chicken is done.

5. Remove the chicken to a serving platter, increase the heat to high, and let the sauce reduce for about 2 minutes. In the end, the sauce will be a creamy pink (*rosé*, Neapolitans say).

6. Pour the sauce over the chicken or use it to dress pasta (reserving some for the chicken) and serve immediately.

VARIATION:

In her 1971 cookbook, *In the Kitchen with Love*, Sophia Loren says that it is sweet red peppers that make chicken cacciatora *really* Neapolitan, although no Neapolitans I have asked—culinary experts, cooks, lifelong residents of the city—seem to agree. "Well, of course, Sophia Loren is from Pozzuoli," they say, as if that was a foreign or far-off town, while it is actually adjacent to Naples. When driving along the sea road, you can't even tell where one ends and the other begins.

Truly Neapolitan or not, Loren's version is particularly delicious. Follow the directions for classic Pollo alla Cacciatora, but leave out the rosemary and add, with the onion, 1 medium to large sweet red pepper, seeded, cut into strips no wider than ½ inch and no longer than 3 inches. Just before removing the chicken from the heat (or when the sauce becomes reduced to taste), add about ⅓ cup torn or cut basil. Stir well and simmer a few seconds before removing from the heat.

POLLO AL LIMONE DI AGATA LIMA

AGATA LIMA'S LEMON CHICKEN

———

AGATA LIMA OF RAVELLO stews her chicken in a large covered pot to make it tender and juicy and deeply impregnated with the flavors of herbs, garlic, and lemon. But then, her chicken is a dry-fleshed bird that has scratched for its life on her terraced hill on the Amalfi Coast, eventually to be cooked in the juice of the very lemons that grew along with it on the same slope. Our chickens need to be cooked in an open skillet to evaporate their excessive moisture and result in a bird that has the flavor complexity and intensity of Agata's and, also just like hers, just enough sauce to glaze it.

Serves 4

1 3½- to 4-pound free-range chicken, cut into 10 pieces

Salt

Freshly ground black pepper

4 or 5 large cloves garlic, lightly smashed

12 or more large sage leaves

2 or 3 6-inch sprigs rosemary, leaves stripped off the stem

½ cup dry white wine

⅔ cup freshly squeezed lemon juice

1 rounded tablespoon finely cut parsley

1. Season the chicken all over with salt and pepper.

2. Arrange the chicken in a skillet or sauté pan that can hold it all in 1 layer—a 10- to 12-inch pan. The chicken *may* crowd the pan. Tuck in the garlic, the sage, and the rosemary. Do not add any oil or fat. Set over low heat and continually shake the pan or jiggle the pieces of chicken so they don't stick to the pan. After a few minutes, the chicken's fat and juices will start running, and this will become less of a problem. Turn the chicken pieces. Continue to cook over low heat, turning the chicken frequently. It will not brown, but it will take on color. If the chicken juices accumulate in the pan, more than just skimming the bottom of the pan (because the chicken is particularly moist), increase the heat slightly.

3. After about 15 minutes, when the chicken has taken on some color, add ½ the white wine. When the first addition of wine has nearly evaporated, in about 10 minutes, add the remaining wine. There should never be more than a skimming of liquid at the bottom of the pan. Keep turning the chicken frequently.

4. When the second addition of wine has evaporated, add ½ the lemon juice. When the first addition of lemon juice has reduced, add the remaining juice. Altogether, the chicken will cook about 50 minutes. In the end, there should be very little sauce—just a few spoons of reduced juices and fat.

5. Arrange the chicken on a platter. Scrape whatever is left in the pan—herbs, garlic, juices—into a strainer. With a spoon or spatula, press the juices out of the solids and let them drip over the chicken.

6. Serve hot, sprinkled with parsley.

CONIGLIO ISCHITANA

RABBIT IN THE STYLE OF ISCHIA

Chef Franco Arcamone of the Bellavista Restaurant in Fiaiano, Ischia, seasons his famous rabbit sauce

THE FAMOUS RABBIT DISH of Ischia is really rabbit cacciatora. Island experts would disagree with this. Neapolitan cooks would disagree with this. Guidebooks and cookbooks sometimes describe something altogether different from what is actually made, with more than one saying it has olives. No one on Ischia has ever heard of rabbit with olives, at least not from their island. But if coniglio ischitana isn't cacciatora, what's the difference?

According to Anna Calise, of the island's famous Calise pastry family, what distinguishes coniglio ischitana from coniglio alla cacciatora is a kind of wild thyme called piperno. "But no one bothers to pick it anymore," she says. Meanwhile, Anna Gosetti, the Italian food authority who has summered on Ischia for decades, uses rosemary and basil in her recipe.

The liver or the intestines of the rabbit must go into the sauce of a true rabbit Ischia-style, some other experts have written. One even gives instructions on wrapping the intestines in basil leaves. Maybe that was the case in the past. Nowadays, it seems no one except an exceptionally old-fashioned cook puts in as much as a chopped liver. In the island's restaurants, and for most contemporary cooks, the dish is essentially rabbit stewed with garlic, tomatoes, and white wine—cacciatora. Maybe Ischitani use more olive oil and more garlic than a Neapolitan making coniglio alla cacciatora, and more than most of us care to, but Ischitani love that oily, rabbit-flavored sauce on spaghetti, with enough left over to mop up with bread.

Serves 4

⅓ cup extra-virgin olive oil

5 large cloves garlic, lightly smashed

1 3-pound rabbit, cleaned and cut into serving pieces

1 cup dry white wine

2 28-ounce cans peeled plum tomatoes, drained of can juices, coarsely
chopped, or 3 pounds fresh plum tomatoes, peeled and coarsely chopped

¾ teaspoon salt

¼ teaspoon hot red pepper flakes

12 ounces spaghetti

1. In a deep 10-inch skillet, sauté pan, or stovetop casserole, combine the oil and
the garlic and place over medium-low heat. Cook the garlic, pressing it into the oil a
couple of times to release its flavor, until it barely begins to color on both sides.
Remove the garlic.

2. Increase the heat to medium and brown the rabbit a few pieces at a time. As
the pieces are done, remove them to a platter.

3. Return all the rabbit to the pan and add the wine ¼ cup at a time, adding more
as the previous addition evaporates and turning the rabbit once or twice.

4. Add the tomatoes, the salt, and the hot red pepper flakes. Stir well, turn the
rabbit in the sauce, and simmer gently but steadily for 45 minutes to an hour, or until
the rabbit is very tender. As the tomatoes cook down, you will probably have to add
water, as much as 2 cups of water, a few tablespoons at a time, to prevent the sauce
from drying out. In the end, however, it should be thick and shiny with oil.

5. Use the sauce to dress 12 ounces of spaghetti, saving some to dress the second
course of rabbit.

ANITRA ALLE LENTICCHIE

ENTRATA DI MALLARDA CON LE LENTI

STEWED DUCK WITH LENTILS

ASK NEAPOLITANS HOW TO cook a duck and they either draw a blank—"Duck? Who cooks duck?"—or offer this recipe. It's from the second edition of Ippolito Cavalcanti's *La cucina teorico-pratica* (*The Theory and Practice of Cooking*), published in 1839, and it is still, although rarely, prepared today. Unfortunately, American-bred Pekin ducks are not as meaty or lean as Italian ducks. When you make this dish with only one of our Pekin ducks, the result is a large quantity of lentils, albeit sensationally seasoned lentils, and not quite enough meat to make as many main course servings as the lentils. Unless you want to make the duck for four and have plenty of lentils left over for a minestra another day, my suggestion is to strip the duck meat off its bones in big pieces—discarding the unattractive, flabby skin while you are at it—returning the meat to the lentils to reheat it, and serving the dish as a grand minestra for an impor-tant dinner. For a more informal meal, it can be a piatto unico, a minestra and main course in one. In that case, stewed cabbage (page 318) is a great accompaniment. The dish also works well with chicken, quail, pigeons, rabbit, even stewing beef or lamb.

Serves 8 as a first course, or 4 as a main course, with leftover lentils

1 pound lentils

½ teaspoon salt

1 4½- to 5-pound duck

4 ounces prosciutto, finely chopped

6 ounces chopped beef

1 medium onion, diced

2 tablespoons extra-virgin olive oil

5 or 6 sprigs fresh parsley

¼ teaspoon dried marjoram

¼ teaspoon dried thyme

2- or 3-inch sprigs fresh rosemary or ½ teaspoon dried rosemary

1 cup dry white wine

2 cups beef broth (homemade, or 1 can, diluted with water to make 2 cups)

Hot red pepper flakes or freshly ground black pepper

1.   Cook the lentils al dente in boiling water with the ½ teaspoon of salt. Set aside in their cooking liquid.

2.   Cut up the duck, removing and setting aside or discarding the fat deposits, the wing tips, the backbone, any flaps of skin and fat that do not have a significant amount of meat attached, and the ribs, which also are covered with fat and skin but not much meat. (Use the fat trimmings to render duck fat; use the bony trimmings to make duck stock. Both can be kept frozen for up to 6 months.)

3.   In a large pot with a cover, combine the pieces of duck, the prosciutto, the ground beef, the onion, the oil, and all the herbs. Place over high heat, and stirring almost constantly, cook the mixture until the ground meat and duck have browned.

4.   Add the wine ⅓ cup at a time, letting it evaporate after each addition.

5.   Add all the broth and cover the pan. Reduce the heat to low and continue cooking for 45 minutes.

6.   When the duck is cooked, remove it from the pan. Spoon off the fat from the sauce. Combine the drained lentils with the sauce. Add some of the lentil cooking liquid if necessary to moisten the lentils further. Season to taste with salt and pepper. Cook for about 10 minutes.

7.   Serve the lentils very hot with the duck pieces, which may be reheated in the lentils. Or strip the meat off the duck bones, discarding the skin, and mix large pieces of duck meat into the lentils.

QUAGLIE DI MONDRAGONE

QUAIL OF MONDRAGONE

MONDRAGONE, THOUGH IT IS on the sea south of Gaeta, is backed by hills and better known as a place for game birds than fish. The quail of Mondragone have whiter flesh than most of the quail we can buy, but this treatment works beautifully for any quail or for squab (pigeons). The braised birds wrapped in pancetta are delicious without peas, but it's the peas that make it in the style of the area. For a dinner party, the quail can be made ahead, gently reheated, and the peas added for the last few minutes.

Serves 4

8 quail

Salt

Freshly ground black pepper

2 large cloves garlic, each cut in quarters

8 3-inch-long sprigs rosemary

8 very thin slices pancetta

3 tablespoons extra-virgin olive oil

1 medium onion, thinly sliced

1½ cups dry white wine

1 10-ounce box frozen small peas, defrosted

1. Rinse and dry the quail. Sprinkle them lightly, inside and out, with salt and pepper. Inside the cavity of each, place a piece of garlic and a sprig of rosemary. Wrap a slice of pancetta around the breasts of the quail, then tie up each bird with string so that its legs and wings are folded over the pancetta and under the string.

2. Place the quail in a pot wide enough to hold them in a single layer. Drizzle on the olive oil, then scatter the onion on top. Place over medium heat and cook, turning the quail and stirring the onions frequently, until the onions are brown and have formed a brown glaze on the bottom of the pot, about 30 minutes.

3. Add the dry white wine and let it simmer, uncovered, for 5 minutes, turning the quail in it while it cooks down.

4.   Partially cover the pan and adjust the heat so the quail simmer gently for another 45 minutes. Make sure to turn the birds frequently and stir up the onions and any browned glaze that develops in the pan, especially toward the end of the cooking time.

5.   When they are done, remove the quail from the sauce. Set aside, covered to keep them warm if you are serving them immediately. Stir the sauce and taste it to see if it is sufficiently reduced and adequately seasoned. Cook it down a little further, if necessary. You will not have more than ½ cup or so of sauce.

6.   Stir the defrosted peas into the sauce. Place the pan over high heat and cook the peas a few moments, until just done.

7.   Serve the quail with the peas and pan juices.

Note: To prepare ahead, complete the recipe up to the point of adding the peas. Just before serving, gently reheat the quail in the pan, adding a few spoons of water if necessary. Then proceed as above.

VEGETABLES

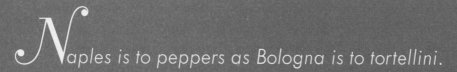
"MY BROCCOLI"

IN ONE OF THE FABLES from the most famous Neapolitan book, *Lo cunto de li cunti* (Story of Stories) by Giambattista Basile (1634–36), the son of a rich merchant has to leave Naples. The boy turns back, looks at the city in the distance, and—full of nostalgia—sees it as a city made of food. He says:

> *Stay strong my beautiful Naples, I'm leaving you! Who knows if I'll ever see you again, with your bricks of sugar and walls of almond paste? Where the stones are made of manna, the beams of sugar cane, the doors and windows of sfogliatelle! . . . Farewell carrots and Swiss chard, farewell zeppole and noodle puddings, farewell broccoli and tuna belly, farewell tripe and sweetbreads, farewell stews and pasticci, farewell flower of all cities, luxury of Italy, painted egg of Europe, mirror of the world, farewell Naples non plus ultra, where virtue resides and grace marks its borders! I am leaving to be forever widowed from pignati maritati, I leave this beautiful hamlet; my broccoli, I turn my back on you.*

Naples, that dangerous red sauce and spaghetti city on the sea. That's the image. The truth is, the city isn't so dangerous anymore and, yes, Neapolitans do eat what seems like an inordinate amount of pasta (and pizza) with tomato sauce, but they also eat as many vegetables as when, before the rise of pasta, they were known to the rest of the peninsula as the leaf eaters (*mangiafoglie*). It's still a vegetable city, "my broccoli!" Everywhere there are vegetables, at every meal except breakfast.

Since the seventeenth century, when frequent fear of famine made dried, storable pasta one of the few foods they could count on, Neapolitans supposedly started eating fewer vegetables and more macaroni. From being the *mangiafoglie* they became the *mangiamaccheroni*. What is rarely mentioned is that when there was no famine, they mixed as many vegetables as they could with that macaroni. Some of these recipes you will find in the pasta chapter, some in the minestra chapter. Almost all the recipes in this chapter are served in small portions as antipasti or side dishes or in more substantial amounts for their own sake. Some recipes here can also be converted into a pasta dish or a minestra, or they could be the main part of the meal.

At the height of summer, after tomatoes, the most important crops are sweet and hot peppers of various colors and kinds, red being the most common; zucchini; and eggplant. Eggplant comes in various sizes, none of which is as large as our typical variety. There are two types of zucchini. In the regular markets, there is a dark green zucchini close to ours, but never grown larger than our medium-size ones. Its flowers—stuffed, battered and fried, unstuffed and fried, chopped into fritters, or folded into crêpes—are even more prized than the vegetable itself. Roadside farmers' stands and residential gardens also provide a long, pale green type of zucchini, sometimes called cucuzza, sometimes called zucchina di pergola because it is a quick-growing vine that can cover a garden pergola in a season. Sometimes it is serpentine, sometimes more like a baseball bat. It's so watery it is used only in soup or boiled in sugar syrup for candy.

A land of traditionalists who have not yet yielded to the temptation of tomatoes in January (other than canned), Campanians tend to wallow in whatever is in season until the next crop is up. ("We grow them, but we wouldn't eat them. We sell them up north," a farmer said of the pallid winter tomatoes he was growing under plastic near Salerno.) In summer, it's not hard to eat tomatoes every day. If not ripe plum, pear, or cherry tomatoes in a sauce or salad, then slightly green and tart salad tomatoes. Of the salad tomatoes, the most coveted is the large, ultra-sweet cuore di bue, the "bull's heart," which grows bigger than a big man's fist.

Pumpkin (zucca) is one of the first signs of fall in Campania, but it is the leafy cool-weather greens that everyone really awaits. Aside from broccoli rabe and leafy broccoli, there are several kinds of escarole (scarola), chicory (cicoria), cauliflower (cavolfiore), a couple of kinds of cabbage (verza and cappuccio), fresh beans (spollichini), and bulb fennel (finocchio), which I have seen grown to the size of a small cabbage and still taste sweet. Thanks to Vesuvius, which destroys in the same hot breath it creates, the soil of Campania produces vegetables (and fruits) in quantity and of the best quality.

In early spring, there are peas, artichokes, and fava beans, before the May heat brings another cycle of "sunny" Italian summer.

CARCIOFI IMBOTTITI

STUFFED ARTICHOKES

LARGE ARTICHOKES STUFFED between the petals with bread and seasonings are a staple of the Italian-American kitchen. Where the more typical and genuine Neapolitan recipe differs is that the filling is based on mollica di pane, the doughy interior of the bread, not on dried bread crumbs, although you'll find plenty of cooks in Campania who swear by bread crumbs, too. These are served as an antipasto in a restaurant or for a feast meal. For every day, a stuffed artichoke, then a hearty pasta or minestra and a salad could be a whole meal.

Serves 4

1 lemon

4 large artichokes

2 tablespoons capers in salt, rinsed and soaked

3 whole anchovies in salt, thoroughly rinsed, filleted and finely cut, or 6 oil-packed anchovy fillets, rinsed and finely cut

½ cup finely cut parsley

4 cloves garlic, finely minced

1 slice (about 5-by-4-by-½ inches) day-old Italian bread, soaked in cold water

5 tablespoons extra-virgin olive oil

⅛ teaspoon hot red pepper flakes

½ teaspoon salt

¼ teaspoon freshly ground black pepper

1 tablespoon fine, dry bread crumbs

1. Before preparing the artichokes, squeeze the lemon into a large bowl- or potful of cold water, reserving the juiced-out lemon halves.

2. To prepare the artichokes: With scissors, snip off the prickly tips of the outer leaves. Cut the stems off flush at the base and reserve the stems in the lemon water.

Spread the artichoke petals so you can get at the center of the artichoke and pluck out the prickly purple-tinged petals forming a cone, then scrape out the fuzzy choke, using a serrated-tipped grapefruit spoon or melon baller.

(continued)

As you work, rub all the cut surfaces with the juiced-out lemon halves to retard browning. As each artichoke is prepared, place it in the lemon water.

With a sharp paring knife or swivel-bladed peeler, trim off the outside green layer of the stems and return them to the water. Let the artichokes and stems soak for 20 minutes or longer.

3.   Meanwhile, prepare the stuffing: Drain the capers and finely chop, then place them in a mixing bowl with the anchovies, the parsley, and the garlic. Squeeze the water from the bread and chop it finely—it should be a generous cup. Add it to the bowl with the other stuffing ingredients. Finely dice the artichoke stems and add them to the stuffing mixture. Add 3 tablespoons of the olive oil and the red pepper flakes. Mix very well.

4.   Drain the artichokes. With a teaspoon, and using a scant ⅓ cup of filling for each artichoke, stuff the bread mixture between as many leaves as you can, and put a small amount inside the central cavity. Try to distribute the filling evenly.

5.   Place the artichokes upright in a 4- to 6-quart saucepan or casserole. Pour 1 cup of water around the artichokes. Over them, drizzle the remaining 2 tablespoons of olive oil. Sprinkle with salt and pepper, then the dry bread crumbs.

6.   Bring the water to a boil over high heat, then cover and adjust the heat so the water simmers gently. Cook for 45 minutes, or until the artichokes are thoroughly tender. Check the amount of liquid in the pan after 20 minutes to make sure there is enough. Add a little more if necessary. Check the artichokes by tasting an outer leaf and by putting the point of a small, sharp knife in the base—it should penetrate easily when they are cooked.

7.   If there is too much liquid when the artichokes are cooked, uncover the pan and let the liquid reduce over high heat for a few minutes. In the end, you should have a few tablespoons of liquid/oil in the bottom of the pan.

8.   Serve warm or at room temperature, drizzling the remaining liquid over the artichokes before serving.

VARIATION:

Pitted and chopped green olives are frequently included in the stuffing, but I feel they take over. If you care to try them, use no more than 2 tablespoons of minced olives in the stuffing above. The large Sicilian green olives are the most commonly available in Campania, but any mild green olive will do.

CARCIOFI E PATATE IN UMIDO

BRAISED ARTICHOKES AND POTATOES

ARTICHOKES WITH POTATOES is a commonplace combination in Campania, either sautéed together or stewed together. I keep thinking it's because the artichokes, plentiful as they are, are relatively precious, while the potatoes are not. When they are cooked together the potatoes carry and extend the flavor of artichokes, if only from the oil in which they cook side by side. You can find this dish served in elegant restaurants, simple trattorias, and at home. It is mainly a side dish, particularly good with roast lamb or goat.

Serves 6 as a side dish

1 lemon

Flour

6 large artichokes or 15 baby artichokes

1½ pounds new potatoes

4 tablespoons extra-virgin olive oil

2 large cloves of garlic, chopped (or more to taste)

⅓ cup finely cut parsley

1 teaspoon salt

¾ teaspoon freshly ground black pepper

1. Cut the lemon in half. Reserve half to squeeze on the artichokes as you prepare them. Squeeze the other half into a large bowl of cold water. Stir in the flour. Use this solution to keep the artichokes from oxidizing and turning brown before they are cooked.

2. To clean the artichokes, whether large or small, remove all the hard outer leaves by snapping them down and off. Trim down to the chartreuse leaves. Trim off the dried or withered bottom of the stems and a thin peel from the stems, as well as the bottom section where the outer leaves were removed. As you go, dip the artichoke in the acidulated water. If using small artichokes, trim off the top ½ inch or so, cut them in halves or quarters, depending on their size, rub and squeeze all their cuts with lemon juice, then place them in the acidulated water. If using large artichokes, quarter them, then cut out the hairy chokes and prickly purple leaves around them. Cut each artichoke into 4, 6, or 8 pieces, as desired and seems appropriate for the size of the artichokes. Make sure to rub and squeeze the artichokes with lemon juice as you go.

3.   Scrub the new potatoes and cut them into quarters or eighths, depending on their size and the size of the artichokes. They should all be about the same.

4.   In a deep 10-inch skillet, a sauté pan, or a stovetop casserole with a cover, combine 2 tablespoons of the olive oil, the well-drained artichokes, and the potatoes. Place over medium-low heat and, with a wooden spoon, turn the vegetables in the oil. Let the vegetables sizzle a minute, then add enough water to come about ¼ inch up the sides of the vegetables. Bring to a simmer.

5.   Sprinkle with the garlic, the parsley, the salt and pepper. Drizzle on the remaining olive oil. Cover the pan and simmer gently until the potatoes and artichokes are very, very tender, about 30 minutes.

6.   Serve warm or at room temperature.

Modestina Evangelista's Fagiolata

Fagiolata, which can be loosely translated as a "mess o' beans," can be a side dish, or an antipasto, or, with some salami or sausage as flavoring, as this one has, a *piatto unico* (one-dish meal). This recipe was served as a first course before an evening of homemade pizza baked in Modestina and Arcangelo Evangelista's new outdoor pizza oven at their home in Pignataro Interamna, a small town next to Cassino. The pizza oven has wheels and is built to trail a car, so it can be taken on picnics, but we ate under an arbor in the backyard, as so many Italians do in the warm weather.

Serves 10

3 tablespoons extra-virgin olive oil

1 medium onion, cut into ¼-inch dice (1 cup)

8 ounces dried sausage, salami, soppressata, or pepperoni, cut into bite-size pieces or ¼-inch-thick rounds, depending on the diameter of the product

2 cups canned tomatoes, coarsely chopped, with their juice

4 cups bottled, boxed, or canned tomato puree

Hot pepper oil to taste (see page 93)

5 tablespoons finely chopped parsley (or basil, sage, or celery leaves)

5 cups cooked cannellini beans (2 cups cooked in 9 cups of water
with 2 teaspoons salt, or use canned)

1 15-ounce can chickpeas, drained

1.   In a large pot over medium heat, warm the oil, add the onion, and sauté until very tender, about 8 minutes.

2.   Add the sausage and toss it with the onion over medium heat for 2 or 3 minutes, then add the tomatoes and tomato puree. Bring to a simmer, then adjust heat so tomatoes simmer gently for about 20 minutes, until the mixture cooks down to a medium-bodied sauce.

3.   Add the remaining ingredients. Heat through for about 10 minutes. The fagiolata is now ready to eat, but it improves after standing for 1 or 2 hours or longer.

4.   Serve hot or warm, with bread to help mop up the sauce.

Broccoli di Rapa Affogati

Smothered Broccoli Rabe

THE NEAPOLITANS' LOVE of broccoli is beyond our imagining. More than 300 years after the poet Basile called it thus in his *Lo cunto de li cunti* (The Story of Stories), a Neapolitan might still think of his "hamlet" as "my broccoli." From fall through early spring, Campanians appear to eat what we call broccoli rabe every day. It is almost unthinkable to eat sausage or braciole without a side of broccoli, and it goes with meatballs, too. It is essential, a law, in Minestra Maritata (see page 110), the king of Neapolitan soups, the mainstay of the people before pasta became the staff of life. It is incredibly popular with pasta, too. Cooked almost into a cream, it is most often tossed with orecchiette, the chewy "little ears" of flour and water pasta; a dish, perhaps originally of Avellino, that is prepared all over the region and the south of Italy today (page 168). In the very traditional kitchens of Salerno and Battipaglia, and also in Benevento, it is stirred into soaked old bread to make one type of the porridgelike minestra, pancotto, which is also called Pane Duro (page 123).

I have counted three types of broccoli in Campania, but I suspect there may be more because there are different dialect names for the same plant, or the same name is used for different plants, or a different way of trimming a plant gives the resulting vegetable a different name. The main types, however, are (1) what we would call broccoli rabe and Campanians call either cime di broccoli, broccoli di rapa, or friarielli, (2) a type we do not have called broccoli di foglia because only the large leaves are eaten, or called broccoli di Natale because it comes into season just before Christmas. Finally, and most rare, there is (3) our kind of flower-head broccoli. Cauliflower, including a green one that is a ringer for our broccoli, is much more common than the North American–style broccoli.

In the end, as a side dish, they are all usually cooked in the same way, which is to say blanched if their deep bitterness needs taming in the opinion of the cook and those he's feeding, then "smothered" (*affogati*) or "pushed around" (*strascinati*) in a pan with olive oil, garlic, and hot pepper. The Neapolitan dialect name friarielli, meaning "little fried things," comes from this mode of cooking.

Against the stereotype they have in the world, Neapolitans use garlic sparingly. With broccoli they would most likely cook but not brown the garlic in the olive oil, then remove it before adding the vegetable. It is not a disaster, however, if you leave the garlic in the pan. As soon as you add the wet vegetable, it will stop browning. To eat it or not is up to the eater who gets it.

I would like to add, as most Campanian cooks would, that if you stretch this vegetable preparation by adding water or broth, it makes a fine minestra, mixed with beans or potatoes, or poured over dried bread.

Serves 2 or 3

1 bunch broccoli rabe (about 1 pound)

2 to 3 tablespoons extra-virgin olive oil

2 large cloves garlic, lightly smashed

Big pinch hot red pepper flakes or a piece of a dried or fresh hot pepper

½ teaspoon salt, or to taste

1. Trim and wash the broccoli well, removing all the tough stems.

2. Bring a large pot of water to a rolling boil. Add salt at a ratio of a teaspoon per quart. Plunge the broccoli rabe into the water and cover immediately. As soon as the water returns to a boil, uncover the pot and let the broccoli boil for 5 minutes. Drain the broccoli.

3. In a 9- to 10-inch skillet, sauté pan, or stovetop casserole with a cover, over medium-low heat, combine the oil, the garlic, and the hot pepper. Cook the garlic, pressing it into the oil a couple of times to release its flavor, until it barely begins to color on both sides. Remove the garlic.

4. Add the blanched broccoli and toss well to coat with oil. Cover the pan and let cook over very low heat for 10 to 15 minutes, stirring a few times, until the broccoli is soft but not totally falling apart. Add salt if desired.

5. Serve hot or at room temperature.

VARIATION:

In Cavalcanti's 1839 *Cucina teorico-pratica* (The Theory and Practice of Cooking), the preceding is his basic method for broccoli, with a few exceptions. He leaves out the hot pepper and adds 6 salted anchovies, washed and filleted, to the oil with the garlic. As soon as the anchovies liquefy in the oil, he adds the blanched broccoli. He removes the garlic when the broccoli is half-cooked and at that point corrects the salt and adds black pepper.

Verza Stufata o Affogata

Stewed or Smothered Cabbage

Cabbage is a workhorse vegetable in Campania, just as it is here. It's something to fall back on during the cold months when nothing more appealing is in season. Once you've stewed it this quick and simple Neapolitan way, however, I'm sure you'll be falling back on it more often.

Serves 6 to 8

½ large head cabbage

2 tablespoons extra-virgin olive oil

2 large cloves garlic, lightly smashed

Big pinch hot red pepper flakes or a piece of fresh or dried hot pepper

¾ teaspoon salt

2 canned and peeled plum tomatoes

1. Remove any blemished outer leaves from the cabbage, then cut out the core. With a sharp knife, cut the cabbage into ¼-inch or finer shreds, or into squarish pieces of from ½ to 1 inch. Rinse the cabbage and place it in a colander, shaking the colander so the cabbage drains very well.

2. In a 2½- to 3-quart saucepan, over medium-low heat, combine the oil, the garlic, and the hot pepper. Cook the garlic, pressing it into the oil a couple of times to release its flavor, until it barely begins to color on both sides. Remove the garlic.

3. Add the shredded cabbage and the salt. Crush each tomato in your hand, letting it fall directly into the pot. (Or chop them first.) Cover the pot, increase the heat to medium, and let cook about 5 minutes, until the cabbage begins to wilt.

4. Toss the cabbage, getting the unwilted top portion to the bottom. Recover and let cook about another 10 minutes, or until all the cabbage is well wilted.

5. At this point there will be too much liquid in the pot, so uncover it, increase the heat again slightly, and tossing the cabbage constantly, let the liquid evaporate almost entirely.

6. Serve hot.

LA SPIRITOSA

"Spirited" Carrots or Green Beans

THIS IS THE RECIPE OF MATILDE Serao, the revered early twentieth-century Neapolitan writer. In her book of essays called *Il Ventre di Napoli* (The Belly of Naples, 1884), which is intended as a pun, because the book is not a cookbook but about life in the formerly impoverished center of Naples, she says la spiritosa was "one of the most economical condiments, which, put on bread, nourished the common people at the end of the 1800s." Though they still make them the same way, nowadays no one seems to know this pickle by the name Serao attributes to it. Whatever the name, they are an attractive and delicious addition to an antipasto napoletano (see page 14) or just nice to have in the house as a snack. Because of their very acidic marinade, the carrots (or any vegetable) keep well for several days at room temperature and for several weeks in the refrigerator. They are good to eat when they are first made, but much better the next day and the few days after, when the flavors have a chance to mellow and meld.

Makes about 3 cups

1 pound (approximately) medium carrots

½ cup white wine vinegar or distilled white vinegar

½ cup water

¼ to ½ teaspoon salt

2 teaspoons dried oregano

1 fresh or dried hot red pepper or ⅛ to ¼ teaspoon hot red pepper flakes

2 large cloves garlic, either smashed lightly or sliced

½ cup extra-virgin olive oil

1. Do not peel or scrape the carrots. Wash them, cut them in half across the width, then place them in a pot of lightly salted boiling water. Boil until they are tender to the center (check with the point of a small, sharp knife), anywhere from 5 to 10 minutes, depending on the carrots. With tongs or a slotted spoon, pull out the thinner ends as they are done, leaving the thicker sections to cook through.

2. Drain the carrots and, as soon as they are cool enough to handle, using the abrasion of a paper towel, rub off the outside skin. It should come off easily. Cut any discolored specks out of the carrots, then cut them into approximately 3-inch sticks that are between ¼ and ½ inch thick.

3.   While peeling the carrots, using your smallest saucepan, boil the vinegar and water together over high heat until the liquid has reduced to almost ½ cup, half its volume, 5 to 8 minutes.

4.   Place the carrots in a flat serving dish and season with salt and oregano. Break the hot pepper into 3 or 4 pieces and add with the garlic. Pour on the vinegar (better hot than at room temperature), then the olive oil. Mix gently but well. Marinate at room temperature for at least 8 hours, but preferably 24, turning the carrots in the marinade every few hours. If desired, keep the carrots refrigerated after the first 8 hours.

5.   Serve at room temperature.

Note: When doubling the recipe, use only half again as much marinade ingredients.

VARIATION:

The exact same treatment—boiling, then marinating in the dressing—works beautifully with green beans, sliced fennel, or peeled baby carrots (which, of course, don't need to be peeled again).

FAGIOLINI IN PADELLA

SAUTÉED GREEN BEANS

THE BASIC NEAPOLITAN WAY with stringbeans or green beans is, as it is with almost any vegetable, to boil them until tender, then finish them in a skillet with olive oil, a hint of garlic, and perhaps a bit of hot pepper—not to make them fiery, just to season them.

1. Head and tail fresh green beans, wash them well, then boil them in salted boiling water until tender, from 4 to 7 minutes, depending on the maturity and thickness of the beans. Drain well, and if you are not finishing and serving the beans immediately, rinse them under cold running water to stop the cooking.

2. To finish the beans, skim a skillet with olive oil and place over low heat with a lightly crushed or thickly sliced clove of garlic and, if desired, a pinch of hot red pepper flakes or a piece of hot pepper. Cook until the garlic is tender and just beginning to color, pressing it into the oil a couple times to release its flavor. Remove the garlic. If desired, remove the pepper pod, too. Add the boiled beans, season with salt to taste, and sauté for 2 or 3 minutes, so the beans pick up the garlic and oil flavor.

3. Serve hot or at room temperature

VARIATIONS:

Let a few halved or quartered cherry tomatoes cook in the oil for a minute before adding the beans, and/or add a few torn basil leaves to the beans for the last 30 seconds.

Insalata di Fagiolini e Patate

Green Bean and Potato Salad

The brilliance of Italian cooking, not just Campanian, is its simplicity, which also necessitates a high regard for ingredients. Made with freshly picked early summer green beans and a delicate, not assertive, condiment-grade olive oil, this very simple salad can take a proud place on an antipasto or buffet table or be a side dish to grilled sausage, fish, any meat or chicken, a frittata, or a slice of grilled cheese. It goes with almost anything and is perfect for picnics, too.

Serves 4 to 6

½ pound green beans

1 pound (or so) boiling-type or yellow-fleshed potatoes

½ cup ¼-inch-dice red onion

3 tablespoons extra-virgin olive oil

½ teaspoon salt

Freshly ground black pepper

1 tablespoon (or so) white wine vinegar

1. Snap off the ends of the green beans and wash well. Bring a small pot of lightly salted water to a boil, then boil the beans for 6 to 8 minutes, depending on taste.

2. Meanwhile, scrub the potatoes and place them in a pot with cold water to cover well. Bring to a boil over high heat, then simmer until the potatoes are tender, but not soft.

3. When the stringbeans are cooked, drain them immediately in a colander and stop their cooking by rinsing them under cold running water. Cut them into 1½-inch lengths. (Cutting on the diagonal makes attractive pieces.) Set aside.

4. When the potatoes are done, drain them and let them cool to tepid. Peel the potatoes and cut them into ¼- to ½-inch quarter-size slices. (The way you cut the potatoes will depend on their size and shape; use your judgment, you can't go wrong.)

5.　In a serving bowl, lightly toss together the potatoes, green beans, and diced onion. Drizzle with the olive oil and toss gingerly again. Sprinkle with salt and pepper, then drizzle on the vinegar. Toss once more.

6.　The salad is best after an hour or so at room temperature and it tastes best the day it is made, although it can be kept refrigerated for a day or so. Serve at room temperature.

MELANZANE O ZUCCHINE
ALLA GRIGLIA

Grilled Eggplant or Zucchini

THIN SLICES OF GRILLED eggplant and zucchini seasoned with salt, raw garlic, and an herb—mint for zucchini, parsley or basil for eggplant—is one of the most popular antipastos of the Campanian summer. You see them in almost every restaurant, arranged neatly on deep platters that can accommodate several, if not numerous layers of the vegetables and a profuse amount of olive oil. I used to think that American chefs simply didn't cook their grilled vegetables long enough, which is why they too frequently are tasteless and leathery. Now I realize the problem is not enough oil. You can't be fat phobic and have great grilled vegetables. As you will see, both vegetables will seem barely cooked after they've been grilled as I describe here. They'll lose that "greenness," becoming supple and succulent, only after an hour or so in oil. Don't stint on the amount of oil or its quality, remembering that although the vegetables will absorb some of it, you don't have to consume all the oil that's around them. This uncooked oil, now flavored with garlic and an herb, can always be turned into a salad dressing or be used to dress a cooked vegetable, such as broccoli or cauliflower, or a bowl of spaghetti. A minimum amount of oil is indicated below, but more is always welcome.

Serves 4 to 6

(continued)

1 eggplant (about 1 pound) or 3 medium zucchini
or more smaller ones (about 1 pound)

¼ cup extra-virgin olive oil, or more to taste

1 tablespoon finely minced garlic, or garlic cut into slivers

¼ teaspoon salt or more to taste

⅓ cup loosely packed mint, parsley, or basil leaves, torn

1. Wash the eggplant or zucchini and dry it. Cut (either one) the long way into ¼-inch-thick slices, discarding the outside, skin-covered slices of eggplant.

2. Heat a frying pan or ridged stovetop grill over high heat, until the palm of your hand placed an inch or so over the pan can feel the heat acutely after 4 seconds. Place a layer of vegetable in the pan. Lower the heat to medium-high. Press the slices with a spatula. After about 4 minutes, check to see if they are turning an uneven brown or getting dark marks from the grill. If they are not, adjust the heat accordingly. Turn the vegetable slices when they are browned in spots without being burned. Grill the second side for about another 3 minutes, checking to prevent burning. Again, adjust the heat if they start to color too much or not enough.

3. Place the cooked vegetable slices on a large platter, without overlapping. Drizzle with olive oil. Scatter on a few pinches of minced garlic or slivers of garlic. Sprinkle with salt and scatter on a few torn leaves of mint.

4. Continue cooking the remaining vegetable slices in batches. Make layers of the vegetables (each layer should cover the bottom of the plate), dressing each layer while still warm with another tablespoon or so of oil, more salt, garlic, and mint leaves.

5. Let stand for at least an hour before serving. The eggplant is even better if made in the morning to serve in the evening, or allowed to marinate for 24 hours. Do not cover the platter with plastic wrap until the vegetables have cooled to room temperature.

Polpette di Melanzane

Eggplant Balls

THESE ARE SOMETIMES SOLD in Naples's snack shops and pizzerias, but above all they are what Mamma makes. I'm told they used to be fried on the street in the poor quarters of the city, along with the many other fritti. These days they seem to be one of the most popular specialties of the Campanian family table, but for some reason they are little known outside the region, much less outside Italy. To extrapolate from the number of times I have been "introduced" to this dish by Campanian hosts and cooks, I'd say the locals are well aware of this and proud of it.

When done well (and small), polpette or palle di melanzane can be an elegant morsel to pass at a party, with or without tomato sauce. Accompanied by a small, interesting salad, they can be served as a plated antipasto for a formal dinner. Following a pasta or minestra, and accompanied by a green vegetable or a salad, they're also a treat as a family main course, as they were meant to be.

Makes about 24, serving 6 to 8 as a second course, more as an antipasto

2 pounds eggplant (size and number are not important), peeled

2 eggs, lightly beaten

1 cup freshly grated Parmigiano-Reggiano

2 rounded tablespoons finely cut parsley

2 rounded tablespoons finely cut basil (or use ¼ cup parsley)

½ teaspoon freshly ground black pepper

¼ teaspoon freshly grated nutmeg

About ¾ cup fine, dry bread crumbs

Salt

1½ to 2 cups bread crumbs for dredging

Optional: 2 cups tomato sauce (see page 46 or 50)

1.   Peel the eggplant and cut into quarters or eighths, depending on the size. Bring a large pot of salted water to a rolling boil. Add the eggplant and cook until just tender enough to break apart easily, about 10 minutes. Remove a piece and check it for doneness. Drain the eggplant pieces in a colander, and when they are cool enough to handle, press them lightly to expel excess water.

(continued)

2. Turn about half of them into a large mixing bowl, and with a table fork or potato masher, make a coarse puree. Cut the remaining eggplant into roughly ¼- to ½-inch pieces and add them to the bowl with the puree.

3. Add the beaten egg to the cooled eggplant and mix well. Stir in the grated cheese, the herbs, pepper, and nutmeg. Add enough bread crumbs to make a mixture that holds together well.

4. Shape the eggplant mixture into patties 2½ to 3 inches in diameter and about ½ inch thick. Dredge them heavily in bread crumbs.

5. Heat ½ inch of olive oil in a frying pan and fry the patties—in batches, without crowding the pan—until browned on both sides, about 5 minutes total.

6. For a second course or plated antipasto, serve hot, with lemon wedges if desired, or with any tomato sauce. The sauce can be served in a boat on the side or under or over the eggplant patties. Some people cook the balls a few minutes in the sauce before serving them, but then they lose their crisp surface. The patties are also excellent as a finger food, served at room temperature with just a sprinkling of salt or a dab of a thick, chunky tomato sauce on top. In that case, you will want to make smaller patties.

VARIATIONS:

Instead of boiling the eggplant, you can bake it whole, in a 350-degree oven until fully tender, but not collapsed.

Some people use soaked and squeezed-out dry bread instead of bread crumbs, which makes a slightly lighter and softer patty, but one that is more difficult to handle. In the eggplant mixture, substitute 3 cups of several-days-old bread soaked for about 30 minutes in water, then squeezed dry. (You should end up with about 2 cups of dampened bread.)

Whether making the dish with bread crumbs or bread, some cooks use flour instead of bread crumbs for dredging the patties. Bread crumbs give a crisper surface, however, which is a nice contrast to the soft interior.

Melanzane al Funghetto in Agrodolce

Sweet and Sour Eggplant

This is two recipes in one. Without the finish of vinegar and sugar the dish is called melanzane al funghetto, eggplant in the style of mushrooms, which is to say sliced and fried. It is one of the most common ways of cooking eggplant. Add the sweet and sour sugar and vinegar seasoning and the dish is melanzane in agrodolce, an almost equally popular preparation.

Sweet and sour was the predominant flavoring of Neapolitan food before the tomato, and before pasta became the main food of the people in the seventeenth century. That taste is still hugely popular today. Interestingly, however, except for the natural sweet-acid flavor of tomatoes, it is rare, if not unheard of, to season pasta with sweet and sour ingredients. Even the ubiquitous raisins of the Neapolitan kitchen—used in combination with olives, and with garlic, with meats, with vegetables, and in many other otherwise savory situations—traditionally never make it into a pasta. So the eggplant cooked without vinegar and sugar is a vegetable a Neapolitan might well mix with some macaroni, but not the sweet and sour version. That's best as a side dish with grilled sausage, lamb, chicken, or dark or oily fish, such as tuna, mackerel, or fresh sardines.

Makes 1 cup

1 1-pound eggplant

1½ tablespoons kosher salt

1 cup extra-virgin olive oil (see note)

¼ cup white wine vinegar

1½ teaspoons sugar

1. Cut the eggplant lengthwise into slices ½ inch thick. Cut the slices about ½ inch wide and 3 inches long. You should have about 2½ cups of eggplant strips. Place the eggplant in a colander and toss with the salt. Place a weight on top. A plate with a couple of cans of tomatoes on it works well. Let the eggplant drain in the sink or over a bowl or tray for at least 30 minutes.

(continued)

2. When ready to fry, heat the oil in a 10-inch skillet, over medium heat, until the oil is hot enough to make a piece of the eggplant sizzle rapidly as soon as it hits it. While the oil is heating, quickly rinse the eggplant under running water, then thoroughly pat dry.

3. Fry the eggplant in two batches, until golden. With a slotted spoon or skimmer, transfer the fried eggplant to absorbent paper to drain, then to a clean skillet.

4. Sprinkle the eggplant with vinegar and place over medium heat. Constantly toss the eggplant while the vinegar evaporates, about 2 minutes. Sprinkle on the sugar and continue tossing the eggplant for another minute, still over medium heat.

5. May be served hot or at room temperature, as an antipasto or contorno (side dish).

Note: Less than ¼ cup of oil is retained in the eggplant. The remaining oil can be used again, but only for eggplant.

Melanzane in Agrodolce al Pomodoro

Sweet and Sour Eggplant in Tomato Sauce

THIS IS SIMILAR TO SICILIAN caponata, which contains, in addition to the fried eggplant, boiled sliced celery, olives, capers, and raisins. Some or all of those can be added to this, but in Naples it is still called sweet and sour eggplant. Caponata in Campania is something else entirely—a tomato and bread salad (page 359).

Makes 4 cups

2 pounds eggplant, cut into 1½-inch cubes

3 tablespoons kosher salt

1 cup extra-virgin olive oil

1 cup plum tomatoes, fresh and peeled or canned and drained,
chopped coarsely or pureed

¼ cup white wine vinegar

2 teaspoons sugar

1.   Place the eggplant in a colander and toss with the salt. Place a weight on top. A plate with a couple of cans of tomatoes on it works well. Let the eggplant drain in the sink or over a bowl or tray for at least 30 minutes.

2.   When ready to fry, heat the oil in a 10-inch skillet, over medium heat, until the oil is hot enough to make a piece of the eggplant sizzle rapidly as soon as it hits it. While the oil is heating, quickly rinse the eggplant, then pat dry.

3.   Fry the eggplant, in 2 batches, until golden. With a slotted spoon or skimmer, transfer the fried eggplant to absorbent paper to drain.

4.   Pour off all but a tablespoon of oil from the skillet. Add the tomatoes and bring to a simmer over medium heat until thickened. Stir in the vinegar and sugar and let the sauce cook for a few more minutes. Stir in the eggplant, making sure all the pieces are covered with tomato.

5.   Let it rest for a couple of hours before serving at room temperature, as an antipasto or contorno (side dish).

Melanzane a Scarpetta

Melanzane a Barchetta

Stuffed Eggplant Shoes or Boats

A SCARPETTA IS A LITTLE shoe or slipper, and that's what the scooped-out small egg-plants look like to a Neapolitan. "Boats" would be the word used by a more cos-mopolitan cook. This is an old, traditional recipe, one that is still prepared regularly and a dish that you might well see on a tray in a *tavola calda*. It's one of those dishes that encapsulates the flavors of the region. Serve it as an antipasto or accompaniment to a simple meat or fish course.

Serves 6 as an antipasto, 12 as a side dish

6 small eggplants (1½ to 2 pounds)

2 tablespoons extra-virgin olive oil

3 to 4 fresh plum tomatoes (about ¾ pound), peeled (not juiced)
and cut into ¼-inch pieces, or 1 cup canned plum tomatoes,
drained well and cut into small pieces

5 to 6 tablespoons fine, dry bread crumbs

2 rounded tablespoons salted capers, rinsed well

2 rounded tablespoons minced, pitted Gaeta olives

Optional: 3 whole salted anchovies, thoroughly rinsed and filleted and finely
cut, or 6 oil-packed anchovy fillets, rinsed and finely cut

½ teaspoon dried oregano

2 rounded tablespoons finely cut parsley or basil

Hot red pepper oil to taste (or freshly ground black pepper)

3 tablespoons extra-virgin olive oil

3 tablespoons water

1.   Rinse the eggplants. Remove the ends with the green calyx and cut the egg-plants in half the long way. Using a small, sharp knife, and a teaspoon when neces-sary, cut and scoop out the inside flesh of the eggplant halves, forming eggplant shells with walls about ¼ inch thick. Place the eggplant shells in a large bowl of lightly salted water and let stand at least 30 minutes, while preparing the filling.

To prepare the filling:

2. Coarsely chop the scooped-out eggplant pulp. (You should have 2 to 2½ cups of chopped eggplant.)

3. In a small skillet, over medium heat, warm the 2 tablespoons of olive oil until a piece of eggplant will sizzle in it immediately and sauté the chopped eggplant, tossing and stirring constantly, until just tender, about 3 minutes.

4. Remove the skillet from the heat and stir in the tomatoes, 5 tablespoons of the bread crumbs, the capers, the olives, the anchovies (if using), the oregano, the parsley or basil, and just enough drops of hot pepper oil to season to taste. (It should not be very hot.) Mix well. If the mixture still seems too loose (it can be when using canned tomatoes), add a tablespoon or so of bread crumbs.

To assemble and bake:

5. Preheat the oven to 375 degrees.

6. Drain the eggplant halves and dry well with paper towel, pressing the insides firmly to sponge up any excess moisture.

7. Grease a large, shallow baking pan with a tablespoon of the remaining olive oil. Pour in the 3 tablespoons of water. Arrange the eggplant halves in the pan and stuff with the filling. Don't pack the filling tightly. Let the stuffing mound slightly higher than the eggplant shells if there's enough to do that. Drizzle the eggplant halves with the last 2 tablespoons of oil, making sure to drizzle some of it over the exposed edges of the eggplant halves and not worrying if some of it runs into the pan.

8. Bake for 1 hour, until the eggplant is tender but has not collapsed totally.

9. Serve hot, warm, or at room temperature. They are even better eaten the day after they are made.

PARMIGIANA DI MELANZANE

EGGPLANT PARMIGIANA

———

THE FIRST PRINTED MENTION of eggplant parmigiana is in Vincenzo Corrado's 1765 *Il cuoco galante* (The Gallant Cook), which is also the first Neapolitan cookbook. He suggests that you can make it with or without tomato sauce but, interestingly, he never mentions baking it. I say "interestingly" because these days, although it is always baked, it is never served piping hot. It is tepid or it is at room temperature. A couple of other ways the classic Neapolitan version has not changed over the centuries, and differs from the way we make it in North America, is that the eggplant is hardly ever breaded before frying, and the sauce and the cheeses—mozzarella and Parmigiano—are used quite sparingly. In short, it is a lighter dish, which is why it is often eaten as a side dish in Campania. It can be a first course, too, or a *piatto unico* (one-dish meal). It can be a thin slip of a dish only a couple of eggplant layers thick, or a sumptuous casserole. In the summer, its real season, it's made with fresh tomato sauce and basil, yet in the winter I've eaten parmigiana made with ragù.

The Italian-American habit of breading the eggplant first may come from the old Amalfitano-Salernitano custom of layering eggplant that has been *indorata e fritta*, dipped in flour and egg and fried. Eggplant is still cooked this way (page 334), but cooks today choose lightness over substance in their parmigiana. Fried eggplant is rich enough, they say. Indeed, the main hurdle in making a first-class parmigiana, which is to say a reasonably light one, is frying the eggplant so it doesn't absorb too much oil. Ironically, the more oil you use for the frying, the less the eggplant will absorb. So don't stint. Use a good one-third inch of oil in a wide skillet. The eggplant must be well salted, too, as salted eggplant absorbs less oil. Some cooks also take the time to let the fried eggplant drain in a colander or on a slotted rack for thirty minutes or so, during which time it should express some of the oil it has absorbed.

Eggplant is by far the most popular vegetable cooked *alla parmigiana*, but not the only one. Zucchini, artichokes, and fennel sometimes get the same treatment.

Serves 6 to 8

3 pounds eggplant (preferably small to medium-size)

3 tablespoons kosher or coarse sea salt

4 cups pureed tomato sauce or ragù (see page 46, 50, 53, or 56)

1 to 1½ cups extra-virgin olive oil

10 ounces thinly sliced mozzarella (about 1 cup)

1 cup basil leaves

1½ cups grated Parmigiano-Reggiano

1. Wash and dry the eggplant. Cut lengthwise into ½-inch-thick slices. Peel only the 2 end slices to expose the flesh on both of their sides. Sprinkle each slice with salt. Place in a large colander set in the sink or over a bowl or tray. Put a plate on top of the slices and cans of tomatoes or other weights on top of the plate. Let drain for an hour. Rinse the eggplant slices quickly under cold running water, then dry thoroughly, pressing firmly to blot out moisture.

2. In a skillet, heat about ⅓ inch of oil until a slice of the eggplant sizzles immediately when you dip it in. Fry a few slices at a time until dark golden on both sides. Drain them on absorbent paper or on a slotted rack as they are done.

3. Spread about ¾ cup of sauce over the bottom of an approximately 8-by-12-inch baking dish that you don't mind bringing to the table. Place a layer of eggplant on the sauce, then a layer of half the mozzarella, another ½ cup sauce, ⅓ cup of the basil leaves, whole or torn if they are very large, and finally ½ cup grated Parmigiano. Repeat with a second layer of eggplant, the remaining ½ cup of mozzarella, ½ cup sauce, ⅓ cup basil leaves, and ½ cup Parmigiano, then a third layer of eggplant. Top the eggplant with the remaining basil leaves, the remaining sauce, and the last of the Parmigiano. May be prepared ahead to this point.

4. Preheat oven to 350 degrees.

5. Bake for 30 minutes, or until bubbly.

6. Let rest for 15 minutes before serving. It can be served at room temperature, but warm is better.

(continued)

Some people put slices of hard-cooked egg in one of the layers.

An old-fashioned but nice variation is to pour some beaten egg between the layers, which not only creates an omelet-like layer but holds the parmigiana together better.

A *Monzù* variation is to dissolve a couple of tablespoons of cocoa in the fresh tomato sauce.

MELANZANE ALL'AMALFITANA
AMALFI-STYLE FRIED EGGPLANT

THE AMALFI-BORN MOTHER of an American friend always made this for her as a treat. JoAnn liked to eat the virtually omelet-encased eggplant slices savory, as they come from the pan, but she says some members of her family sprinkled them with sugar at the table. Though JoAnn Napoli's mother came to America nearly 100 years ago, things have not changed much. Amalfitani still use eggplant in dessert—see page 399 for the famous eggplant with chocolate sauce—and they make exactly what JoAnn's mother did as a savory snack or main course or side dish. It is also the base for the white eggplant parmigiana that follows—from an Amalfitano chef.

Serves 4 to 6

2 pounds eggplant (2 medium-size)

5 eggs

3 tablespoons water

⅛ teaspoon salt

½ cup grated Parmigiano-Reggiano

⅓ cup finely chopped parsley or basil

Flour

Extra-virgin olive oil for frying

1. Prepare the eggplant recipe.

2. Preheat the oven to 350 degrees.

To assemble the dish:

3. Lightly butter a 9-by-13-inch baking pan.

4. Arrange a layer of eggplant slices in the baking pan, trying to cover the bottom as closely and completely as possible without cutting the slices to fit or overlapping them. Arrange slices of cooked ham over the eggplant, this time cutting the ham (if necessary) so it covers the eggplant completely and covers gaps that may be between slices. On top of the ham, arrange half of the Gouda or Fontina, then half of the sliced hard-cooked eggs (don't worry if the slices are not perfect), ¼ cup of the grated Parmigiano, and a good sprinkling of freshly ground black pepper. Repeat a layer of eggplant, then the remaining ham, eggs, cheese, and Parmigiano, and another good sprinkling of pepper. For the last layer, arrange eggplant slices attractively and so they cover completely, even overlapping slightly.

5. About 30 minutes before serving time, bake for 20 minutes. Remove from the oven and let rest for 10 minutes before slicing.

6. The dish is best served hot, but it can be reheated.

Melanzane sott'Olio Estive

Summer-Pickled Eggplant

THIS IS A VINEGARY PICKLE that keeps well in the refrigerator for several weeks but is really meant for consumption within several days of its preparation. It's handy to have on hand for antipasto plates, to garnish or toss into a green salad, or to serve as a condiment/vegetable with grilled fish. I particularly like the way the eggplant picks up the capers' flavor by being boiled with it.

Makes 3 cups

2 pounds eggplant, cut into strips about ½ inch thick,
¼ inch wide, and 3 inches long

3 cups white wine vinegar

3 cups water

1 tablespoon salt

2 tablespoons salted capers, unrinsed

1 teaspoon oregano

2 tablespoons mint leaves

¾ cup olive oil

3 cloves garlic, cut in slivers

¼ teaspoon hot red pepper flakes

1. In a 2½-quart saucepan, combine eggplant strips, the vinegar, the water, the salt, and the capers. Bring to a boil and simmer until the eggplant is tender, about 10 minutes. The eggplant will absorb much of the liquid. Drain. Reserve the capers with the eggplant. Let cool.

2. Place the cooled eggplant in a bowl with the remaining ingredients and toss delicately to combine. Let marinate at least an hour, or keep refrigerated for up to 10 days.

3. Serve at room temperature.

MELANZANE SOTT'OLIO

EGGPLANT PRESERVED IN OIL

THIS IS THE CLASSIC PICKLED eggplant that is served as part of an antipasto napoletano. The eggplant comes out looking like short lengths of twine, and almost as
chewy as meat. There is often a jar of it tucked into the corner of the kitchen, sometimes homemade but these days usually store-bought or made by a relative who spe-
cializes in it. It is a production, but one you will feel was well worth doing when you
have a store of pickled eggplant to pull out for last-minute situations. Cutting the eggplant takes time, then it needs to be salted for twenty-four hours, under weights, to
squeeze out as much moisture as possible. Only then does it get treated in vinegar and
put up in olive oil.

Makes about 6 cups

3 pounds long, narrow eggplants, peeled, sliced lengthwise into ⅛-inch
matchstick strips, 3 to 4 inches long

2½ tablespoons kosher salt

1 quart or 1 liter white wine vinegar

4 cups water

4 cloves garlic, cut in slivers

1½ tablespoons dried oregano

Hot red pepper flakes

Olive oil

1. As you cut the eggplant, place the strips in a very large bowl and sprinkle with
a little salt every time you lay down a covering layer. Toss with the salt each time you
add it, too. Weigh down the eggplant by placing a plate on top of it, then large cans
of tomatoes or a filled water kettle on top of the plate. Let the eggplant stand at
room temperature for 24 hours. Press down the weight every once in a while, as you
remember. Drain well.

2. Place the vinegar and water in a large nonreactive pot. Cover and bring to a
boil. Add the drained eggplant. Cover and return to a boil. As soon as the liquid
returns to a boil, drain the eggplant, discarding the vinegar solution, and spread the
eggplant out to dry on clean cotton dishtowels or absorbent paper.

(continued)

3.   After the eggplant has air-dried for a couple of hours or longer, pack the strips tightly into sterilized jars (see preparation instructions for jars, page 351), adding slivers of garlic and pinches of oregano and hot pepper flakes to each layer, and tamping the layers gently now and then.

4.   Pour in the olive oil slowly, making sure it seeps into the bottom of the jar. If the eggplant has been packed tightly, it will be necessary to wedge a spoon or fork between the eggplant and the sides of the jar for the oil to get to the bottom.

5.   Close securely with hot rings or seals. Italians would store these in a cold larder, but United States authorities recommend the refrigerator. The eggplant should keep for several months. The oil will solidify, so remove the desired amount and bring to room temperature before serving.

Scarola Affogata

Smothered Escarole

THIS IS THE MOST COMMON way of preparing any dark, leafy green vegetable, so you can use this recipe for spinach, beet greens, Swiss chard, curly chicory (also called curly endive), kale, dandelions, wild chicory, borage, and the most popular of all in Campania, broccoli rabe (page 316). Some greens—like broccoli rabe and turnip tops, dandelion greens and wild chicory—for some tastes—those that are super-sensitive to bitter—should be blanched for a minute to five minutes before they are smothered. Spinach, sweet beet greens, and Swiss chard can go in the pan with only their rinsing water clinging to them. Escarole can go either way. In this recipe, it keeps its bitter character. Blanch it and drain it if you want it less so.

Serves 2 to 4

1 large head escarole (about 1 pound)

2 to 3 tablespoons extra-virgin olive oil

2 large cloves garlic, lightly smashed, cut in half, or coarsely chopped

½ teaspoon salt

⅛ teaspoon hot red pepper flakes, or to taste

1. Cut off the very bottom, the usually dirty root end of the escarole, then separate the leaves and wash them very well. Just shake a few times to remove excess water. Don't dry. In 2 or 3 batches, cut the leaves across the ribs into 1-inch-wide or narrower strips. Set aside in a colander.

2. In a deep, 9- to 10-inch skillet or sauté pan that can be covered (if it doesn't have its own cover, a dinner plate will do), combine the olive oil and garlic. Place over medium-low heat and when the garlic begins to sizzle, if using smashed or halved garlic, press it into the oil slightly to release its flavor. When the garlic shows the first signs of coloring, remove the big pieces, if using, and immediately add the escarole. Toss to coat it with oil. Season with salt and red pepper, then cover and let steam and sizzle for 3 or 4 minutes.

3. Toss again, cover again, then cook another few minutes, until the heavy white ribs are just tender, about another 4 or 5 minutes. If there is too much liquid for your taste or use—personally, I like to mop up the pot liquor with bread—uncover the pan and let the liquid evaporate, tossing the escarole frequently. Adjust salt and pepper as necessary.

4. Serve hot or at room temperature with or without lemon wedges.

VARIATIONS:

See Pizza di Scarola (page 80) for smothered escarole with the full array of Neapolitan condiments.

SCAROLA IMBOTTITA

MUCILLI

STUFFED ESCAROLE

STUFFING HEADS OF ESCAROLE with the usual Neapolitan condiments—olives, capers, raisins, pine nuts, parsley, garlic, grated cheese, and some bread crumbs—is a tedious job that is rarely done these days except for a Christmastime meal. That doesn't mean Neapolitans deprive themselves of the pleasure of the combination. It is one of their favorites, but it is essentially the same as in an elaborately seasoned pan of smothered escarole (see previous recipe), which becomes the filling for the very popular double-crusted Pizza di Scarola (page 80), also called Calzone di Scarola, either of which can also be called pizza piena di scarola, stuffed pizza with escarole.

The stuffed version is an interesting but not beautiful presentation. Its dialect name, mucilli, means "kittens," which is supposed to make adorable what ends up looking like a rag-mop of greens. That's why instead of offering the classic recipe, I've devised the following recipe using endive, an escarole cousin. It looks much better and tastes quite as good.

INDIVIA IMBOTTITA AFFOGATA

SMOTHERED STUFFED ENDIVE

ENDIVE IS NOT A VEGETABLE eaten in Campania, except in fancy restaurants, but it is a kind of chicory, which is much appreciated in the region. I created this dish myself after struggling one day with tying up stuffed heads of escarole (see the preceding recipe). I thought for all this effort the escarole doesn't look like much, but endive, its botanical first cousin, would be handsome.

To turn this into an even more elaborate side dish, or an elegant antipasto, after they are cooked, wrap each stuffed endive in a paper-thin slice of prosciutto. Besides being even more elaborate, the salty and sweet prosciutto tempers the bitterness of the endive.

Serves 4

4 whole medium endives, about 1 pound total

For the stuffing:

1 large clove garlic, very finely chopped, about 1 rounded teaspoon

2 tablespoons pine nuts

2 tablespoons raisins, soaked and chopped

2 tablespoons grated Parmigiano-Reggiano

2 tablespoons finely chopped parsley

½ teaspoon salt

For braising:

¼ teaspoon salt, if desired

½ cup water

2 tablespoons olive oil

Plus:

Optional: 2 ounces thinly sliced prosciutto

1.   Trim off the brown root end of each endive. Cut each endive in half lengthwise and, with the tip of a sharp knife, remove the inner leaves from each half, to form a cavity. (Use those inner leaves for a salad.)

2.   In a small bowl, combine the stuffing ingredients and mix well.

3.   Fill 1 cavity of each pair of endive halves with ¼ of the filling mixture. Close with the other half, then temporarily secure the halves with toothpicks.

4.   Tie the endives tightly closed with string. (You can remove the toothpicks now.) Place them in a skillet just large enough to hold them in one layer.

5.   Sprinkle with more salt, if desired, then pour in the water and the oil.

6.   Set over moderate heat, cover, and when the water begins to boil, adjust the heat so it simmers gently. Cook for 10 minutes, then turn the endives (using 2 spoons or tongs) and continue cooking for another 10 minutes, or until the water has evaporated and the endives are soft.

7.   Uncover, turn the heat to low, and turn the endives gently as they take on a light brown color, another 5 minutes or so.

8.   Remove the strings and serve hot or at room temperature, each endive wrapped in a slice of prosciutto, if desired.

Peperoni Arrostiti

Roasted Peppers

As much as Campanians love to fry anything, if given the choice between fried peppers and roasted peppers, most would have to say they prefer them roasted . . . but couldn't they then fry them a little afterward? Roasting peppers not only concentrates their sweetness but adds a haunting smoky tone to their flavor. Some cooks will, in fact, fry peppers after they are roasted—say, for a gratin. That's gilding the lily Neapolitan style.

Roasting peppers over coals or a gas flame is ideal. I manage to balance them on the grates of my stove burners. Keep them over a low flame; the peppers should be directly above the point of the flame, not in it. Turn them regularly with tongs, making sure to turn the bottom and top toward the flame. For most purposes the peppers should not become too soft. The point is to blister and char the skin and to tenderize the peppers, not to make them soft.

When the peppers are done on all sides, place them in a paper bag, plastic bag, or covered pot to steam until they cool. They will soften more.

Peel the peppers with a sharp paring knife.

When you cut them open, catch any pepper liquid in a small bowl. Trim off the stem end, scrape out the seeds, and cut out the ribs.

Proceed as another recipe may suggest, or serve the peppers, cut into strips or wide pieces, dressed with their own juices, salt, black or red pepper, olive oil, perhaps parsley or lemon juice. For a more elaborate dish, add olives, capers, and/or anchovies.

Peperoni in Padella

Fried Red Peppers

Roasted first or not, there's nothing that says summer more in Campania than a huge pan or platter of oily, slightly crinkled, fried sweet peppers. To me they are the color of Naples—red, yellow, and orange, but mostly red, sometimes singed black at the edges—and delicious with everything, including just a piece of bread.

Serves 6

6 medium sweet red peppers or a mix of red, yellow, and orange

3 to 4 tablespoons extra-virgin olive oil

¾ teaspoon salt

Finely cut fresh parsley or basil

1.   Wash the peppers. Cut in half, core, and seed. Cut the peppers into lengthwise strips from ¼ to ½ inch wide.

2.   In a 10-inch or larger skillet or sauté pan, heat the oil over medium heat. Add the peppers, salt them, and fry them, tossing them frequently until they are wilted. Cook until tender, 12 to 15 minutes.

3.   Remove from the heat and toss with the parsley.

4.   Serve anywhere from hot to room temperature.

VARIATIONS:

If desired, add 1 or 2 cut or lightly smashed cloves of garlic to the pan after about 5 minutes, just to add its flavor to the oil. Remove the garlic if it begins to brown. Discard it before serving the peppers.

You might also add whole or cut-up olives, capers, or anchovies for the last few minutes of cooking.

The following more elaborate and rustically seasoned recipe for Peperoni Aglio e Aceto, peppers with garlic and vinegar, was given to me by an old gentleman from Avellino who now lives in New Jersey. (The uncharacteristically large dose of garlic may be his Italian-American addition, but he says no.) When the peppers are almost done, add 6 cloves of coarsely chopped or sliced garlic and ⅓ to ½ cup Gaeta olives (pitted if desired). Cook another 2 to 3 minutes. Take the pan off the heat and immediately add 3 tablespoons of red wine vinegar. It will sizzle and deglaze the pan. Toss and season with freshly ground pepper to taste. Serve hot, warm, or at room temperature, garnished with whole leaves of parsley, which are meant to be eaten with the peppers.

Peperoni Gratinati

Peperoni al Gratin

Baked Pepper Casserole

After plain roasted or fried peppers, this is the most popular pepper dish of the region. Every cook I worked with wanted to show me how she or he makes it, which is how I learned that some like lots of crunchy, oily bread crumbs on top and some want the bread crumbs to be soft, blended with the peppers, absorbing pepper juices and oil, and melding with the condiments. This recipe tends toward the second idea. If you'd like more crust, before putting the casserole under the broiler, sprinkle the surface with an additional two tablespoons of crumbs and drizzle the crumbs with another two teaspoons of olive oil.

Serves 6

3 pounds sweet red peppers, roasted, peeled, and cut into strips ½ inch wide

1 or 2 whole salted anchovies, thoroughly rinsed and filleted and finely cut,
or 2 or 3 oil-packed anchovy fillets, rinsed and finely cut

6 to 8 Gaeta olives (or other purple-black olives), pitted and cut into small
pieces (about ¼ cup)

1 tablespoon salted capers, thoroughly rinsed and chopped coarsely if large

5 tablespoons extra-virgin olive oil

1 teaspoon dried oregano

2 cloves garlic, finely chopped (about 2 rounded teaspoons)

½ cup dried bread crumbs

1. Preheat the oven to 400 degrees.

2. In a shallow baking dish just large enough to hold the peppers (about 2-quart capacity), combine the sliced peppers, anchovies, olives, capers, olive oil, oregano, and garlic. Toss and mix well.

3. Toss again with the bread crumbs.

4. Bake for 20 minutes, then place the dish under the broiler for 5 minutes or until the top crumbs are lightly toasted.

5. Serve warm or at room temperature, as an antipasto or contorno (side dish).

PEPERONI IMBOTTITI SALERNITANI

SALERNO-STYLE STUFFED PEPPERS

IN BENEVENTO, THEY STUFF peppers with soaked bread, too—as opposed to bread crumbs or croutons—but they use mostly their local, small but sweet red or green variety called cornetti, because of their horn shape. These are not available in North America (yet). Large, meaty peppers like the ones we grow in the United States and get from Holland are the ones preferred in Salerno and into these goes a filling that is, like many of our Thanksgiving stuffings, mostly bread, but each bite studded with a piquant flavor—a piece of olive, a caper, a hint of anchovy, and with the overall background flavors of grated cheese, garlic, and parsley. Ironically, the stuffing in Salerno, the province where the modern tomato was born and thrives like almost nowhere else, rarely has tomato, while in Benevento it does. On the other hand, some Salernitani can't resist serving their stuffed peppers—or stuffed eggplant or zucchini—in fresh tomato sauce.

Serves 6

For the stuffing:

6 cups stale bread that has been cut into 1½-inch cubes

½ cup grated Parmigiano-Reggiano

½ cup grated pecorino

¾ cup Gaeta olives, pitted and halved

⅓ cup salted capers, thoroughly rinsed, coarsely chopped if large

3 salted anchovies, thoroughly rinsed, filleted, and cut into ¼-inch pieces, or
6 oil-packed anchovy fillets, rinsed and cut into ¼-inch pieces

1 tablespoon finely minced garlic

¾ cup loosely packed parsley leaves, finely cut

3 eggs

½ teaspoon salt

¼ teaspoon freshly ground black pepper

Plus:

6 medium red peppers, weighing about 2 pounds

⅓ cup extra-virgin olive oil

(continued)

1. Preheat the oven to 400 degrees.

2. In a large bowl, soak the bread cubes in water.

3. In another bowl, combine the cheeses, the olives, the capers, the anchovies, the garlic, and the parsley.

4. Slice the tops off the peppers, removing as little as possible. Remove the seeds and cut out the white membrane.

5. By handfuls, squeeze the water out of the soaked bread and crumble it into the bowl with the other stuffing ingredients. Add the eggs, the salt, and the pepper. With a fork, mix very well, but do not compact the mixture.

6. Fill each pepper to the brim without packing it densely.

7. Place the peppers on their sides in a baking dish large enough to hold them without touching. Drizzle them with the oil, letting a little drip down onto the stuffing.

8. Bake for 45 minutes, turning the peppers 2 or 3 times so that every side has a chance to cook on the bottom of the pan with the oil. When done, the skins will have started to char slightly and the stuffing will be lightly toasted.

9. The peppers are best when served within an hour, but they are also good, if a little heavier, served at room temperature. If prepared a day ahead, the peppers should be reheated in a 350-degree oven, split in half or butterflied so the stuffing reheats without overcooking the pepper. Serve each pepper with a spoon of oil from the pan.

VARIATION:

To make Salerno-Style Melanzane Imbottite (Stuffed Eggplant), cut small eggplants in quarters—cut the long way, then across. Make a deep slit in each quarter, running it parallel to the long way of the eggplant, making 2 flaps connected at the end. Soak the eggplant in salt water for 30 minutes, then drain well and pat dry. Stuff the slit in each eggplant quarter with the bread filling above, neatening the sides so that the stuffing is not running out. Fry the eggplant quarters in olive oil until browned and tender, then drain. Serve as they are, or with tomato sauce, or simmered a few minutes in tomato sauce.

Peperoni Imbottiti di Ida Cerbone

Ida Cerbone's Stuffed Peppers

IDA CERBONE, WHO COOKS at Manducatis, the restaurant she owns with her husband, Vincent, in Queens, New York, still makes the recipes of her hometown. She comes from Pignataro Interamna, a village only a few miles north of the Campania border, near Cassino, in Lazio, where the Cerbones also have a home. Still, says Vincent, a native of Naples, citing ancient history to rationalize his wife's credentials as a bona fide Campanian, "For the Romans it's Campania Felix." That's true, but Ida's food is her Campanian credential. This style of stuffed pepper is pretty typical of Caserta, the Campanian province north of Naples and right over the border from Pignataro, and some would call it Piedigrotta-style, after the section of Naples where the old Neapolitan song festival used to be held.

Serves 8

For the filling:

⅓ cup extra-virgin olive oil

½ cup Gaeta olives, pitted and cut into quarters

1½ tablespoons salted capers, thoroughly rinsed, coarsely chopped if large

⅓ cup loosely packed finely cut parsley

1 tablespoon pine nuts

¼ teaspoon hot red pepper flakes

2 to 3 teaspoons finely minced garlic

Optional: A few anchovy fillets, and/or 2 tablespoons raisins

3 cups of stale bread cut into ½-inch cubes

Plus:

4 medium to large red peppers (about 1½ pounds), washed

1. In a small bowl, combine the filling ingredients except for the bread. Toss to mix. Let stand for at least 15 to 20 minutes. Toss in the bread cubes and mix well so they absorb some of the oil.

2. Cut the peppers in half lengthwise and remove the seeds and ribs.

(continued)

3. Divide the bread cube mixture evenly among the peppers. It should almost fill each.

4. Arrange the peppers in an oiled baking dish large enough to hold them without touching.

5. Preheat the oven to 400 degrees.

6. Bake for 45 minutes, or until the peppers are cooked but still slightly firm and the bread cubes are browned and crisped.

7. Serve hot.

VARIATIONS:

For a different pepper flavor, you can roast and peel the peppers before baking, in which case reduce the cooking time to 30 minutes.

Another traditional filling would include eggplant, sometimes tomato, sometimes both. For Peperoni Imbottiti di Melanzane (Peppers Stuffed with Eggplant), add to the above filling, after the bread cubes: 1 pound eggplant, peeled, cut into ½-inch cubes, salted, drained, dried, and fried until just tender in a skillet with olive oil; 3 fresh plum tomatoes, peeled and cut into ¼-inch pieces; and ½ teaspoon dried oregano. Bake as above.

Peperoni sott'Olio

Red Peppers Preserved in Oil

THESE ARE SO MUCH BETTER than anything you can buy in a jar and so easy to prepare that I urge you to try them when peppers are at their peak in summer. During the winter, you will be thrilled to have jars of these on hand for serving as an antipasto, either by themselves or with sliced cold cuts, cheese, olives, and perhaps some other pickled vegetables for an antipasto napoletano (page 14). You can also use them instead of vinegar peppers in any of the recipes for pork with peppers (page 297). Store them in the coolest, darkest place you can find (other than the refrigerator) for maximum shelf life. When I've kept them in my overheated apartment I find the color of the peppers fades and the peppers become too soft after a couple of months. In a cool place, they should keep almost until the next pepper crop is in—unless they are eaten before then, which is highly likely.

Makes about 9 cups

6 pounds sweet red peppers

2 quarts or liters white wine vinegar

6 cloves garlic, cut in slivers

1 rounded tablespoon kosher salt

2 tablespoons dried oregano

Olive oil

To prepare the jars:

1.   Wash wide-mouthed glass jars in hot soapy water. Rinse well and sterilize them by placing them in water and boiling them for 20 minutes. Do not boil the rubber rings or seals. Just before you are ready to cover the jars, place these in boiling water. Leave the jars in the boiling water while you prepare the peppers.

To prepare and cook the peppers:

2.   Wash the peppers. Halve them and remove the seeds and white membranes. Cut them into ¼-inch-wide strips.

(continued)

3.   In a pot large enough to hold the peppers, combine them with the vinegar. Bring to a boil over high heat. As soon as the vinegar boils, remove from the heat and drain the peppers in a colander. If you want to reserve the vinegar for another batch of peppers, place the colander over a bowl.

4.   Spread the drained peppers on clean dishtowels or sheets of absorbent paper to dry for about 10 minutes.

To pack the peppers:

5.   Using tongs, which have also been sterilized in the water, remove one jar at a time from the hot water bath. Drain it well and put it upside down for a few minutes on a clean dishtowel.

6.   Still using the tongs, pack the peppers into the jars, adding 1 or 2 slivers of garlic to each layer and sprinkling each layer with a bit of salt and oregano. Keep building layers, tamping the peppers down slightly with a sterilized spoon, until the peppers are within ½ inch of the top of the jar.

7.   Pour on the olive oil slowly, making sure it seeps into the bottom of the jar. If the peppers have been packed tightly, it will be necessary to wedge your spoon or fork between them and the sides of the jar for the oil to get to the bottom.

8.   Finally, press the peppers down to release any air bubbles caught in the oil.

9.   Remove the rings or seals from the hot water and seal.

10. Italians would store these in a cold larder, but United States authorities recommend the refrigerator. The peppers are good to eat within a few days, but they continue to improve for a month. The oil will solidify in the refrigerator, so remove the desired amount and bring to room temperature before serving.

GATTÒ

POTATO CAKE

———

The name "gattò" is a vulgarization of the French word *gâteau,* meaning "cake," demonstrating the influence of the French language on the Neapolitan dialect and of French cooking in the Neapolitan kitchen. Anything with a French name is likely to be a fancy dish, and this is the most elaborate potato dish of the region. It is also one of its most famous outside the region. As "potato cake," a direct translation of the Neapolitan, or by other names, it is prepared in many Italian-American restaurants. Full of cheese—often smoked cheese—and salami, it is a rich side dish, usually served in winter and usually accompanying something very plain—such as grilled meat or sausage. It is perfect with a roasted chicken, which is even these days more feast food than everyday food in Campania.

Serves 8

3½ pounds all-purpose potatoes, preferably yellow-fleshed, washed and peeled

3 cups loosely packed grated Parmigiano-Reggiano

4 tablespoons butter

4 ounces Neapolitan-style salami or soppressata, cut into ¼-inch cubes

1 egg, beaten

¾ cup milk

2 rounded tablespoons finely cut parsley

2 teaspoons salt

1 to 2 tablespoons butter (for greasing the pan)

¼ cup dried bread crumbs (for the pan)

4 ounces smoked provola or smoked Gouda, cut into ½-inch or smaller cubes

8 ounces mozzarella, cut into ½-inch or smaller cubes

Optional: Freshly ground black pepper

1 tablespoon butter

1. Boil the potatoes in plenty of salted water until just tender. Rice the potatoes into a bowl. (Do not mash.)

(continued)

2. Add the Parmigiano, butter, salami, egg, milk, parsley, and salt, stirring only enough to incorporate everything evenly.

3. Preheat the oven to 425 degrees.

4. Heavily butter a 10-inch pie dish or cake pan, then coat with bread crumbs.

5. Turn ⅔ of the potato mixture into the prepared pan. Smooth out gently, using a spatula or the back of a spoon, making the layer even. Do not press down. Try not to disturb the bread crumbs coating the pan.

6. Sprinkle evenly with the smoked cheese and mozzarella cubes, but don't bring them to the very edge. Season with freshly ground black pepper, if desired. Top with the remainder of the potato mixture. Smooth gently again. With a fork, make a decorative pattern on the surface of the potatoes; sprinkle lightly with bread crumbs, then dot with 1 tablespoon of butter.

7. Bake for 15 to 20 minutes, or until the top is lightly browned.

8. Serve hot, cut into wedges or spooned out of the pan.

PATATE ARRIGANATE

POTATOES BAKED WITH OREGANO

POTATOES PREPARED THIS WAY do not get crusty, as you might think and want them to. As a sublime consolation, they become melting, almost fonduelike slices with traces of crispness at their edges.

Serves 4 to 6

3 tablespoons extra-virgin olive oil

2 pounds all-purpose potatoes, peeled and sliced ¼ inch thick

1 small onion, cut in half, then thinly sliced

1 generous tablespoon oregano

2 to 3 canned peeled tomatoes, coarsely chopped or chunked up

1¼ teaspoons salt

1. Preheat the oven to 400 degrees.

2. Pour the oil into a shallow baking dish of about 2-quart capacity. Combine all the ingredients in the pan and toss well to mix.

3. Bake for 45 minutes. If you like crusty bits, do not turn the potatoes while baking. They will stick a little on the bottom, but can be easily scraped up with a metal spatula. When done, the potatoes should be very tender.

4. Serve hot or warm.

POMODORI AL GRATIN

BAKED TOMATOES

––––––––––

THIS MAY BE ONE of the oldest European ways of preparing tomatoes. An almost identical recipe, a variation that is still made, was described in *Of Pythagorean Food or, Herbaceous Food for the Use of Noblemen and Literati* by Vincenzo Corrado, in 1781. He recommends stuffing tomatoes with anchovies, garlic, parsley, oregano, salt, and pepper, then sprinkling them with bread crumbs and oil and baking in the oven. Keep in mind that these tomatoes are supposed to collapse. They will not be pretty, firm tomato halves when they come out of the oven, but they will be intensely, irresistibly savory.

Serves 6

6 medium salad-type tomatoes

1½ teaspoons salt

For the filling:

½ cup dried bread crumbs

3 tablespoons salted capers, rinsed thoroughly, coarsely chopped if large

1 teaspoon very finely minced garlic

1 teaspoon dried oregano

½ teaspoon freshly ground black pepper

5 tablespoons extra-virgin olive oil

1. Preheat the oven to 400 degrees.

2. Halve the tomatoes across the center. With a grapefruit knife, a melon baller, or a teaspoon, scoop out the seeds and discard them. Use a melon baller to scoop out the rib pulp and reserve it in a strainer over a mixing bowl. Sprinkle the insides of the tomato shells lightly with salt, then place them upside down on a rack to drain while preparing the filling.

3. To the drained tomato pulp, add the filling ingredients and 2 tablespoons of the olive oil.

4.   Fill each tomato half lightly—about 2 tablespoons filling. There will be barely enough.

5.   Grease a 9-by-13-inch or similarly sized baking dish with 1 tablespoon of the olive oil. Arrange the tomatoes in the pan. Drizzle the tops with the remaining 2 tablespoons of oil.

6.   Bake for 50 minutes to 1 hour, until the tomatoes have collapsed and the filling has browned lightly on top.

7.   Serve hot or at room temperature. (The baked tomatoes can be kept refrigerated for several days. Allow to return to room temperature before serving.)

INSALATA DI POMODORO

TOMATO SALAD

NOTHING COULD BE MORE BASIC or important than tomato salad. Or is it tomato sauce? Some Neapolitans would argue that tomato salad is raw sauce. One could think of it that way. So why is macaroni dressed with diced raw tomatoes often called pasta all'insalata? Who says Italians never eat macaroni salad?

It's well known that tomatoes should never be chilled or refrigerated. Their flavor and fragrance are diminished by cold. Tomatoes should be stored at room temperature. But in my readings, I found a lovely technique for cooling tomatoes on a hot summer day, to make a salad of them more refreshing: Let the whole tomatoes—theoretically vine-ripened and still warm from the sun (or your hot kitchen)—stand for 30 minutes in a bowl of cool tap water.

Serves 4

1 pound ripe tomatoes, diced

3 tablespoons extra-virgin olive oil

1 large clove garlic, sliced or finely minced

½ teaspoon dried oregano

¼ teaspoon salt

1. In a mixing bowl, combine the diced tomatoes, the olive oil, the garlic, the oregano, and the salt. Stir gently but well.

2. Let stand at room temperature for 30 minutes to an hour. Remove the sliced garlic, if using. (Do not add vinegar.)

VARIATIONS:

When available, use torn basil leaves instead of oregano or with the oregano. Or add torn fresh parsley leaves.

Instead of garlic, add ½ cup finely minced red onion.

Capers and pieces of pitted Gaeta olives are always options, too.

La Caponata Napoletana

Acqua Sale

Tomato and Bread Salad

The true caponata is made with toasts that are not sweet; they can be either rectangular or the round kind with a hole in the middle, as they make them in Castellammare di Stabia, moistened with water, broken in pieces, then put in a bowl and seasoned with salt, oil and vinegar.

On this base, the caponata can be constructed in a thousand ways, following the whim of the cook: with a clove of garlic lightly crushed, with oregano, with some baby eggplant preserved in vinegar, with slices of tomato, with pitted black olives, with capers, with anchovy fillets. Some people add a pinch of hot pepper. . . . In any case, the caponata . . . suits our Southern taste.

—Achille Talarico, *Gastronomia salernitana*
(The Gastronomy of Salerno)

I suppose caponata is so basic to the Neapolitan kitchen—you might say it is one of the primal foods—because from its simplest form to its most complex presentations it does showcase, as Achille Talarico says, for better and for worse, the taste (and tastes) of southern Italy. Cecilia Bellelli Baratta made absolutely sure to explain it to me the very first time I visited her farm in Paestum. I had spent several days cooking and eating with her and her family, and I'd already packed the car to get on the road to Naples when she called me to the kitchen. It was an emergency. She had forgotten to give me a lesson on caponata.

It's nothing but tomato salad and moistened dry, toasted, (often whole wheat) bread called pane biscottato and sometimes simply biscotti, which is why Talarico makes a point of specifying "not sweet" toasts. It is a product one buys, not makes. "But you have to be careful about softening the bread," Cecilia said, the two of us standing in the kitchen in winter overcoats, the car running outside, she dipping toasts into salt water to show me how and for how long. (Hence the dish's other name, acqua sale.) "The bread needs to be softened, but not turned to mush," Cecilia explained, "and you also have to consider that the tomatoes will give off liquid as they marinate."

(continued)

It was January, so there were no tomatoes to demonstrate, but I got the picture. Now I get the "big" picture and see how this originally very primitive salad can become a catch-all of the grandest proportions. It has at my house, and Cavalcanti has a much-quoted recipe for a caponata of fish that is an architectural construction reminiscent of Liguria's extravagant capon magro. Liguria has a simpler capponadda of its own, too, and both the Ligurian and Neapolitan dishes are bread salads based on the mariners' hard tack, the dried bread that would be taken to be eaten aboard ship because of its keeping quality. Capone is a fish, and it's thought that's where the word for the salad must come from. Sea water would be, of course, the convenient moistener. Sicilian caponata is better known than either Liguria's or Naples's, and it makes one wonder how it got its name, as it is a sweet and sour eggplant stew, neither a fish nor a bread salad.

Both pane biscottato and freselle are imported from Italy in cellophane bags and are available at specialty markets. In addition, many Italian-American bakeries make freselle, the ring-shaped dried bread, or what they might call bread biscotti. When you find them you can stock up because they keep well in a tin for a few months—at least as long as the tomato season.

Serve 4

1 teaspoon salt

2 cups water

4 to 6 whole-grain freselle or pane biscottato,
or oven-dried whole grain "country-style" bread

1 tablespoon red or white wine vinegar

1 recipe Insalata di Pomodoro (see preceding recipe),
the tomatoes sliced or diced

Optional ingredient suggestions:

Fresh basil or parsley leaves, torn or shredded

Sliced or diced sweet onion

1 6-ounce can solid light tuna in olive oil

Gaeta olives

Capers

Anchovy fillets

Cooked stringbeans, cut into 1-inch lengths

Sweet or hot red peppers in vinegar or preserved under oil
(see pages 14 and 351), cut into strips or diced

Eggplant preserved in oil (see page 339)

Marinated mushrooms, halved or quartered

1. In a medium bowl, make a saltwater bath by dissolving the salt in the water. Dip the freselle into the salted water to soften it slightly. Some products require only a few seconds, some as long as a minute. After you do the first 1 or 2 slices you will be able to adjust the time.

2. Depending on whether you are making a composed salad or a tossed one, either arrange the freselle or dried bread slices on a platter or break them up into approximately ½-inch chunks and place them in a serving bowl. Sprinkle the vinegar over the bread.

3. If using sliced tomatoes, arrange them over the bread on the platter, then pour on the marinade and tomato juices. Otherwise, to the pieces of bread in the bowl, add the diced tomato salad and toss well.

4. Add optional ingredients as desired.

5. Serve immediately, or let stand a few minutes or up to several hours—at room temperature.

A note on leftovers: Once refrigerated, the salad loses its appeal—although you may still find it quite acceptable. It can be turned into a delicious version of pancotto (or pane cotto), "cooked bread," a minestra, which should be served hot with extra-virgin olive oil drizzled over the top—or better, hot pepper oil. Turn the soggy salad into a saucepan and place over medium heat. With a wooden spoon, beat the mixture, adding a little water as necessary, to form a thick gruel. It should not be perfectly smooth, rather more like the consistency of thick oatmeal.

ZUCCHINE A SCAPECE

MARINATED FRIED ZUCCHINI

SCAPECE MUST COME FROM the early era of Spanish occupation in the sixteenth century because it is a derivative of the Spanish *escabeche*, the Iberian technique of frying a food, usually fish, then marinating it in vinegar. In Campania, the method is today used mainly for zucchini and sometimes for eggplant, but also for fresh anchovies, sardines, and other small fish, which are lumped together under one Neapolitan word, "fragaglie."

Scapece, without qualification, usually means zucchini. And the dish is everywhere during the summer, not only because zucchini are in season but because it is perfect summer food. It's served at room temperature, keeps well for several days, is refreshing with the acid of vinegar and menthol of mint, piquant with raw garlic and pepper—all perking up sluggish summer appetites. With its chewy, substantial texture, a scapece sandwich is not an unlikely lunch on a stifling August afternoon. I like a plate of scapece with a piece of caciocavallo or provolone, some bread and white wine. Scapece is also an excellent antipasto or a side dish to anything from the grill.

This recipe calls for air drying or, even better, sun drying the zucchini slices before frying them. Because the zucchini have so much moisture, it's a necessary step if they are to be chewy, as they should be.

Serves 4 as an antipasto or side dish

1 pound zucchini, as small as possible and no larger than 4 to the pound

¼ cup extra-virgin olive oil

¼ teaspoon salt

¼ teaspoon freshly ground black pepper

⅓ cup mint leaves, torn

¼ cup white vinegar

¼ cup water

1 clove garlic, minced

1. Wash and dry the zucchini. Slice them into rounds no more than ¼ inch thick. Place on racks to dry for 12 hours or more. (Or, if you have a sunny and hot day without much humidity, place them outside in the sun to dry.)

2. In an 8- to 9-inch skillet, heat the oil over medium-high heat and, when hot, fry the zucchini slices in small batches. They will brown quickly, so do not leave the pan unattended. Fry on both sides. With a slotted spoon or skimmer, remove the zucchini as soon as they are browned on both sides. Drain them on absorbent paper if desired, although they do not absorb much of the oil.

3. Place the fried zucchini in a bowl. As you add another small batch, sprinkle each layer with a tiny bit of salt and pepper, and some torn mint leaves. Reserve the frying oil. You should have about 2 tablespoons.

4. In a small saucepan, combine the vinegar, the water, and the garlic. Bring to a boil and let boil for 10 minutes. Stir in the zucchini frying oil and pour the hot mixture over the zucchini. Cover (with a plate or plastic wrap) and let stand for at least 2 hours, or overnight.

5. Serve at room temperature.

CIANFOTTA (CIAMBOTTA) NAPOLETANA

VEGETABLE STEW

MORE THAN MOST DISHES in the region-wide repertoire, ranking along with pasta and beans, cianfotta highlights the old and sometimes still staunch provincialities of Campania. The fact that it is pronounced and spelled many different ways says everything. In Naples, the hub, the place where everything grown and made in the region can be had, cianfotta is most often an appropriately elaborate stew of tomatoes, eggplant, peppers, potatoes, and onions seasoned with capers, olives, and parsley. But in Capri, where peppers never used to grow, they never use peppers in this dish—an important distinction, a proud Caprese will tell you. And in the spring on Capri, they make a stew of garden peas and their famous fava beans that they call cianfotta. In Salerno, an old-style cianfotta could be just peppers, eggplant, and potato, each fried separately, then baked together in the oven with chopped garlic, salt, pepper, and lard or olive oil. In the rural parts of Salerno, a stew of wild spring greens and potatoes might be called cianfotta, too.

"The important thing is the fat," a home cook in Salerno told me. "You should cook each vegetable separately, so that each one gets done just so." She tilted her head, indicating that "just so" wasn't so easy to obtain or that important anyway. "But then, if they haven't cooked in the same fat, you have to let their fats mingle." Another housewife, this one from Benevento, told me: "I put in every fat I find in the refrigerator—a little butter, a little lard, a little olive oil, some prosciutto fat if I have it. But I don't tell my children about the lard. They'd kill me for using lard."

This recipe uses a classic Neapolitan combination and technique. Only the peppers are fried separately, and to their oil are added the other vegetables, one at a time, from those that cook the longest to those that need the least time. So, for instance, if you want to add zucchini to the mixture, add it last. If you want to add green beans (stringbeans) or fresh cranberry beans, add them at the beginning. Like any vegetable stew, cianfotta can be made ahead and kept for several days in the refrigerator. But eat it at room temperature or warmed. It is usually served as an antipasto or side dish, but, with bread and a piece of cheese, you can easily make a meal of it.

Makes 9 to 10 cups, at least 8 servings as an antipasto or side dish

2 pounds eggplant, peeled and cut into ¾-inch cubes

1 teaspoon fine salt

½ cup extra-virgin olive oil

2 pounds red peppers, washed, cored, seeded, and cut into ¾-inch squares

1 pound onions, peeled, cut in half through the root end and sliced thinly

1½ pounds potatoes, peeled and cut into ¾-inch cubes

1 pound (2 large) tomatoes, cored and cut into roughly 1-inch pieces

1½ teaspoons salt

½ teaspoon freshly ground black pepper

½ cup Gaeta olives, pitted or not (or other black-purple olives,
such as Greek or Niçoise)

3 tablespoons salted capers, rinsed thoroughly, coarsely chopped if large
(or use small capers in vinegar or brine, rinsed, but not chopped)

1½ cups loosely packed basil or parsley leaves, finely cut

1. Salt the eggplant.

2. Meanwhile prepare the rest of the vegetables as specified in the ingredient list.

3. In a large casserole, preferably terra-cotta or enameled cast iron, heat the olive oil over medium heat and when hot enough to make a piece of pepper sizzle immediately, add the peppers and fry, stirring frequently, until they are just tender, about 8 minutes. With a slotted spoon or skimmer, remove the peppers, leaving the oil in the casserole.

4. Add the onions to the hot oil and sauté until onions are well wilted, 5 to 8 minutes.

5. Add the potatoes and cook them, stirring frequently, for about 5 minutes.

6. Dry and squeeze the eggplant with paper towels, then stir the eggplant cubes into the casserole. Cook with the rest of the vegetables for about 5 minutes.

7. Add the tomatoes, the salt, and the pepper, stir well, then adjust heat to lowest possible. Cover the pot and let the vegetables simmer very gently until the potatoes and eggplant are just tender, stirring frequently, from 15 to 30 minutes, mainly depending on the size of the pot.

(continued)

8. Add the reserved fried pepper and continue simmering gently, still covered, for at least another 15 minutes, still stirring frequently, until the eggplant and potatoes are totally cooked and tender.

9. Add the olives, the capers, and the basil or parsley. Stir, uncovered, for about 3 minutes, to blend the flavors.

10. Cool and serve warm or at room temperature, correcting the salt and pepper just before serving.

INSALATA DI RINFORZO

CAULIFLOWER SALAD FOR CHRISTMAS

Basilio Avitabile

AS CHEF BASILIO AVITABILE of La Cantinella, one of Naples's top restaurants, was tossing together this salad one December 22, he complained. "No one really eats this here, but you have to have it." Colorful, with strips of pickled red pepper and orange carrot rounds, green and purple olives, pale green pickled celery, and darker green gherkins, all set off by cloudlike pieces of white cauliflower, rinforzo has become a kind of Neapolitan Christmas decoration. It does look good on the sideboard. And every Neapolitan does have to at least look at one during the season.

The name, which means to reinforce or strengthen, can be interpreted as a triple pun: (1) rinforzo in the sense that it's the additional dish on the table, no matter what else is served, (2) rinforzo because it holds up for days and can be supplemented with additional cauliflower, pickles, anchovies, etc., and (3) rinforzo in the figurative meaning of the word, a pick-me-up.

Insalata di rinforzo is not the same as giardiniera. The cauliflower in giardiniera is fully pickled (boiled in vinegar), and in rinforzo, among other quibbling differences, the cauliflower is merely dressed with oil and vinegar and only becomes marinated when it stands for a day. Still, many Neapolitans buy bottled giardiniera and use it in their rinforzo, discarding the bottled cauliflower and using fresh cauliflower as the base for the salad. You can do the same. Giardiniera in bottles is well distributed in American supermarkets and Italian delicatessens.

Serves at least 8

1 medium head cauliflower

½ cup pickled sweet red pepper strips, ¼ to ½ inch wide

½ cup mixed pickled vegetables: carrots, celery, sour gherkins (cornichons)

12 Gaeta olives, pitted

12 large green Sicilian olives, pitted and each cut into halves or slices

3 tablespoons extra-virgin olive oil

2 tablespoons white wine vinegar

¼ to ½ teaspoon freshly ground black pepper

Salt

4 to 6 whole salted anchovies, thoroughly rinsed and filleted,
or 8 to 12 oil-packed anchovy fillets, rinsed

1. Cut any green leaves off the cauliflower and cut out the heavy central stem. Rinse well, then boil in salted water until just tender, about 8 minutes. Drain the cauliflower, let it cool enough to handle, then cut it into small flowerettes. Place in a salad bowl.

2. Add the pickled peppers and vegetables, and the two kinds of olives, and toss.

3. Add the oil and toss again.

4. Add the vinegar and toss again.

5. Season with pepper and salt. Toss again.

6. Drape the anchovies on top decoratively.

7. Serve at room temperature.

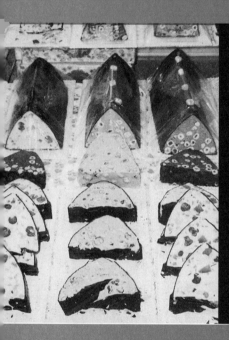

DESSERTS

CAMPANIANS START THEIR DAY with sweets, end their day with sweets, and punctuate their day with sweets. It's no wonder the English love Campania. Naples has many great bakeries and pastry shops, and every city of the region has at least one outstanding one. I've stopped at tiny combination grocery-cafés in the countryside and eaten sublime graf, the ubiquitous fried donut, and fresh, warm sfogliatelle perfumed with orange flower water. There are poorly made pastries in Campania, but it's hard to find them.

The region also excels at frozen desserts. As Eskimos have many words for snow, Neapolitans have many names for frozen desserts. There are gelati (ice creams) and semifreddi (a general category of not-quite ice creams that includes coviglie and perfetti, each made with a different type of beaten egg base). Then there are sorbetti (frozen juices and purees); spumoni (molded layers of several frozen desserts); ghiacciate (shaved ice with flavored syrup); and granite (flavored slush that is now dispensed from machines similar to frozen cocktail contraptions).

And there are the iced drinks, based on fruit syrups, coffee, chocolate, and nut milks. A frappè at Naples's famous Mexico café-bar, iced coffee whipped with milk and crushed ice into a thick froth, is one of those things to which locals proudly point tourists. Frullato is a whipped fruit and milk drink. Cremolata is a frozen, but not solid, sweetened fruit puree or chocolate served from a cup.

American Neapolitan ice cream is not Neapolitan, by the way. But it derives from something Neapolitan—spumoni, elaborate, molded frozen desserts. A true spumone (literally "big foam") is at least two layers. The outer one is usually a gelato. The inner one is not a true ice cream but a semifreddo or just frozen whipped cream. They can be studded with candied fruit, nuts, chocolate, chestnuts, nut brittle, you name it. They're bought, not made at home, and never what they used to be in Italian-American restaurants—a slice of striped ice cream—vanilla, strawberry, and pistachio (or nowadays chocolate), imitating the Italian flag.

FRUIT

*T*he fruits of Campania are considered the best in Italy, and particularly the peaches. Peaches love warm weather, and southern Salerno especially provides it. In Rome and up north, you can see market signs touting the Campanian origins of peaches, but also the region's figs, apricots, plums, lemons, and oranges. The Sorrento peninsula is so hospitable to lemons, citrons, and other citrus fruits that from some angles it looks like one enormous terraced orchard. Up and down the steep hills, the lemon groves are covered with black netting to protect them from the wind that whips off the sea.

Where did all this ice come from? Naples is a hot city. In the seventeenth century, when all these frozen desserts started, ice would be gathered from the mountains of the Sorrento peninsula, loaded on donkeys, and brought in by boat to Naples and the coast. It was kept covered with straw in caves and cellars.

The true inventor of modern ice cream was a Tuscan, according to Jeanne Carola Francesconi. His name was Bernardo Buontalenti, and he lived in the early sixteenth century. We know that Florentine Catherine de Medici brought ice cream to the French court in 1533, when she married Henry II, but it was kept a court secret and only the court ate it.

It wasn't until 1660, when Procopio Coltelli, a Sicilian, opened his famous Café Procope in Paris, that the French started enjoying "Italian" ice creams. Imitating and competing with Coltelli was another Sicilian named Tortoni. He opened a café bearing his name and became just as famous. The toasted almond semifreddo called tortoni in Italian-American restaurants is named after him, but unknown in Naples. So, as Francesconi and every Neapolitan says, even if frozen desserts were not invented in the Kingdom of Naples, the Sicilians and Neapolitans certainly made it their domain.

Most frozen desserts can't be made at home—not well at least—but you'll find here the semifreddi served in cups, which are easy and work perfectly in a home freezer without any special equipment or cooking skills.

Campanians don't usually bake their own pastries, either. They have bakeries that provide everything. Still, I've included recipes for the complicated sfogliatelle—it's a good project for a hobbyist baker—and for the two cakes that are hallmarks of the Neapolitan *pasticceria*: babà, the yeast-risen crown, and torta caprese, the chocolate and almond torte of Capri. I've concentrated on baked fruit, simple pound cakes, puddings, and delizie, the group of assembled desserts of cookies or sponge cake with cream and flavorings. These are the Neapolitan desserts that any home cook might make.

Actually, having asked numerous cooks what home dessert their families like most, I discovered that pineapple upside-down cake is a favorite. They are always surprised to find out it is American.

CREMA PASTICCIERA I

THICK PASTRY CREAM

CAMPANIANS ARE WILD for pastry cream. Thickened with flour, rich with eggs, flavored with vanilla, lemon, chocolate, or coffee, it fills cream puffs, sponge cakes, and ladyfingers in all the composed desserts called delizie (delights), and the grandest of all, Zuppa Inglese (page 378). It goes under fruits and fruit preserves in tarts, which are called either crostate or pizze. It forms a topknot in the hole of the famous fried zeppole di San Giuseppe, the bignè—or French crullers, you might call them—made in honor of St. Joseph on March 19. Pastry cream is also one of the bases for frozen desserts. It can be lightened with whipped cream, thinned with liquid cream. It also makes a fine sauce, the same as French crème anglaise.

This recipe requires total concentration and a quick eye and hand. The eggs must be heated just to the point that they do their maximum thickening and never so much that they scramble. The starch must be kept in constant motion, too; otherwise it will lump. I find that even with the best technique it is always prudent to be prepared with a strainer placed over a bowl. No matter how careful you are, there are frequently at least a few lumps that need to be smoothed out.

Makes 5 cups

1¾ cups all-purpose flour, sifted before measuring

2 cups sugar

4 eggs

1 quart milk

⅛ teaspoon salt

1 tablespoon vanilla

1. Set a clean, dry, nonreactive bowl and a sturdy rubber spatula near the stove. Put a large, fine strainer over a large bowl, ready to pour hot pastry cream through it.

2. In another bowl, mix the flour with 1 cup of the sugar. Whisk in the eggs until smooth. The mixture will be very thick.

3. In a 2½- to 3-quart, heavy-bottomed saucepan, mix the milk, the remaining cup of sugar, and the salt. Scald over medium heat, stirring frequently so it doesn't scorch or form a skin. When the milk has a ring of small bubbles around the edge of the pan, remove it from the heat and, with a whisk, stir 1 cup of the milk, a little at a time, into the flour and egg mixture. Whisk in another cup of hot milk, then pour the now-tempered flour and egg mixture into the saucepan with the remaining milk, whisking constantly. Still whisking constantly, but slowly, over medium to medium-low heat, cook the mixture until it thickens. Pull it off the heat at the first sign of a boil—as soon as the first bubble breaks on the surface. This will take about 5 minutes.

4. Immediately pour the hot pastry cream through the strainer and into the bowl, using the spatula to remove it all from the pan and to push it through the sieve. Stir in the vanilla.

5. Cover the very surface of the cream with wax paper or plastic wrap to prevent a skin from forming. Refrigerate for at least several hours, or until chilled. Pastry cream can be kept refrigerated for several days, sometimes up to a week, depending on the efficiency of the refrigeration.

CREMA PASTICCIERA II

THIN PASTRY CREAM

THIS VERSION OF PASTRY CREAM is used to fill baked pastries, such as the Neapolitan favorite, Pizza di Amarene, made with sour cherries (page 410). It can also be used as a dessert sauce or a base for a frozen dessert. For the latter, simply fold in an equal volume of whipped cream sweetened and/or flavored to your fancy. Freeze for at least two hours in individual serving cups—ramekins, custard cups, paper "soufflé" cups, or coffee cups.

Makes 6 cups

¾ cup all-purpose flour, sifted before measuring

1 cup sugar

Pinch of salt

6 eggs

1 quart milk

2 teaspoons vanilla

1. Set a clean, dry, large nonreactive bowl and a sturdy rubber spatula near the stove. Put a large, fine strainer over the bowl, ready to pour hot pastry cream through it.

2. In another bowl, mix the flour with the sugar and a pinch of salt. Whisk in the eggs until smooth.

3. In a 2½- to 3-quart heavy-bottomed saucepan, scald the milk over medium heat. When the milk forms a ring of small bubbles around the edge of the pan, remove it from the heat and, with a whisk, stir in 1 cup of the milk, a little at a time, into the flour mixture. Whisk in another cup of hot milk, then return the tempered flour and egg mixture to the saucepan with the remaining milk, whisking constantly. Whisking constantly but slowly over medium to medium-low heat, cook the mixture until it thickens and starts to boil. This will take about 10 minutes.

3. Immediately pour the hot pastry cream through the strainer and into the bowl, using the spatula to remove it all from the pan and to push it through the sieve. Stir in the vanilla.

4. Cover the very surface of the cream with wax paper or plastic wrap to prevent a skin from forming. Refrigerate for at least several hours, or until ready to use. After chilling, the cream is firm enough to use as a filling or base for crostate (tarts). Pastry cream can be kept refrigerated for several days, sometimes up to a week, depending on the efficiency of the refrigeration.

Scorzette di Arance Candite

Candied Orange Peel

THIS CANDIED PEEL, from pastry chef, teacher, and cookbook author Nick Malgieri's *Great Italian Desserts*, is so far superior to anything you can buy that it is well worth the time to prepare it. Use it for the Torta di Ricotta Gregoriana (page 415), the Migliaccio di Ischia (page 401), the Pastiera (page 412), or cut in fine strips as a garnish for the Neapolitan composed desserts called delizie. It will make all the difference.

Makes about 1½ pounds, drained—about 3 cups

6 large oranges

Sugar equal to the weight of the peel (2 cups per 1 pound of peel)

Light corn syrup equal to half the weight of the sugar
(1 cup per 1 pound of peel)

Water equal to ¼ the weight of the sugar (½ cup per 1 pound of peel)

1.   Score the oranges in 5 or 6 places from stem to blossom ends and remove the peel (both the colored part and the white part beneath it). Weigh the pieces of peel. There should be about 1 pound.

2.   Place the peel in a large saucepan or casserole and cover with water. Bring to a boil and drain. Repeat the process 7 more times to remove the bitterness from the peel and to soften it.

3.   In a large saucepan or casserole, combine the sugar, corn syrup, and water. Bring the syrup to a boil and add the blanched orange peel. Bring to a boil again. Adjust the heat so the syrup gently simmers for about 30 minutes.

4.   Add ¼ cup water, return to a boil, and cool.

5.   Pack the candied peel with its thick syrup in glass jars. Cover tightly and store in the refrigerator. It should keep for several months.

Delizia di Marmellata

Zuppa Tartara

Marmalade Delight

DELIZIA, MEANING "DELIGHT," not delicious, is the word Campanians often use for their composed desserts built on ladyfingers (savoiardi), cream puffs (profiteroles), or sponge cake (pan di Spagna), with pastry cream or another creamy filling, and usually another element, like the marmalade (or jam) in this recipe. (The same desserts are also called *dolce* of whatever flavor or major ingredient.) Often the cake part is doused with a diluted liquor or spirit. Frequently it is Strega in Benevento, where it's made; likely limoncello in Sorrento, Amalfi, and Capri, where it is made; or another liqueur, or rum, or brandy. The same spirit might also flavor the filling. Delizie can be elaborately decorated, or not at all, a homey dessert or one for a fancy dinner.

Zuppa tartara is a name I've seen only once and it struck me as characteristically Neapolitan in its attempt to make something quite modest into something very grand, associating this simple "delight" made with marmalade and packaged cake with the aristocratic zuppa inglese. But aggrandizement with the word "zuppa" wasn't enough for the amateur pastry chef who invented this. He uses tartara to romanticize beyond reason the dessert's uncooked ricotta filling. It's what Americans call a refrigerator cake, and it can be assembled in minutes. Use this recipe as a general outline for creating your own flavor combinations. Keep in mind that alcohol is not a necessity. For moistening cake, use coffee or fruit juices.

This sweet is also related to tiramisù in that it is an assemblage of soaked cake and creamy filling meant to be spooned up, not cut up, into servings. I have, however, come up with a configuration using ladyfingers that presents well on an attractive oval platter or a wide dinner plate and can be neatly portioned for six.

Serves 6

(continued)

For the filling:

1 cup ricotta

2 tablespoons confectioners' sugar

2 tablespoons heavy cream

To assemble the dessert:

½ cup orange marmalade or other fruit jam

½ cup orange juice plus 2 tablespoons orange liqueur, rum, or brandy, or
about ½ cup dry sherry, or 3 tablespoons rum or brandy diluted with about
⅓ cup water, or ¼ cup limoncello diluted with ¼ cup water

18 savoiardi (there are usually 22 to 24 in a 7-ounce package)

Optional: Dark chocolate (so-called semisweet or bittersweet) for grating as a
garnish, or better, 6 pieces chocolate-covered, candied orange peel

Whipped cream, if desired

1. Using a rubber spatula, press the ricotta through a fine sieve into a mixing bowl. (Ricottas vary, and this step is unnecessary if the texture of the ricotta is creamy.)

2. In a cup, with a table fork, beat the sugar into the cream until the sugar is dissolved. (If using imported ricotta, which has less moisture than domestic, you will probably want to add a teaspoon or so more cream.)

3. Using the rubber spatula, blend the cream mixture into the ricotta. It should be easily spreadable, but not at all runny. Set aside.

4. Melt the marmalade slightly by putting the measuring cup of marmalade into a pan of hot water. Set aside. (Or later, just before you are ready to use it, melt the marmalade in a microwave for 15 to 30 seconds on high, stirring once.)

5. Pour the dipping liquid—orange juice and liqueur, or other choice—into a small, shallow bowl, one in which a savoiardo can lie flat on the bottom.

6. Put before you the dinner plate or small oval platter on which you want to assemble and serve the dessert. Dipping the savoiardi one at a time, and rolling each very quickly in the juice mixture, arrange 6 savoiardi snugly next to each other on the plate or platter.

7.   Using the rubber spatula, spread the first layer of savoiardi with half the ricotta cream, pouring the cream down the middle of the biscuits and leaving about ½ inch on either side without cream. Drizzle on about half the marmalade, distributing it evenly over the cream.

8.   Dip 6 more savoiardi, 1 at a time as above, and arrange over the filling and lining up with the bottom layer, pressing each biscuit down slightly. Spread, as above, with the remaining ricotta. Now, either drizzle with remaining marmalade and top with another layer of 6 dipped savoiardi, or place dipped savoiardi directly on the cream and glaze the top layer of the savoiardi with the remaining marmalade. (I top with a glaze of marmalade when serving this without whipped cream.)

9.   Refrigerate for at least 1 hour before serving, but preferably 3 or 4 hours. It keeps perfectly for at least 3 days. Each 3-biscotti section is 1 serving. If desired, serve the whole dessert decorated with gratings or curls of chocolate, or whipped cream and grated chocolate, or garnish each serving with a piece of candied or chocolate-covered orange peel.

ZUPPA INGLESE

THIS IS ONE OF THE MOST famous desserts of the Neapolitan repertoire, one that enjoyed a vogue in the United States for many years but has now been out of favor for at least twenty. It is, as its Italian name implies, a Neapolitan take on English trifle. In its most classic form, it is a dome-shaped composition of cake doused with spirits, layered with pastry cream and sour cherry preserves, and topped with baked meringue. It is, in effect, the most elaborate of delizie.

There are several stories of how it came to be and was given its name, but the one that is the most likely, or at least the most amusing to believe, involves an infamous adulterous love affair. Lady Emma (Hart) Hamilton, the young wife of the much older Sir William Hamilton, the archaeologist, art collector, and long-standing and very powerful ambassador to the court of Naples from England, had a scandalous relationship with Admiral Horatio Nelson, the British naval hero whose statue graces Trafalgar Square in London. It would end in tragedy for them all.

Emma was, as they used to say, "compromised at a young age," and by about sixteen was the mistress to William Hamilton's nephew Charles Greville in London. Greville was a gambler and lost all his money, but not his art collection. Sir William bailed him out, but on the condition that the young man send his collections to Naples.

Along with the art, the nephew sent Emma, sure that she would settle any debt to his uncle. Emma was eventually thought to be one of the most beautiful women of her day, the late eighteenth century, although there is a current revisionist idea that it was more her intelligence and "charms" than beauty that gained her the reputation. She produced, directed and performed *tableaux vivants* of mythic, historical, or biblical scenes in which she often appeared topless.

It speaks volumes about Ferdinand and Maria Carolina's court that Emma Hart's past did not prevent her from being presented at court. She became a fast friend and confidante of the queen.

In 1795, Horatio Nelson arrived in Naples to have the Bourbons fulfill their treaty with England and give him replacements and supplies to continue fighting Napoleon in Egypt. Lady Hamilton to the rescue. When Sir William could not get an audience with the king fast enough, Emma appealed to the queen, to whom she had immediate access, and secured help for Nelson, who did indeed defeat Napoleon in Alexandria.

When they next met, in 1798, Nelson arrived triumphant in the Bay of Naples. He was the hero of the day for having successfully defended the city against an attack of Napoleon's navy.

Now comes the zuppa inglese. A huge banquet was given in Nelson's honor by King Ferdinand and Maria Carolina. One version of the story has it that zuppa inglese was created in imitation of the English trifle and thus named by a *Monzù* at the court to honor Nelson and his fellow Englishmen, the Hamiltons. The more vicious version has it that the chef, who may have been trained in France or was at least not intending to truly honor the English, threw a disrespectfully homey dessert together—just some doused dried cake and pastry cream with preserves, something those gastronomically backward English would appreciate.

Serves 8

10 ounces stale sponge or yellow cake, sliced ⅓ inch thick

3 tablespoons Alchermes or (red) maraschino liqueur

2 cups thick pastry cream (see page 371; made with egg yolks only, and reserving the whites for a meringue), well chilled

½ cup morello cherry preserves

1 tablespoon rum mixed with 1 tablespoon water

3 egg whites

1 tablespoon sugar

2 tablespoons confectioners' sugar

1. Select an attractive, round, oven-proof platter that has a flat central surface of at least 9 inches in diameter. If that is not available, construct the dessert on a baking sheet lined with parchment paper or aluminum foil. The finished dessert will be a dome about 9 inches wide at the base and 5 inches high.

2. Arrange a layer of cake slices on the platter or baking sheet to roughly form a 9-inch circle. Because the dessert will eventually be covered with meringue that can be spread to make a more even shape, there's no need to make a perfect circle. Still, to make it fairly regular, cut the cake slices (with a serrated knife) as necessary.

3. Sprinkle the first layer of cake with Alchermes or maraschino. Spread on a ¼-inch-thick layer of cold pastry cream, then drop dots of preserves over the cream.

(continued)

Arrange another layer of cake on the cream, making this circle smaller than the first, then sprinkle this layer with some of the rum and water mixture. Repeat layers of pastry cream, dots of preserves, layers of cake—alternating rum mixture and red liqueur on each cake layer—and build a dome by making each successive cake layer smaller than the last.

4. Refrigerate for at least 1 hour, or for as long as a few days, covered with plastic wrap.

5. Finish the dessert on the day it will be served, even just before serving. Preheat the oven to 400 degrees.

6. In a clean mixing bowl, beat the egg whites until they hold soft peaks and are glossy. Sprinkle on the granulated sugar and continue to beat until stiff.

7. With a spatula, gently and carefully spread the meringue over the dessert dome, covering it entirely to the base. Sift the confectioners' sugar over the meringue.

8. Bake for 6 minutes, or until very lightly browned.

9. Let cool thoroughly—at least 15 minutes—before serving, cut into wedges. (If the dessert has been formed on a baking sheet, it can be transferred to a serving platter by carefully sliding it to the edge of the sheet by pulling the sheet's parchment or foil liner, then folding the liner under the sheet as you slide the dessert off it—difficult but possible.)

Mele al Forno con Marmellata di Albicocca

Baked Apples with Apricot Preserves

One of the myths of southern Italy is that it is "sunny" Italy; that its climate is like that of Hawaii or the Caribbean—eternal summer. The stately palms that line the seaside public parks in Naples and Salerno give that impression. When the first chill winds and rain come in October and everyone from Naples to Avellino starts donning new fashions, however, it becomes clear that all these stylish sweaters and leather coats will actually be necessary by Christmas.

During the cool late fall and often cold and dreary winter of Campania, there is no sunny fruit, just apples. And baked apples are a very popular home dessert. "Of course baked apples," I've heard over and over again when I've asked home cooks what desserts they make, not buy. Cooked fruit is usually considered mainly for children, the elderly, and the infirm, but evidently baked apples are an exception.

Serves 4

4 medium Rome apples

2 tablespoons butter, melted

½ cup sugar

4 tablespoons apricot preserves

1. Preheat the oven to 400 degrees.

2. Wash the apples, core them, and peel the top ⅔.

3. Brush the peeled portion of each apple with melted butter. Brush the extra butter onto the bottom of a pie plate or shallow baking pan.

4. Place the sugar in a small bowl, then roll the buttered portion of each apple in the sugar. (You will have extra sugar, but the full amount is needed to be able to coat the apples well.) Arrange the apples in the pie plate or pan. Spoon a tablespoon of preserves into the cavity of each apple.

5. Bake for 50 to 60 minutes, or until the apples are lightly browned and tender.

6. Serve hot, warm, or at room temperature, with or without liquid or whipped cream.

Mele al Forno con Vino Bianco

Baked Apples with White Wine

IF YOU CATCH THESE at the right moment, the insides are soft and the skins are still firm enough to stand straight and act as cups. With the buttery, caramelized syrup made with the pan juices, you might even consider these dress-up baked apples.

Serves 4

4 medium Rome, Cortland, Golden Delicious, or other good baking apple

3 tablespoons butter plus 1 teaspoon

4 tablespoons sugar

1⅓ cups white wine

1. Preheat the oven to 400 degrees. With 2 teaspoons of butter, grease a flame-proof baking pan that will hold the apples snugly in one layer.

2. Wash the apples and cut them in half perpendicular to the stem and blossom ends, so that the stem and blossom ends are the bottoms of each half. With a sharp knife or melon baller, remove the cores and place 1 teaspoon of butter in each half.

3. Place the apples in the prepared pan and sprinkle a little sugar on each half and add the rest of the sugar and all the wine to the pan. Bake for 30 to 35 minutes, or until the apples are cooked through.

4. Place the apples on a serving dish.

5. Over medium high heat, reduce the cooking juices to a syrupy sauce, stirring occasionally. Pour the sauce over the apples and serve warm or at room temperature. Use a teaspoon to scoop the soft flesh out of the skin.

SFOGLIATELLE RICCE

*Whoever invented the "sfogliatella," that most disconcerting
of Neapolitan pastries?*

*A Baroque architect, who perhaps wanted to duplicate in his kitchen the curled
play of a molding, or a capricious clam fisherman, so enchanted by the lovely
shape of their shells that he succeeded in repeating their mysterious, spiral
geometry, or a very patient, gentle nun who unconsciously created a pastry so
similar to her tender heart.*

MARIO STEFANILE, *Partenope in cucina* (PARTHENOPE IN THE KITCHEN)

SFOGLIATELLE, OR SFOGLIATE, as Neapolitans call them, are the supreme and most
amazing Neapolitan pastry. The ricotta- and semolina-filled shell-shaped sweets are
consumed by the thousands every morning in *caffès* all over the region. They are kept
warm all day in special display cases, but by the afternoon there are rarely any left. Pasticceria Scaturchio is considered to have the best, meaning the crackling, fat-layered
pastry is not tough or greasy and the filling is soft and fragrant with orange and real
vanilla. But almost every Naples neighborhood or Campanian town of any size has a
good bakery for sfogliatelle. They are not something that would be baked at home.
Even the version with the much easier to prepare short pastry, pasta frolla—called
sfogliatelle frolle—that always fill a tray next to the ricce, are not something home
cooks attempt. Those who like big baking projects might like to try this recipe, however. It has been worked out by pastry chef and master teacher Nick Malgieri, and
appears in his book *Great Italian Desserts*.

Makes 16 to 18 pastries

(continued)

For the dough:

3 cups all-purpose flour

1 teaspoon salt

¾ cup warm water

For the filling:

1 cup water

½ cup sugar

⅔ cup semolina or cream of wheat

1½ cups whole milk ricotta

2 large egg yolks

2 teaspoons vanilla extract

¼ teaspoon ground cinnamon

⅓ cup candied orange peel, rinsed and finely chopped (page 374)

Plus:

4 ounces lard

8 tablespoons (1 stick) butter

To prepare the dough:

1.   In a mixing bowl, combine the flour and salt. Stir in the water. The dough will be very dry.

2.   Scrape the contents of the bowl onto a work surface, and press and knead the dough together so that all the dry bits are incorporated.

3.   Press or roll out about ⅓ inch thick and pass repeatedly through the widest setting of a pasta machine to work the dough smooth. Fold the dough in half after each pass through the machine and change the direction of inserting the dough occasionally. After about 12 or 15 passes, the dough should be smooth.

4.   Knead the dough into a ball, wrap in plastic wrap, and allow to rest in the refrigerator for about 2 hours.

To prepare the filling:

5.   In a 2-quart saucepan, combine the water and sugar. Bring to a boil.

6.   Sift the semolina or cream of wheat over the boiling water gradually, stirring constantly to avoid lumps. Lower the heat and cook, stirring often, until very smooth and thick, 1 to 2 minutes.

7.   Press the ricotta through a fine sieve, or puree it in a food processor fitted with the metal blade.

8.   Stir the ricotta into the cooked semolina mixture. Cook several minutes longer, stirring often. Remove from the heat and stir in the egg yolks, vanilla, cinnamon, and candied orange peel. Scrape the filling into a shallow bowl or glass pie pan and press plastic wrap against the surface. Refrigerate until cold and set.

9.   In a mixing bowl, combine the lard and butter and beat until soft, fluffy, and completely mixed.

10.   Flour the dough and divide it into 4 pieces. Flour each piece of dough and pass it through the pasta machine at the widest setting. Make sure the dough emerges in a neat rectangular strip as wide as the opening of the machine. If the dough is uneven, fold it over on itself so that it is as wide as the opening and pass it through again. Pass all 4 pieces of dough, one after the other, through every other setting, ending with the last setting.

11.   Place 1 of the strips of dough onto a lightly floured surface and paint it generously with the lard-and-butter mixture. Begin rolling the dough into a tight cylinder from a short end. Pull gently on the sides of the strip of dough as you roll it up to make it thinner and about 8 or 9 inches wide.

12.   Paint another strip of dough with the fats and position the rolled piece on it so that the end of the first strip meets the beginning of the second; continue to pull and roll up. Proceed with the third and fourth strips in the same way. Cover the remaining lard and butter and reserve, in the refrigerator, for baking the sfogliatelle. The dough should form a tight cylinder about 2½ inches in diameter and 8 to 9 inches long. Wrap in plastic and chill several hours, until firm. The dough may be frozen at this point; defrost it in the refrigerator overnight before proceeding.

13.   Preheat the oven to 400 degrees and set a rack in the middle level. Line 2 jelly-roll pans with parchment.

(continued)

14. Remove the roll of dough from the refrigerator. Place it on a cutting board and trim the ends straight. Cut the roll into about 16 to 18 slices, each about ½ inch thick.

15. Place the filling in a pastry bag that has a ¾-inch opening; a tube is not necessary.

To form the pastries:

16. Take 1 slice of the dough at a time and, using the heel of your hand, flatten it from the center outward in all directions—north, south, east, and west. Form it into a cone by sliding the layers away from each other with the thumbs underneath the dough and the first 2 fingers of each hand on top, manipulating the dough (with your thumbs) from the center outward. Holding the cone of dough on the palm of one hand and the pastry bag with the other, squeeze in the filling so that the pastry is full and plump. There is no need to seal the open end; the filling is too firm to run during baking.

17. Bring the lard-and-butter mixture to room temperature to soften it. Position the formed and filled sfogliatelle on the paper-lined pans and paint the outside of each with the lard and butter.

18. Bake them about 20 to 25 minutes, basting once or twice with the remaining fats, until they are a deep gold.

19. Remove from the pans to racks to cool. Serve the sfogliatelle warm on the day they are baked.

Note: To reheat, place on a paper-lined pan and heat at 350 degrees for about 10 minutes.

ZEPPOLE DI SAN GIUSEPPE

St. Joseph's Day Crullers

THE BIGNÈ FORM of these donuts or crullers was invented for St. Joseph's Day (March 19), 1840, by Don Pasquale Pintauro, who was given a noble title by King Ferdinand II of the Two Sicilies for his creation. The Pintauro *pasticceria* still stands at Via Roma, 275, and it is still among the most highly regarded in the city, although some Neapolitans are fond of saying, "It isn't what it used to be." Until Pintauro adopted the French cream puff pastry dough—*pâte à choux*, in French—for his bakery's zeppole, only the much cruder kind of zeppole existed. These are still made for Christmas and are called either zeppole di Natale, or, in dialect, scauratielli. They are made from a dough of only flour and water or flour and milk, with no leavening, not even an egg. After the Christmas zeppole are formed into rings, actually more the shape of an AIDS ribbon, and fried, they are dipped in hot honey. As you might imagine, they are considerably heavier than the bignè form of zeppole, and because they become even weightier and rather indigestible as they stand, they have to be eaten almost as soon as they emerge from their honey bath. These light, eggy bignè, on the other hand, although they are best when just cooled, can be made hours ahead and re-crisped in a 350-degree oven for a few minutes. The dough can be made a day ahead and kept refrigerated.

Makes about 12 crullers

1 cup water

6 tablespoons butter

Pinch salt

1 tablespoon sugar

1 cup all-purpose flour

4 eggs

Oil for frying

Thick pastry cream (page 371)

Sour cherry preserves

1. In a 2-quart saucepan, combine the water, butter, salt, and sugar. Place the mixture over medium heat and bring to a simmer, stirring a few times. As soon as the liquid begins to boil (and the butter is completely melted), remove the pot from the heat. Add all the flour and stir very well and vigorously, until the mixture comes together as a dough.

2. Return the saucepan to low heat and stir until the mixture is very smooth, glossy, and begins to form a slight film on the bottom of the pan, about 3 minutes. (If using a nonstick pan, there will be no film formed as an indicator.)

3. Break the eggs, 1 at a time, into the dough, and, before adding the next, beat each egg in very well until it is incorporated into the dough and the dough has become smooth again. (I use a handheld electric mixer because this is a tight dough and otherwise requires considerable strength and stamina to beat it.) When all the eggs have been added, you should have a smooth, thick paste. It may be prepared a day ahead, but the zeppole should be fried within hours before eating them.

4. Cut the parchment paper into 12 4-inch squares.

5. Using a pastry bag or piping tube fitted with a ½-inch star tip (#6), pipe 3- to 3½-inch circles of dough onto the parchment squares.

6. In a 10- to 12-inch skillet, heat ½ inch of oil to 375 to 380 degrees and fry the zeppole a couple or a few at a time, depending on the size of the skillet. Place the zeppole in the oil with the parchment paper on the top. Using tongs, remove the parchment paper after about 10 seconds. This will require a little up-and-down jiggling of the paper, and a motion of peeling the paper back and off the frying dough.

The zeppole should not fry very fast. It should take more than a minute for the first side to become a medium golden. Do not let it get fully, deeply golden. You know the temperature is correct if, after turning the zeppole to the second side, the first fried, already golden side starts splitting open. This indicates that the center is cooking and expanding. Let the second side get golden, then turn over again to finish the first side. If the temperature is correct—about 375 degrees—the whole process takes 3 to 4 minutes. Drain the zeppole well on absorbent paper before topping with pastry cream and serving.

For the traditional St. Joseph's Day presentation, arrange the zeppole on a serving plate. Pipe or spoon into the center of each a couple of tablespoons of pastry cream, then garnish with a small spoonful of sour cherry preserves or a candied cherry.

QUARESIMALI

Lenten Biscotti

QUARESIMA IS *ITALIAN* for Lent, and quaresimali qualify as Lenten because they are made without fat—at least no butter, oil, or lard. More than making up for that lack, however, is the fat in the huge amount of almonds. Ground almonds are the base of the dough, which is seasoned both sharply and sweetly with a "pisto" of white pepper, nutmeg, cinnamon, and clove. Whole almonds stud every bite. Similar quaresimali are made in other regions of Italy, often with hazelnuts.

Makes 50 to 54 biscotti, 1½ inches wide by ½ inch thick

For the dough:

1¼ cups whole, unblanched (with their skins) almonds, toasted and roughly ground in a food processor or blender

1 cup sugar

1½ cups all-purpose flour

For the "pisto":

1 teaspoon finely ground white pepper

½ teaspoon finely grated nutmeg

¼ teaspoon ground cinnamon

¼ teaspoon ground cloves

Plus:

2 eggs

1¼ cups whole, unblanched (with their skins) almonds, toasted

⅓ cup finely chopped candied orange peel (page 374) and candied citron

1 egg, beaten, for the wash

1. Preheat the oven to 325 degrees. Line a baking sheet with parchment paper.

2. On a board, or in a large bowl, mix together the ground almonds, the sugar, the flour, and the pisto.

3. Make a well and break in the eggs. Using a fork, or your fingers, gradually incorporate the eggs into the dry ingredients, as if you were making pasta dough.

(continued)

Once you have obtained a sticky dough, work in the whole almonds and the candied peels. If you are using a bowl, turn the dough out onto a lightly floured board.

4. Shape the dough into 3 logs, each 9- by 1½ inches and about ¾ inch high. Place the logs on a cookie sheet lined with parchment. Brush them with beaten egg.

5. Bake for 35 minutes. Remove from the oven and let cool on the pan for 15 minutes. Reduce the oven temperature to 300 degrees.

6. With a metal spatula, remove the logs from the paper and place them on a cutting board. Cut them into ½-inch-wide, crosswise slices. Return the biscotti to the baking sheet, arranging them standing up and not touching each other.

7. Bake another 25 minutes. Cool the cookies on a rack.

8. Store in a tin.

MOSTACCIOLI

THESE ARE ONE OF CAMPANIA's several Christmas spice cookies. They are sometimes half-covered with chocolate fondant, half with white, sometimes only with chocolate. They are also made imbottiti, stuffed with dried fruits or a chocolate cream, which seem always to be chocolate-coated and shaped more like bon bons than cookies. Indeed, having eaten more than my share of mostaccioli imbottiti, I've observed that these days they are most often more chocolate truffle with the thinnest layer of spice cookie than a cookie with filling. This recipe is from New York–based, Neapolitan-American pastry chef, teacher, and writer Nick Malgieri, who worked out a better recipe than I could manage in his *Great Italian Desserts*.

Makes 36 cookies

For the cookie dough:
2 cups bleached all-purpose flour

1 cup sugar

⅓ cup water

½ teaspoon ammonium bicarbonate
(or ½ teaspoon each baking powder and baking soda)

¼ teaspoon ground cinnamon

¼ teaspoon ground pepper

¼ teaspoon ground cloves

Grated zest of 1 orange

For the chocolate icing:

6 ounces semisweet chocolate

¼ cup water

¼ cup light corn syrup

¾ cup sugar

1. Preheat the oven to 325 degrees.

2. In a mixing bowl, combine the flour and sugar.

3. Pour the water into a small bowl and stir in the remaining dough ingredients. Stir the water mixture into the dry ingredients and continue mixing until the dough begins to hold together. If it seems dry, add more water, no more than a tablespoon at a time, sprinkling the water on the dough. Do not add so much water that you will have to add more flour.

4. Turn the dough out onto a lightly floured surface and knead a minute or so, just until the dough becomes homogenous and smooth. Do not knead too much or the dough will be difficult to roll and the cookies will be tough.

5. Shape the dough into a flat disk about 6 inches in diameter, then wrap it in plastic. Let the dough rest at room temperature for at least 30 minutes before shaping and baking it. (Other Campanian bakers suggest letting the dough "ripen" for from 1 to 3 days, in the refrigerator.)

6. Place the dough on a lightly floured surface, dust the top very lightly with flour, then roll it out to a 12- by 9-inch rectangle no more than ¼ inch thick.

7. With a floured knife or (pizza or pastry) cutting wheel, cut the dough into 6 strips, each 2 by 9 inches. Cut each strip diagonally at 2-inch intervals to make 6 diamonds. You should get 36 in all. (Malgieri suggests that you do not mass the scraps back together—the resulting cookies will be overly tough—but bake them as they are.)

(continued)

8. Transfer the mostaccioli to greased cookie sheets, or to cookie sheets lined with greased parchment paper. Brush them lightly with cold water.

9. Bake in the middle level of the oven for about 20 minutes, until they are very lightly colored. Remove the cookies to a cooling rack and let cool completely.

For the icing:

10. Chop the chocolate finely and set aside.

11. In a small saucepan, combine the water, the corn syrup, and the sugar. Bring to a boil, stirring often.

12. Remove the pan from the heat and add the chopped chocolate, swirling the mixture around the pan to make sure the chocolate is immersed in the syrup. Allow to stand 3 minutes.

13. Whisk the icing smooth.

14. With a pastry brush, paint icing on the underside of each mostacciolo. Allow the mostaccioli to dry, icing up, on a rack for 5 minutes.

15. Turn the cookies over and brush the tops with icing. (If, as you work, the icing becomes firm, add 1 tablespoon water and reheat it gently over low heat, stirring constantly.) Allow the icing to dry at room temperature for at least 1 hour, then ice them again and let dry again.

16. Pack them into a tin between layers of wax paper. They keep well.

STRUFFOLI

FRIED HONEY-DIPPED DOUGH BALLS

STRUFFOLI ARE ONE OF the many Christmas sweets that Campanians dote on. Every bakery makes struffoli, packing the honey-coated little fried dough balls into baskets, cornucopias, and other fanciful, edible containers made of croccante (almond brittle).

At home, struffoli may be shaped on a plate into a Christmas wreath and decorated with glacéed fruits and multicolored sugar sprinkles, or simply heaped into a mound.

The dough is essentially an egg pasta that is formed into long, thin ropes, cut into tiny pieces, then deep fried. The dough puffs out in the hot oil, forming light, crunchy dough nuts. Some people mix sugar and honey together for the candy glaze, because sugar used to be more economical than honey. Today, the better struffoli are cooked entirely in honey. A mound of struffoli will keep well, out on a table for nibbling at will, for at least a week—if they haven't been devoured before then.

Makes 1 dinner plate–sized mound or wreath

1 to 1¼ cups all-purpose flour

¼ teaspoon salt

2 eggs

Peanut or canola oil for frying

1 cup honey

Optional: ¼ cup finely diced candied orange peel (page 374) or mixed candied peels; 2 tablespoons to ¼ cup chopped or slivered almonds or coarsely chopped hazelnuts or pistachios; multicolored sprinkles and/or candied cherries for garnish

1. In a large mixing bowl, combine the flour and the salt. Make a well in the flour, then break in the eggs. With a fork, little by little, beat the flour into the eggs until a stiff dough forms.

(continued)

2.   Turn the dough out onto a lightly floured board and knead vigorously until you have a smooth, compact dough, 8 to 10 minutes. Shape it into a disk, wrap in plastic or wax paper, and let rest for 20 minutes.

3.   Cut the dough into ½-inch slices. Between the palms of your hands, and not on a board, roll the dough slices into ¼-inch-thick ropes. Cut the ropes into ¼-inch pieces.

4.   In a skillet (the wider it is, the more struffoli can be fried at one time), heat ¼ to ½ inch oil until a piece of dough sizzles immediately. Fry the struffoli until a dark nutty brown on all sides, using a slotted spoon or skimmer to keep turning them in the hot oil. They will expand to more than double their size. Do not crowd the pan with more dough balls than can fry on the surface of the oil when they have expanded. When done, drain the struffoli on a rack or absorbent paper.

5.   In a large saucepan, heat the honey over low heat until very hot but not boiling. Add the struffoli and, with a wooden spoon, turn and stir the struffoli into the honey, until all the balls are well coated. Remove the pan from the heat and continue to stir until the honey has cooled and thickened and is sticking well to all the dough balls.

6.   Stir in any optional ingredients, reserving a few for garnish.

7.   Pour the struffoli onto a dinner plate, mounding them or fashioning them into a wreathlike ring. Scrape any syrup out of the pan and let it drip on the struffoli. Garnish as desired.

8.   Let stand until thoroughly cool before serving. The struffoli keep well at room temperature for at least a week.

Coviglia al Caffè

Coffee Semifreddo

The word "coviglia" is unique to Naples and Campania and it refers to the little china, crystal, or metal (often silver) cup in which this frozen mousse or semifreddo (not a true ice cream or gelato) is served. I have yet to see it served that way, but I did find old silver-plate coviglia cups at the weekend flea market in Naples's Villa Municipale, the city park along the bay. Nowadays, coviglia most often comes in a disposable, clear plastic cup and is sold out of the self-serve ice cream cases at *pasticcerie* and bars. As made at home, it can be egg yolks beaten with sugar, then lightened with whipped cream and possibly egg whites and frozen, or it can be a classic cooked pastry cream with whipped cream and/or egg whites folded into it. This coffee version based on beaten egg yolks sometimes separates slightly, leaving a concentrated coffee liquid on the bottom, but even when that happens, it is delicious and velvety.

Serves 6 to 8

4 whole eggs, separated

¼ cup very strong prepared espresso coffee or 2 teaspoons instant espresso powder or crystals dissolved in ¼ cup hot water

1 cup superfine sugar

1 cup heavy cream

1. In a mixing bowl, beat the egg yolks, gradually adding half the sugar, until they are light and lemon colored.

2. Dissolve the remaining sugar in the coffee, then blend the mixture into the egg yolks.

3. In another bowl, beat the cream until it holds soft peaks, then fold the whipped cream into the coffee and egg mixture.

4. In a clean bowl, with clean beaters, beat the egg whites until stiff. Fold them into the mousse base.

5. Pour into individual cups and place in the freezer for about 2 hours, until firm but not solid. If the coviglie are kept frozen for longer, take them out of the freezer to soften somewhat before serving.

SEMIFREDDO DI STREGA

ONLY A FEW YEARS AGO, when the Alberti family decided it was about time they published a book of recipes using the Strega liqueur they'd been producing since 1860, they turned to the people who cook with it, their retail customers, professional chefs, and noted gastronomes. The result is a little paperback, *Le ricette ed i consigli Strega* (Strega Recipes and Tips), filled with some recipes that are new and often outrageous and many that have become family traditions, even local classics. The desserts with Strega have the most appeal, and this frozen, cream-enriched zabaglione somehow opens up and rounds out the liqueur's complex, tight flavor blend of seventy spices and herbs, softening it and making it appealing even to those who say they don't like Strega or liqueur-based desserts. It is worth buying a bottle if only to make this over and over again. It is extremely rich; hence the small suggested serving size.

Serves 8

3 eggs

¾ cup sugar

3 tablespoons Strega

1½ cups heavy cream

1. Make a zabaglione: In a mixing bowl, preferably stainless steel, whisk together the whole eggs, the sugar, and the Strega. Place the bowl over a pot of barely simmering water and whisk constantly, but not very fast or vigorously, scraping down the sides of the bowl occasionally, until the mixture thickens. Be careful about the heat under the bowl. The water should never really boil. At the first sign of egg sticking to the side of the bowl, remove it from the heat and beat it vigorously. You do not want to curdle or scramble the eggs. When the mixture is very thick, remove the bowl from the heat and continue whisking for a minute, just to cool it down a bit. Set aside.

2. In a large bowl, beat the cream until it holds soft peaks. If you make it too stiff, it will be difficult to fold it evenly into the zabaglione.

3. Carefully fold the whipped cream into the zabaglione, then pour the mixture into small, individual serving bowls or cups. Each of 8 servings should be ¾ cup.

4. Place in the freezer for at least 2 hours before serving. Serve direct from the freezer, although after 2 or 3 minutes the texture gets better.

Variation:

For a Semifreddo di Limoncello, in the zabaglione, use 3 tablespoons of limoncello instead of the Strega, plus the grated rind of 1 lemon. Then beat 1 tablespoon of the liqueur into the whipped cream after the cream is in soft peaks.

Palline al Cocco

Coconut Balls

These little bonbons are from Dr. Rosa Serio, who lives in Pagani, a small industrial town between Salerno and Naples. Rosa is an obstetrician-gynecologist, married to a cardiologist, and they are the parents of two charmingly precocious sons. As one might imagine, their lives are as busy as any American family's, and Rosa doesn't have much time for cooking. Still, she insists the family eat together every night, enlisting the help of her maid to do some of the cooking. And when she has guests she turns out an elegant spread all by herself, perhaps only with a little help from something her mother has cooked. For instance, the afternoon I visited with some American members of her family, she indulged us with a bowl of fresh egg pasta (made by a local shop) that was dressed with her mother's ragù. Then she served breaded fried chicken cutlets at room temperature, as many Italians would, with a salad. Then we went on to a grand cheese course, featuring several of the local products, including one that's among the most highly prized of the region—a crock of bocconcini di cardinale, small balls of buffalo mozzarella in thick, clotted buffalo cream. After fruit and a homemade semifreddo, along came a plate of these sweets. When I asked for the recipe, Rosa was at first embarrassed to admit she'd gotten it from the back of a box of coconut flakes. As we read the recipe together, however, she realized she'd made a major change. Instead of "Philadelphia," as Italians call the eponymous cream cheese, she used ricotta. The result is unusually refreshing and light.

Make 6 to 7 dozen

(continued)

2½ cups sweetened flaked coconut (1 7-ounce package and, optionally, more for coating the balls)

1 15-ounce container whole milk ricotta

¼ cup sifted confectioners' sugar

4 teaspoons dark rum or cream sherry

½ cup sifted, unsweetened cocoa powder, for coating some of the balls

Optional: Miniature paper cups for the balls

1.   In a mixing bowl, combine the coconut and ricotta. With a wooden spoon or, even better, a heavy rubber spatula, work them together until well blended, making sure you have broken up any lumps of coconut.

2.   Add the confectioners' sugar and work it in, then add the rum or sherry and work it in.

3.   Pinching up no more than about a teaspoon at a time, roll balls no bigger than a large marble between the palms of your hands. They should be small enough so they don't have to be bitten into, just popped in the mouth. At some point, your palms will become too sticky to continue rolling easily. Wash them and begin again. As you make the balls, arrange half of them on a platter, in tiny paper cups or not. (If desired, you can roll all or some of the balls in more flaked coconut. I personally like them best that way.)

4.   Make about half the balls white; roll the remaining balls in cocoa and intersperse them on the platter, in or out of cups. (Do not try to roll balls in cocoa while you are rolling white ones. You will have to wash your hands too often.)

5.   Refrigerate the balls for at least an hour before serving, during which time the cocoa-rolled balls will turn dark or spotted dark as the cocoa absorbs moisture. For longer storage, cover the balls with plastic wrap. They keep well enough for 24 hours, but are best eaten the day they are made.

MELANZANE AL CIOCCOLATO

EGGPLANT WITH CHOCOLATE

A FEW TRAVEL AND RESTAURANT guides have characterized this dish as a *nuova cucina* novelty. It may seem so when savored in the rarefied international atmosphere of Don Alfonso 1890, the Michelin three-star restaurant in Sant'Agata sui Due Golfi, near Sorrento, where chef-owner Alfonso Iaccarino likes to astonish his jet-set diners with it. Chef Iaccarino readily admits, however, that the dish is a very old one.

Legend has it (although it could be history) that the dish originated in a monastery in Tramonti, in the mountains above the Amalfi Coast town of Maiori, where sometime in the Middle Ages the prior started dipping fried eggplant in the black liqueur made by his monks. Concerto d'Erbe is the name of the liqueur. Recipes still exist for it. The one I have says to steep in alcohol unspecified herbs, spices, and roots that one can supposedly buy in a package in the store. The flavored alcohol is then mixed with a sugar syrup based on barley-thickened water and flavored and colored with coffee.

Alfonso Iaccarino of the restaurant Don Alfonso 1890

Sometime later, one has to suppose no earlier than the mid-sixteenth century, when chocolate was introduced to Europe from the New World, the people of Maiori took the monks' idea of eggplant sweetened with a black alcoholic syrup and changed the sauce to melted chocolate. Now on the Amalfi Coast it is the traditional dish of the Feast of the Assumption, August 15, which is also Ferragosto, the celebration of summer.

"The 15th of August is the pick of the summer," explains Chiara Lima, who has a custom travel service in neighboring Ravello. "The weather is very hot. Everybody is on holiday and a lot of people organize parties and wait for the midnight fireworks that are done from Maiori. At these parties, just for the occasion, they serve eggplant with chocolate. For children and adults it is a big and awaited event, not only for the fireworks but also for this delicious dish. It's seldom sold in restaurants or bakeries. It is a very family tradition. It takes a long time to cook, but it's worth doing at least once a year!"

(continued)

As it has been made better known at Don Alfonso 1890, the dish is much different from the traditional one. Chef Iaccarino takes a piece of sponge cake, spreads on a ricotta filling, drapes a slice of steamed eggplant over this, then pours on a chocolate sauce. Traditionally, there is no sponge cake or ricotta. Slices of eggplant are fried, then dipped in flour and egg and fried again, which is why Chiara says it takes a long time to cook. The double-fried slices are then layered with chocolate and a filling of either pine nuts and candied citron or raisins—just a scattering—or chopped almonds and minced candied fruits, always including citron. Netta Bottone, the chef-owner of Trattoria Cumpà Cosimo in Ravello, tops hers with coarsely crushed candy-coated almonds, called Jordan almonds in English, confetti in Italian—an appropriately named garnish for a festival dish. You can eat it at her restaurant only on August 15. It is like a cream-filled candy, except the eggplant is what's creamy. There is actually no need to fry the eggplant twice, so I don't.

Serves 8

½ recipe Melanzane all'Amalfitana,
made without herbs and cheese (page 334)

12 ounces semisweet or bittersweet chocolate, melted

3 to 4 tablespoons coarsely chopped or slivered almonds or whole pine nuts

5 to 6 tablespoons finely minced candied citron
(or mixed citron and candied orange peel, page 374)

¼ cup Jordan almonds, coarsely crushed

1. On a platter large enough to hold the eggplant in 2 layers, cover the bottom with eggplant, overlapping the slices very slightly.

2. Pour on ⅓ the melted chocolate. Sprinkle all the nuts and half the candied fruits evenly over the sauced eggplant.

3. Arrange the second layer of eggplant over the first, pouring on the remaining chocolate. Garnish with the remaining candied peels and crushed Jordan almonds.

4. Serve at room temperature. The dessert keeps well in the refrigerator for 1 day.

MIGLIACCIO DI ISCHIA

CAPELLINI PUDDING

ON ISCHIA, SAY "CALISE" and you're referring to dessert. The Calise family owns the two largest *pasticcerie-gelaterie* on the island. The one in Casamicciola Terme is one of the social hubs for the island's young people. The one in Port'Ischia is surrounded by a Calise-owned park where locals as well as tourists from all over the world take coffee, pastry, or ice cream. Or a walk! Headed by two sisters and a brother, Anna, Elsa, and Emilio, whom Anna's daughter Francesca calls respectively "the heart, the head, and the body" of the company, Calise also bakes and provides frozen desserts to restaurants, hotels, and smaller pasticcerias. The Calise kitchens under the Port'Ischia location are vaster than those of many resort hotels and have the latest baking and ice cream equipment. It's really not possible for an amateur to reproduce their fantastic and ever-evolving line of cakes and confections. This recipe is, instead, a popular, local home dessert that Anna Calise (the heart) makes herself. Serve it to the family when you want them to have a special treat or afternoon snack. It's delicious both warm from the oven (but not hot) and at room temperature. Or serve it at a party, cut into smaller squares, even tiny squares that you can present in the fluted paper cups meant for truffles and petit fours.

The word "migliaccio" comes from the Latin word for the millet gruel that sustained the Romans, but in Campania today it is used for both savory and sweet cornmeal and semolina puddings, and at least in this application, to mean noodle pudding.

Serves 4 to 12

¼ **pound capellini, broken into thirds or fourths**

6 **eggs**

½ **cup milk**

5 **tablespoons sugar**

5 **tablespoons minced candied orange peel (page 374)**

1. Preheat the oven to 350 degrees. Butter a 9-inch round cake or pie pan.

2. Cook the capellini al dente in plenty of lightly salted boiling water. Drain well.

3. Meanwhile, in a mixing bowl, beat the eggs until well blended, then beat in the milk and the sugar.

(continued)

4. Add the drained capellini and mix well.

5. Add the finely diced candied orange peel and toss to mix well again.

6. Spread the pasta mixture evenly in the pan and bake for 20 minutes, or until the pudding is lightly browned around the edges and set in the center. Let cool to warm or room temperature before cutting into squares and serving.

BABÀ

The babà is not a Neapolitan sweet but, certainly,
one of Polish origin that in Naples has had its success.

—ACCADEMIA ITALIANA DELLA CUCINA, *GUIDA AI RISTORANTI D'ITALIA*
(GUIDE TO THE RESTAURANTS OF ITALY)

A FRENCHMAN MIGHT ARGUE with the Italian Culinary Academy about that. They might well say that the cake christened "babà," after Ali Baba, by King Stanislas Leczinsky in the early 1700s, "found its success" not in Naples but in France. King Stanislas was exiled to Lorraine, and in 1725 his daughter Maria married Louis XV. The king's cake was, in fact, probably not at all like the babà of today or even the babà of the nineteenth century. More likely it was similar to the yeast-risen babka of Poland today, the kugelhopf of Germany, and the gubana made in Friuli, in the northeastern and very Austrian corner of Italy. In any case, the king found the cake too dry for his taste, so he doused it with rum, creating a sensation at his court in exile in Nancy. It is said that it was one of his pastry cooks, a man named Sthorer (his first name seems to be unknown), who perfected the recipe, making it more like a brioche, and who eventually popularized it in Paris.

In Paris, in the 1850s, the name was changed to Brillat-Savarin by the Julien brothers, pastry chefs, in honor of their friend, the famous philosopher, who is said to have furnished the recipe for the rum syrup (highly unlikely). Eventually, the name in France became simply savarin while it has remained babà in Naples. In Paris it is just another cake. In Naples it is the king of cakes. There are taste differences, too. A good Neapolitan babà has a melt-in-the-mouth lightness. A superior savarin is closer knit, with a more buttery mouth feel.

This is the family recipe of Maria Giovanna Fasulo Rak, a restoration expert at the National Archives in Rome and author of *La cucina napoletana in cento ricette tradizionali* (Neapolitan Cooking in 100 Traditional Recipes). The mixing procedure is most unusual, but it is the only recipe of the many I have tried that gives the real Neapolitan texture. Beaten egg whites are incorporated into the dough, but not folded in, to retain their airiness, and the yeast is not beaten into the dough until the very end. The mixing requires a heavy-duty mixer with a paddle to do it well and easily. Individual babàs au rhum, which are shaped like stout mushrooms and are submerged in bowls full of syrup, are also popular in Naples, but most cafés and pastry shops proudly display a huge crown of only lightly doused babà. After each portion is cut and put on a plate, it is doused again, moistening the cake more thoroughly.

Serves 8 to 10

1 envelope active dry yeast (2½ teaspoons)

½ cup warm milk

4 large eggs, at room temperature, separated

8 tablespoons butter (1 stick), at room temperature

2 tablespoons sugar

½ teaspoon salt

3½ cups cake flour, measured then sifted

For the syrup:

2 cups sugar

2 cups water

Zest of 1 lemon

2 tablespoons to ¼ cup rum

Optional: Heavy cream, whipped, or thin pastry cream (page 372)

1. Dissolve the yeast in the milk and set aside.

2. Beat the egg whites until stiff and set aside.

3. In a heavy-duty electric mixer, using the paddle, cream the butter with the sugar and salt until the mixture is light colored and fluffy.

4. Add the egg yolks one at a time, beating to incorporate each before adding the next.

(continued)

5. Add 1 cup of the sifted flour, ½ cup at a time, beating each addition until it is incorporated and scraping down the bowl and beaters between additions.

6. Add half the beaten egg whites and beat until incorporated. The dough will loosen up. Add another cup of flour, ½ cup at a time, again scraping down the bowl and beaters between additions. Beat in the remaining egg whites. Add the last 1½ cups of flour, ½ cup at a time.

7. Finally, beat the milk and yeast mixture into the dough and let the machine run about 90 seconds, until the dough loses enough of its stickiness to pull away cleanly from the bowl when scraped with a rubber spatula.

8. Turn the dough out into the bowl used to beat the egg whites. Cover with a towel and set aside to rise for 1 hour. It should be doubled in bulk.

9. Generously butter a 9-inch tube pan.

10. When the dough has risen, using a rubber spatula, dislodge the dough from the bowl and ease it into the tube pan, turning the bowl or the pan so that the dough stretches around to fill the pan. Using the rubber spatula, prod and poke the dough so it fills the pan more or less evenly. (You will not be able to get the top of the dough smooth. Don't worry about it.) Cover with a kitchen towel and set aside to rise for another 1½ hours. At this point, the dough should have risen to fill about ¾ of the pan.

11. Preheat the oven to 375 degrees.

12. Bake for about 35 minutes, until the cake begins to pull away from the sides of the pan. Remove and let the cake cool in the pan, on a wire rack, for about 10 minutes. Unmold the cake and place it in a deep dish.

13. While it cools more, make the syrup: Combine the sugar, water, and lemon zest in a small saucepan. Bring to a boil over high heat, stirring until the sugar has dissolved. Reduce heat and simmer gently for 10 minutes. Remove the syrup from the heat and add the rum. Allow to cool slightly before drenching the cake.

14. With a toothpick or thin bamboo skewer, make a couple of dozen tiny holes in the top of the cake. Spoon syrup over the cake very slowly. As syrup accumulates in the platter, spoon back over the cake. Use all the syrup.

15. Serve with whipped cream or thin pastry cream, if desired.

TORTA DI LIMONE DI AGATA LIMA

AGATA LIMA'S LEMON CAKE

AGATA LIMA IS A PROFESSIONAL cook in Ravello. What does that mean? That she has been hired to do everything from being the personal chef to many of the illustrious people who come to Ravello—for its remoteness and relative tranquillity, medieval charm, and stunning views from its perch above the Amalfi Coast—to frying 100 pizzette for a local church supper. Flavored with lemon rind and moistened with lemon syrup, Agata's is a particularly rich, moist example of a standard pound cake from the Sorrento peninsula, where the hills are terraced with lemon groves. As moist and sweet and lemony as Agata's version already is, her husband, Salvatore, likes to pour a little limoncello on his slice, as you can see many people do in the bars of Amalfi. As you might imagine, the commercial version often needs a little "freshening," as one bartender put it.

Makes 1 9-inch bundt cake, serving at least 8

6 ounces (1½ sticks) butter

1 cup sugar

4 eggs

4 large lemons, juiced (to make ½ cup), the rind grated

3 cups all-purpose flour, measured after being sifted

Pinch salt

2 teaspoons baking powder

½ cup milk

¼ cup water

½ cup sugar

Slivered almonds

1. Preheat the oven to 350 degrees. Butter and flour a 9-inch bundt pan.

2. In a large mixing bowl, cream together the butter and sugar until light and fluffy, about 5 minutes.

3. Add the eggs 1 at a time, beating very well between additions. Beat in the lemon peel.

(continued)

4.   In a small bowl, stir together the flour, the salt, and the baking powder.

5.   Fold in half the flour, then stir in half the milk. Fold in the remaining flour, then stir in the remaining milk.

6.   Pour into the prepared 9-inch bundt pan.

7.   Bake for 40 to 45 minutes.

8.   While the cake is baking, make a sugar syrup: In a small saucepan, combine the water and the sugar. Stir over high heat until the mixture boils—the sugar should be dissolved and the syrup crystal clear. Let the syrup cool a few minutes, then add ½ cup lemon juice.

9.   When the cake tests done, remove from the oven and let cool on a rack for 15 minutes.

10.   While the cake is still in the pan and still warm (but not hot), make holes in the cake with a skewer or toothpick, then slowly spoon the lemon syrup over the cake, letting it absorb each dose before adding another. Reserve a few tablespoons of the syrup.

11.   Turn the cooled cake out onto a serving plate.

12.   Boil the reserved few spoons of syrup until it is thick—the bubbles will become larger as it thickens. Brush the outside of the cake with this thickened syrup. It should form a light glaze, or at least make the surface sticky. Press slivered almonds onto the sticky surface of the cake.

TORTA CAPRESE DI GIOVANNA TAFURI

ALMOND AND CHOCOLATE TORTE FROM CAPRI

DESPITE ITS IDENTIFICATION with Capri, this cake can be seen in almost every bakery window in Campania, always finished with powdered sugar, almost always stenciled with either the word "Caprese," the word "Capri," or a silhouette of the distinctive-looking pair of rocks just off Capri—the Faraglioni, where the Sirens of Greek mythology were supposed to have called irresistibly to sailors (from which we get the phrase "siren call," as well as the name for the noise ambulances make). Like anything that has turned as commercial as the torta caprese—which, ignoring its large chocolate content, is also sometimes called torta di mandorle (almond cake)—it is hard to find a great example. At Christmas Eve dinner at the home of Laura and Savj Marano in Salerno, however, their niece Giovanna Tafuri served, among the good half-dozen other desserts on the Marano table, this incredibly moist, rich, and almost light example.

Giovanna Tafuri

Torta caprese is a true torte, which means it contains no starch and no leavening. Only the ground almonds give it body. Eggs form the structure and leaven it. It's not a tricky cake to bake, but you must, as always, be careful when folding in the egg whites.

Makes 1 10-inch cake, serving at least 12

12 ounces blanched and peeled almonds, finely ground

6 tablespoons sugar

8 ounces bittersweet or semisweet chocolate

8 ounces (2 sticks) butter, at room temperature

6 eggs, separated

10 tablespoons sugar

¼ cup sugar

1. Preheat the oven to 325 degrees. Butter and flour a 10-inch springform pan. Line the bottom with wax paper or baking parchment. Butter and flour the lining.

(continued)

2. In the bowl of a food processor, using the metal blade, grind the almonds in 3 batches, pulsing each with 2 tablespoons of sugar, for a total of 6 tablespoons. Set aside.

3. In a double boiler, melt the chocolate and butter together.

4. In a mixing bowl, using an electric mixer, beat the egg yolks until lemon colored, about 5 minutes, then gradually beat in the 10 tablespoons of sugar.

5. Add the melted chocolate and butter to the egg yolks. Stir to mix well. Fold in the ground almonds and stir well to incorporate.

6. In a clean bowl, beat the egg whites with the final ¼ cup sugar until they are stiff.

7. Fold the egg whites into the chocolate batter in 2 additions.

8. Pour the batter into the prepared cake pan. Bake on a cookie sheet, in the lower third of the preheated oven for 90 minutes, or until a toothpick inserted in the center comes out clean.

9. Let cool on a rack 15 minutes before removing the sides of the springform.

10. When the cake has cooled, turn it upside down onto a serving plate. Remove the wax paper or parchment. Before serving, sift confectioners' sugar over the top (which was formerly the bottom).

Torta Secca di Mandorle e Arance

Almond and Orange Sponge Cake

THIS TYPE OF SPONGE CAKE is called dry cake (torta secca), but it's not. In this case it is beautifully moist with almonds. It's called dry because so many other Neapolitan cakes are either wet with syrup, full of cream, or otherwise elaborated upon. Not that you can't turn this high, single layer into something Baroque. I can easily see it split horizontally and—doused with spirits or not—filled with a ricotta cream or pastry cream and candied peels, then iced with more pastry cream and decorated with colorful glacéed fruits.

Serves 12

3 cups (12 ounces) slivered blanched almonds

1½ cups sugar

6 eggs, separated

⅔ cup orange juice

Grated rind of 1 orange

1 cup plus 1 tablespoon flour, sifted

Confectioners' sugar

1.   Butter and flour a 9-inch springform pan. Preheat the oven to 325 degrees.

2.   Place the almonds in the bowl of a food processor with 2 tablespoons of the sugar and pulse until the mixture is as fine as possible. Some roughness is inevitable and even desirable for the texture of the finished cake, so don't worry if not all the almonds are pulverized evenly.

3.   In the large bowl of an electric mixer, beat the yolks with the rest of the sugar until foamy. Add the ground almonds in 3 batches, beating well after each addition. Moisten the mixture by beating in a few tablespoons of orange juice, then the rind. Add the flour alternately with the rest of the juice, ending with the flour.

4.   In a medium bowl, beat the egg whites until stiff but not dry. Stir about ½ cup whites into the batter to loosen it. Fold in the rest.

5.   Pour the batter into the pan and bake in the middle of the preheated oven for 40 minutes. The cake should have shrunk slightly from the sides of the pan and be light brown. Pass a knife around the sides of the cake and place on a rack to cool. Sprinkle with confectioners' sugar just before serving.

Pizza di Amarene

Sour Cherry Pie

THE SOUR CHERRIES CALLED AMARENE in Italian and morello in English are the most prized fruit of Campania. And they are expensive. So expensive that a Neapolitan friend points out that you don't always get much cherry preserve in a run-of-the-mill pizza di amarene. They are often filled mostly with pastry cream. I'm afraid he might be critical of this version because it does have more cream than preserves. As an American with a lower tolerance for the intense sweetness a Neapolitan appreciates, I find the following to be well balanced. Amarene are called sour, but once they've been boiled in sugar, they are as sweet as any fruit preserve. Wilkin & Sons' morello cherry preserves from Tiptree, England, are an ideal stand-in for Italian cherry preserves and they are widely available. They are, in fact, the brand of English marmalades and preserves most coveted in Naples, where they are sold in the fanciest food shops for four times what they cost in our supermarkets.

This dessert must be eaten the day it is made, but both the dough and the pastry cream can be made as many as several days ahead.

Makes a 10-inch tart

For the pasta frolla:

3 cups all-purpose flour

½ cup sugar

1 teaspoon baking powder

12 tablespoons cold butter

3 eggs, lightly beaten

For the filling:

3 cups thin pastry cream, well chilled (page 372)

¾ cup morello cherry preserves

1 egg (for the egg wash)

For the pasta frolla:

1. In the bowl of a food processor fitted with the metal blade, combine the flour, sugar, and baking powder. Chunk in the butter. Pulse until the butter is well distributed and the mixture resembles very coarse meal. Add the eggs and pulse again until the dough comes together in clumps, but not a ball. Gather the dough into a ball.

2. Divide the dough into 2 flattened disks in portions ⅓ and ⅔ of the whole amount. Wrap each disk with wax paper and chill the dough at least 1 hour. It is important to work with the dough cold.

3. Butter a 10-inch round cake pan no less than 1½ inches high.

4. Roll the larger disk of dough into a 16-inch-diameter circle. Transfer it to the cake pan and line the pan, allowing the dough to overlap the rim slightly.

To assemble and bake the tart:

5. Preheat the oven to 350 degrees.

6. Fill the pastry with the pastry cream and dot with the cherry preserves. Brush the rim of the pastry with egg wash.

Roll out the remaining disk into a 10-inch-diameter circle and cut 10 strips, each 1 inch wide. Use every other 1-inch strip, and lay each of the 5 strips diagonally across the filling, an inch apart. Turn the pan about 15 degrees and lay the remaining 5 strips across the filling, creating a lattice.

7. Brush the strips with egg wash and trim the overlapping dough to be even with the edge of the cake pan.

8. Bake on a dark cookie sheet, in the lower third of the oven, for 55 to 60 minutes. Turn the tart after the first half hour to ensure even baking.

9. Let cool in the pan, on a rack, for 30 minutes.

10. Have 2 plates ready, one a serving plate. Run a knife around the edge to loosen the tart. Turn upside down on a plate. Immediately reverse right side up on a serving plate. The tart is best served the same day it is made, but may be refrigerated for several days, in which case the pastry suffers slightly.

PASTIERA

Ricotta and Grain Cake

THIS IS ONE OF THE MOST famous of all Neapolitan pastries. It used to be an Easter specialty, but nowadays pastiera can be purchased in a bakery any time of the year. It is a typical ricotta cheesecake-type filling distinguished by an addition of soaked, hulled, whole-wheat berries. These can be found in Italian markets around Easter, and in some health food stores all year (but be careful not to buy unhulled wheat, which never softens as much as is necessary to make a pleasant texture). Because the wheat can be difficult to find, this recipe calls for pearled barley as an alternative. The barley gives a similar texture, but the flavor is not nutty, like the wheat. Still, it makes an excellent pastry. When Neapolitans first arrived in North America—and until fairly recently—it was impossible to find the wheat, and many of the Italian-American recipes that have been handed down do indeed call for rice or barley, as even some old Neapolitan recipes do.

Makes 1 10½-inch-diameter cake or a 9- by 13- by 2-inch cake

For the pastry:

3 cups bleached all-purpose flour

1 cup sugar

¼ teaspoon salt

14 tablespoons (7 ounces) butter, at room temperature

4 egg yolks

½ teaspoon grated lemon rind

For the filling:

15 ounces whole milk ricotta

1 cup sugar

¼ teaspoon cinnamon

1 tablespoon orange flower water (see note)

½ cup finely minced mixed candied orange, citron,
and lemon peel (you can use all orange if you made
the candied orange peel recipe on page 374)

6 eggs, separated (reserve 4 whites)

⅓ cup hulled wheat, soaked for 12 hours and boiled in lightly salted water
for 40 minutes, until tender, or ¼ cup pearl barley, boiled until tender,
about 30 minutes

Plus:

Confectioners' sugar

To prepare the pastry:

1. In a large bowl, combine the flour, sugar, and salt. Mix well.

2. With a pastry blender or with 2 forks, cut in the soft butter. The mixture should resemble coarse meal. Add the egg yolks and lemon rind and stir to moisten the butter/flour mixture. Clumps of dough will start to form. The dough should not be overworked. Sprinkle ice water over the dough, a tablespoon at a time, as necessary to form larger clumps.

3. Place the dough onto a lightly floured work surface. Knead it just enough to form it into a cohesive, soft and yellow dough. Shape it into a loaf about 9 inches long. Wrap it in a clean, wet, and squeezed-out dishtowel. Set aside while you prepare the filling.

To prepare the filling:

4. In a large mixing bowl, whisk together the ricotta, sugar, cinnamon, orange flower water, and candied peels. Whisk in the egg yolks. Then mix in the drained wheat or barley.

5. In a clean mixing bowl, beat 4 egg whites until stiff but not dry. Fold them into the barley mixture.

To assemble and bake the pastiera:

6. Preheat the oven to 350 degrees.

7. Place a sheet of wax paper about 20 inches long on a work surface. Dust it with flour and place ⅔ of the dough on top. Flatten it with a floured rolling pin and cover it with another sheet of wax paper. Roll it into a rectangle that will fit the bottom and sides of the baking pan—about 13 by 16 inches and ¼ inch thick.

(continued)

8.   Peel off the top sheet of paper and turn the pastry into the pan. Peel off the remaining sheet of paper while fitting it into the pan. Trim off the excess dough with a sharp knife. The dough may break in the process, but it is very easy to patch.

9.   If using a springform pan, roll the dough into a circle at least 18 inches in diameter—large enough to cover the bottom and sides of a 10- to 10¼-inch-diameter pan.

10.   Pour the filling into the pastry-lined pan.

11.   Roll out the remaining dough into a rectangle 9 by 13 inches and ⅜ inch thick. Cut it into ¾-inch-wide diagonal strips. Arrange strips diagonally and very loosely over the filling and over the sides of the baking pan. Arrange the remaining strips in the opposite direction, to form a lattice top. Again, if the strips break, they patch easily and you will be sprinkling the finished cake with confectioners' sugar anyway.

12.   Trim off the excess pastry and, using a table fork, pinch the ends of the lattice strips to the pastry lining.

13.   Bake in the middle of the oven for 1 hour, or until a knife inserted near the edge comes out clean. If using a springform, bake it on a baking sheet. Turn the pastiera halfway through baking to ensure even cooking. The filling will puff up during baking and retract when it cools. It will turn a nutty brown, while the lattice top will turn only a shade of beige.

14.   Let the cake cool thoroughly, then refrigerate for at least 12 hours. The pastiera should be served dusted with confectioners' sugar and at room temperature.

Note: In a pinch you can use 2 teaspoons orange extract instead of the classic orange flower water.

TORTA DI RICOTTA GREGORIANO

RICOTTA CAKE FROM SAN GREGORIO MAGNO

WHENEVER I VISIT Cecilia Bellelli Baratta in Paestum she manages to have just heard about an interesting restaurant "only 45 minutes from here." So up into the arid hills behind the Sele river valley we drove one evening, not technically to the higher Monti Alburni, but close—to San Gregorio Magno, a town hit badly by the 1980 earthquake. The new houses, lined up on the crest of a hill, down a road with street lamps, like an American subdivision, are not as picturesque as the mortarless stone buildings that stood here before. You can still see portions of the ancient rubble walls and houses. But the town is doing better economically than when it was quaint and before light industry mingled with the olive trees on the hillsides.

Al Triangolo is in the center of San Gregorio and next to a gas station, in what we call a strip mall. Both the dining room and the kitchen are antiseptic and modern. But the restaurant has a wood-burning fireplace on which to cook the local lamb and a brick oven to bake the bread you are served. Down a staircase from the kitchen is an ancient, moldy, low-ceilinged cellar where aging soppressate, capicolli, and salsicce (sausage)—all handmade by Maria and Gregorio Leo—share space with old vintages of local and regional wine. We drank Gregorio's own rich, purple red in a pitcher, ate all the salumi, including a dense but not too salty prosciutto, dried sausage with enough peperoncino to remind me of American pepperoni sausage, local olives marinated in olive oil with fresh peperoncino, Maria's fusilli with fresh tomato sauce, her ricotta-filled ravioli dressed with porcini and a bit of cream, bony cuts of lamb grilled over wood, fried potatoes, sautéed red peppers, and, for dessert, this crostata, the only thing one could ever even vaguely reproduce at home.

I would say this recipe turns out reasonably close to Triangolo's, but it cannot be exact because the ricotta in Campania is so different from ours. Theirs is the true ricotta, made from the recooked whey left from cheesemaking. Our is a much creamier and looser whole milk product. More typically going by the name crostata, not torta, ricotta cakes and pies are one of the most popular home desserts of the region.

Serves 12

(continued)

For the pastry:

3 cups bleached all-purpose flour

½ cup sugar

4 ounces cold butter (1 stick), cut into tablespoons

2 eggs

1 tablespoon milk

For the filling:

2 pounds whole milk ricotta

1 cup sugar

3½ tablespoons Strega

6 tablespoons finely minced mixed candied peels
(I use 2 tablespoons each of citron, orange, and lemon, but you can use
all orange if you made the candied orange peel recipe on page 374)

3 eggs, lightly beaten

Plus:

6 ounces bittersweet chocolate, grated

1 tablespoon butter

Egg wash (1 egg yolk beaten with 1 tablespoon water)

3 tablespoons granulated sugar

To prepare the pastry:

1. In the bowl of a food processor fitted with the metal blade, combine the flour, sugar, and butter. Pulse until the butter is well distributed and the mixture has a mealy consistency. Add the eggs and milk and pulse on and off until the dough comes together in clumps, but not in a ball.

2. Scrape the dough out of the bowl onto a lightly floured work surface. Knead together a few times, adding just enough flour so the dough doesn't stick to the surface, and form into a ball.

3. Divide it into 2 flattened disks in portions ⅓ and ⅔ of the whole amount. Wrap each disk with wax paper and chill the dough at least 1 hour. It is important to work with the dough cold.

To prepare the filling:

4. In a mixing bowl, combine the ricotta, sugar, Strega, and candied peels. Mix well. Add the beaten eggs and mix well again.

To assemble and bake the crostata:

5. Preheat the oven to 350 degrees. Butter a 9- by 13-inch baking pan, preferably metal.

6. On a floured surface, pat the larger disk of dough into a rectangle. Then, always keeping the dough very lightly dusted, roll the dough out into a very thin rectangle that will fit the bottom and sides of the baking pan—about 13 by 16 inches.

7. Fit the dough neatly into the buttered pan and trim off the excess dough with a sharp knife.

8. Spoon about ⅓ of the ricotta filling, about 2 cups, into the pastry-lined pan. Scatter the grated chocolate over the ricotta. Pour the remaining ricotta filling gently over all.

9. Roll out the remaining dough into a rectangle 9 by 13 inches. If the dough becomes too soft, transfer it to a small baking sheet and refrigerate it briefly so that it is easier to handle. Cut it into 13 1-inch-wide strips in the 9-inch direction.

10. Brush the rim of the pastry lining with egg wash so that the strips adhere. Arrange strips diagonally and very loosely over the filling and over the sides of the baking pan. Arrange the remaining strips in the opposite direction, to form a lattice top. Trim off the excess pastry and, using a table fork, pinch the ends of the lattice strips to the pastry lining.

11. Brush the lattice strips with egg wash—it's fine if the egg drips onto the topping slightly. Sprinkle the top with the 3 tablespoons sugar.

12. Bake in the lower third of the oven for 45 minutes. Turn the crostata halfway through baking to ensure even cooking.

13. Allow to cool thoroughly before cutting into squares for serving. The torta is best served the day it is made, but it can be kept refrigerated for several days, in which case the pastry may suffer slightly.

LIQUORE DI FRAGOLE

STRAWBERRY LIQUEUR

I KNOW NO BETTER WAY to capture the perfume, flavor, and color of fragile, locally grown strawberries at the peak of their season. The strawberries need to infuse in the alcohol for at least a day, but altogether the liqueur takes only minutes to make, and it will retain its intensity for at least a year—until a new crop of strawberries is harvested.

Makes about 1 quart

1 pint ripe strawberries, washed and hulled

1½ cups grain alcohol

2 cups water

1½ to 2 cups sugar (depending on how sweet you want the liqueur)

1. Place the strawberries in a clean glass jar. Cover with the alcohol. Let stand at room temperature for about 24 hours, shaking the jar several times—whenever you think of it.

2. Strain out the berries. They will be pale in color and very alcoholic. You can save them and put them back in the bottle or decanter with the finished liqueur, but they are not particularly attractive. I discard them.

3. In a small saucepan, combine the water and sugar. Stir over medium heat until the sugar has dissolved completely and the syrup begins to boil. When it is crystal clear, which is almost immediately, remove the syrup from the heat and allow it to cool to room temperature.

4. Combine the syrup and the alcohol and pour the liquor into a decorative bottle or stoppered decanter.

5. The liquor may be drunk immediately, but the flavor rounds out after a week or so.

LIMONCELLO

Lemon Liqueur

LIMONCELLO IS KNOWN as a liqueur of Amalfi, Capri, and Sorrento, where lemons grow in profusion, but it is made all over Campania. In the last few years, it has become a fashionable after-dinner drink all over Italy. As a rationalization for drinking so much of it, Italians north of Rome are prone to say it is a *digestivo*, a digestive, although on home ground it's considered pure indulgence, a *rosolio*. There are many commercially made products these days, often artificially colored yellow, but only the homemade and artisanally made liqueur has the fresh and refreshing edge that makes it such a wonderful drink. From Rome to Milan, the trendy way to serve it is icy cold and syrupy thick from the freezer, but most Campanians keep it in a decanter on the sideboard and serve it at room temperature.

The fresher the lemons, the more plump with oil their skins will be and the more fragrant and flavorful the liqueur. Campanian recipes usually call for a couple or a few green lemons (not limes) along with the yellow, as the greener lemons are the most fragrant, while the yellow the most flavorful. In the United States, it's difficult to find still-green lemons, but mottled green and yellow ones are often in the supermarket bins. Choose them.

Makes 2 quarts

2 pounds very fresh, mottled green and yellow lemons (give or take
a few ounces), which is anywhere from 12 small to 8 large lemons, washed

1 quart grain alcohol

6 cups water

2½ cups sugar

1. Peel the lemons with a swivel-bladed peeler, taking care not to remove any of the white pith. (The pith gives an unpleasantly bitter taste.)

2. Put the lemon zests into a half-gallon jar with a tight-fitting lid. Pour on the alcohol. Let stand for 2, 3, or perhaps 4 days, out of the sunlight, shaking the jar several times a day.

(continued)

DESSERTS

419

3. When the lemon zests are pale and as crisp as parchment, you've extracted all their oil. Strain the lemon-flavored alcohol and discard the zests.

4. Make a sugar syrup: In a saucepan, combine the water and sugar and stir over medium heat until the sugar dissolves and the syrup is clear. Do not let it boil. Let it cool to room temperature.

5. Stir the syrup into the infused alcohol. The mixture will turn cloudy. Into 2 clean, dry bottles, pour the liquid through a funnel. Some people strain the liqueur through fine gauze or cheesecloth, but I've found it unnecessary if the lemons have been peeled carefully. Close with clean corks.

The limoncello can be drunk immediately, but its flavor will round out if allowed to sit for a week or so. Serve in tiny glasses—special decorative pottery ones are made in Vietri sul Mare, the ceramics town next to Salerno—at room temperature or direct from the freezer.

Note: This recipe makes a rather dry liqueur; if a sweeter one is desired, increase the sugar to 3¾ cups and reduce the water to 5⅓ cups.

Acton, Harold. *The Bourbons of Naples (1734–1825)*. London: Methuen; New York: Barnes and Noble, 1956, 1974. *The Last Bourbons of Naples (1825–1861)*. London: Methuen, 1961. The definitive English language history of the dynasty that ruled Southern Italy from 1743 until the unification of Italy in 1861, first as the Kingdom of Naples, then as the Kingdom of the Two Sicilies.

Agnesi, Vincenzo. *E' tempo di pasta: scritti 1960–1976*. Roma: Gangemi Editore, 1992. A collection of essays on the history and manufacture of pasta, written by a scion of the Agnesi pasta family. Many antique pasta labels reproduced in color from the collections of the Vincenzo Agnesi Foundation.

Anonimo. *Ricette gastronomiche: la cucina di Pulcinella*. Napoli: Edizioni Marotta, 1989. Nearly 500, mostly traditional, inconsistently reliable recipes, without annotation. Chapter introductions are amusing comment on the recipe category, and there is an excellent, concise listing of Campanian wines, with a short description of each. A popular Neapolitan cookbook.

Bacco, Enrico, Cesare D'Engenio Caracciolo, and others. *Naples: An Early Guide*. New York: Italica Press, 1991. A reproduction of a 1671 guide with a contemporary historical introduction. The old guide includes lists and capsule biographies of the viceroys and kings, the noble families, important military and church figures, as well as historical maps.

Barendson, Marino. *Addio Cicerchia: piccola storia della cucina caprese*. Capri: Edizioni La Conchiglia, 1991. Short essays and recollections about food and eating on Capri, by a contemporary writer and resident of the island. Published locally.

Cafiero, Antonio. *Sorrento e le sue delizie*. Sorrento: Franco Di Mauro Editore, 1993, 1995. Recipes, mostly unreliable in the American kitchen, for Neapolitan pastries, cakes, and other desserts, written by a professional baker from Sorrento.

Camera di Commercio Industria Artigianato e Agricoltura di Napoli. *Neapolitan Meetings on Tourism and Gastronomy: Cuisine in Art; Incontri turistico gastronomici napoletani; la cucina nell'arte*. Napoli: 1996. Essays on Neapolitan cuisine by various authors.

Cavalcanti, Ippolito. *Cucina teorico-pratica*. Napoli: Tommaso Marotta Editore, 1986. A reprint of the 1847 edition. One of the cornerstones of the literature on Neapolitan cooking, written by a nobleman for noble families.

Convivialis. Finmeccanica Public Relations Office, 1996. A privately published monograph of essays on Neapolitan cuisine distributed as a Christmas gift by a large Italian union.

D'Abbraccio, Maria Antonietta. *Semplicità: ricette di cucina & pensieri d'amore*. Piedimonte Matese: Ikonia, 1995. A privately published book of homey recipes and motherly advice on love and life by a young homemaker in the province of Benevento. Locally published.

De Bury, Gianni. *Le ricette di frijenno magnanno*. Sorrento: Franco Di Mauro Editore, 1989. The more than 1,001 recipes in this compendium were contributed by home cooks who are identified by name. They range from the most humble antique food of the countryside through the traditional repertoire to contemporary dishes with slight foreign accents.

Ferretti, Lya. *Gran natale alla napoletana: minestra, capitone, ciociole, strufoli e tombola: la canzone de lo capo d'anno*. Sorrento: Franco Di Mauro Editore, 1988. A monograph collection of the important Neapolitan Christmas recipes, with lyrics to New Year's songs.

Francesconi, Jeanne Caròla. *La cucina napoletana*. Roma: Newton Compton Editori, 1992, 1995. This is considered "the bible" of Neapolitan cooking. The life work of a dedicated culinary scholar, obviously good cook, and meticulous recipe writer, it was revised several times. The last revision was completed about four years before her death in 1996. The book covers the entire scope of Neapolitan cuisine, from the antique dishes of la cucina povera through the noble dishes created at the Bourbon court and by the chefs of the aristocracy to fare created after the Second World War by the author herself and many of her upper-middle-class and titled friends. Extensive historical introductions and recipe notes make this by far the most important book on the subject.

Gerli, Fabrizia Villari. *Napoli in cucina*. Verona: Arnoldo Mondadori Editore, 1993.

Fundamental and dependable recipes of the cuisine, with color photographs of their preparation.

Gleijeses, Vittorio. *A Napoli si mangia così*. Nuova ed. Napoli: La Botteguccia, 1990. A contemporary collection of mostly reliable traditional recipes with a short historical/cultural introduction.

Gosetti della Salda, Anna. *Le ricette regionali italiane*. Milano: Case Editrice "Solares," 1967, 1993. A compendium of the most important dishes from Italy's twenty regions. Concise introductions to the regions start each chapter of precisely written recipes, which often have historical or insightful notes. Written by the founder of *La Cucina Italiana,* now Italy's most popular food magazine.

Headlam, Cecil. *The Story of Naples*. Illustated by Major Benton Fletcher. Nendeln, Liechtenstein: Kraus Reprint, 1971. Reproduction of a 1925 history and guide to the city.

Lewis, Norman. *Naples '44: An Intelligence Officer in the Italian Labyrinth*. New York: Henry Holt and Co., 1978, 1994. The diary of a British officer stationed in Naples during the Allies' first year of occupation.

Malgieri, Nick. *Great Italian Desserts*. New York: Little Brown, 1990. Totally reliable recipes from all the regions of Italy by an American pastry and baking teacher.

Oliviero, Nello. *Storie e curiosità del mangiar napoletano*. Napoli: Edizioni Scientifiche Italiane, 1983. The purple prose and hyperbole make some of the stories as believable as the book's admitted legends, but these essays by a recently deceased, prolific

Neapolitan food writer are always amusing and demonstrate the Neapolitan's passion for his food.

Pane, Mariano. *L'Immaginario e' servito*. Napoli: Casa Editrice Fausto Fiorentino, 1995. A treatise on mock Neapolitan dishes.

Pasticceria napoletana. Orlando Editorie, 1995. A paperback collection of Neapolitan pastry recipes that are not very reliable for an American kitchen.

Penta de Peppo, Marinella. *L'arte della cucina secondo la tradizione napoletana*. Milano: Arnoldo Mondadori Editore, 1994. A contemporary, not strictly traditional collection of recipes from an upper-middle-class hostess. It reflects how affluent Neapolitans eat today.

Rak, Maria Giovanna Fasulo. *La cucina napoletana in cento ricette tradizionali*. Roma: Tascabili Economici Newton, 1995. A small paperback with an excellent and concise history of Neapolitan food, introducing the 100 recipes that most represent the Neapolitan kitchen. Many of the recipes are from the family of the author, an archivist at the National Library in Rome. Part of a series on Neapolitan culture and history.

Reale, Angela. *La cucina sannita: le ricette del passato: 208 ricette antiche*. Benevento: SPES Editrice, 1996. Antique recipes from Benevento are introduced with erudite comment on the old ways.

Reale, Angela. *La cucina sannita: ricettario e saggio storico*. Benevento: SPES Editrice, 1994. The only serious book on the food of Benevento, it has well-researched history and reliable recipes from a contemporary writer.

Le Ricette ed i consigli Strega. Benevento: Strega. A small, promotional book of recipes gathered by the Alberti famiily, manufacturers of Strega liqueur, from users of their product.

Santasilia di Torpino, Franco. *La cucina aristocratica napoletana*. Napoli: Sergio Civita Editore, 1996. A large format, glossy book with color photographs and recipes for dishes developed by the *Monzù* chefs for the aristocratic families of Naples. The author, a well-known scholar of Neapolitan food, is from a titled family that itself has a *Monzù* chef.

Santolini, Antonella. *Napoli*. Bologna: Edizioni Mida, 1989. Part of the well-known corrugated cardboard–covered cookbook series that offers recipes in Italian, regional dialect, and English.

Scialò, Pasquale. *La canzone napoletana dalle origini ai giorni nostri*. Roma: Tascabili Economici Newton, 1996. A paperback history of Neapolitan songs and music. Part of a series on Neapolitan culture and history.

Scicolone, Michelle. *A Fresh Taste of Italy*. New York: Broadway Books, 1997. A collection of traditional and contemporary recipes from all over Italy by an American writer.

Serra, Anna and Piero. *La cucina della Campania*. Sorrento: Franco De Mauro Editore, 1988, 1991. A comprehensive collection of more than 500 recipes from all over the region, including glossaries of dialect food, cooking terms, and dialect names of fish, plus descriptions of the region's wines.

Serra, Piero, and Lya Ferretti. *Il grande libro della pasticceria napoletana*. Napoli: Il Libro in Piazza, 1983, 1994. Inconsistently reliable recipes for all the traditional Neapolitan pastries, cakes, and other desserts, plus jams, marmalades, and liqueurs.

Sontag, Susan. *The Volcano Lover: A Romance*. New York: Farrar Straus Giroux, 1992. A novel about the obsessive collecting habits of Sir William Hamilton, the great eighteenth-century archaeologist, art collector, and ambassador to Naples from England, husband of Emma Hart Hamilton, who was the lover of Lord Admiral Horatio Nelson.

Sorrentino, Lejla Mancusi, and Germana Militerni Nadone. *Menù napoletani*. Napoli: Guida Editori, 1990. A cookbook of very reliable traditional and contemporary Neapolitan recipes arranged by the season.

Stefanile, Mario, and Nello Oliviero. *Partenope in cucina (con la Pasta Chirico).*

A cura di Noura Korsch, con 200 ricette di piatti di pasta. Napoli: Fausto Fiorentino, 1993. Essays and 200 workable recipes by two of Naples's most prolific twentieth-century food writers, with a separate introduction commissioned by the Chirico pasta company.

Talarico, Achille. *Gastronomia salernitana di ieri e di oggi*, 3rd. ed. Salerno: Edizioni Salernum, 1989. The only cookbook devoted to the cooking of the province of Salerno, with recipes detailed enough to work for a good cook and extensive, amusing notes on dining and cooking habits of the area, past and until the post–World War II era.

Vellino, Sergio. *Momenti della cucina caprese*. 2nd ed. Napoli, Roma: L.E.R., 1997. A small color paperback with color photos and recipes for the most distinctive recipes of Capri. Published as a tourist souvenir.

INDEX